AN EXPLORER'S GUIDE

DRAWN

Virginia

Candyce H. Stapen

with photographs by the author

F I R S T   E D I T I O N

The Countryman Press ✻ Woodstock, Vermont

Explorer's Guide Virginia
978-0-88150-911-3

Interior photographs by the author unless otherwise specified
Maps by Erin Greb Cartography © The Countryman Press
Book design by Bodenweber Design
Composition by PerfecType, Nashville, TN

Published by The Countryman Press, P.O. Box 748, Woodstock, VT 05091

Distributed by W. W. Norton & Company, Inc., 500 Fifth Avenue, New York, NY 10110

Printed in the United States of America

10 9 8 7 6 5 4 3 2 1

As always, to Matthew, Alissa, and David,
my favorite traveling companions

EXPLORE WITH US!

Welcome to the first edition of a comprehensive guide to Virginia, a state whose attractions stretch from the shores of the Atlantic Ocean in the east to the peaks of the Appalachian Mountains in the west. U.S. history in Virginia spans more than 400 years, dating from the 1607 establishment of Jamestowne, the first permanent English settlement in the New World. You can also explore contemporary Virginia in the art galleries, trendy shops, and restaurants in the state's big cities, as well as enjoy the old-time music and country culture and crafts in the southwestern mountain towns.

Virginia: An Explorer's Guide is designed to appeal to a wide range of visitors: beach lovers, birders, crafters, eco-adventurers, hikers, history buffs, arts enthusiasts, music lovers, museum-goers, foodies, families, solo travelers, couples seeking romantic getaways, as well as those simply curious about what the next bend in the road reveals. This book is designed to enable you to find what you want quickly and to discover something new easily.

Please note that no attraction, lodging, restaurant, outfitter, or shop has paid to be in this book. All entries were chosen for their merits. Here's a quick guide to the book.

WHAT'S WHERE

As the title suggests, this introductory section presents a quick summary of where you can find items of particular interest, whether you are searching for crafts, historic plantations, gardens, wineries, Civil War sites, and much more.

LODGING

Whenever possible, the lodging section presents a choice. Sometimes a bed in a budget chain is fine. For other occasions, you may want a big city hotel, a historic lodge, a secluded bed-and-breakfast home, or a romantic inn. The properties included reflect these options. The prices listed for rooms are the rack rates exclusive of taxes. Prices change and properties create money-saving packages. Be sure to check with any prospective hotel and search for deals online and with travel agents.

RESTAURANTS

A range of restaurants is included as well. After all, you may want a quick bite at a local diner, a moderately priced lunch at a café, or a leisurely dinner at the region's top dining room. The listed prices are for dinner entrées.

KEY TO SYMBOLS

- ♈ **Bar/Nightspot.** Look for this symbol when searching for nightlife. The symbol appears next to dance venues, clubs, and restaurants that have popular bars,
- ✎ **Child-friendly.** This symbol indicates an attraction, lodging, or restaurant that's especially appealing to kids.

- ⊸ **Eco-friendly.** We have used this symbol sparingly. Because *eco-friendly* is the new buzz word, and because the criteria for receiving an eco-friendly label varies, we indicate only those establishments that have made significant efforts in reducing their carbon footprints by using recycled/eco-friendly materials and also by employing alternative energy sources.
- 🏵 **Extra value.** This indicates places that are great budget-stretchers.
- 🐾 **Pet-friendly.** If you like traveling with your pets—primarily dogs and cats—look for this symbol. Some lodgings are more pet-friendly than others and most places that accept Fido or Fluffy limit the number of rooms available to pets and restrict the size and the number of animals that can bunk with you. Always call ahead.
- ♂ **Weddings/Civil Unions.** Some inns and hotels specialize in weddings or offer a particularly good venue.
- ♿ **Wheelchair accessible.** Places that are partially or completely accessible by wheelchair feature this symbol. Please remember that even though this symbol appears, wheelchair accessibility may be limited. In a historic building, access may be restricted to the first floor. A national or state park may feature just a few, short accessible trails and frequently a lodging may have only one or two accessible rooms. It's always wise to call ahead to be sure that what's offered meets your needs and, in the case of an accommodation, is available.
- ((ᵢ)) **Wi-Fi.** This symbol prefaces places with wireless Internet connections that are either free or available for a fee.

We would appreciate any comments or corrections. Please write to:
Explorer's Guide Editor
The Countryman Press
P.O. Box 748
Woodstock, Vermont 05091

Thank you and we hope you enjoy this book as much as we have enjoyed researching and writing it. Happy travels.

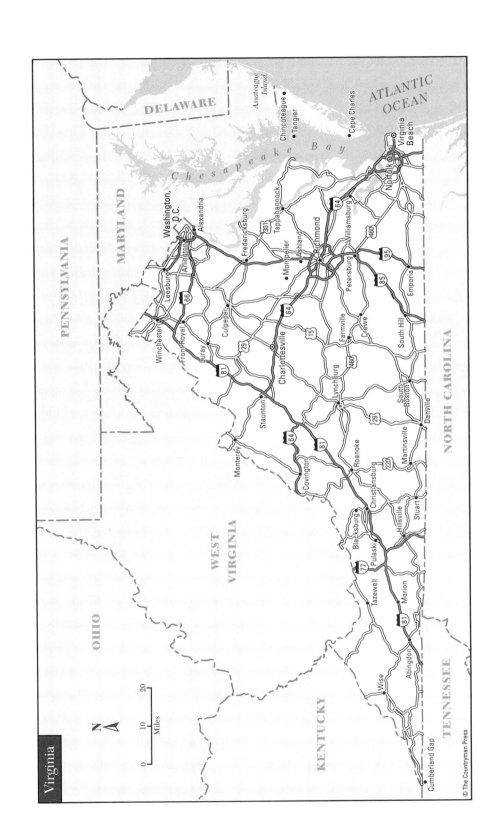

Virginia

ATLANTIC OCEAN

© The Countryman Press

CONTENTS

INTRODUCTION

M y fascination with Virginia started in grade school, when I wrote a book report on Patrick Henry. The fiery patriot's "Give me liberty or give me death" speech amazed and inspired me, although at age nine I didn't have any particular rebellion of my own planned. I did, however, nag my parents to take me to Colonial Williamsburg with a zeal that Mr. Henry would have recognized. That trip fueled my fascination with all things colonial, especially candle making, wig wearing, and blacksmithing. I am still captivated by crafts and history (less so with wigs). Growing up, I gained an appreciation for wildlife sanctuaries, craggy mountains peaks, rolling farmlands, vineyards, and country roads. Virginia has all these in abundance plus 400-years of history that reach back to the first English

ALEXANDRIA WATERFRONT

Virginia Myers

settlers who established a permanent foothold in the New World at Jamestown in 1607. Alexandria was a flourishing seaport in 1749, long before rebelling from the Crown was even a whisper.

As a resident of Washington for more than 30 years, I have had the good fortune to spend time exploring Virginia. It is easy in Virginia to combine history with a soothing natural setting. In Virginia, you are never far from a hiking trail, a bicycle path, a river perfect for canoeing and kayaking, or a sunlit beach. Virginia has two of America's great roads—Skyline Drive and the Blue Ridge Parkway. The rich land nurtures more 170 wineries. Virginia has much to offer, from seacoast to mountains and history to space-age science. There are intriguing museums, underground caverns, fertile farmlands, wildlife sanctuaries, and thrill parks with gut-wrenching roller coasters. The mountain heritage of handcrafting and old-time music remains alive and well in the Blue Ridge Highlands and southwestern regions. Drive the back roads to discover artisans fashioning fine furniture and jewelry, quilts, pottery, and contemporary sculpture. In Galax and Floyd, join a jamboree where pickin' and playin' of old-time and bluegrass music pulls you into dancing. You will enjoy Virginia. The terrain is diverse; the people, friendly; and the resorts and lodges, inviting.

I want to thank Virginia Myers for her contributions to the writing and Rebecca Crockett, with whose help the final maps were created.

WHAT'S WHERE IN VIRGINIA

ACCESSIBILITY Divided by region, the online guide *Accessible Virginia* (www.accessiblevirginia.org), lists detailed information about the accessibility of many of the state's attractions. In addition to providing facts about wheelchair accessibility, the guide explains what accommodations a site has made for those with special hearing or visual needs.

AMUSEMENT AND WATER PARKS In northern Virginia, **Splash-Down Waterpark**, Manassas, has 13 acres of water features, from a 770-foot Lazy River to a 25-meter lap pool, two four-story waterslides, plus two slippery-fast cannonball slides. In the Tidewater Region, take a break from colonial history to visit **Busch Gardens Williamsburg**, which has roller coasters and other fun rides with ersatz English, Scottish, Irish, German, French, and Italian villages. Voted the "Most Beautiful Park" for 20 consecutive years by members of the National Amusement Park Historical Association, Busch Gardens features hills, greenery, lovely landscaping, a lake, and lots of animals. Or cool off at its sister park, **Water Country USA**, Williamsburg, whose 40 acres have pools and water slides. The **Great**

Wolf Lodge–Williamsburg combines themed rooms with a mammoth 67,000-square-foot indoor water park. **Kings Dominion**, 20 miles north of Richmond, comprises 15 roller coasters, rides for little kids, plus a water park. At Virginia Beach's **Ocean Breeze Waterpark**, zip down 16 waterslides and tackle the surf in Runaway Bay, a wave pool.

APPLE AND ADDITIONAL FRUIT PICKING In Charlottesville, pick your own peaches in spring and apples in fall at the **Carter Mountain Orchard**. In Nelson County, pick bushels full at **Dickie Brothers Orchard**, Roseland, and **Drumheller's Orchard**, Lovingston. In the Shenandoah Region, **Winchester** and the surrounding Frederick County also have apple orchards. The Visitor Center offers a **Follow the Apple Trail** audio driving tour for purchase. Along the way, visit **Marker-Miller Orchards**, known for its apple cider doughnuts, and **Pumpkin Patch at Hill High Farms**, noted for its apple dumplings and fall display of pumpkins.

ART MUSEUMS AND GALLERIES In northern Virginia, visit the **Torpedo**

VisitNorfolk

Factory, Alexandria, to watch potters, painters, glass artists, and others work. Their creations are available for sale. Colonial Williamsburg's **Abby Aldrich Rockefeller Folk Art Museum** houses one of the country's best collections of folk art from the 17th through 19th centuries. Also, in the Historic Area, the **DeWitt Wallace Decorative Arts Museum** showcases fine furnishings and decorative arts. Norfolk's **Chrysler Museum of Art** is renowned for its 20th-century European and American art as well as its 10,000-piece collection of glass that includes a Tiffany gallery.

Among Central Virginia's museums are two interesting art facilities. Charlottesville has the **Kluge-Ruhe Aboriginal Art Collection**, a noteworthy collection of Australian Aboriginal works. The **Virginia Museum of Fine Arts** houses an exceptional collection of jewel-encrusted Fabergé eggs as well as paintings by 20th-century masters. Roanoke, in the Shenandoah Valley, also has two interesting art spaces. The **O. Winston Link Museum** is a must-see for both lovers of photography and train buffs.

The museum exhibits hundreds of Link's black-and-white photographs of trains, primarily 1950s Norfolk & Western Railway's steam locomotives, the last of their era. At the **Taubman Museum of Art**, an 81,000-square-foot facility with a striking glass façade, peruse American modern and contemporary art, as well as 19th-century works.

BEACHES White sands grace much of Virginia's miles of coastline The U.S. Fish and Wildlife Service and National Park Service share management of more than 14,000 acres of pristine ocean beaches and protected dunes. **Chincoteague National Wildlife Refuge** is the Virginia portion of Assateague Island, a barrier island that stretches across the Virginia/Maryland border. In **Chincoteague**, enjoy dune-bordered

David Hills, VisitNorfolk, Virginia Tourism Corporation

beaches, the famous wild ponies, wide sands, and swimmable surf. For the classic beach with a 3-mile boardwalk (a paved path adjacent to the beach), come to **Virginia Beach**, a destination that lures beach lovers with 20 miles of continuous sandy shores. Virginia Beach also offers unspoiled beaches for strolling—not swimming. Enjoy the dune-bordered sands and the sound of surf at both **Back Bay National Wildlife Refuge** and the even more rustic **False Cape State Park**.

Virginia Tourism Corporation

BICYCLING The Virginia Department of Transportation Office of Public Affairs (www.virginiadot.org) will send you a map, "Bicycling in Virginia." The **Washington Area Bicyclist Association** (www.waba.org) offers a dozen different maps, available online or by mail, of bicycle trails in northern Virginia, including in Arlington, Alexandria, and Fairfax County. Northern Virginia has an extensive network of bike trails, including one of our favorites, the 18-mile **Mount Vernon Trail**, which runs along the Potomac River from Theodore Roosevelt Island to Mount Vernon Estate. The **Northern Neck Heritage Trail Bicycle Route Network** (www.northernneck.org) has seven paved trails that weave through the Northern Neck and also connect in several places with the Potomac Heritage National Scenic Trail (www.nps.gov/gewa), a developing system for cyclists that follows the Potomac River. Miles of flat roads, water views, and small-town life on the **Eastern Shore** attract leisurely cyclists as well as serious athletes. Seaside Road, or State Road 600, is a country-road alternative to the more commercial US 13. Bike routes wind

past the general stores and bait shops, historic homes, and small farms of quaint bay and seaside communities. In Chincoteague, bikes are a great way to get around to explore the island, and kids love to pedal over to the ice-cream shops on their own. In **Virginia Beach**, you can cycle the boardwalk on two-wheelers or pedal your family along the path using four-wheeled bikes with awnings. In **Blue Ridge Highlands** and **southwestern Virginia**, many of the state parks as well as the **Mount Rogers National Recreation Area** have

Virginia Tourism Corporation

multiuse bicycle and hiking trails. **Radford Mountain Bike Park** overlooks Claytor Lake Dam and offers 12 trails built according to International Mountain Biking standards. Other useful contacts for cyclists include **BikeWalk Virginia** (www.bikewalk virginia.org), **Adventure Cycling Association** (www.adventurecycling .org), and **Captain John Smith Chesapeake National Historic Trail** (www.nps.gov/cajo).

BIRDING Virginia's 43,000 square miles of diverse natural habitat shelter 400 species of birds. You can find them by following the **Virginia Birding and Wildlife Trail** (804-367-1000; www.dgif.virginia.gov/vbwt/), a network divided into three areas. The coastal trail offers 18 loops, the mountain trail has 34 loops, and the Piedmont trail has 13 loops through forests, pinelands, and grasslands. Also, the eastern shore and Virginia Beach are on the Atlantic flyway, so in season you see thousands of migrating birds. At the Northern Neck's **Caledon Natural Area**, you can reserve a tour to see one of the East Coast's largest colonies of bald eagles. On a **Rappahannock River Cruise**, also on the Northern Neck, bring binoculars to spot some of the 50 resident bald eagles that nest in the trees along the shore. In Virginia Beach, the **Seashore to Cypress Birding Trail** links several of the beach's prime birding places, connecting 130,000 natural acres. In September and May, the **Chesapeake Bay Bridge-Tunnel** affords birdwatchers a prime spot to view the migrations.

BLUE RIDGE MOUNTAINS AND BLUE RIDGE PARKWAY The Blue Ridge Parkway (www.blueridgepark way.org) winds for 469 miles, linking Virginia's Shenandoah National Park to North Carolina's Great Smoky Mountains National Park. In Virginia, the parkway starts in central Virginia's Nelson County in the Blue Ridge Mountains and continues south and west. (See the Central Virginia and Shenandoah Valley chapters.)

BOAT EXCURSIONS (See also *Lakes.*) From Reedville, board a boat for a cruise across the Chesapeake Bay to Tangier Island or to **Smith Island**, Maryland, the self-proclaimed "Softshell Crab Capital of the World," or to **Tangier Island**, on Virginia's Eastern Shore. Captain Rick Kellam, a fifth-generation waterman, runs **Broadwater Bay Ecotours** (www.broadwaterbayecotour.com), which takes visitors to the barrier islands. The **Hampton Roads** area, **Norfolk**, and the **Northern Neck** offer many opportunities to get out on the water. Boat excursions give you a wind-in-your-hair exhilaration and a view of the region's attractions. On a boat outing in Norfolk, you get a good perspective of just how big are some of the U.S. Navy's huge ships in port. **Nauticus**, Norfolk's maritime museum, offers dolphin-watching cruises in season. From Norfolk, board the passenger ferry for a **day trip to Portsmouth** across the Elizabeth River.

BREW TRAIL Like many destinations, Virginia is home to a burgeoning selection of microbreweries. **Capital City Brewing Company** (www.capcitybrew.com), has three locations in the D.C./northern Virginia area. In Arlington, the taps run with seven or eight different brewed choices every night. Fredericksburg's

Capital Ale House has no fewer than 60 beers on tap, 250 in bottles, plus two cask-conditioned ales for beer aficionados. In Alexandria, **Bilbo Baggins** is a cozy bar and comfy restaurant that has 10 beers on tap (or choose from 80 bottles). In the Tidewater Region, **Williamsburg AleWerks** brews ales. Also in Williamsburg, **Green Leafe** has two locations, each with 50-plus beers on tap. Try them at **Green Leafe Café Downtown** and **Green Leafe New Town**. Nelson County, in Central Virginia, has created a **BrewRidge Trail.com** (www.brewridgetrail .com) that shows off the region's microbreweries and hard cideries (yes, that's a word). Among the brewpubs are **Blue Mountain Brewery**, Afton; **Devils Backbone Brewing Company**, Roseland, not far from Wintergreen Resort; and **Wild Wolf Brewing Company**, Nellysford, also near Wintergreen Resort. In Central Virginia, a region with abundant apples, it's no wonder that hard cideries are being established. Central Virginia has **Albemarle Cider-Works**, North Garden. In the Blue Ridge Highlands and southwestern Virginia, try **Foggy Ridge Cider**, Dugspur.

CANOEING, KAYAKING, PADDLING, ROWING In northern Virginia, **Potomac Paddle Sports** (potomacpaddlesports.com) offers a four-hour flatwater trip setting off from the Virginia side of the river at Columbia Island. The Northern Neck and Middle Peninsula's many inlets and rivers make the area a prime paddling spot. **Captain John Smith Chesapeake National Historic Trail** (www.smithtrail.net), is America's first national water trail. This 3,000-mile route takes paddlers along waterways explored by Captain John Smith in the 17th century as he sailed the Chesapeake Bay, Northern Neck, and Middle Peninsula rivers and their tributaries in Virginia and Maryland. Virginia has three of the trails six "smart buoys," along the James River near Jamestown, the Elizabeth River near Norfolk, and the Rappahannock River near Stingray Point, which relay weather, water quality, and other information. Simply put down your paddle and input www.buoybay.org /m on your mobile phone; from your computer, check www.buoybay.org; to find out what the Chesapeake was like in that area during Smith's time, phone 1-877-BUOYBAY. In the Williamsburg/Jamestown area, the **Powhatan Creek Blueway**, an 8-mile roundtrip, takes you between the York and James rivers through an area that belonged to the Powhatan Indian Confederacy. In the Northern Neck area, **Calm Waters**, Lancaster, is a combined bed-and-breakfast inn and sculling camp. In **Belle Isle State Park**, explore miles of the Rappahannock River on a guided canoe or kayak trip. Paddle the James River from several areas: Charlottesville's outfitters include **James River Runners**. In Lexington, take a guided trip with **Twin River Outfitters** (www .canoevirginia.net) or the **Wilderness Canoe Company** (http://wilderness canoecampground.com). On the Eastern Shore, two kayak companies offering guided expeditions are **Assateague Explorer** (www.assa teagueisland.com/kayaktours.htm), based in Chincoteague, and **South-East Expeditions** (www.southeast expeditions.net), Cape Charles. In the Shenandoah region, the **Front Royal Canoe Company** (www.frontroyal

canoe.com) as well as **Shenandoah River Outfitters** (www.shenandoah river.com) have guided paddle trips on the Shenandoah River.

CAVERNS As pretty as the Shenandoah Region is above ground, it also harbors a world of underground wonders. In the area's many caverns, view limestone pillars, "secret tunnels," flowing streams, and "rooms" as big as cathedrals. Another plus, especially on a steamy Virginia afternoon, is that the temperatures in the caverns hover around 56 degrees F, all the time. **Luray Caverns**, Luray, is Virginia's largest and the most popular cavern on the East Coast. **Skyline Caverns**, Front Royal, gains fame for its clusters of shimmering white calcium carbonate crystals, known as anthodites. These rare, slow growing formations gain only 1 inch every 7,000 years. **Endless Caverns and RV Resort**, New Market area, has more than 5 miles of trails. Along with a cavern, **Shenandoah Caverns**, Quicksburg, adds above-ground attractions, including a barn with historic vehicles, floats from parades, and farm animals.

CHILDREN, ESPECIALLY FOR (See also *Amusement and Water Parks* as well as *Caverns*). Attractions, restaurants, and experiences of special interest to kids appear with the 🐾 (Kids icon) in front the listing. In northern Virginia, children like the **Claude Moore Colonial Farm at Turkey Run**, an 18th-century tenant farm brought to life with period interpreters going about their chores, planting vegetables, cooking over an open fire, weeding, and harvesting tobacco.

Any of the Shenandoah region's **caverns** will delight kids; just make

sure they are old enough to walk on their own for an hour or so. You don't want to have to carry a tired child on the tour, and especially not up the many steps required to climb out of most caverns. On the Eastern Shore, you and your kids can climb to the top of the **Assateague Lighthouse**, at Assateague Island National Seashore. At the **Virginia Living Museum**, children discover Virginia's natural heritage from the state's coast to its mountains. The facility showcases thousands of the reptiles, mammals, birds, and sea critters that inhabit Virginia, and sea turtles and schools of fish swim in a 30,000-gallon tank. **Colonial Williamsburg** has many special programs for children; ask at the Visitors Center. Life is more than living history museums. In Williamsburg, take a break from the 18th century to visit **Busch Gardens Williamsburg**, a park that combines roller coasters and other fun rides with ersatz European villages. On a hot and humid Virginia summer day, make time to cool off at Busch Gardens' sister park **Water Country USA**, Williamsburg.

In Hampton, the birthplace of America's space program, the **Virginia Air and Space Center** features more than 100 hands-on exhibits and has historic aircraft hanging in its atrium. Next door, the **Hampton Carousel** delights little kids (big ones, too) with its prancing steeds and chariots. The **Virginia Discovery Museum**, located in Charlottesville's Downtown Mall, is also great fun for young kids. Richmond's **Science Museum of Virginia** offers hundreds of hands-on exhibits. **Nauticus**, which comprises the National Maritime Center and the USS *Wisconsin*, Norfolk, offers a tour of one of the largest battleships of its kind as well as uses some hands-on exhibits to engage children. At the facility's Aegis Theater, make rapid-fire decisions in a high-tech naval battle, and in Design Chamber: Battleship X, race against others to design a World War II battleship. The city's **Virginia Zoo** is a manageable 53 acres, and the Zoo Train makes it easy to get around when little ones tire of walking. The **Virginia Aquarium & Marine Science Center**, Virginia Beach, is a good place to go when you have to get out of the sun. With 800,000 gallons of exhibits, there's much to see. The kid-friendly exhibits mostly focus on Virginia's marine habitats from marshes to the bay and the ocean. Skateboarders can't get enough of Virginia Beach's **Mount Trashmore Park**, whose jewel is a skateboarding park.

Along with spectacular outdoor recreation and underground caverns, the Shenandoah Valley features some interesting museums and attractions. At the 180-acre **Virginia Safari Park**, Natural Bridge, the exotic animals roam in large enclosures and the people stay in their cars and drive through. The park gives kids (and adults) the chance to see zebras, antelope, ostriches, elk, bison, and other animals roaming "free," or at least more freely than in traditional zoos. In Roanoke, children learn about science and the ecology of western Virginia through the many hands-on exhibits at the **Science Museum of Western Virginia**. Planes, automobiles, and especially trains—more than 40 big behemoths—intrigue at the **Virginia Museum of Transportation**. Kids discover pioneer life at Staunton's **Frontier Culture Museum** at six re-created homesteads where costumed

interpreters darn, cook, and plant as did the early settlers.

CIVIL WAR Virginia commemorates the **Sesquicentennial of the Civil War**, the war's 150th anniversary, from 2011 to 2015 by hosting special events at the state's many Civil War sites. Contact **Virginia Civil War** (www.virginiacivilwar.org) for the specific attractions as well as the applicable tourist offices. The **Civil War Heritage Trail** road map, which includes a brief history and timeline with a complete map of Civil War sites and trails in Virginia and Maryland, is available from many local tourist offices. Northern Virginia's **Manassas National Battlefield Park**, Manassas, is where the Civil War began: its first major battle, known as First Manassas or the Battle of Bull Run, erupted here on July 21, 1861. At **White Oak Civil War Museum and Research Center**, you can imagine life as a Civil War soldier when you see the hand-dug replicas of the huts they built for themselves in winter. The **Fredericksburg/Spotsylvania National Military Park** commemorates the Civil War battles that raged through the area. View four major battlefields: Fredericksburg, Chancellorsville, Wilderness, and Spotsylvania Court House. Author Virginia Morton, who wrote *Marching Through Culpeper*, leads two-hour **Civil War Walking Tours** through downtown Culpeper. In the Tidewater region, **Hampton Roads** was the site of the first battle of the ironclads. **The Mariners' Museum**, Newport News, uses recovered parts of the noted Civil War battleship *Monitor* to detail both the significance of the vessel and the science of conservation.

Central Virginia likely has the most sites, including such significant ones **Appomattox Court House National Historical Park**, the place where General Robert E. Lee surrendered to General Ulysses S. Grant on April 9, 1865. **Richmond**, the capital of the Confederacy from 1861 to 1865, is rich in sites related to the Civil War. Start your history tour at the **American Civil War Center at Historic Tredegar**. The museum interprets the Civil War from three perspectives: Union, Confederate, and African American. The site conveniently has a Visitor Center for the **Richmond National Battlefield Park**. The park commemorates the four sieges to control Richmond; a complete battlefield tour requires an 80-mile drive of 13 sites. **The Museum and White House of the Confederacy** doesn't glorify the confederates or the Confederacy, but does present artifacts and a historical interpretation.

The **White House of the Confederacy** was home to President Jefferson Davis and his family during the Civil War. The last decisive battle of the war took place in **Petersburg**, 23 miles south of Richmond. **Petersburg National Battlefield**, a 2500-acre site, explicates the extraordinary 10-month siege of the city. **Pamplin Historical Park and the National Museum of the Civil War Soldier** provides additional information on the war's last significant fight, the April 2, 1865, battle that took place on the site. Pamplin's **National Museum of the Civil War Soldier** immerses you in the life of an everyday soldier fighting in the Civil War as you tour the exhibits with an audiotape that relates the experiences of one of 13 "soldier comrades," based on real warriors. At the end of the

visit, you discover what happened to your "comrade." The grounds of Petersburg's **Old Blandford Church** contain the graves of 30,000 Confederate soldiers. The church, however, is known for its extraordinary collection of Tiffany windows. (See *Historic Churches*). The **Battle of Lynchburg Driving Tour**, on CD, takes you to eight sites that proved crucial to the Battle of Lynchburg, June 17–18, 1864.

The Shenandoah Valley saw fierce fighting during the Civil War. The northern valley has some 10 battle sites. Contact the **Shenandoah Valley Battlefields Foundation** (www .shenandoahatwar.org), New Market, for a comprehensive list of sites. During the Civil War, **Winchester**, the northernmost city under Confederate control, changed hands more than seventy times. **Middletown** saw the **Battle of Cedar Creek**, also known as the Battle of Belle Grove, the last significant encounter in the Shenandoah Valley. The **New Market Battlefield State Historical Park and Hall of Valor Civil War Museum** commemorates the 257 Virginia Military Institute students whose fighting on May 15, 1864, contributed much to the Union retreat. In Lexington, in the southern Shenandoah Valley, pay homage to General Stonewall Jackson at his burial site in the **Stonewall Jackson Memorial Cemetery** and learn about the leader's civilian life at the **Stonewall Jackson House**. More than 1,700 Confederate soldiers are buried in Staunton's **Thornrose Cemetery.**

COLONIAL HISTORY (See also *Historic Homes and Plantations*.) Williamsburg, Jamestown, and Yorktown, known as Virginia's Historic Triangle, make the colonial era come to life. **Colonial Williamsburg** depicts the town of Williamsburg on the eve of the American Revolution. From 1699 to 1776, Williamsburg served as the capital of Virginia, England's oldest, largest, and richest colony. Nearby, **Historic Jamestowne** is the site of the first permanent English settlement in the New World. The adjacent **Jamestown Settlement** is a living history museum that brings the era and the colonists' struggles to life. **Yorktown**, on the York River, is best known for the **Yorktown Battlefield**, the site of the last major battle of the Revolutionary War. **The Yorktown Victory Center** is a museum of the American Revolution. Less well known but worth a visit is the Richmond area's **Henricus Historical Park**, a re-creation of the second successful English settlement in the New World, Henricus, established in 1611.

CRAFTS The Torpedo Factory in northern Virginia's Alexandria hosts 160 artists in a beehive of studios and galleries. **Charlottesville**, **Richmond**, and **Williamsburg** all have craft galleries. In the towns of the **Blue Ridge Highlands** and **southwestern Virginia**, the legacy of handcrafted items remains. Long known for quilts, baskets, wood carvings, and pottery, the region blooms with craft galleries, artists' studios, and craft shops. **Round the Mountain: Southwest Virginia's Artisan Network** (www.roundthemountain .org) offers an interactive trip planner that allows you to find crafts and artists whose work interests you.

CROOKED ROAD MUSIC TRAIL
The **Crooked Road** is Virginia's music heritage trail. The path, part of the **Blue Ridge Highlands** and **southwestern Virginia**, zigzags and meanders for 253 miles through 10 counties of the Appalachian Mountains. Joe Wilson in his book, *The Crooked Road: A Music Heritage Trail,* details the venues from local country stores to 40-year-old festivals where you can admire, listen to, learn about, and dance to the lively mountain tunes.

CRUISE PORT Carnival and **Holland America** are among the major cruise lines that depart from Norfolk or make a port stop in the city.

FACTORY OUTLETS Williamsburg Premium Outlets has more than 135 shops, including BCBG, Burberry, Calvin Klein, Carter's, Coach, Cole Haan, Gap Outlet, Nike, and Polo Ralph Lauren.

FARMERS' MARKETS Virginia still has farms. You can find fresh produce and local foods at the area's many farmers' markets. When applicable, the larger of the markets are included in each chapter. Check **Buy Local** (www.buylocalvirginia.org) for a listing near your destination. In northern Virginia, Alexandria's **Market Square** is thought to be the site of the oldest farmers' market in the country, one that once included produce from George Washington's Mount Vernon farm. On the Northern Neck, at **Westmoreland Berry Farm & Orchard**, Oak Grove, pick your own bushels of peaches, blackberries, raspberries, or strawberries—whatever is in season. Don't forget to put a coin in the feed dispenser to watch the farm goat walk ramps and platforms 20-feet high to get his reward. Yours can be an ice-cream sundae topped with fruit just off the trees. In central Virginia, visit Charlottesville's **City Market**; Nelson County's **Nelson Farmers' Market**, Nellysford; and Richmond's **17th Street Farmers' Market**. In the Shenandoah Valley, the **Virginia Farm Market**, Winchester, sells farm-fresh fare and displays 15,000 pumpkins in fall. In Lexington, browse the **Lexington Farmers Market** and **Rockbridge Farmers' Market**, and in Staunton, stroll the **Staunton/Augusta Farmers' Market**. The **Historic Roanoke City Market**, also known as the Farmers' Market, dates to 1882, making the place one of the oldest, continuously operated open-air markets in Virginia. In the Blue Ridge Highlands and southwestern Virginia, browse farmers' markets in **Abingdon** and **Blacksburg**.

GARDENS Norfolk Botanical Garden features 30 themed gardens on 155 acres; its rose garden delights with more than 3,000 plants. Richmond blooms with two spectacular botanical gardens: **Lewis Ginter**

Botanical Garden has 40 acres of plants and pathways, including a rose garden with 1,800 roses, and **Maymont House and Park** has 100 acres of trees and gardens.

GOLF Virginia Golf (www.virginia golf.com) describes the state's many courses. For the most part, we list those places easily available to visitors—public and resort courses. The **Williamsburg area** has the most golf courses. Among those open to the public are **Golden Horseshoe Golf Club's**, which has one 9-hole and two 18-hole courses; **Kingsmill Resort** has three courses; the **Williamsburg National Golf Club** has two; and **Virginia Beach** has several golf courses as well.

In Central Virginia, follow the **Monticello Golf Trail** to five courses in the Charlottesville area; and **Wintergreen Resort**, Nelson County, has both a mountaintop and a valley golf course. In the Blue Ridge Highlands and southwestern Virginia, **Primland Resort's Highland Course**, Meadows of Dan, offers good golf and great mountain views.

HIKING In Central Virginia's Nelson County, hike to **Crabtree Falls**, the highest cascading waterfall east of the Mississippi River. Experienced hikers can tackle 25 miles of the **Appalachian Trail. Shenandoah National Park** (www.nps.gov), which has more than 100 trails that cover 500 miles. Hundreds of miles of hiking trails lace the Blue Ridge Highlands and southwestern Virginia, home to several state parks and thousands of acres of the **George Washington and Jefferson National Forests**.

Alexandria Convention and Visitors Association

Virginia Tourism Corporation

HISTORIC CHURCHES In northern Virginia's Alexandria, **Christ Church** was frequented by George Washington and Robert E. Lee. In Williamsburg, the **Wren Building**, on the campus of the College of William and Mary, was designed by Christopher Wren and built at the turn of the 18th century. **St. John's Episcopal Church**, Hampton, was established in 1610, and is believed to be the oldest English-speaking parish in continuous service in America. The current structure dates to 1728. The Northern Neck's **Historic Christ Church**, on the National Register of Historic places, dates to 1735 and is the best example of colonial Anglican parish churches in Virginia. Norfolk's **St. Paul's Church** is the city's oldest building and the only structure that survived the British bombardment on January 1, 1776. Lord Dunmore, who had fled Williamsburg for Hampton Roads on the eve of the Revolution, fired a cannonball that still remains lodged in the church's southwestern wall. The church also has a Tiffany window. In 1775, in **St. John's Church**, Richmond, Patrick Henry declared his famous "Give me liberty or give me death" speech. The cemetery at Petersburg's **Old Blandford Church** contains the graves of 30,000 Confederate soldiers. To honor them, the town's Ladies Memorial Association chose Louis Comfort Tiffany to design 15 memorial windows, now one of the largest collections of Tiffany windows in the world. The **Lee Chapel and Museum**, on the Washington and Lee University campus, Lexington, was constructed in 1867 under the supervision of General Robert E. Lee. The chapel is noted for Charles Willson Peale's portrait of George Washington and Edward Valentine's recumbent sculpture of Lee, who served as president of the college from the end of the Civil War until his death in 1870. Staunton's **Trinity Church** features 12 stained-glass windows by Tiffany Studios.

HISTORIC HOMES AND PLANTATIONS (See also *Colonial History*.)

In northern Virginia, George Washington's beloved **Mount Vernon Estate** interprets colonial life and Washington's private world. The property's **Donald W. Reynolds Museum and Education Center** uses state-of-the-art exhibits in 23 galleries to reveal Washington's life from his early boyhood to his death. **Woodlawn Plantation**, originally part of the Mount Vernon Estate, is the home Washington gifted to his stepgranddaughter, Eleanor ("Nelly") Parke Custis, whom he raised with his wife, Martha; and her husband, Washington's nephew, Lawrence Lewis. **Gunston Hall**, Mason Neck, is an outstanding example of Federal-style architecture. The home once belonged to the influential George Mason IV, who ran the 5,500-acre

C. Stapen

tobacco and corn plantation during the 18th century. Along the Northern Neck, visit **George Washington Birthplace National Monument**, Popes Creek, and also nearby **Stratford Hall Plantation**, a stately great house completed in the 1740s that was a family home of the Lees of Virginia.

Colonial Williamsburg features original and re-created colonial-era buildings. Explore colonial life from a different point of view by touring the historic plantations across the James River. These plantations give a glimpse into the pomp and pleasures of a life grown prosperous in the New World. **Shirley Plantation**, Charles City, is among Virginia's most impressive plantations. Founded in 1613—just six years after Jamestown—it is still owned and operated by the descendants of Edward Hill. The imposing brick Queen Anne–style manor house dates to 1723. **Berkeley Plantation**, Charles City, is 2 miles down the road from Shirley Plantation. Berkeley Plantation's brick Georgian manor house was built in 1726 by Benjamin Harrison IV. Only the grounds of **Sherwood Forest Plantation**, Charles City, are open to the public on a regular basis. The manor house, built around 1720, is believed to be the longest frame house in the United States. The descendants of U.S. president John Tyler, who purchased the property while still in office in 1842, still live on property. The 1665 **Bacon's Castle**, a National Historic Landmark, is the oldest documented house in Virginia as well as a rare example of Jacobean architecture in the New World.

Explore three presidents' homes in the Charlottesville area: Thomas Jefferson's **Monticello**, James Monroe's

Ash Lawn–Highland, and James Madison's **Montpelier**. Not far away in Lynchburg is Jefferson's retreat **Poplar Forest**. Although surrounded by suburban homes, it offers insight on Jefferson's exceptional skills as an architect. Richmond has **Agecroft Hall**, an authentic 15th-century manor house brought over from England and reconstructed. The Northern Neck has two interesting historic homes: Popes Creek Plantation, at the **George Washington Birthplace National Monument**, Colonial Beach, is where the George was born on February 22, 1732. Even though only the footprint of the original Washington home remains, you do gain insight into what early life was like for the future president. **Stratford Hall Plantation**, Stratford, a stately great house completed in the 1740s, was the family home of the Lees of Virginia. Richard Henry Lee and Francis Lightfoot Lee, both signers of the Declaration of Independence, grew up at the plantation whose green lawns roll toward the Potomac River. Robert Edward Lee was born in the residence and resided there until he was almost four.

INNS AND BED-AND-BREAKFASTS When applicable, each section contains listings of that region's bed-and-breakfast establishments and inns.

ISLANDS Theodore Roosevelt Island, off George Washington Memorial Parkway, is an oasis of green, minutes from Washington, D.C. Trails wind through woods and paths afford great views of the Potomac. Twelve miles out in the Chesapeake Bay, **Tangier Island** sits like a world unto itself. About 500 people live on the 3 by 1½-mile spit of land. Tangiers's best asset is seafood. Take a day cruise to the island via **Broadwater Bay Ecotours** (www .broadwaterbayecotour.com).

LAKES In northern Virginia, **Lake Anna State Park**, Spotsylvania, has a 13,000-acre lake. Central Virginia has

Virginia Tourism Corporation

the state's two biggest freshwater lakes. **Smith Mountain Lake**, with 500 miles of shoreline, is the second largest; at a whopping 48,000 acres, **Buggs Island Lake (John H. Kerr Reservoir)**, which lies within **Occoneechee State Park** near the North Carolina border, is Virginia's largest lake. In the Blue Ridge Highlands and southwestern Virginia, several parks offer boating, fishing, and swimming in their lakes. The dam-created **Claytor Lake State Park** is big: 4,500 acres, 21 miles long, with 101 miles of shoreline. **Hungry Mother State Park** is noted for its woodlands and its 108-acre lake.

MILITARY HISTORY, SITES, MEMORIALS (See also *Colonial History* and *Civil War History.*) More than 300,000 soldiers from every U.S. military conflict, from the Revolutionary and Civil wars to the two world wars and those in Iraq and Afghanistan are buried at **Arlington National Cemetery**. The northern Virginia site also houses the Tomb of the Unknown Soldier as well as the burial plot for President John F. Kennedy and his brothers Robert and Edward. **Women in Military Service for America Memorial**, near Arlington National Cemetery, pays tribute to all women who have served in the military. Three simple spires gracefully arcing into the air create the **Air Force Memorial**. The elegant **Pentagon Memorial**, just outside the Pentagon itself, honors the 184 people who died here when terrorists crashed an airplane into the building on September 11, 2001. **The National Museum of the Marine Corps** presents two centuries' worth of artifacts that detail the marine experience.

In Newport News, the **Virginia War Museum** traces the development of the U.S. military from 1775 to the present, using exhibits of uniforms, weapons, posters, and personal items. In Norfolk, **Nauticus** details U.S. maritime history. You can tour the battleship the **USS *Wisconsin*** berthed alongside the museum as well as learn about the region's naval history at the **Hampton Roads Naval Museum** housed in Nauticus. Also in the city, tour the **Norfolk Naval Station Tours**, reputed to be the world's largest, with 4,300 acres. The **Mariners' Museum**, Newport News, features the USS Monitor Center that delves into the science and history of the recovery of the Civil War battleship *Monitor* that sank off the coast of Cape Hatteras, North Carolina. Bedford's **National D-Day Memorial** commemorates the epic Normandy invasion of June 6, 1944 (also called D-Day).

MUSEUMS (See also *Art Museums, Children, especially for*, and *Military History, Sites, Memorials.*) In Chantilly, adjacent to Dulles International Airport, the **Smithsonian Air and Space Museum–Steven F. Udvar-Hazy Center** owns the largest collection of air and space artifacts in the world. The facility houses the Smithsonian's biggest pieces: hangars full of historic airplanes, space ships, and other items hanging from 10-story-high trusses. Hampton is the location of the **Virginia Air and Space Center.** Yes, it's much smaller than Washington, D.C.'s National Air and Space Museum, but it's also much less crowded. Virginia Beach's **Atlantic Wildfowl Heritage Museum** is a must-see for those for whom carved decoys are a passion. Richmond's

Edgar Allan Poe Museum possesses one of the largest collections of Poe originals in the world.

OUTDOOR RECREATION (See also *Parks and Forests, National* and *Parks, Forests, Preserves, and Refuges, State and Regional.*) **Virginia Outdoors** (www.virginiaout doors.com) offers a wealth of information about where to hike, canoe, kayak, horseback ride, swim, fish, boat, and picnic.

PARKS AND FORESTS, NATIONAL Shenandoah National Park, gem of the Shenandoah Valley, celebrated its 75th anniversary in 2011. The park's 197,438 acres of forests, mountains, and streams preserves the region's legendary beauty. Enjoy the park by foot, hiking some of its more than 100 trails that cover 500 miles, and also drive through the park on legendary **Skyline Drive**, a road that stretches 105 miles across the crest of the Blue Ridge Mountains from Front Royal to Rockfish Gap.

PARKS, FORESTS, PRESERVES, AND REFUGES, STATE AND REGIONAL Check the state's Web site (www.dcr.state.va.us/parks) for a comprehensive listing of its state parks. In northern Virginia, enjoy **Great Falls Park**, an 800-acre park with views of Great Falls, where the Potomac River funnels into narrow, rocky passageway, as well as miles of hiking and walking trails. **Prince William Forest Park** is a 15,000-acre wooded park crisscrossed with 37 miles of hiking trails. At **Lake Anna State Park**, Spotsylvania, get out on the 13,000-acre lake in a pontoon boat, swim at a lifeguarded beach, or go fishing. The Northern Neck's

Westmoreland State Park extends about 1½ miles along the Potomac River, and its 1,311 acres neighbor the former homes of both George Washington and Robert E. Lee. On the Eastern Shore, **Kiptopeke State Park**, Cape Charles, located on the bay, has a swimming beach. **The Eastern Shore of Virginia National Wildlife Refuge**, off US 13 near the terminus of the Chesapeake Bay Bridge Tunnel, is a 1,393-acre refuge. A good portion of the **George Washington and Jefferson National Forest**'s 1.9 million acres lie in the Shenandoah region; the forest also includes most (200,000 acres) of **Mount Rogers National Recreation Area**. In Virginia, the forest runs from near Winchester in the north continuing through the Blue Ridge Highlands and southwestern Virginia to Abingdon in the south. The region's many state parks include **Claytor Lake State Park**, Dublin, which has a 4,500-acre lake; **Fairy Stone State Park**, in the Meadows of Dan region; **Grayson Highlands State Park**, Mouth of Wilson, about 35 miles from Abingdon; **Hungry**

pcopros

pcopros

Mother State Park, Marion; **Natural Tunnel State Park**, Duffield; and **New River Trail State Park**, in the Radford area.

RATES Every attempt has been made to list up-to-date rates, but always check with the property and look online for special rates and packages.

RESORTS A stay at the AAA Four Diamond **Williamsburg Inn** puts you in the heart of the Colonial Williamsburg's Historic Area. Nearby, the **Kingsmill Resort & Spa**, also an AAA Four Diamond resort, extends to 2,900 acres fronting the James River. **Great Wolf Lodge Williamsburg**, bigger than the average hotel but without the golf and fine dining typically found at resorts, attracts families to its mega-size indoor water park. **The Tides Inn**, Northern Neck, has an on-site sailing school in season. In Central Virginia, try **Keswick Hall at**

Monticello, an Orient-Express property that unfolds on 600 acres; and **Wintergreen Resort**, a golf and ski resort, encompasses nearly 11,000 acres in the Blue Ridge Mountains. In the Shenandoah Valley, go downhill at **Bryce** or **Massanutten** resort. The **Homestead Resort**, a grande dame property, takes up 3,000 acres in the Allegheny Mountains. In the Blue Ridge Highlands and southwestern Virginia, you can choose plain or fancy mountain accommodations. The **Mountain Lake Conservancy and Hotel** Pembroke, with its serviceable lodge rooms and cottages, offers 2,600 acres for your enjoyment. This traditional lake resort served as the set for the movie *Dirty Dancing*. **Primland Resort Lodge at Primland**, Meadows of Dan, offers luxury on 12,000 acres that have 18-hole golf course, a spa, tennis courts, an indoor pool, horseback riding, and stargazing at the property's own observatory equipped with a high-powered telescope.

SCENIC DRIVES Much of Virginia's countryside offers a treat to the eye. Here are some highlights: In the Tidewater/Hampton Roads area, you can travel across the **Chesapeake Bay Bridge Tunnel**. The Shenandoah Region has two legendary roads: **Skyline Drive**, which winds through Shenandoah National Park, as well as the **Blue Ridge Parkway**. The latter drive starts near Waynesboro and winds for 469 miles through the Shenandoah Valley, connecting Shenandoah National Park to the Great Smoky Mountains National Park, North Carolina, crossing into North Carolina at milepost 218. In the Blue Ridge Highlands and southwestern Virginia, the road cuts through southern Appalachia, offering access to scenic views, lush woods, state parks, and country towns.

In the Williamsburg area, drive the 24-mile, wooded **Colonial Parkway** that connects Colonial Williamsburg, Jamestown, and Yorktown. The winding road, with its occasional views of the James and York rivers, is scenic and soothing. The **Journey Through Hallowed Ground**, a scenic byway, stretches for 180 miles from Gettysburg, Pennsylvania, to Charlottesville. If you prefer to pick it up in central Virginia, the suggested 52.6-mile drive begins at Montpelier, continues to the Barboursville Ruins located on the winery, then leads to Ash Lawn–Highland, James Monroe's home, and onto Monticello, Thomas Jefferson's estate, before ending in downtown Charlottesville.

SKIING Yes, Virginia, there is skiing in the state. A popular ski (and four-season resort) is **Wintergreen Resort**, Wintergreen, 43 miles southwest of Charlottesville. The resort has comprehensive ski programs. Part of Lynchburg's Liberty University, the **Liberty Mountain Snowflex Centre**, offers skiing on synthetic snow year-round. In the Shenandoah Valley, go downhill at **Bryce** or **Massanutten** resort. The **Homestead Resort Ski Area**, part of the famed Homestead Resort, is best for beginners and those looking for fun, not thrills.

SPAS The **Williamsburg Inn** offers a variety of soothing treatments from massages to soaks, many of which are based on colonial use of herbs and other botanicals. **Kingsmill Resort**, Williamsburg, and **Wintergreen Resort**, Wintergreen, also have nice spas. The **Homestead Resort**, Hot Springs, was founded its healing mineral springs. You can still soak in its historic **Jefferson Pool** that dates to 1761 and is named for the third president who stayed at the Homestead in 1818 and soaked in the waters in hopes the healing minerals would ease his arthritis.

WILD PONIES Every year, at the end of July during **Pony Penning Week**, Chincoteague, "saltwater cowboys" mount their horses and herd ponies across the channel between the wildlife preserve on Assateague Island, where they live, and Chincoteague Island, where the foals are sold to families eager to own a cute little piece of history.

WINERIES Virginia, with more than 180 wineries, boasts that it is the fifth-largest producer of wine in the United States. See **Virginia Wine** (www.virginiawine.org) for a list of wineries as well as regional wine trails and events. The **Williamsburg Winery** produces about 60,000 cases per year, making it one of the state's largest wineries. The Monticello and Albemarle County region is called the "birthplace of American wine" because of Thomas Jefferson's early but unsuccessful attempts to grow wine-producing grapes. The **Monticello Wine Trail** features 23 vineyards in Albemarle and other nearby counties. Our favorites to visit, for the wine and/or the scenery, include **Barboursville Vineyards**, Barboursville; **Jefferson Vineyards**, Charlottesville; **King Family Vineyards**, Crozet; **New Kent Winery**, New Kent (listed on the Chesapeake Bay Wine Trail even though the facility is between Richmond and Williamsburg); and **Prince Michel Vineyards & Winery**, Leon. The Bedford Wine Trail leads to four wineries, including the Peaks of Otter Winery, known for its fruit wines. The **Chesapeake Bay Wine Trail** leads to nine wineries. Among the Eastern Shore's wineries are **Bloxom Winery**, Bloxom; **Chatham Vineyards**, Machipongo; and **Holly Grove Vineyards**, Exmore. Among the wineries in the Shenandoah Valley are **Linden Vineyards**, Linden, whose owner keeps his winery peaceful by not allowing groups larger than six people to tour. Founded in 1976, **Shenandoah Vineyards**, Edinburg, is the oldest winery in the Shenandoah Valley. **Vino Curioso**, Winchester, a boutique winery, is open by appointment only. Among the wineries in the Blue Ridge Highlands and Southwest Virginia are two in the Floyd area, **Château Morrisette** and **Villa Appalaccia Winery**.

Tidewater Virginia

VIRGINIA'S HISTORIC TRIANGLE:
WILLIAMSBURG, JAMESTOWN,
YORKTOWN

HAMPTON ROADS

CHESAPEAKE BAY:
NORTHERN NECK AND
THE MIDDLE PENINSULA

INTRODUCTION

Rivers, primarily the James, York, and Potomac, rising and falling with tides from the Chesapeake Bay, define Virginia's Tidewater region. When Captain John Smith landed on the Powhatan (later known as the James River) in 1607, these fertile lands had long been home to Native Americans who fished along the shores and hunted the abundant wildfowl. The explorer, or interloper, established the Jamestown Settlement, named after his king. The next year, Smith and his crew explored the Chesapeake Bay by oar and sail, traveling up the Potomac and the Rappahannock rivers and the latter's tributaries. The Northern Neck, adjacent Middle Peninsula, and the Colonial Williamsburg regions are historically rich, not just for themselves or for Virginia, but for the United States. In the Northern Neck, on a walk along the shores of Popes Creek at the George Washington Birthplace National Monument, Westmoreland County—the plantation where the first U.S. president was born on February 22, 1732—you can sense the culture of farms and access to water that shaped him and other important families—the Carters, the Fairfaxes, and the Lees. At Stratford Hall, a mere 7 miles from Popes Creek, Richard Henry Lee and Francis Lightfoot Lee, both signers of the Declaration of Independence, grew up. Robert E. Lee was born at that impressive plantation on January 19, 1807. Land meant security and wealth.

Water was the way to move goods. For convenience, we've divided the Tidewater region into three sections. It was between the James and York rivers that America took root. In section one, **Virginia's Historic Triangle: Williamsburg, Jamestown, Yorktown**, learn about the lives of the early settlers, the forces that led to revolt, and the battles that won a new nation. In section two, **Hampton Roads**, discover how the region's development was and remains linked to the sea. Norfolk—heart of the Hampton Roads region and the "0–mile" marker on the Intracoastal Waterway—is home to one of the world's largest naval installations. In section three, **Chesapeake Bay: Northern Neck and the Middle Peninsula**, find thousands of miles of shoreline. Along with attracting history buffs, the Tidewater region lures boaters, birders, beach lovers, and eco-adventurers. The Northern Neck alone has 1,200 miles of tidal coastline as well as 6,500 acres of natural areas, including marshes, state parks and preserves.

In season, sun and sand enthusiasts flock to Virginia Beach's 20 miles of soft, white sands.

And don't forget to sample the local, water-blessed fare: oysters, crab cakes, and really fresh seafood.

VIRGINIA'S HISTORIC TRIANGLE: WILLIAMSBURG, JAMESTOWN, YORKTOWN

You never know who you'll meet in Virginia's Historic Triangle. And that's part of the fun. At Historic Jamestowne, you could be pacing the palisade with an officer who made the long, treacherous journey from England to settle in the colony. At Colonial Williamsburg, you might chat with Thomas Jefferson, listen to Patrick Henry argue for independence, and even join ranks with fellow rebels to learn how to march and to handle a musket. Virginia's Historic Triangle—Williamsburg, Jamestown, and Yorktown—is where America took root. That history is played out at several attractions, each providing a different slant on the birthing of America. With costumed interpreters and guides, Colonial Williamsburg and the two "Jamestowns" focus on the people, the pioneers, and the patriots in the New World. Yorktown Battlefield, the site of the last major battle of the American Revolution, adds a military perspective. The historic plantations along the James River, including Bacon's Castle, built in 1665, showcase how the old-world gentry lived once they crossed the Atlantic. The region, however, provides much more than history. Unofficially dubbed "Virginia's golf capital," Williamsburg's greens and fairways are a challenge. The area's resorts please vacationers who can opt for first-class service at

A PERSON FROM THE PAST, COLONIAL WILLIAMSBURG

C. Stapen

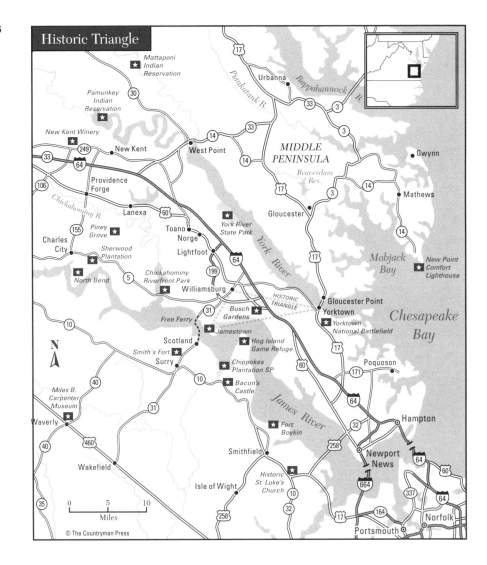

the Williamsburg Inn, homelike condominiums at Kingsmill, pioneer-themed rooms plus a gigantic indoor water park at Great Wolf Lodge, or good deals at a variety of roadside hotels. Combine these lodging options and varied attractions with expansive outlet malls, Virginia's largest winery, and an array of restaurants from down-home Southern fare to trendy, upmarket meals, and you can see why the region is a major tourist draw.

TOWNS Jamestown. There are actually two "Jamestowns." While neither is a "town" as we know the term and each as a Williamsburg mailing address, both are interesting attractions that make up part of Virginia's Historic Triangle. Historic Jamestowne is the site of the first permanent English settlement in the

New World. The adjacent Jamestown Settlement is a living history museum that brings the era and the colonists' struggles to life.

Williamsburg. Colonial Williamsburg is the most famous—and popular—attraction in the region, but there's more to the area. Like any city, this one has its downtown, or "New Town," with services that support the residents as well as the students at William and Mary, a four-year university not far from the Historic Area. The Williamsburg region is also known for its winery and shopping outlets as well as for Busch Gardens Williamsburg, a theme park.

Yorktown. This small town on the York River is best known for its battlefield, the site of the last major battle of the Revolutionary War.

GUIDANCE Greater Williamsburg Chamber and Tourism Alliance (757-229-6511; www.williamsburgcc.com), 421 North Boundary Street, Williamsburg. Weekdays 8:30–5. In addition to providing information about Colonial Williamsburg, the chamber has information on the nonhistoric attractions, shops, and restaurants in the Williamsburg area, including those in Jamestown and Yorktown.

Colonial Williamsburg's Visitor Center (757-229-1000; 1-800-HISTORY; www.history.org), P.O. Box 1776 or Visitor Center Drive, Williamsburg. Open daily 8:45–5, summer 8:45 AM–9 PM. Begin your Historic Area visit with a stop at the Visitor Center, If you haven't purchased tickets already, you can buy them here. It's essential to obtain the calendar of events for the week. Along with containing a map, the brochure lists the special programs, exhibits, and attractions. One-Day Basic $37 adults, $18 ages 6–17. One-Day Plus includes the Governor's Palace $46 adults, $23 ages 6–17. Annual Pass $59 adults, $29 ages 6–17. Often the Williamsburg area offers multiattraction passes.

America's Historic Triangle (www.historictriangle.com) also offers information.

The Gallery at York Hall (757-890-3300; www.yorkcounty.gov), 301 Main Street, Yorktown. Open Mon.–Fri. 8:15–5. The office has brochures about area attractions.

GETTING THERE Williamsburg, 150 miles south of Washington, D.C., can be reached from I-64. Williamsburg is located midway between Richmond and Virginia Beach.

By air: The **Newport News/Williamsburg International Airport** (757-877-0221; www.nnwairport.com) is 14 miles (about 15 minutes) from Williamsburg; the **Norfolk International Airport** (757-857-3351; www.norfolkairport.com) is about 45 miles (about 50 minutes) from Williamsburg; and the **Richmond International Airport** (804-226-3052; wwwflyrichmond.com) is about 45 miles or 50 minutes from Williamsburg.

By bus: The **Greyhound** bus terminal (1-800-231-2222: www.greyhound.com), 468 North Boundary Street. The historic area is a short cab ride or a long walk from the station.

By car: From Washington and Baltimore, take I-395 south toward Richmond to I-95 south onto I-295 south toward I-64 east. Continue on VA 143 toward US 60.

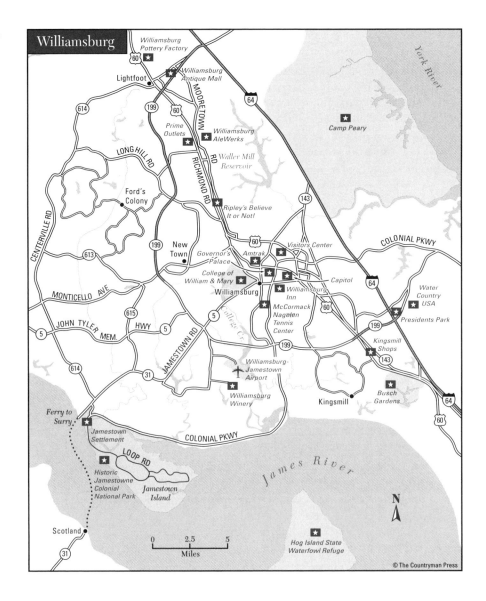

From Richmond, take I-95 north toward I-64 east toward VA 143. From Norfolk/Hampton Roads, take I-64 west toward VA 199 west.

By train: **Amtrak** (757-220-3399; www.amtrak.com), 468 North Boundary Street, Williamsburg, services Williamsburg. The historic area is a short cab ride or a long walk from the station.

GETTING AROUND Local bus transportation is provided by **Williamsburg Area Transit Authority** (WATA) (757-220-5493; www.williamsburgtransport .com), open winter Mon.–Sat. 6 AM–8 PM, summer Mon.–Sat. 6 AM–10 PM. However, it's easiest to get around the region by car, especially if you plan to visit the wineries, plantations, and other attractions in the outlying areas.

WATA also operates the **Williamsburg Trolley** (757-220-5493; www.williams burgtransport.com), which makes roundtrips from New Town and Merchants Square, stopping at the Williamsburg Shopping Center and High Street. Open Mon.–Thu. 3–10 PM, Fri. and Sat. 3–11 PM, Sun. noon–8 PM.

The **Historic Triangle Shuttle** (757-898-2410; www.nps.gov/colo) operates a free shuttle that connects Colonial Williamsburg with Jamestown and Yorktown from mid-March through October.

The **Jamestown Area Shuttle** links Historic Jamestowne, Jamestown Glasshouse, and Jamestown Settlement. Operates daily 9–5 in season.

The **Yorktown Trolley** stops at Yorktown Battlefield Visitor Center, Yorktown Victory Center, and Riverwalk Landing. Operates daily 10–6 in season.

Colonial Williamsburg Shuttle Buses, available to any Historic Area ticket holder, transports guests from the Visitor Center to select stops on the periphery of the Historic Area. Operates daily 8:50 AM–10 PM.

WHEN TO COME Spring and summer are high seasons, whereas fall brings nice walking weather and fewer crowds. Although winter is cold, the Historic Area looks lovely dappled with snow and decorated with real wreaths, fragrant pinecones, and flickering candles. Forget about plastic blow-up Santas or strings of lights. Such modern decorations aren't permitted. In addition, the special balls and other holiday events make this a good time to visit.

MEDICAL EMERGENCY Sentara Williamsburg Regional Medical Center (757-984-6000), 100 Sentara Circle, Williamsburg.

✴ To See
Colonial Williamsburg
Colonial Williamsburg depicts the town of Williamsburg on the eve of the American Revolution. From 1699 to 1776, Williamsburg served as the capital of Virginia, England's oldest, largest, and richest colony. In the years leading up to the American Revolution, Williamsburg bred independent politics and drew radicals such as Thomas Jefferson and Patrick Henry. Colonial Williamsburg is one of the most well-known living history museums in the United States and also one of the world's largest such facilities. The Historic Area consists of 301 acres and has more than 500 buildings. Of these, 88 homes, taverns, shops, and other structures are original to the 18th and early 19th centuries. The remaining buildings were re-created based on meticulous plans.

Colonial Williamsburg is the kind of place you can visit many times. Spring and summer bring military drills, garden tours, and other special programs. During the December holidays, there are fireworks and a candlelit ball, the perfect place to show off your hoop skirt. During every season, the Colonial Williamsburg Foundation hosts various lectures, music recitals, and other changing programs.

Colonial Williamsburg offers a variety of admission passes. Prices vary by season and often discounts are available online. A one- or two-day pass permits access to most major buildings, including the Capitol, the Governor's Palace, Raleigh Tavern, all trade sites, the Courthouse, Gaol, Magazine, Peyton Randolph House, George Wythe House, the Abby Aldrich Rockefeller Folk Art Museum, Bassett Hall, and the DeWitt Wallace Decorative Arts Museum. One-day pass $38 adults, $19 ages 6–17. Two-day pass $46 adults, $25 ages 6–17.

MUSEUMS ⅃ **Abby Aldrich Rockefeller Folk Art Museum** (757-220-7724; www.history.org), 326 West Francis Street. Open daily 10–7. This museum houses one of the country's best collections of folk art from the 17th through the 19th centuries. Although the exhibits change, you are likely to see landscapes and portraits of kids in period attire (yes, that young child in the long dress is a boy), furniture, quilts, and whimsical weather vanes adorned with hogs and cows. The museum's changing exhibits have focused on quilts, whirligigs and other items. Take young children to see Down on the Farm, a display of three-dimensional scenes from a storybook. Inspired, kids can sit at the room's table, draw their own scenes and display them. Admission included in the one-day, annual and some other passes. Otherwise, one-day pass $10 adults, $5 ages 6–17; annual pass $20 adults, $10 ages 6–17.

TOWNSWOMAN AT REVOLUTIONARY CITY, COLONIAL WILLIAMSBURG

C. Stapen

⅃ **The DeWitt Wallace Decorative Arts Museum** (757-220-7724; www .history.org), 326 West Francis Street. Open daily 10–7. Enter through the Public Hospital of 1773. For those who like antiques and fine furnishings, the DeWitt Wallace Museum is a gift to the eye. The Masterworks Gallery showcases expertly crafted tall case clocks, sideboards, and chairs. Other galleries feature early examples of harpsichords, grand pianos, and violins; delicate porcelain dinnerware; and impressive silver tea services. Even though Teen Takes: A New Angle on Art, a free audio tour of 17 objects, provides comments narrated by teens, the narrative provides insight on the objects useful for adults, too. Admission included with general pass.

HISTORIC BUILDINGS AND SITES Most all of Colonial Williamsburg's structures, whether re-creations or built upon original foundations or footprints, are considered historic. Not all of the buildings are open for tours and of those that are, some have restricted hours, so it's important to check the program guide, *Colonial Williamsburg This Week*, available at the Visitor Center.

The Historic Area's richness comes from its diversity of buildings—public, private, and trade shops—combined with special interpretive programs. Among the grandest buildings and the must-sees are those built to govern the burgeoning community—the Capitol and Governor's Palace. Among the rich and famous family homes on tour are the Peyton Randolph House and the George Wythe House.

✍ **Benjamin Powell House**, Waller Street near Nicholson Street. Open summer Fri.–Sat. 9–5, Sun. 2–5, and other selected times. Powell, a carpenter and contractor, built the Public Gaol, the steeple for the Bruton Parish church, and a few other Williamsburg landmarks. A guide in period attire teaches children how to play with colonial-era toys. Try "catching" a ball in a wooden cup, putting together alphabet puzzles, and playing pick-up sticks. Kids don't seem to mind that the non-air-conditioned building can get uncomfortably warm.

&. **The Capitol** (757-220-7645; www.history.org), east end of Duke of Gloucester Street. Guided tours daily 9–4:30. The imposing brick building is the third on this site. On a guided tour, see the halls where such stalwart supporters of revolution as Thomas Jefferson, Patrick Henry, and George Washington delivered impassioned speeches. On May 15, 1776—almost two months before the Continental Congress in Philadelphia—legislators in the Capitol unanimously voted for a resolution seeking independence from Britain.

George Wythe House (757-220-7645; www.history.org), Palace Green. Open daily 9–1. Guided tours daily 9–4:30. This grand house, the home of George Wythe, a prominent lawyer, was built in the mid-1750s. It is likely that Thomas Jefferson and his family stayed here in 1776. Guided tours included with admission.

&. **Governor's Palace** (757-220-7645; www.history.org), Palace Green. Guided tours daily 9–4:30. Grand by Williamsburg standards, the Governor's Palace was built to impress and to remind the townspeople of the Crown's power. Bayonets, muskets, and swords line the entrance hall and gilt mirrors hang on the walls, some

MUSIC RECITAL, GOVERNOR'S PALACE
C. Stapen

of which are covered with hand-tooled leather. The tour takes in the public rooms, including the ballroom where Thomas Jefferson once danced, as well as the private bedrooms. Sensing trouble, the last royal governor, the Earl of Dunmore, sent his wife and six children back to England. After Dunmore removed the gunpowder from the Magazine in 1775, he had 40 sailors surround the palace to protect him from the citizens' rage. On June 8, 1775, Dunmore fled his former lavish residence and never returned. After the guided tour, allow time to explore the gardens adorned with topiary, a bowling green and a holly maze. Included with a Plus admission.

Peyton Randolph House (757-220-7645; www.history.org), Nicholson Street and Market Square. Hours vary. One of the Historic Area's outstanding homes, the structure was originally built in 1715. Peyton Randolph, from a wealthy Virginia family, served as the first president of the Continental Congress. Typically, you take a self-guided tour and can ask questions of guides in various rooms. Sometimes special programs take place in the house. On one of our visits we watched a ghost tour presentation in the home. Guided tours are included with admission.

SPECIAL PROGRAMS An effective way to get into the spirit of time travel and to see beyond the Historic Area's commercialism is to take part in one or more of the special programs. The clash between the 18th-century world and ours makes the time travel lively. Programs change seasonally and the scripts vary. Among the many options are garden tours, furniture talks, meetings with a founding father (Mr. Jefferson is particularly witty), musical interludes, and witch trials. For families, there are children's orientation tours, dance and music (Dance, Our Dearest Diversion) and African American tales (Listen, My Children: Legends, Myths and Fables for Families). We recommend participating in at least one day and one evening tour (such as the Tavern Ghost Walk). After all, moonlight makes time travel easy. Some programs, such as In Their Own Words: African Americans in the Revolutionary Era, are included with a regular admission; others require a more expensive admission ticket, whereas others, including many of the evening programs, require a separate ticket. Some highlights include the following:

♿ **Great Hopes Plantation** (757-220-7645; www.history.org), Colonial Williamsburg. Great Hopes represents a plantation that existed in York County, Virginia, during the 18th century. Not the estate of the well-born, Great Hopes re-creates what Patrick Henry called the world of the "middling," those who weren't shop owners but who worked 100 acres or so. At Great Hopes, Colonial Williamsburg interprets farming—and because slave owning was typically a part of that world, Great Hopes presents field slave interpreters and offers, at select times, special African-American programs.

Order in the Court (757-220-7645; www.history.org), Courthouse, Duke of Gloucester Street and the Palace Green. Your first lesson about colonial justice comes when the clerk calls for white, land-owning, Protestant men 21 years of age or older. Only these people could serve as jurors. Other volunteers serve as plaintiffs, defendants, and witnesses. The trails vary. On one visit we watch a husband, whose tipsy wife sang a ditty belittling the king, receive a £2 fine. On cue, the poor man, a visitor, complained that such a fee was beyond his means—how then was justice served? The judge ordered the wife to be lashed to a stool and dunked six times. "As you grow wet, may you grow wise," he intoned. Included with admission.

♿ **Revolutionary City**, east end of Duke of Gloucester Street. Mid-Mar.–mid-Oct. daily 3–5, weather permitting. Part street theater, part history lesson, this outdoor program puts you in the middle of the town's central controversy. Do you support revolution or not? Walk along the street and eavesdrop on the locals arguing. Depending on the program, you may be pulled by a bewigged gentleman into a rally for independence, or asked by a bonneted woman with hoop skirts as broad as barn whether you're a traitor. With children in tow, arrive 15 minutes early for Get Revved. Geared to kids, this introductory segment includes songs and typically lessons in how to curtsy. Revolutionary City, rich with "persons from the past," can be entertaining and informative. Sometimes, however, the "speechifying" goes on too long, especially in the vignette about the royal governor. He does, however, arrive impressively in a horse-drawn coach. If you must choose just one program to watch, we recommend either Citizens at War or Building a Nation, because these allow more opportunity to chat with the characters. Included with admission.

✐ **Trade Shops** Visit the trade shops to learn about the realities of 18th-century life. Check the weekly guide for times. It's most fun to visit when a tradesperson is present or conducting a special program. While it might be boring to look at a row of hats at the milliner, it's engaging to chat with the shop owner, especially when he talks about creating baby clothes in Welcome, Little Stranger. Many of the 21 craft sites are on Duke of Gloucester Street. These include: the **Apothecary**; ♿ **Blacksmith**; **Milliner and Tailor**, Margaret Hunter Shop; ♿ **Printer and Binder**, Printing Office and Post Office; **Shoemaker**; **Silversmith**, Golden Ball; **Weaver**, Taliaferro-Cole Shop; **Wigmaker**, Kings' Arms Barber Shop.

Other trades are: **Brickmakers**, brickyard off Nicholson Street; **Cabinetmaker**, Nicholson Street; **Carpenter and Joiner**, Ayscough house, Francis Street; ♿ **Cooper**, Ludwell-Paradies stables; **Gunsmith**, James Geddy Workshop off the Palace Green.

Wren Building (757-221-4000; www.wm.edu), west end Duke of Gloucester Street, College of William and Mary campus. Call for tours. A jewel of the College of William and Mary, the Wren Building, designed by Christopher Wren, was built between 1695 and 1700. Although the building was destroyed by fire three times, much of the outer walls date to the original construction. The Chapel looks much as it might have in the 18th century. Although William and Mary is the second-oldest college in the United States (Harvard is older), it is believed that the Wren Building is the oldest college building in the United States.

Jamestown

♿ **Historic Jamestowne** (757-229-1733; www.historicjamestowne.org), western end of the Colonial Parkway, 9 miles from Colonial Williamsburg. Open daily

AFRICAN SLAVES AND THE AMERICAN REVOLUTION AT COLONIAL WILLIAMSBURG

In the 1770s, patriots such as Patrick Henry and Thomas Jefferson argued for rebellion from Britain because the motherland had violated their rights with excessive taxation and other punitive acts. But what about the slaves? To find out what choices they had, we sign up for In Their Own Words: African Americans in the Revolutionary Era, a one-hour walking tour included free with Historic Area tickets.

On the eve of the rebellion, the period depicted at Colonial Williamsburg, Africans accounted for more than 52 percent of the population. The first thing Louise, our guide, does is to line up our group of 25 shoulder to shoulder in tight rows to simulate the "loose pack" formation slaves endured for 70 days on the voyage from West Africa. We march across the street to Bruton Parish Church, a few minutes' walk. Despite being unshackled and upright (real slaves had been prone on the floor), the forced closeness makes us feel encroached upon.

Then, Louise points to one row, saying, "Move over there; you didn't make it." About 20 percent of the captives died en route. Louise reminds us that in the New World, we are property. "Like a chair or a table, slaves had no rights," she says.

The first Africans arrived in Jamestown in 1619. A 1670 proclamation declared that all non-Christians entering the colony by ship would be in servitude for life, as would their children, their children's children, and all the

8:30–4:30. Closed Thanksgiving, Dec. 25, and Jan. 1. Historic Jamestowne marks the original 1607 site of the first permanent English community in America. Although the earliest, enduring toehold in the New World beats Plymouth in Massachusetts by thirteen years, the Virginia locale lacks the Pilgrim landing's name recognition. Unlike Colonial Williamsburg, as part of Colonial National Historical Park this site on the James River is, more natural than developed, despite an obelisk memorial and a 1907 re-creation of a historic church.

The video in the Visitor Center uses nine computers to show 3,000 images that introduce visitors to the perils faced by the community of 104 men and boys who came ashore. Their landing marked the beginning of America's colonization. The site has been an active dig since 1994. Remarkably, the head archaeologist, William Kelso, discovered the original post molds, remnants of the stains left in the ground by the decayed wood of the fort's palisades. Two rows of rough wooden planks re-create two sides of the original, triangular fort. (The third side now can't be depicted, as it would be in the water.)

following generations. Some owners had their slaves converted to Christianity. No matter, Louise states; Christian slaves, the Church pronounced around 1677, will continue to be property. However, the master of a baptized slave, the Church declared, will reap a reward in heaven.

A few lucky slaves obtained freedom by purchasing it. One of Colonial Williamsburg's 11 free blacks, Matthew Ashby, worked for years to buy his wife and three children from their owner for £150, a fortune in the 1770s. Governor Dunmore, in November 1775, provided another option. With the colony in near open revolt, the governor retreated to a ship in Norfolk harbor. From there he mandated freedom for any slave who joined the British forces to fight the patriots.

"What would you do?" Louise asks, "Remain a slave to your master?" Likely to encounter hard times in war, your master could sell you and your children to separate owners at any moment. Even though the British promised freedom, as a slave you had to reach the royal troops in Norfolk, a formidable 45 miles away.

We arrive at a surprising decision. Despite our patriotic zeal, we say, "Go with the British." Although the odds are against us even making it to Norfolk, at least there, we reason, we have a chance to keep our children and someday, if we survive, be free.

About 100,000 slaves made that choice. Many died en route and in battle. Some were caught, returned, and severely punished or killed. Despite losing the Revolution, the British kept their promise, resettling 20,000 to 25,000 former slaves as free people in Nova Scotia.

The wine bottles, brass candlesticks, clay pipes, potshards, tailor's shears, horse bones, a gold ring, a silver ear picker (employed by well-bred gentlemen to scoop wax out of their ears), and a rare slate with New World flowers and birds on display at the Archaerium, the site's museum, detail aspects of the first colonists' daily lives. JR, the skeletal cast of a 19- to 22-year-old man with a musket shot still embedded in his leg, testifies to the era's dangers. To get more of a sense of what the New World looked like to the first English settlers, drive the park's 5-mile loop that cuts through acres of natural woodlands and marsh. $10, free for age 15 and younger. Four-site ticket good for Historic Jamestowne, Jamestowne Settlement, Yorktown Battlefield, and Yorktown Victory Center $30 adults, $19.25 ages 13–15, $9.25 ages 6–12, free for age 5 and younger.

✂ ♿ **Jamestown Settlement** (757-253-4838; 1-888-593-4682; www.historyisfun.org), 2110 Jamestown Road, Rte. 31 south, Williamsburg. Open mid-Aug.–mid-June daily 9–5, summer daily 9–6. This attraction fills in much of the history

HISTORIC JAMESTOWNE'S SPECIAL PROGRAMS

In the Trenches, typically the first and third Mondays of the month, April through October. History buffs can walk the settlement led by Dr. Kelso, the archaeologist whose persistence unearthed much of the original Jamestowne. Reserve ahead by purchasing tickets online or at the museum the day of the tour. $30.

Curator's Artifact Tour, typically the second and fourth Wednesdays of the month, April through October. Learn how artifacts are recovered from the site and get a behind-the-scenes tour of the archaeological lab that includes viewing items not displayed in the Archaerium. Reserve ahead by purchasing tickets online, or buy at the museum the day of the tour. $20.

Living History Tour, four times daily in summer, weekends only September through October. Hear about life at the James Fort from a costumed inter-preter who relates details of the pioneers and their daily struggles. Free.

and background pertaining to the original Jamestowne. Although we've marked this with a children's icon because of the living history areas, Jamestowne Settle-ment appeals to adults, too, especially the 30,000-square-foot gallery. Interest-ingly, the gallery's focus isn't just on the settlers. Instead, the exhibits detail the relationships between the region's three cultures—Native Americans, English, and African. The Powhatans already inhabited the New World when the first English settlers arrived in 1607. The first documented Africans arrived in Vir-ginia in 1619.

In the area devoted to the Powhatans, learn about their camps and listen to a recording of their actual language. Find out about the investors of the Jamestown colony and their difficult voyage to the New World. The film *From Africa to Virginia* details the slave trade. Among the exhibits for children are a walk through a planter's house, slave quarters, and a native home covered in bark. Outdoors, at the three living history areas, guides wear period clothing, but speak in contemporary English. At the Powhatan Village, depending on the day, you might watch guides—and assist them—in tanning hides, crafting pottery, or cooking food. Replicas of the *Susan Constant,* the *Godspeed,* and the *Discovery,* the three ships that left England with the future colonists, are moored at the riverfront. Aboard a ship you can chat with a crew member, see the cramped quarters, and try to figure out latitude with an astrolabe, an early navigational tool. At the Riverfront Discovery Area, kids—or anyone—can watch and chat with interpreters about boat-building, learn early fishing techniques, and help carve a canoe from a tree trunk. James Fort, a triangular structure, recreates the 1610–14 Jamestown Settlement, including its church, storehouse, and guard-house. Kids can try on armor and watch musket drills. $14 adults, $6.50 ages 6–12. Four-site ticket good for Historic Jamestowne, Jamestowne Settlement, Yorktown Battlefield, and Yorktown Victory Center $30 adults, $19.25 ages

13–15, $9.25 ages 6–12, free for age 5 and younger. Check with the **Greater Williamsburg Chamber and Tourism Alliance** (757-229-6511; www.williams burgcc.com) for additional multiattraction passes.

Yorktown area

Colonial National Historical Park (757-898-2410; www.nps.gov/colo), between the York and James rivers; write to P.O. Box 210, Yorktown 23690. Stretching for more than 9,000 acres on a peninsula between the York and James rivers, Colonial National Historical Park includes Historic Jamestowne, Yorktown Battlefield, and the 24-mile Colonial Parkway that connects Colonial

THE REAL POCAHONTAS

Long before the region became Virginia's Historic Triangle, it served as home to the Native American nation the Powhatans, an Algonquin-speaking people. When the English settlers arrived, the Powhatans numbered roughly 14,000, divided into about 30 tribal groups. The real Pocahontas, the daughter of Wahunsonacock, sometimes called Wahunsenacawh or Chief Powhatan, was born in the area in 1596. Although Amonute and Matoaka were her formal names, history has come to refer to the Indian maiden as Pocahontas, a nickname she had that means "playful one."

According to Captain John Smith, he first met Pocahontas in 1607 when she was about 11 years old. Smith states that he had been captured by the Powhatans and brought to the chief's capital on the York River. After a feast, the Native Americans placed Smith's head on two stones as if to kill him. Pocahontas, writes Smith, "got his head in her armes, and laid her owne upon his to save him from death."

In 1608, Pocahontas came to Jamestowne with gifts of food, to persuade the English to release some Native American prisoners. When Smith left Virginia in 1609, other colonists told her that he had died. Pocahontas later married Kocoum, a Native American. In 1613 Samuel Argall kidnapped Pocahontas. As a result, Powhatan released seven English settlers taken prisoner along with some guns and permitted Pocahontas to live among the English.

Baptized in 1614, she was given the name Rebecca. Soon afterward she married John Rolfe, who introduced tobacco to Virginia as a cash crop. In 1616, after Pocahontas, her husband and young son traveled to England to encourage new settlers to come to Virginia, she met briefly with John Smith. In 1617, before she could return to the colony, Pocahontas became ill and died at Gravesend, England. In Jamestown Settlement's museum, you can compare various images of Pocahontas from early paintings to a cell from Disney's popular movie named for her.

Williamsburg, Jamestown, and Yorktown. (See "Historic Jamestowne" and "Yorktown Battlefield" in *To Do*.)

In Yorktown

Cape Henry Memorial (757-898-2410; www.nps.gov/colo), between the York and James rivers; write to P.O. Box 210, Yorktown 23690. Open daily, dawn–dusk, but call first. Because the memorial is located on Fort Story Military Reservation, the site maybe closed due to security concerns. The memorial marks the actual landing site of the pioneers who settled Jamestown, who landed at Cape Henry at 4 AM on April 26, 1607. The site consists of memorial cross, plaque, and interpretive panel.

♿ **Yorktown Battlefield** (757-898-2410; www.nps.gov/yonb), eastern end of the Colonial Parkway. Open daily 9–5. Closed Thanksgiving, Dec. 25, and Jan. 1. The Visitor Center's film, *Siege of Yorktown*, places the battle, the last major one of the American Revolution, in a historical context. The British general Lord Charles Cornwallis surrendered to General Washington on October 19, 1781. Among the museum's exhibits are parts of General Washington's campaign tents. The way to see the most of the battlefield is to drive. The 9-mile Encampment Road tour shows the location of the revolutionary forces as well as Washington's headquarters. The 7-mile Battlefield tour follows the events of the siege. $10 adults, free for age 15 and younger.

♿ **Yorktown Victory Center** (757-253-4838; 1-888-593-4682; www.historyisfun.org), 200 Water Street, Rte. 1020. Mid-Aug.–mid-June daily 9–5, summer daily 9–6. Operated by the Jamestown-Yorktown Foundation that also manages Jamestown Settlement, the Yorktown Victory Center is a museum of the American Revolution. Road to Revolution, an outdoor walkway, features timelines and information pods detailing significant events that fueled the rebellion, from tax increases to the founding of the First Continental Congress. Witness to the Revolution, among the indoor museum's most interesting exhibits, details how the Revolutionary War affected 10 people, including soldiers, farmers, a Mohawk chief, and two slaves who joined the war—one for the Continental Army and one for the British. At the year-round Continental Army Encampment, intriguing for adults as well as children, interpreters in period costumes bring aspects of the war to life. Depending upon the program, you might chat with a physician about battlefield surgery or learn how to fire a canon (it took 15 men). Also on site is a 1780s farm that has a kitchen garden for vegetables and tobacco plants. $9.50 adults, $5.25 ages 6–12.

James River plantations

Bacon's Castle (757-357-5976; www.apva.org/BaconsCastle), 465 Bacon's Castle Trail, Rte. 617 north of Rte. 10. Open Apr.–Oct. 31 Wed.–Sun. noon–4, Mar. and Nov. weekends only noon–5. An important colonial site, Bacon's Castle, a National Historic Landmark, is the oldest documented house in Virginia as well as a rare example of Jacobean architecture in the New World. Dating to 1665, the brick structure's distinctive features include curvilinear gables, triple chimneys, and a cruciform plan. Although built for prosperous planter Arthur Allen, the house takes its name from the rebels, supporters of Nathaniel Bacon, who occupied the structure in 1676. Furnishings in parts of the house reflect the early to mid-18th century. Allow time to stroll the castle's garden planted with species that were grown in the 17th century. $8.

Berkeley Plantation (804-829-6018; 1-888-466-6018; www.berkeleyplantation .com), 12602 Harrison Landing Road, Charles City. Open daily 9:30–4:30. Closed Thanksgiving and Dec. 25. Berkeley Plantation is a brick Georgian manor built in 1726 by Benjamin Harrison IV. His son, Benjamin Harrison V, signed the Declaration of Independence. Another Harrison—William Henry Harrison—became the ninth president of the United States. The grounds served as the site of the first Thanksgiving in the New World, when 38 settlers from the Berkeley Company landed in December 1619 and gave thanks. British troops occupied and sacked the plantation during the American Revolution and Union troops under General George McClellan did much the same during the Civil War. In 1907, John Jamieson, who has been a drummer boy in McClellan's army, purchased the plantation, and his son restored it. $11 adults, $6 ages 6–12, $7.50 ages 13–16.

&. **Chippokes Plantation and State Park** (757-294-3625; www.dcr.virginia.gov /state_parks/chi.shtml), 695 Chippokes Park Road, Surry. Open daily 8 AM–dusk; museum Apr.–Oct. Mon. and Wed.–Fri. 10–3, Sat. 10–5, Sun. 1–5. Closed Tue. and Nov.–Mar. Tours of the mansion are available at select times. Chippokes' land grant for 550 acres dates to 1619, just 12 years after the colonists landed at what they came to call Jamestown. In 1646, Colonel Henry Bishop expanded the

BERKELEY PLANTATION

Virginia Tourism Corporation

plantation to more than 1,400 acres. The 1854 manor house survived the Civil War. That's because, as legend has it, Chippokes had one of the few legal distilleries in Virginia and the owner, Albert Jones, shrewdly sold his brandies to both Union and Confederate soldiers. Farmed ever since 1619, Chippokes grows corn, peanuts, and soybeans, making it one of the oldest working farms in the United States. The Chippokes Farm and Forestry Museum interprets the 1850s farming era through exhibits and displays of 19th-century farm tools. Despite the plantation's historic significance, most visitors come for the recreation. $3. (See *Green Spaces,* and *Lodging* for overnight information.)

& **Sherwood Forest Plantation** (804-829-5377; www.sherwoodforest.org), 14501 John Tyler Highway, Charles City. Grounds open daily 9–5, home open by appointment. In 1842, while still president of the United States, John Tyler purchased this 1,600-acre property and renamed it Sherwood Forest as a reference to his reputation as a political outlaw. After his presidency ended in 1845, Tyler resided at the plantation. His descendants still live on property. The manor house, built around 1720, stretches to 300 feet and is reputed to be the longest frame house in the United States. The self-guided grounds tour leads to good views and some ancient trees, including what's thought of as America's oldest gingko tree. There's also a resident ghost, the "Gray Lady." Family members hear her in one of the mansion's rooms as she sits in a rocking chair, holding a child. $10 adults, free for age 15 and under.

Explore colonial life from a different point of view by touring the historic plantations along the James River. Among the most impressive are Shirley and Berkeley, which still thrive a short drive from Williamsburg. These plantations give a glimpse into the pomp and pleasures of a life grown prosperous in the New World. Two that may especially delight children are Shirley Plantation and Berkeley Plantation; both boast lawns that sweep to the river and ancestry tracing back to England's Queen Elizabeth I. Combination admission tickets are available for Shirley, Berkeley, Evelynton, and Sherwood Forest plantations.

Shirley Plantation (804-829-5121; 1-800-232-1613; www.shirley plantation.com), 501 Shirley Plantation Road, Charles City. Open daily 9:30–4:30. Closed Thanksgiving and Dec. 25.

A SLAVE INTERPRETER, SHIRLEY PLANTATION

Virginia Tourism Corporation

Among Virginia's most impressive plantations, Shirley is situated along the James River, 35 miles west of Williamsburg and 2 miles up the road from the Berkeley Plantation. Founded in 1613—just six years after Jamestown—the plantation is still owned and operated by the descendants of Edward Hill. The imposing brick Queen Anne–style manor house dates to 1723, when Elizabeth Hill, great-granddaughter of Edward Hill who established a farm on the site, married John Carter, son of noted colonial landowner Robert "King" Carter. The property remains both a home—the 11th generation of the Hill-Carter descendents reside at Shirley—and a working plantation. The 30-minute guided tour points out such noteworthy architectural details as the "flying staircase" and highlights the family antiques and history. Shirley, with its sweeping lawn and dependencies, affords a glimpse into the privileged life of the colonial gentry. Special programs take place during the year, including April garden tours, Memorial Day military history, and a July Fourth ice-cream social. $11 adults, $7.50 ages 6–18.

Yorktown
Watermen's Museum (757-887-2641; www.watermens.org), 309 Water Street. Open Apr.–Dec. Tue.–Sat. 10–5. The museum displays skipjacks and other wooden boats used by Chesapeake watermen, as well as tools for oyster harvesting and crabbing. It also has a wooden boat-building program where you can watch and/or participate. $5, students $2.

✳ To Do

AMUSEMENT PARKS

Williamsburg
♂ ♿ **Busch Gardens Williamsburg** (1-800-343-7946; www.buschgardens.com), One Busch Gardens Boulevard. Open mid-May–Labor Day daily 10–8, special hours for October's Howl-O-Scream and late Nov.–Dec. 31 Christmas Town. This theme park combines roller coasters and other fun rides with ersatz English, Scottish, Irish, German, French, and Italian villages. Besides munching on bratwurst, brioche, pizza, or pasta and tapping along with the sidewalk serenades in several languages, you and your kids will love the rides. At Sesame Street Forest of Fun, a KIDsiderate attraction (the park's designation for kid-friendly fare), Elmo, Bert, Ernie, Big Bird, and other of the furry television stars sing and dance and meet and greet the kids at photo ops. Children can ride a mini roller coaster and get wet at Elmo's Castle, fountain and water jet play area. It's best for kids to wear bathing suits and bring a change of clothing. Little ones also like Land of the Dragons, a climb-and-play area with treetop houses, a mini Ferris wheel, and other kid-friendly rides.

Europe in the Air, a ride simulator, makes you feel as if you are flying over Paris's Eiffel Tower, Rome's Colosseum, England's Stonehenge, and other European must-sees. The park features several gut-wrenching roller coasters, perfect for 'tweens, 20-somethings, and anyone else who likes thrill rides. Griffon, among the world's tallest, floorless coasters, drops riders from 205 feet at speeds up to 75 mph; and Alpengeist, a tall, twisting coaster, flips riders six times and hurtles them at speeds up to 67 mph. Busch Gardens debuts its tallest thrill ride in spring 2011: Mach Tower lifts riders 246 feet in the air, then rotates the platform they are on by 360 degrees, providing them with panoramic views, before dropping the platform at speeds up to 60 mph.

Busch Gardens draws in those who don't especially like theme parks—and also those who do—with its landscaping, animals, and special Up-Close Tours. It has been voted the "Most Beautiful Park" for 20 consecutive years by members of the National Amusement Historical Association. Among the critters are bald eagles at Eagle Ridge, gray wolves at Wolf Valley, and the impressive Clydesdale horses at Highland Stables. The Up-Close Tours enable you to go behind the scenes to learn more about cer-

Busch Gardens Williamsburg,

ALPENGEIST COASTER, BUSCH GARDENS

tain attractions. At Wolf Training Up-Close, you'll discover how the smart and sleek animals learn, after which you will watch in amazement as Kashmir, a blue-eyed female wolf, rings a bell in response to your command. On the Roller Coaster Insider, you'll see the inner workings of Loch Ness Monster and Griffin coasters; on the Steam Engine Insider, you can take a special ride on the park's

SESAME STREET FOREST OF FUN, BUSCH GARDENS

C. Stapen

steam engine; and on the one-hour Gardening Insider, you'll learn about some of the park's more than 120 varieties of plants. Busch Gardens also offers a host of seasonal events. October brings Howl-O-Scream, a just-scary-enough collection of evening haunted houses and shows; and from Thanksgiving through December, the park typically opens for Christmas Town on weekends—a combination of carolers, holiday performances, and crafts. In 2010, Busch Gardens inaugurated IllumiNights, a summer festival of light shows. Park fees vary depending upon season and whether you purchase a single day, multiday, annual pass, two-park (admission to Water Country USA also), or other packages. Open spring–summer daily $63.99 age 10 and older, $53.99 ages

3–9, free for age 2 or younger; $22 Christmas Town, $20-plus Up-Close Tours; parking $13. The park offers discounts to military personnel and their families.

✐ ♿ **Water Country USA** (757-253-3350; 1-800-343-7946; www.watercountry usa.com), 176 Water Country Parkway, Rte. 199. Late May–early June 10–6, early June–mid-Aug. 10–8, mid-Aug.–near Labor Day 10–7, Labor Day weekend 10–6. This 40-acre water park, sister park to the better-known Busch Gardens Williamsburg, cools you off with waterslides, pools, and rides. Float down Hubba Hubba Highway, a 3½-acre river ride laced with geysers and sprays; zip down Malibu Pipeline, a slippery chute with a partially enclosed tube; and get your thrills on Aquazoid, a slide with a dark section and laser lights. New in spring 2011, Vanish Point mixes thrills with water fun. You can either zip to the bottom of the ride on a 300-foot speed slide or opt to plunge into the drink from the 75-foot tower when the floor beneath you vanishes. Those in wheelchairs are likely to need assistance because of the steep hills. Although the shows and restaurants are accessible, many of the water attractions are not. Call ahead. $45.

BICYCLING

Jamestown
Historic Jamestowne's Island Loop Trail (757-229-1733; www.historicjames towne.org), western end of the Colonial Parkway. Open daily 8:30–4:30. Closed Thanksgiving, Dec. 25, and Jan. 1. Pedal along the James River past natural wetlands on a 2- or a 3-mile loop. Stop along the way at Black Point for an expansive view of the James River similar to the one that the first settlers saw. Further on the Travis Graveyard holds the remains of the family that began farming the area in 1633. See also "Museums and Historic Sites."

Williamsburg
Contact the **Greater Williamsburg Chamber & Tourism Alliance** (757-229-6511; www.williamsburgcc.com), 421 North Boundary Street, Williamsburg, for a brochure of area biking trails. A favorite is the easy, mostly flat, 5.2-mile route from Merchants Square through the Historic Area and the College of William and Mary.

♿ **York River State Park** (757-566-3036; www.dcr.virginia.gov/state_parks /yor/shtml), 5526 Riverview Road. Open daily dawn–dusk. A coastal estuary, this 2,550-acre park has six bike trails. Although four share paths with hikers and horseback riders, two trails are reserved exclusively for mountain biking: the 2-mile, beginner/intermediate Laurel Glen Trail and the 6-mile, advanced Marl Ravine Trail. There are some wheelchair accessible trails.

Yorktown
Cycle along the 1.1-mile Riverwalk in **Historic Yorktown** and also pedal the trails of Yorktown Battlefield. Obtain a map at the Visitor Center.

BOAT EXCURSIONS

Yorktown
Schooner Alliance (1-800-979-3370; www.schooner alliance.com), Riverwalk Landing near Water Street and George Washington Highway. Apr.–Oct. 11 AM and 1 PM. Explore the Chesapeake aboard the schooner *Alliance*, a gaff-rigged

105-foot boat, or her sister ship, the *Serenity,* a 65-foot gaff topsail boat. The ships depart from Riverwalk Landing for scenic 60- to 90-minute cruises of the Chesapeake. $30 adults, $18 ages 12 and under; two-hour sunset sail $35.

BREWERIES

Williamsburg

Williamsburg AleWerks (757-220-3670; www.williamsburgalewerks.com), 189-B Ewell Road. Brewery store open Mon.–Sat. noon–5:30, guided tours Mon.–Sat. 2 and 3. Geoff Logan, brewmaster, likes the big bold flavors of ales. That's why, for now, Williamsburg AleWerks, a microbrewery founded in 2006, produces only ales. For summer, he brews a light white ale and for fall, his pumpkin ale is popular. Logan likens his tavern ale to something colonial gents would have downed centuries ago. Year-round, you can also toast the founding fathers with pints of Wheat Ale, Washington's Porter, and Chesapeake Pale Ale. (We also like the labels.) $3 tastings of all the beers on tap, $5 guided tour.

GOLF

Williamsburg area

Golden Horseshoe Golf Club (1-800-648-6653; www.goldenhorsehoegolf .com), 401 South England Street. This public club offers two 18-hole courses, the Gold Course and the Green Course. For a quick round, there's the nine-hole, executive Governor Spotswood course, named for the colonial governor. $40–100.

Kingsmill Resort (757-253-1703; 1-800-832-5665; www.kingsmill.com), 1010 Kingsmill Road. Rated by *Golf Digest* as among the top 75 golf resorts in the United States, Kingsmill offers three courses that are open to the public. The Plantation Course is ranked by *Golf Digest* as among the 10 best for women. The River Course and the Woods Course, named for their scenic views, challenge golfers as well. $45–160.

Williamsburg National Golf Club (1-800-826-5732; www.wngc.com), 3700 Centreville Road, features the Jamestown and the Yorktown courses. $35–80.

HORSEBACK RIDING

Williamsburg area

Lakewood Trails (757-566-9633; www.stonehousestables.com), 2116-A Forge Road, Toano, offers one-hour trail rides year-round by reservation as well as a three-hour ride through York River State Park. One hour $65, three hours $275. Specialty celebration rides are available as well.

Stonehouse Stables (757-566-0666; www.stonehousestables.com), 2116-A Forge Road, Toano, is the sister business to Lakewood Trails. Stonehouse offers lessons, boarding, and other services. Call for prices.

CANOEING, KAYAKING, PADDLING, ROWING

Captain John Smith Chesapeake National Historic Trail (410-260-2470; www.smithtrail.net), National Park Service Chesapeake Bay Office, 410 Severn

Avenue, Annapolis, MD. America's first national water trail, this 3,000-mile route includes the Chesapeake Bay, Northern Neck and Middle Peninsula rivers, and their tributaries in Virginia and Maryland. The routes follow regions explored by Captain John Smith in the 17th century. In places, the trails have "smart buoys" that relay weather, water quality, and other information. Simple put down your paddle and input www.buoybay.org/m on your mobile phone; from your computer, check www.buoybay.org; to find out what the Chesapeake was like in that area during Smith's time, call 1-877-BUOYBAY. In Virginia, there are three smart buoys, one of which is on the James River near Jamestown.

In the Williamsburg/Jamestown area, the **Powhatan Creek Blueway**, an 8-mile roundtrip, takes you between the York and James rivers through an area that belonged to the Powhatan Indian Confederacy. Tuckahoe plants, a staple for the Native Americans, still grow in along some of the shores.

SCENIC RIDES

Jamestown to Surry County
Jamestown–Scotland Ferry (1-800-VA-FERRY), Glass House Point, Rte. 31 Jamestown to Scotland Wharf, Surry County. A scenic—and easy way—to get from the Jamestown area to Surry County is to board the Jamestown–Scotland Ferry. While admiring the scenery on the 15-minute crossing, it's easy to imagine what the New World looked like to the first settlers. Free.

Williamsburg and Yorktown
Colonial Parkway (757-898-2410; www.nps.gov/colo), between the York and James rivers; write to P.O. Box 210, Yorktown 23690. A drive along the wooded, 24-mile Colonial Parkway that connects Colonial Williamsburg, Jamestown, and Yorktown is not only a good way to get from one of these attractions to another, but the winding road with its occasional views of the James and York rivers is scenic and soothing. The parkway is part of the Colonial National Historical Park (see under "Museums and Historic Sites"). Free.

SPAS

Colonial Williamsburg
Williamsburg Inn (757-253-2277; 1-800-HISTORY; www.history.org), 136 East Francis Street. The spa offers a variety of soothing treatments from massages to soaks. Several literally reach back to historic roots by employing botanicals the early settlers used. The two-hour Colonial Herbal experience, for example, includes an herbal bath of sage, rosemary, and juniper followed by a ginger and orange body scrub and a warm wrap Colonial Herbal $265, one-hour massage $120.

WINERIES

Williamsburg
Williamsburg Winery (757-229-0999; www.williamsburgwinery.com), 5800 Wessex Hundred. Tours and tastings Open Apr.–Oct. Mon.–Sat. 10:30–5, Sun. 11:30–5; Nov.–Mar. Mon.–Sat. 10:30–4, Sun. 11:30–4. Patrick and Peggy Duffeler

acquired a 300-acre farm in 1983, planted the first grapes in 1985, and released 2,000 cases of their first wine in 1988. Now the winery produces about 60,000 cases per year, making it one of Virginia's largest winery. The winery's Gabriel Archer Reserve won a bronze medal in 2005. Bottles of wine are sold in the wine shop. The guided tour includes a video on winemaking, a tour through the barrel cellar, and a tasting of seven wines, $10. The Reserve Wine Tastings, available by appointment, feature the estate's reserve wines, $30.

✴ Green Spaces

BEACHES

Yorktown

Yorktown Beach (757-890-3500; www.riverwalklanding.com/market), 425 Water Street, Riverwalk Landing. Open Apr.–Oct. 19. By most standards, the 2-acre, dirt-sand stretch along the river isn't much of a beach, but locals, especially teens and 20-somethings, flock here for sun and fun in summer. You can fish from the pier as well as picnic on the 10 acres of grass adjoining the beach.

PARKS

Jamestowne

Historic Jamestowne (757-898-2410; www.historicjamestowne.org; also 757-229-1733; www.historicjamestowne.org), western end of the Colonial Parkway. (See "Museums and Historic Sites" under *To See.*)

Surry

& **Chippokes Plantation and State Park** (757-294-3625; ww.dcr.virginia.gov /state_parks/chi.shtml), 695 Chippokes Park Road, Surry. Open daily 8 AM–dusk; farm museum Apr.–Oct. Mon. and Wed.–Fri. 10–3, Sat. 10–5, Sun. 1–5. Closed Tue. and Nov.–Mar. Tours of the mansion are available at select times. Although the land grant for Chippokes dates to 1619 and mansion to 1854, most visit Chippokes for recreation. Fish, hike 3.5 miles of trails, and swim in an Olympic-size pool in summer. A lift provides pool access to those in wheelchairs. The park also has overnight cabins and camping facilities. $3 parking fee. (See *Lodging* for overnight information.)

Williamsburg

York River State Park (757-566-3036; www.dcr.virginia.gov/state_parks/yor /shtml), 5526 Riverview Road. Open daily dawn–dusk. Just 11 miles west of Williamsburg, enjoy the peace of a 2,550-acre coastal estuary. The park offers 25 miles of hiking, bicycling, and horseback riding trails. Two trails are for mountain bikers only: the 2-mile, beginner/intermediate Laurel Glen Trail and the 6-mile, advanced Marl Ravine Trail.

Yorktown

Riverwalk Landing (757-890-3370; www.riverwalklanding.com), 425 Water Street. In addition to being a shopping and restaurant complex, Riverwalk Landing is a park and the hub of "happenings" in Historic Yorktown. Shaggin' on the Riverwalk, the free Friday evening dance-alongs with lessons in summer, are popular. On Yorktown Day, October 19, holidays, and other occasions, the park hosts free performances. From the park, you can walk a scenic, mile-long path along the river to the Yorktown Battlefield.

✳ Lodging

The Williamsburg area has a great many lodgings. Most convenient are those operated by the Colonial Williamsburg Foundation within the Historic Area, as well as those just outside the Historic Area that offer guests access to Colonial Williamsburg's shuttle buses. Contact the **Greater Williamsburg Chamber and Tourism Alliance** (757-229-6511; www.williamsburgcc.com) for more information.

Colonial Williamsburg

✦ **Colonial Houses** (757-253-2277; 1-800-HISTORY; www.history.org), 136 East Francis Street. Located throughout the Historic Area are 26 period properties that accommodate two to twelve people. Just close your door and walk into the 18th century. Some rooms are part of multiunit buildings and others are independent houses with sitting areas. The Chiswell-Bucktrout Tavern comes with a private garden and the Ewing House has a first-floor suite with a sitting area and two upstairs bedrooms, nice for families. The rooms vary and so do the prices, although these can be at the upper end of Historic Area lodgings. Remember that some rooms are small and may feel cramped with their dormer ceilings. Tavern rooms $149–269, houses and suites $239–459.

✦ **Williamsburg Inn** (757-253-2277; 1-800-HISTORY; www.history.org), 136 East Francis Street. A stay here puts you in the heart of the Historic Area. Constructed in 1937 to repre-sent the early 19th-century Regency style, the hotel reigns as the Historic Area's grande dame. Each of the 62 guest rooms at this AAA Four Diamond property covers at least 500 square feet and comes with a sumptuous bathroom. Queen Elizabeth II stayed here when she commemorated the 400th anniversary of the Jamestown Settlement. In season, play croquet on the sweeping back lawn; year-round, pamper yourself at the resort's spa. In summer, there's an outdoor swimming pool. Guests have priority at the hotel's two affiliated golf courses. The restaurant is known for its fine dining. Rooms $319–629, suites $439–799.

✦ **Williamsburg Lodge** (757-253-2277; 1-800-HISTORY; www.history .org), 310 South England Street. Family-friendly, this lodge, renovated in 2007, offers 323 rooms in several buildings. When we can't do the big splurge at the Williamsburg Inn or a Colonial House, we stay here. This property, located within the Historic Area, is about 1½ blocks from the inn, and lodge guests have the use of the indoor and outdoor pools at the inn. Pencil-post beds and folk art reproductions add a colonial feel to the room. The rocker and a shawl plus the paperback books add to the cozy feel. South-wing rooms are somewhat smaller than others; rooms in Tazewell Hall have a more contemporary style and come with balconies and courtyards. Rooms $129–299, suites $199–459.

Greater Williamsburg area

& **Governor's Inn** (757-253-2277; 1-800-HISTORY; www.history.org), 506 North Henry Street. You can walk the three blocks from the Governor's Inn to the Historic Area or board a shuttle bus. Rooms are basic at this most budget-friendly of the lodgings operated by the Colonial Williamsburg Foundation. The property has an outdoor swimming pool and guests may enroll kids in the programs at the Williamsburg Woodlands (see following listing). $59–109.

✒ & **Great Wolf Lodge–Williamsburg** (1-800-551-9653; www.greatwolf.com), 549 East Rochambeau Drive. A faux Northwoods-themed log cabin, this 405-room property is the kind you stay at for the kids: The Great Wolf Resorts chain lures youngsters with its water parks. The lodge comes with a 300,000-gallon, indoor one that occupies a whopping 67,000 square feet. Little ones can splash in the toddler area and older ones will want to zip down the waterslides, tackle the wave pool, and climb on Fort Mackenzie—a tree house outfitted with water sprays, guns, and a big, bad bucket dump. In warm weather, there's an outdoor pool, too. If you can get your kids out of the water, the resort has a Cub Club, a supervised craft and play area for young kids, a GR8 Space for teens, and a build-a-remote-controlled race car shop. Choose from a variety of log cabin–themed rooms. In the Wolf Den Suite, bunk beds occupy a section of the room. In the KidCabin Suite, an in-room log cabin contains bunk beds plus a day bed, great for families with three children. You can choose from a variety of other configurations as well. $190–660.

& **Kingsmill Resort & Spa** (757-253-1703; 1-800-832-5665; www.kingsmill.com), 1010 Kingsmill Road. Sprawled on 2,900 acres, this AAA Four Diamond resort fronts the James River. Choose from hotel rooms as well as one- to three-bedroom condominiums that come with complete kitchens. The resort has a nice spa, an indoor swimming pool, several restaurants, and three golf courses. In summer, a supervised children's program operates for ages 5–12. $109–999.

& **Williamsburg Woodlands Hotel & Suites** (757-253-2277; 1-800-HISTORY; www.history.org), 105 Visitor Center Drive. Just outside of the Historic Area adjacent to the Colonial Williamsburg Visitor Center, the Woodlands' standard hotel rooms are well located and also a good buy, more expensive than the Governor's Inn but less costly than the Williamsburg Lodge. In summer, the property has a swimming pool and hosts the Colonial Kids Club, an activities program. The shuttle stops here as well. Rooms $69–159, suites $119–209.

OTHER LODGINGS

Many chain hotels have properties in the Greater Williamsburg area.

& (ᵗ) **Embassy Suites** (757-229-6800; www.williamsburg.embassysuites.com), 3006 Mooretown Road. The property has an interior atrium and an indoor pool. The two-room suites have a separate bedroom and a pull-out sofa in the living room. All guests receive a complimentary hot breakfast. $109–229.

& (ᵗ) **Homewood Suites by Hilton** (757-259-1199; www.homewoodsuites.com), 601 Bypass Road. All the rooms are suites that have a living area and a full kitchen as well as a bedroom. Rates include a complimentary hot breakfast and a light meal on Mon.–Thu. evenings. The property has an indoor pool. $109–159.

&. ((·)) **Williamsburg Hospitality House** (757-229-4020; www.williamsburghosphouse.com), 415 Richmond Road. 296 rooms. Within walking distance of the Historic Area and located across from the campus of the College of William and Mary, this AAA 3 Diamond hotel has a courtyard, outdoor pool, and two restaurants. $80–240.

BED & BREAKFASTS AND INNS

Liberty Rose Bed & Breakfast (757-253-1260; 1-800-545-1825; www.libertyrose.com), 1025 Jamestown Road. This romantic bed-and-breakfast on an acre of land surrounded by oak, beech, and poplar trees is about 1⅛ miles from Colonial Williamsburg's Merchants Square. Choose from among four rooms, each with a private bath, a four-poster bed, and a Victorian rather than colonial décor. Rates include a full breakfast. Mon.–Thu. $195–215, Fri.–Sun. $205–245.

Wedmore Place at the Williamsburg Winery (757-941-0310; www.wedmoreplace.com), 5810 Wessex Hundred. Stay in one of Wedmore Place's 28 rooms and you get the privacy of a lodging set on 300 acres plus vineyard views and, if you want, wine tastings. (See "Wineries" in *To Do*). Part of the Small Luxury Hotels of the World, Wedmore Place exudes a European flair. The guest rooms, named for European regions, combine antiques with reproductions, and each room has a wood-burning fireplace, Internet access, a dual-line phone, and a television. Located

under the eaves, the Tradition Rooms are among the smallest, ranging from 277 to 325 square feet. Classic Rooms are the same size, but do not have sloping ceilings. Superior Rooms are larger corner rooms ranging from 326 to 430 square feet. The three large suites range from 500 to 1100 square feet and have a separate sitting room. Rates include continental breakfast for two. Guests are welcome to use the property's biking trail that runs along the river. There are two restaurants on the property. The Gabriel Archer Tavern, open Apr.4–Dec. 31., serves lunch daily and dinner Thu.–Mon. The Café Provençal serves dinner. Rooms $175–395, suites $300–750.

CABINS AND CAMPING

Chippokes Plantation and State Park (757-294-3625; ww.dcr.virginia.gov/state_parks/chi.shtml), 695 Chippokes Park Road, Surry. The 1,683-acre park has cabins and camping facilities. One-bedroom cabins $77–104 per night, $457–617 per week, two-bedroom cabins $88–119 per night $585–791 per week. Camping Mar.–Dec. $25 per night; sites have electricity and water.

WHERE TO EAT

Colonial Williamsburg
Colonial Taverns (757-229-2141; www.history.org) comprises four taverns in the Historic Area. Consider dining the first night at one of them to get into the spirit of the place. Even though the entrées are more adequate than memorable (AAA rates most with two diamonds), the wooden tables aglow in candlelight and the costumed wait staff help transport you back 200 years. Plus, sampling such

18th-century Southern staples as spoon bread, Carolina fish muddle (a stew), and peanut pie is fun. Although the taverns feature several items that are the same from one establishment to the other, each tavern is known for a particular type of cuisine. Because dinning at the taverns is extremely popular, book your meal when you make your lodging reservations.

& **Chowning's Tavern** (757-229-2141; www.history.org), 109 East Duke of Gloucester Street. Open daily 11 AM–10 PM; reservations not accepted. An ale house, Chowning's serves such lighter fare as soups, salads, and sandwiches such as smoked turkey, ham, and pork barbecue. Don't forget to sample the peanut pie. Entrées $9-11.

Christiana Campbell's Tavern (757-229-2141; www.history.org), 101 South Waller Street. Open Tue.–Sat. dinner 5–9. Closed Sun. and Mon. Reputedly a favorite of George Washington's, the tavern specializes in crab cakes, sherried shrimp, and other seafood. Entrées $20–40.

King's Arms Tavern (757-229-2141; www.history.org), 416 East Duke of Gloucester Street. Open Thu.–Mon. lunch 11:30–2:30 and dinner 5–9:30. Closed Tue. and Wed. In the tradition of a period chop house, this tavern serves roast beef, pork, duck, and their signature peanut soup. Lunch offerings include a ham-and-cheese or turkey sandwich. Entrées lunch $12–14, dinner $27–34.

& **Shields Tavern** (757-229-2141; www.history.org), 422 East Duke of Gloucester Street. Open Tue.–Sat. lunch 11:30–2:30 and dinner 5–8:30. Closed Sun. and Mon. Colonial Williamsburg dubs the menu "comfort foods inspired by colonial recipes." Lunch features hamburgers, grilled sausage, and chicken and dumplings. The dinner entrées include barbecued ribs, braised pork, chicken, and ale-potted beef. Entrées lunch $10–14, dinner $18–24.

Williamsburg

Adjacent to the Historic Area, **Merchants Square** offers shops and cafés, and three stand-out restaurants.

Blue Talon Bistro (757-476-BLUE; www.bluetalonbistro.com), 420 Prince George Street, Merchants Square. Open daily 8 AM–9 PM. This bistro, with its pressed-tin ceiling, mosaic tiles, and folk art, creates a warm setting, suitable for what Chef David Everett calls his "serious comfort food." The burgers are big, the meat loaf tasty, and the mac and cheese much better than the one you ate as a child. You can also usually order seafood or lamb shanks or other "grown-up" entrées. Enjoy a continental breakfast on the outdoor patio. Entrées lunch $12–14, dinner $19–25.

Carrot Tree Kitchens (757-229-0957; www.carrottreekitchens.com), 1782 Jamestown Road. Open Mon. 8–4, Tue.–Fri. 8–5:30, Sat. 8–4, Sun. 10–4. This café serves soups, salads, sandwiches, wraps, barbecue, and crab cakes. $5–11.

Cheese Shop (757-220-0298; www.cheeseshopwilliamsburg.com), 410 West Duke of Gloucester Street. Open Mon.–Sat. 10–8, Sun. 11–6. Come here for cheese as well as sandwiches to eat in or take out. There's a wine shop, too. $5–8.

Fat Canary (757-229-3333; www.fatcanarywilliamsburg.com), 410 West Duke of Gloucester Street. Open daily 5–9. This AAA Four Diamond–rated restaurant serves seasonal

American cuisine in a stylish setting. Entrées may include quail with sage and truffle stuffing, soy-glazed salmon, and braised boneless beef short ribs. Entrées $27–38.

Pierce's Pitt Bar-B-Que (757-565-2955; www.pierces.com), 447 East Rochambeau Drive. Open daily 10–9. Locals keep returning for Pierce's hickory-smoked, Tennessee-style barbecue. $3.50-19.

The Trellis (757-229-8610; www.thetrellis.com), 403 West Duke of Gloucester Street. Open daily 8 AM–9 PM. Chef David Everett, proprietor of the noted Blue Talon Bistro, also oversees food at the Trellis, where he prepares modern American cuisine. Salads and sandwiches dominate lunch. The dinner offerings may include Idaho rainbow trout, salmon, chicken, or Angus strip steak. Save room for the dessert, especially Death by Chocolate, a rich cakelike concoction that chocoholics "die for." Entrées lunch $7–15, dinner $24–30.

OTHER RESTAURANTS

Surry County
Surrey House Restaurant (757-294-3389; www.surreyhouserestaurant.com), 11865 Rolfe Highway, Surry. Open Tue.–Sat. 8–8, Sun. 8-6. Locals have been coming to this restaurant since 1954. The down-home fare includes such regional delights as crab cakes, fried chicken, peanut soup, and, of course, Virginia country ham. Nearby Smithfield, after all, is known for its ham. $12–18.

Williamsburg Jamestown area
Dale House Café (757-229-1733; www.historicjamestowne.org), western end of the Colonial Parkway. Open daily 9–5. Conveniently located in Historic Jamestowne, this café serves predictable salads, pizza, hot dogs, and wraps, but the view of the James River is wonderful. $7–10.

Jamestown Pie Company (757-229-7775; www.buyapie.com), 1804 Jamestown Road. Open Mon.–Sat. 10–9, Sun. noon–8. The motto of this take-out restaurant, located near Jamestown Settlement, is "because round food is good." That's the answer to why they serve dessert pies, potpies, and pizzas. Wraps and sandwiches are also available. $7–30.

ℰ **Retro's Good Eats** (757-253-8816; www.retrosgoodeats.com), 435 Prince George Street. Open daily 11–9. In an atmosphere redolent of a 1950s soda fountain, Retro's serves burgers, hot dogs, chicken sandwiches, fries, draft root beer, and frozen custard. Entrées $2.50–5.

The Whaling Company (757-229-0275; www.whalingcompany.com), 494 McLaws Circle. Open daily 4:30–10. Located near Busch Gardens, this is a good place for seafood. Chicken and steak are also served. Entrées $14–55.

Yorktown
Carrot Tree Kitchens (757-988-1999; www.carrottreekitchens.com), Cole Diggs House, 411 Main Street. Open daily 11:01–3:29; tea Tue.–Wed. 4, Thu.–Sat. 5:01–8:29. Located in a house that dates to 1720s, the oldest house in Yorktown, Carrot Tree serves good soups, sandwiches, stew, and pastries. $5–14.

The Rivah Café (757-875-1522; www.riverwalkrestaurant.net), 323 Water Street, Suite A-1. Open Apr.–Aug. daily 11:30–9. Closed Mon. Sept.–Mar. The café serves salads, soups and sandwiches. In warm

62

TIDEWATER VIRGINIA

weather, dine on the outdoor patio overlooking the river. After lunch, munch on pizzas, mini-sandwiches, and other bar fare. Lunch $9–15.

The Riverwalk Restaurant(757-875-1522; www.riverwalkrestaurant .net), 323 Water Street, Suite A-1. Open Apr.–Aug. daily lunch 11:30–2:30, dinner 5–9. Closed Mon. Sept.–Mar. The sister restaurant to the Rivah Café, the Riverwalk Restaurant's dining room has big glass windows facing the river. Seafood is the specialty—try the she-crab soup with sherry. For non-seafood lovers, the restaurant has a vegetarian selection and also lamb chops or beef. Dinner $17–29.

NIGHTLIFE: BARS, CLUBS, EATERIES

Williamsburg

Ⓨ **415 Grill** (757-229-4020; www .williamsburghosphouse.com), 415 Richmond Road. Open Mon.–Thu. 11:30–9, Fri. and Sat. 11:30 AM–2 AM, Sun. 11:30–9. Crab cakes and bean soup are among the favorites for dinner at this restaurant located in the Williamsburg Hospitality House hotel. On weekends, the grill has DJs and karaoke. $10–15.

Ⓨ **Corner Pocket** (757-220-0808; www.thecornerpocket.us), 4805 Courthouse Square. Open Mon.–Thu. 11:30 AM–1 AM, Fri. and Sat. 11:30 AM–2 AM. The Corner Pocket has 13 pool tables and live music—often Blues and Zydeco—on Thursday nights. The restaurant serves salads, sandwiches, and crab cakes. $7–22.

Ⓨ **Green Leafe** has two locations: **Green Leafe Café Downtown** (757-220-3405; www.greenleafe.com), 765 Scotland Street and **Green**

Leafe New Town (757-221-9582; www.greenleafe.com), 4345 New Town Avenue. Both locations open Mon.–Thu. 11 AM–1 AM; Fri.–Sat. 11 AM–2 AM; Sun. 10 AM–2 AM. Beer is the big draw at both—50-plus drafts and 150 bottled versions. The pub grub—soups, salads, burgers, and pizza—is accompanied by fish-and-chips, ribs, meat loaf, and other dinner entrées. $9–18.

Ⓨ **J. M. Randalls** (757-259-0406; www.jmrandalls.com), 4854 Longhill Road. Open Sun.–Thu. 7 AM–1 AM, Fri. and Sat. 7 AM–2 AM. Calling itself a "classic American grill," J. M. Randalls features live music on Friday and Saturday nights and sometimes on other evenings.

✳ Selective Shopping

Williamsburg

Merchants Square (757-229-1000; merchantssquare.org), the west edge of the Historic Area, office 427 Franklin Street. Open fall–spring Mon.–Sat. 10–6, Sun. noon–5; summer Mon.–Sat. 10–8 or 9, Sun. noon–5. Standouts among the more than 40 shops, restaurants, and cafés in this open-air mall include:

Everything Williamsburg (757-565-8476; www.williamsburgmarketplace .com) for those de rigueur logo shirts, mugs, and needlepoint pillows.

J. Fenton Gallery (757-221-8200; www.quiltsunlimited.com), 110 South Henry Street, Henry Street Shops. Browse a good selection of pottery, wooden boxes and toys, jewelry, and kaleidoscopes. The Fenton Gallery's sister shop located just across the hall is **Quilts Unlimited** (757-253-8700; www.quiltsunlimited.com). Among the items the shop sells are bed quilts, quilted wall hangings, and colonial clothing.

Gallery on Merchants Square (757-564-1787; www.galleryonm sq.com), 440A West Duke of Gloucester Street. The eclectic gallery features paintings, prints, antiques, and jewelry

Nancy Thomas Gallery of Folk Art (757-259-1938; www.nancythomas .com), 407 West Duke of Gloucester Street. Nancy Thomas, a well-known artist, does colorful work in a variety of media. Much of her work has the feel of a modern rendition of folk art mixed with a touch of whimsy. Various prices.

&. **Williamsburg Premium Outlets** (757-565-0702; www.premiumoutlets .com), 5715-62A Richmond Road. Open Mon.–Sat. 10–9, Sun. 10–7. The more than 135 shops include BCBG, Burberry, Calvin Klein, Carter's, Coach, Cole Haan, Gap Outlet, Nike, and Polo Ralph Lauren.

✳ Special Events

Colonial Williamsburg
July: **Fireworks and parades** in the Historic Area commemorate July 4.

October: **Military reenactors** make camp as they prepare for General Washington's siege of Yorktown.

December: **Grand Illumination** features fireworks and Christmas decorations in the colonial area, along with music and a grand ball.

Yorktown
October: On **Yorktown Day**, October 19, experience patriotic music, fife and drum performances, and food from vendors.

HAMPTON ROADS

This region's history and development are inextricably tied to the sea. Hampton Roads has one of the world's largest natural deepwater harbors, and the peninsula location drew settlers from Native Americans to English colonists. In 1610, a group of pioneers left disease-ridden Jamestown for the fertile soil of Hampton Roads. Initially, the Kecoughtan peoples befriended the newcomers, but after an English settler was killed, the peaceful coexistence ended and the English took control, changing the region's name from Kecoughtan to Elisabeth City, after the daughter of King James I. Later on, the region was renamed Southampton, in honor of the Earl of Southampton, a major stockholder in the Virginia Company. Eventually, the town's name was shortened to Hampton.

The harbor is formed by the merging of the James, Elizabeth, and Nansemond rivers with the Chesapeake Bay. Here, you can sail the waters explored by Captain John Smith. Hampton's Old Point Comfort Lighthouse was built in 1802. Because the colonies' riches and English goods passed through the harbor, Hampton attracted merchants, shippers, and also pirates, including the notorious Blackbeard. The former scourge of the Caribbean, Blackbeard (a.k.a. Edward Teach) had settled in North Carolina but soon began looting Hampton and other ports, until stopped by Virginia governor Spotswood in 1718, who sent two ships to root out the pirate in North Carolina.

The port of Hampton Roads is the second largest in the United States (New York City's is the largest). Consequently, the region saw the birth of the modern navy, with the Civil War battle of the first fight between two ironclad ships, the USS *Monitor* and the CSS *Virginia* (*Merrimack*). Several military installations anchor in the region. Among them are Fort Eustis, Langley Air Force Base, and the Naval Station Norfolk.

TOWNS Newport News. The name "Newportes Newes," spelled eight different ways, first appears in 1619 in the Virginia Company's records. That reference makes the area the one of the oldest English place names in the New World, according to the Newport News Tourism Development Office. Whether the city name is the first reference or not, it's an early reference. One theory is that Newport News was named after the English sea captain Christopher Newport whose three-ship fleet landed at Jamestown Island in 1607.

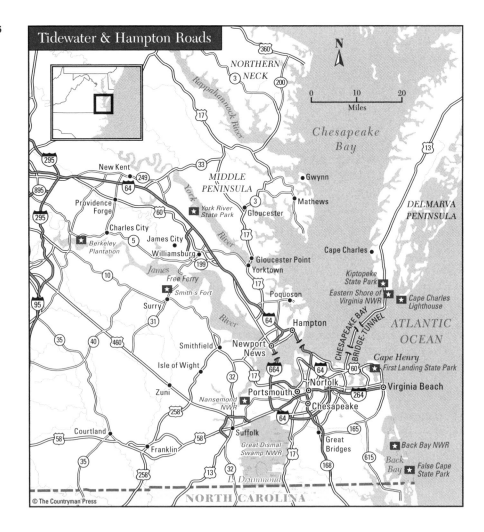

Tidewater & Hampton Roads

Norfolk. Norfolk—heart of the Hampton Roads region, the "0-mile" marker on the Intracoastal Waterway—is home to the world's largest naval installation, Naval Station Norfolk. You can also explore, the town's interesting neighborhoods: Stroll the cobblestone streets of the Freemason Historic District, check out the trendy restaurants and bars in Granby, and burrow through the antique shops in Ghent.

Virginia Beach. Sand and surf lovers come to Virginia Beach for its 20 miles of white sand beach. Most kids—and many adults—get their photo taken with King Neptune, a 24-foot high, 12-ton statue poised at the entrance to Neptune Park. He sets a tone. After all, with beauty in the eye of the beholder, people either find Neptune festive or a bit tacky. In any event, Virginia Beach is no picturesque, quaint New England seaside village. And we're glad of that. With a 3-

mile long, bustling boardwalk, lots of cotton candy and ice cream, white sands, and breaking surf, Virginia Beach delivers a modern and affordable beach getaway, one that also enables visitors to savor undeveloped, dune-lined beaches and marshlands filled with birds. Together, Back Bay National Wildlife Refuge and False Cape State Park feature more than 13,000 acres of unspoiled land with miles of pristine shore.

GUIDANCE **Hampton Convention &Visitor Bureau** (1-866-657-9392; www.hamptoncvb.com), 120 Old Hampton Lane, Hampton. Open daily 9–5. Closed Thanksgiving, Dec. 25, and Jan. 1.

Nauticus Welcome Desk, One Waterside Drive. Open Sat. and Sun, noon–5.

Newport News Visitor Center (757-886-7777; 1-888-4-WE-R-FUN; www .newport-news.org), 13560 Jefferson Avenue, Newport News. Open daily 9–5. Closed Thanksgiving, Dec. 24–25, and Jan. 1.

Norfolk Convention and Visitors Bureau (757-664-6620; 1-800-368-3097; www.visitnorfolktoday.com), 232 East Main Street, Norfolk. Open Mon.–Fri. 8:30–5.

Portsmouth Visitor Information Center (757-393-5111; 1-800-PORTSVA; www.visitportsva.com), 6 Crawford Parkway, North Ferry Landing, Portsmouth. Open Mon.–Fri. 9–5.

Starboards (757-478-0056; www.starboards.biz), 101 High Street, offers visitor information and maps as well as coffee. Open spring Mon.–Fri. 6:30–5 PM, Sat. and Sun. 8–2; summer Mon.–Fri. 6:30–5 PM, Sat. and Sun. 8–5; winter and fall Mon.–Fri. 6:30–3 PM, Sat. 8–2, closed Sun.

Virginia Beach Convention and Visitors Bureau (1-800-822-3224; www .vbfun.com), 2100 Parks Avenue, Suite 500, Virginia Beach. Summer daily 9–7; fall, winter, and spring daily 9–5.

GETTING THERE *By air:* **Newport News/Williamsburg International Airport** (757-877-0221), 900 Bland Boulevard. The airport is 13 miles from Newport News, 18 miles from Hampton. US Airways Express, Delta. Air Tran and Frontier are among the carriers serving the airport.

Norfolk International Airport (757-857-3351), 2200 Norview Avenue, is about 6 miles from Norfolk and 13 miles from Virginia Beach. Among the carriers are American, Delta, Southwest, United Express and US Airways.

By bus: **Greyhound terminal** (1-800-231-2222; www.greyhound.com). **Hampton**, 2 West Pembroke Avenue; **Norfolk**, 701 Monticello Avenue; **Virginia Beach**, 1017 Laskin Road. There is no bus service into Newport News.

By car: **Hampton:** From Washington and Baltimore, take I-95 south to I-295 south and continue onto I-64 east and take VA 195 east. From Richmond, take I-95 north toward I-64 east and then take US 60. From Norfolk/Hampton Roads, take I-1264 east onto I-64 west toward US 60 west. **Newport News:** From Washington and Baltimore, take I-395 south to I-95 south onto I-295 south and then merge onto I-64 east toward I-664 south. From Richmond, take I-95 north

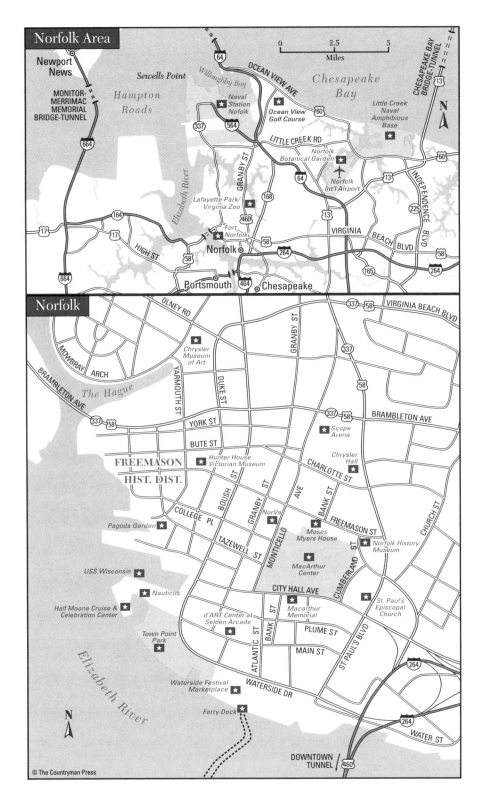

Norfolk Area

Newport News

MONITOR-MERRIMAC MEMORIAL BRIDGE-TUNNEL

Sewells Point

Hampton Roads

Willoughby Bay

OCEAN VIEW AVE

Chesapeake Bay

Naval Station Nofolk

Ocean View Golf Course

Little Creek Naval Amphibious Base

CHESAPEAKE BAY BRIDGE-TUNNEL

LITTLE CREEK RD

GRANBY ST

Norfolk Botanical Garden

Norfolk Int'l Airport

INDEPENDENCE BLVD

Elizabeth River

Lafayette Park/ Virginia Zoo

Fort Norfolk

VIRGINIA BEACH BLVD

HIGH ST

Norfolk

Portsmouth

Chesapeake

0   2.5   5
Miles

N

Norfolk

OLNEY RD

MOWBRAY ARCH

Chrysler Museum of Art

GRANBY ST

VIRGINIA BEACH BLVD

BRAMBLETON AVE

The Hague

YARMOUTH ST

DUKE ST

YORK ST

BUTE ST

Scope Arena

BRAMBLETON AVE

FREEMASON HIST. DIST.

Hunter House Victorian Museum

Chrysler Hall

CHARLOTTE ST

COLLEGE PL

BOUSH ST

GRANBY ST

AVE

BANK ST

CHURCH ST

Pagoda Garden

NorVa

FREEMASON ST

Norfolk History Museum

TAZEWELL ST

Moses Myers House

USS Wisconsin

MONTICELLO ST

MacArthur Center

CUMBERLAND ST

Nauticus

CITY HALL AVE

St. Paul's Episcopal Church

Half Moone Cruise & Celebration Center

d'ART Center at Selden Arcade

BANK ST

Macarthur Memorial

PLUME ST

ST PAUL'S BLVD

Town Point Park

ATLANTIC ST

MAIN ST

264

Elizabeth River

Waterside Festival Marketplace

WATERSIDE DR

Ferry Dock

264

WATER ST

N

DOWNTOWN TUNNEL

460

© The Countryman Press

VisitNorfolk

ARCHWAY

toward I-64 east toward I-664 south. From Norfolk/Hampton Roads, take I-264
west to I-464/US 460 west to I-664 north.

Norfolk: From Washington and Baltimore, take I-95 south to I-295 south and
continue onto I-64 east toward I-263 west. From Richmond, take VA 195 east to
I-95 north and continue onto I-64 east toward I-264 west.

Portsmouth: From Williamsburg and Richmond, take I-64 East to I-664 South
and cross the Monitor-Merrimack Memorial Bridge Tunnel. From Norfolk, drive
through either the Downtown or the Midtown Tunnel.

Virginia Beach: From Washington and Baltimore, take I-395 south to I-95
south. Continue on I-295 south to I-64 east onto I-264 west to I-264 east/VA
Beach. From Richmond, take I-95 north to I-64 and continue on I-64 east
toward I-264 west toward I-264 east. Virginia Beach is about 20 miles east of
Norfolk/Hampton Roads. Take I-264 east, turn left at Arctic Avenue, and then
turn right at 25th Street.

By ferry: Portsmouth: From Norfolk, board the Elizabeth River Ferry (757-222-6100; www.gohrt.com), at Norfolk's Waterside to Olde Town Portsmouth, about a 20-minute boat ride.

By train: **Amtrak** (1-800-872-7245; www.amtrak.com) services **Williamsburg** and **Newport News**.

GETTING AROUND Newport News and Hampton: Hampton Roads Transit (www.newportnews.worldweb.com/Transportation/PublicTransit) provides public transportation, but cars are also advisable.

Norfolk: The Norfolk Electric Transit (NET) (www.norfolk.gov/visitors/net.asp), the free electric trolley system, runs along 2.2 miles downtown. The Tide, Norfolk's light rail system, is scheduled to open sometime in 2011.

Portsmouth: Walk the Olde Town area. Otherwise, take taxis or use a car. Car rental companies are available.

Virginia Beach: Hampton Roads Transit (HRT) Beach Trolley (757-222-6100; www.gohrt.com) is a good way to get around. Parking is scarce, so it's best to leave your car at your hotel or rental unit.

WHEN TO COME For the entire Hampton Roads region, summer is high season, whereas spring and fall bring nice walking weather and fewer crowds. Winter is low season.

LIVE THE LIFE IN VIRGINIA BEACH

Virginia Beach Convention & Visitors Bureau

pcopros

FALSE CAPE STATE PARK DUNES, VIRGINIA BEACH AREA

✳ To See

MUSEUMS AND HISTORIC SITES

Hampton

Cousteau Society Headquarters (757-722-9300; www.cousteausociety.org),
710 Settlers Landing Road. Summer Tue.–Sun. 10–4; call for winter hours.
Jacques-Yves Cousteau established the Cousteau Society in 1973. The now
worldwide organization is dedicated to exploring and rehabilitating the world's
oceans and educating the public about the necessity for protecting the ocean's
natural environment. At the headquarters, view photographs from expeditions
and see videos of the society's expeditions as well as models of sea exploration
vessels *Calypso* and *Alcyone.*

Fort Monroe and the Casemate Museum (757-788-3391; www.monroe.army
.mil/monroe), 20 Bernard Road. Open daily 10:30–:30. Located in Old Point
Comfort, Fort Monroe, the largest stone fort ever built in the United States, is
currently the only moat-encircled fort still in active use, but on September 2011,
the U.S. Army will leave the fort and the base will close. The 565 acres of land
will be reused: The fort and the museum is expected to remain; apartments and
other housing plus areas for restaurants and shops will be built, and much land
will be reserved for parks and open spaces. The Casemate Museum, located in a
network of caverns once filled with Fort Monroe's massive guns, details the fort's
Civil War history. During the war, Fort Monroe's nickname was "Freedom
Fortress" because Union general Benjamin Butler allowed runaway slaves to stay
at the fort, thus enabling them to obtain freedom after the war. Also on view is
the cell that held Confederate president Jefferson Davis after the war. Free
admission.

✦ **Hampton Carousel** (757-727-0900; www.vasc.org), 602 Settlers Landing Road. This handsome 1920 merry-go-round with prancing steeds and chariots is in a pavilion next to the Virginia Air and Space Center. Originally made for Buckroe Beach Amusement Park, the carousel is one of only 170 antique wooden ones still in use in the United States.

Hampton History Museum (757-727-1610; www.hampton.gov/history_museum), 120 Hampton Lane. Open Mon.–Sat. 10–5, Sun. 1–5. Closed Thanksgiving, Dec. 25, and Jan. 1. The museum's nine galleries trace Hampton's development from the home of the Kecoughtan Native Americans to a center for space travel and defense. Learn about 17th-century Port Hampton, the 18th-century pirate Blackbeard, the city's role in the 19th-century Civil War, and Hampton's modern role as a military base. $5 adults, $4 ages 4–12.

&. **Hampton University and Hampton Museum** (757-727-5000 university, 757-727-5308 museum; www.museum.hampton.edu), 11 Frissell Avenue. Open Mon.–Fri. 8–5, Sat. noon–4. Closed Sun. The sprawling 98-foor-diameter oak tree at the entrance to the university is called the "Emancipation Oak" because it was here on January 1, 1863, that residents gathered to hear the reading of President Lincoln's Emancipation Proclamation. It was also under this tree that in 1861 Mary Peake, a free African American, taught her first class of 20 students: escaped former slaves. Many had fled to this area after Union general Butler, in control of Fort Monroe, Hampton, declared that escaping slaves would be "contraband of war" and therefore not returned to slavery. The school became the Butler School for Negro Children in 1863. In April 1868 the Hampton Normal and Agricultural School was opened. Booker T. Washington enrolled in the school in 1872. Eventually the school became the Hampton Institute and then Hampton University. Established in 1868, the museum has a distinctive collection of African and African American works. Free

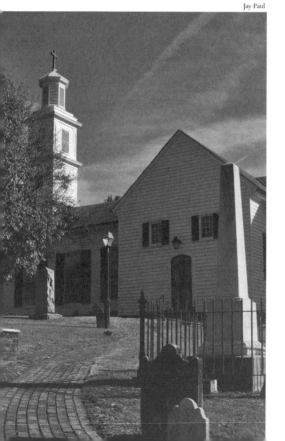

ST. JOHN'S CHURCH

Jay Paul

&. **St. John's Episcopal Church** (757-722-2567; www.stjohnshampton.org), 100 West Queens Way. Open Mon.–Fri. 9–3, Sat. 9–noon, Sun. during services. Established in 1610 as Elisabeth City Parish, the parish is the oldest English-speaking parish in continuous service in America. The current structure dates to 1728 and is the only building to sur-

HAMPTON AND BLACKBEARD, THE PIRATE

English goods sailed into Hampton's harbor and the colonies' riches sailed out. That attracted merchants, shippers, and also pirates. The notorious scourge of the Caribbean, Blackbeard (a.k.a. Edward Teach), settled in North Carolina with his 14th wife. Pardoned by the governor, Blackbeard, for a time, he the life of a gentleman, but all that booty floating along the Chesapeake's docks and the east coast proved too much to resist. He gathered his men, including William Howard, a captain from Hampton, and began once again looting ships, or, as he stated to North Carolina officials, "salvaging abandoned cargo." Legend has it that the North Carolinian powers kept a hands-off policy for Blackbeard as long as he handed over a portion of the goods.

That's why Virginia's Governor Spotswood felt he had to stop the looting. In 1718, Spotswood sent two Royal Navy ships led by Lt. Robert Maynard to Ocracoke, North Carolina. Blackbeard, his men, and fellow pirates were celebrating at a feast—drinking, among other things, rum punch spiked with gunpowder—when Maynard's ships landed at Ocracoke. In the hand-to-hand battle, Blackbeard sustained 25 wounds, fighting fiercely until Maynard decapitated him. Maynard, as the story goes, brought Spotswood Blackbeard's flag, treasure, and severed head. To warn other pirates, Spotswood placed the head on a stake at the entrance to the Hampton River. And that's why, in July, Hampton hosts a pirate festival, with tall ships, a ball, pirate skirmishes, food, and fireworks.

vive the burning of Hampton in August 1861 by the townspeople so that the town's facilities would not be of use to Union soldiers. After the fire, the walls remained. After the Civil War, the church became St. John's. The communion silver dating to 1618 and the 1887 stained-glass window depicting the baptism of Pocahontas are among the church's highlights. Free.

Old Point Comfort Lighthouse (757-723-3473), McNair Drive, Fort Monroe. Although closed to the public, the 1802 lighthouse can be viewed from the street. Legend has it that the name derived from the fact that Captain Christopher Newport anchored his ship, the *Susan Constant,* here before sailing on to what would be called Jamestown.

Newport News

& **Endview Plantation** (757-887-1862; www.endview.org), 362 Yorktown Road. Open Mon, Thu., and Fri. 10–4, Sat. 10–5, Sun. noon–5. Closed Tue. and Wed. and major holidays. Parts of this Georgian-style home, originally built by William Harwood, date to 1769. When Virginia seceded from the Union on April 17, 1861, the plantation was owned by Dr. Humphrey Harwood Curtis, William Harwood's great-grandson. Curtis organized the volunteer company the Warwick

Beauregards, which became Company H of the 32nd Virginia Volunteer Infantry Regiment. In their battle to defend the peninsula in May 1862, Confederate troops were defeated by Union general Joseph E. Johnston's army. The Confederates used Endview briefly as a hospital. After that, Union troops occupied Endview and remained in the area until almost the war's end. Guided tours of the home are available. What makes the plantation special are the spring Civil War Reenactments, typically held in April, as well as the Civil War Children's Camps held in summer. $6 adults, $4 ages 7–18.

Lee Hall Mansion (757-888-3371; www.leehall.org), 163 Yorktown Road. Open Mon., Thu., and Fri. 10–4, Sat. 10–5, Sun. noon–5. Closed Tue. and Wed. and major holidays. The only large antebellum plantation remaining on the lower Virginia peninsula, Lee Hall, situated on a rise, was completed in 1859. Because of its commanding view, Confederate generals John Magruder and Joseph E. Johnston headquartered at the mansion during the 1862 Peninsula Campaign. Exhibits in the mansion, which has been restored to its antebellum appearance, present material on the battle for the peninsula. $6 adults, $4 ages 7–18.

& **The Mariners' Museum** (757-596-2222; 1-800-581-7245); www.mariners museum.org. Open Wed.–Sat. 10–5, Sun. noon–5 Sun. Closed Mon. and Tue. The Mariners' Museum, the largest maritime museum in the United States, delves into various aspects of man's use of the sea. Exhibitions cover exploration, transportation, fishing, pleasure craft, and warfare. The USS Monitor Center, a museum highlight, employs recovered parts of the noted Civil War battleship Monitor that sank off the coast of Cape Hatteras, North Carolina, to showcase both the science of conservation and the significance of the vessel. Come aboard a replica of the ship and, in the Battle Theater, experience the historic encounter. On March 9, 1862, in what came to be called the Battle of Hampton Roads, the USS Monitor clashed with the CSS Virginia, formerly the USS Merrimack, inaugurating the era of iron and steam warships. To commemorate the Civil War, the museum typically hosts special lectures and workshops in the spring.

MARINERS' MUSEUM
Newport News Tourism Development Office

For those who like ships' models, the museum's Crabtree Collection of Miniature Ships showcases a simple dugout canoe paddled by one figure, an ancient Egyptian oar powered ship, a Venetian galley with 359 crew members, and other interesting vessels. The Chesapeake Bay Gallery details the eastern shore's shipbuilding legacy as well as boat replicas and an actual lens from the Cape Charles lighthouse. Peruse old maps and navigational tools at the Age of Exploration Gallery, and view nearly 150 boats from more than 30 countries at the International Small Craft Center.

Another museum delight is the 550-acre parklike setting that features the 167-acre Lake Maury. The 5-mile-long trail that hugs the shoreline has picnic benches and 14 footbridges. In season, you can rent boats by the hour, $4–7, or the day, $15–25. Admission $12 adults, $7 ages 6–12.

Newsome House Museum and Cultural Center (757-247-2360; www.newsomehouse.org), 2803 Oak Avenue. Open Thu.–Sat. 10–5, by appointment Mon.–Wed. The restored 1899 Queen Anne–style home of African American attorney and community leader J. Thomas Newsome serves as an art gallery that displays works by African-American

Newport News Tourism Development Office

VIRGINIA LIVING MUSEUM

and other artists. The facility also holds workshops, lectures, and other programs. $2 donation.

✐ ♿ **Virginia Living Museum** (757-595-1900; www.thevlm.org), 524 J. Clyde Morris Boulevard Open Memorial Day–Labor Day daily 9–5; Labor Day–Memorial Day Mon.–Sat. 9–5, Sun. noon–5. Discover Virginia's natural heritage from the state's coast to its mountains at this facility showcasing thousands of the reptiles, mammals, birds, and sea critters that inhabit Virginia. Sea turtles and schools of fish swim in the 30,000-gallon Noland Chesapeake Bay Aquarium, the star of the Coastal Plain Gallery. Smallmouth bass, catfish, yellow perch, and red squirrels live in the Piedmont and Mountains Gallery. Lobsters, bats, and tree frogs are some of the nocturnal creatures on view in the World of Darkness exhibit. Re-created habitats transport you to a Cypress Swamp alive with alligators and an Appalachian Cove with birds, a waterfall, and a mountain stream. For a closer look at either the red wolves or the otters, sign up for a curator-led, guided Animal Confidential tour, available Wednesdays at 3 for an additional $12.

The museum also details the heavens and earth-friendly gardens and architecture. The Abbitt Planetarium holds various shows, including an afternoon program for preschoolers, and on the second Saturday of the month, an evening show, which may include a rock-and-roll laser show. The Living Green House and Conservation Garden exhibits the latest techniques and products for constructing an earth-friendly home. From the outdoor boardwalk overlooking the lake, you may be able to spot gray foxes, coyotes, deer, wild turkeys, and bald eagles. In season, at the outdoor Butterfly Garden, hundreds of delicate butterflies hover over the colorful host plants.

For a different take on the 1861–65 battle years, read the museum's Naturalist's Walking Guide to the Civil War. The compilation of diary quotes, letters, and other items focuses on how people met some of their basic challenges and how the difficulties affected Virginians' use of animals and plants. $17 adults, $13 ages 3–12; museum and planetarium $21 adults, $17 ages 3–12.

& **Virginia War Museum** (757-247-8523; www.warmuseum.org), 9285 Warwick Boulevard. Open Mon.–Sat. 9–5, Sun. noon–5. Closed Thanksgiving Day, Dec. 25, and Jan. 1. This museum traces the development of the U.S. military from 1775 to the present, using uniforms, weapons, posters, and personal items. Among the galleries are Women at War, which focuses on the changing role of women, and Marches Toward Freedom, which details the contributions made by African Americans from the Revolution to the Gulf War. Among the displayed items—part of a collection of 60,000 artifacts—are an 1883 Gatling gun, a section of wall from a World War II German POW, and a Gulf War Iraqi antiaircraft gun. $6 adults, $4 ages 7–14.

Norfolk

& **Chrysler Museum of Art** (757-664-6200; www.chrysler.org), 245 West Olney Road at Mowbray Arch. Open Wed. 10–9, Thu.–Sat. 10–5, Sun. noon–5. Closed major holidays. After the original facility, the former Norfolk Museum of Arts and Sciences, received the 30,000-object collection of industrialist Walter Chrysler in 1971, the renamed museum became one of Virginia's top art museums. Spanning 5,000 years of history, the galleries showcase textiles, ceramics, bronzes, and paintings from pre-Columbian, African, and Asian artists as well as European paintings and American art from the 17th to the 21st centuries. The museum has works by Mary Cassatt, Frederick Childe Hassam, Peter Paul Rubens, Alexander Calder, Henri Matisse, Roy Lichtenstein, and Georgia O'Keeffe. In addition, the museum contains a 10,000-piece collection of glass that's one of the most notable such collections in the United States. Our favorite space is the Tiffany Gallery, aglow with the rich colors and intricate patterns of Tiffany lamps and vases. Free admission. The museum manages two historic houses in downtown Norfolk, the **Moses Myers House** and the **Willoughby-Baylor House**.

TIFFANY GLOBE, CHRYSLER MUSEUM OF ART

VisitNorfolk

Fort Norfolk (757-625-1720; www.norfolkhistorical.org), 801 Front Street. Self-guided tours Mon.–Fri. A brick and earthwork fort, the facility is the last remaining of 19 harbor-front forts that George Washington authorized as president. Occupied by the U.S. Army until the 1820s, the fort remained unoccupied until 1851, when the navy used it to store ammunition. At the outset of the Civil War's, the Confederate Army captured the fort, but after the Union conquered Norfolk, the structure served as a Union hospital as well as a Confederate prison. The navy took over the fort in 1863 but left in 1880 because locals did not want ammunition stored so close to the city. From 1923 to now, it is home to the Norfolk District, U.S. Army Corps of Engineers. On the self-guided tour, you can walk the ramparts, visit the dungeon, and tour the Officers' Quarters. The Norfolk Historical Society provides information about the fort and oversees reenactments, typically held in June and August. Free admission.

& **Hampton Roads Naval Museum** (757-322-2987; www.hrnm.navay.mil/), One Waterside Drive. Open daily 10–5. Contained within Nauticus, this separate museum operated by the U.S. Navy presents 234 years of Hampton Roads naval history. Find out about area battles, starting with Lord Dunmore's decision in January 1776 to bomb Norfolk in the Revolutionary War, as well as learn about the Civil War battle of the *Monitor* and the CSS *Virginia* (formerly the *Merrimack)*, the first meeting of ironclad naval vessels that took place in the Hampton Roads area. Free admission.

MacArthur Memorial (757-441-2965; www.norfolk.gov/MacArthurMemorial), MacArthur Square. Tue.–Sat. 10–5, Sun. 11–5. Learn about Douglas MacArthur's military career in the galleries and pay your respects to the illustrious general, who is entombed in the rotunda along with his wife. Donation suggested.

✍ **Mermaids on Parade** (www.MermaidsOnParade.com). What started as a fundraiser for the arts has turned into iconic street art and a symbol for Norfolk. More than 24 of these 4- to 10-foot-long mermaids adorn city sites. Find your favorites by following the map.

Moses Myers House (757-333-6283; www.chrysler.org), 331 Bank Street. Fri.–Sun. noon–4. Moses Myers, a prosperous Jewish merchant, built this home in 1792. About 70 percent of the furnishings are true to the period and the home contains Gilbert Stuart's portraits of Myers and his wife, Eliza. Free admission.

✍ & **Nauticus, the National Maritime Center, and the USS *Wisconsin*** (757-664-1000; 1-800-664-1080; www.nauticus.org), One Waterside Drive. Open Memorial Day–Labor Day daily 10–5; Labor Day–Memorial Day Tue.–Sat. 10–5, Sun. noon–5. It's only fitting that Norfolk, home to the second-biggest U.S. port and to one of the largest U.S. Navy installations, pays homage to the sea and U.S. maritime history. Each of the three attractions located at the Nauticus site showcase different aspects.

Although **Nauticus's** hands-on exhibits engage kids, the museum also has many text-heavy galleries, such as the 1907 Jamestown Exposition and the Launching of the Steel Navy that has an informative 26-minute film best appreciated by older teens and adults. Even so, the exhibit targets young children with a sailor's ditty box to explore and a sailor's hat to wear. In the **National Oceanic and Atmospheric Administration's (NOAA)** Science on a Sphere, view satellite images of hurricanes forming as well as compare these to the images of Australia's dry deserts. This is an interesting exhibit for weather-curious teens and adults.

Other exhibits interest youngsters as well as your "inner child." At the Aegis Theater, make rapid-fire decisions in a high-tech naval battle, and in Design Chamber: Battleship X, race against others to design a World War II battleship. You can also land navy warplanes on an aircraft carrier, pilot a ship through the river and into the Chesapeake Bay, and spell your name in Morse code. At Horseshoe Crab Cove, handle horseshoe crabs, sea stars, and whelks; and at the Nauticus Theater, view screen-size high-definition images of spectacular sea life.

Norfolk's role in war preparedness and battle history is also represented at Nauticus by two independent agencies. The city of Norfolk has jurisdiction over the **USS *Wisconsin***, one of the largest battleships, at 887 feet 3 inches. Each of the ship's dozen 16-inch/50-caliber guns can fire a 1,900-pound projectile 23 nautical miles. (The weight is equivalent to a VW Beetle; Nauticus suspends an actual vehicle to demonstrate this point.) Walking on the deck as part of the self-guided tour gives you a sense of how truly gigantic the ship is. Fee includes admission to Nauticus and to the decks of the battleship USS *Wisconsin.* $12 adults, $9.50 ages 4–12.

The privately owned ***Victory Rover*** (757-627-7406; www.navalbasecruises.com), docked at Nauticus, One Waterside Drive, offers two-hour, narrated cruises of the of the Elizabeth River and Hampton Harbor. The cruise goes by some of the navy's aircraft carriers, submarines, and guided missile cruisers. Apr.–late May, and after Labor Day–Oct. daily 11 AM and 2 PM; late May–Memorial Day daily 11 AM, 2 PM, and 5:30 PM; Nov.–Dec. and Mar. daily Tue.–Sun. 2 PM but call to confirm. No tours Jan.–Feb. Note: Possible security restrictions may result tour cancellations. Call ahead. $18 adults, $10 children. Combo ticket with Nauticus and battleship admission: $25 adults, $17 children.

Norfolk History Museum at the Willoughby-Baylor House (757-41-1526; www.chrysler.org), 601 East Freemason Street. Open Fri.–Sun. noon–4. This 1794 house was built by Captain Thomas Willoughby and renovated as the Norfolk History Museum. The facility has changing exhibits highlighting Norfolk's maritime and military heritage, as well as the city's decorative arts. Free admission.

Norfolk Naval Station Tours (757-444-7955; www.norfolkvisitor.com), 9079 Hampton Boulevard. You can tour Norfolk's 4,300-acre naval station, reputed to be the world's largest, home port to 75 ships and 134 aircraft. The navy operates 45-minute **bus tours** from the Naval Base Tour Office. Conducted by navy personnel, the bus rolls you past a few of the ships in port and then to the area of the base where the houses constructed for 1907 Jamestown Exhibition are located. Be aware that security restrictions may result in canceled tours. Those over 18 are required to show photo ID and vehicle registration. Free.

St. Paul's Church (757-627-4353; www.saintpaulsnorfolk.com), 201 St. Paul's Boulevard. Open Tue.–Fri. 10–4. Sun. services 8 AM and 10:30 AM. St. Paul's, built in 1739, is Norfolk's oldest building, an active Episcopal church, and the only structure that survived the British bombardment on January 1, 1776. Lord Dunmore, who had fled Williamsburg for Hampton Roads on the eve of the Revolution, fired a cannonball that still remains lodged in the church's southwestern wall. The church also has a Tiffany window and in its cemetery some tombstones that date to the 17th and 18th centuries. Donation suggested.

🎐 **Virginia Zoo** (757-441-2374; www.virginiazoo.org), 3500 Granby Street. Open daily 10–5. Closed Dec. 24–25 and Jan. 1. The 53-acre facility doesn't overwhelm kids and the Zoo Train makes it easy to get around when little ones tire of walking. Among the newer of the 350 animal inhabitants are five Aldabra tortoises, the second-largest land tortoise in the world. The male weighs a hefty 475 pounds. Other highlights include African elephants, giraffes, lions, and white rhinos. $8 adults, $6 ages 2–11; Zoo Train $2.

Virginia Beach

Atlantic Wildfowl Heritage Museum (757-437-8432; www.awhm.org), 1113 Atlantic Avenue. Open summer Mon.–Sat. 10–5, Sun. noon-5; off-season Tue.–Sat. 10–5, Sun. noon–5. This museum is a must-see for those for whom carved decoys are a passion. Antique and contemporary duck, geese, and decoys of other waterfowl are exhibited. At times, a volunteer carver is at work in the carving room, providing a chance to chat about his art. On the second floor are photographs of Virginia Beach in bygone eras. Donation suggested.

Old Cape Henry Lighthouse (757-422-9421; www.apva.org), Northeastern tip of Virginia Beach, on the grounds of the U.S. Army's Fort Story. Photo ID cards required for visitors 18 and older to enter Fort Story. Open mid-Mar.–Oct. daily 10–5, Nov.–mid-Mar. daily 10–4. The picturesque lighthouse, built in 1791–92, marked the entrance to the Chesapeake Bay until 1881. For a panoramic view, climb the 191 steps to the top. To tackle the stairs, you must be at least 42 inches tall. $5 age 13 and older, $3 age 12 and under (if taller than 42 inches).

🎐 **Virginia Aquarium & Marine Science Center** (757-385-3474; www.virginiaaquarium.com), 717 General Booth Boulevard. Open daily 9–5. Eventually, you have to get out of the sun and this aquarium with 800,000 gallons of exhibits is a great place to go. The clever and kid-

OLD CAPE HENRY LIGHTHOUSE
Virginia Tourism Corporation

friendly exhibits mostly focus on Virginia's marine habitats from marshes to the Bay and the ocean. View turtles, seals, river otters, sand tiger sharks, and touch stingrays—surprisingly velvety—and horseshoe crabs. Restless Planet, the heart of a $25 million renovation, presents critters and habitats indigenous to four world environments that are similar to stages in Virginia's natural evolution. Among them are the Malaysian Peat Swamp, home to snakehead fish and Malayan leaf frogs, and the Red Sea habitat whose highlight is a clear 40-foot tunnel you walk through as eagle rays and colorful fish swim above and around you. The IMAX theater presents movies on a screen six stories high. $17 adults, $12 ages 3–11; with IMAX movie, $25 adults, $20 ages 3–11.

Virginia Myers

HORSESHOE CRAB

✳ To Do

AMUSEMENT PARKS

Virginia Beach
𝒮 **Ocean Breeze Waterpark** (757-422-4444; www.oceanbreezewaterpark.com), 849 General Booth Boulevard. Open third week in May–early Sept. Sun.–Thu. 10–7, Fri. and Sat. 10–10. Kids who prefer pools get splash-happy at this water park located 2 miles from the ocean. They can zip down 16 waterslides and tackle the surf in Runaway Bay, a wave pool. Little kids can climb on Buccaneer Bay's pirate ship and float along on Little Amazon, a "lazy river." $25 adults, $18 ages 3–9.

BEACHES

Hampton
𝒮 **Buckroe Beach and Park** (757-727-8311; www.hampton.gov/parks), North First Street. Open daily 8–6. Lifeguards on duty Memorial Day–Labor Day. Stroll and sun on this 8-acre beach along the Chesapeake Bay. The beach has a playground plus picnic shelters with grills available by reservation. In summer, enjoy concerts on Sunday nights and outdoor, family movies on Tuesday nights.

Newport News
Huntington Park Beach (757-886-7912; www.newport-news.org/things-to-do /outtdoors), 361 Hornet Circle. The 60-acre park has a sandy stretch along the James River. Swimming and boating are allowed. The park also has a rose garden and a tennis center.

CIVIL WAR SESQUICENTENNIAL AND MORE CIVIL WAR SITES

Virginia commemorates the 150th anniversary of the Civil War from 2011 to 2015 by hosting special events at the state's many Civil War sites. For more information about the attractions as well as the applicable tourist offices, contact **Virginia Civil War** (www.VirginiaCivilWar.org).

Newport News

Endview Plantation (757-887-1862; www.endview.org) hosts Civil War Reenactments in spring and Civil War Camp for children in summer.

Mariners' Museum (757-596-2222; 1-800-581-7245); www.marinersmuseum.org) typically hosts lectures and workshops.

Monitor–Merrimack Overlook, Chesapeake Avenue near Sixteenth Street. From here view the site of the first fight between two ironclad ships: the USS *Monitor* and the CSS *Virginia* (*Merrimack*). The battle took place on March 9, 1862. After four hours of combat, both sides claimed victory.

Newport News Visitor Center (757-886-7777, 888-4-WE-R-Fun; www.newport-news.org).

Virginia Living Museum (757-595-1900; www.thevlm.org) offers the Naturalist's Walking Guide to the Civil War that details how the war impacted Virginians' use of animals and plants.

Norfolk

Civil War Trails, a free driving brochure available from the city's Convention & Visitors Bureau, lists nine sites. Among them are the U.S. Customs House, an impressive building that the Federal troops used as a dungeon between 1862 and 1865; Camp Naglee, situated in and around the current Chamber of Commerce Building, was Union camp and hospital, as well as Fort Norfolk, see "Museums and Historic Sites."

Nauticus Welcome Desk, One Waterside Drive. Open Sun. noon–5.

Norfolk Convention and Visitor's Bureau (757-664-6620; 1-800-368-3097; www.visitnorfolktoday.com), 232 East Main Street, Norfolk. Open Mon.–Fri. 8:30–5

BIKING

Norfolk

Go Green Bikes (757-635-3202; www.gogreenbikerentals.com). Open daily 9–7. Go Green will deliver your bicycle to your hotel as well as pick it up. The company can provide helmets, locks, and child trailers. Three-day minimum weekend rental, $35 per day, seven-day minimum weekly rental, $10 per day.

PICK YOUR SANDS IN VIRGINIA BEACH

Where to put your beach blanket depends on what you want. Virginia Beach, with 35 miles of coastline, 20 of continuous sandy shores, and 3 miles of "boardwalk" (actually a flat, paved, no-cars-allowed path), provides several options.

Back Bay National Wildlife Refuge (757 721–2412; backbay.fws.gov), 4005 Sandpiper Road. Visitor Center Mon.–Fri. 8–4, Sat. and Sun. 9–4. Although you can't swim or sunbathe here, you can bicycle and hike through the 9,000 acres of this waterfowl refuge. The 1-mile boardwalk beach loop leads past dune barriers to the Atlantic and the 4-mile dike loop winds through marshlands. Stay on the boardwalk as venomous cottonmouth snakes inhabit the marshes. $2 entrance fee walkers and bikers, $5 per car.

Boardwalk. Stretching from around 2nd Street to 39th, the 28-foot-wide boardwalk lined with shops and cafés is a big draw. We love strolling, people watching and pedaling those four-wheeled bikes with the fringed awnings. (See "Biking" in To Do.)

Chesapeake Bay. For relatively calm surf, go to the bay beaches. Head north along Atlantic or Pacific Avenue. Around 83rd Street the road changes to Shore Drive and the bay beach entrance is nearby.

False Cape State Park (757-426-7128; 1-800-933-7275; www.dcr.virginia.gov /state_parks/fal.shtml), 4001 Sandpiper Road, 5 miles south of Back Bay. In southern Virginia Beach, False Cape is a gift for the eye: 6 miles of beautiful shoreline graced by dunes, gulls, and sandpipers but visited by a relatively small number of people at any one time. The park is a 4,321-acre, mile-wide barrier spit between Back Bay and the Atlantic Ocean. Along with unspoiled beaches, the

SURFING AND KAYAKING AT VIRGINIA BEACH

Virginia Tourism Corporation

Virginia Beach Convention & Visitors Bureau

TERRA GATOR

park has thousands of acres of marshlands and woods filled with songbirds. To reach False Cape, you must hike or mountain bike the 5 miles through Back Bay National Wildlife Refuge. Two vehicles offer access. The Blue Goose Express, a tram, runs in spring, summer, and fall, and from November through March, False Cape's Terra Gator, a big-wheeled vehicle, operates on weekends. Both rides are round-trips, allowing two hours of exploring. Bring snacks and plenty of water. $2 entrance fee for walkers or bikers. $8 for either the tram or the Terra Gator.

Fort Story (757-422-7755), Shore Drive and Atlantic Avenue. Open 5:30 AM–9 PM. Situated in northern Virginia Beach on an army base, the Fort Story beach is much less crowded than the sands in the resort area. However, call ahead as security concerns may close the Fort Story beach to civilians.

Less busy beaches. Head to Sandbridge at the southern end of town or to the north beaches, 40th Street and above.

Nature reserves and parks. Virginia Beach has three interesting options for quieter shores: **Bay National Wildlife Refuge**, **False Cape State Park**, and **Fort Story**.

Resort area. Roughly defined, this region runs from Rudee Inlet in the south to North Beach (around 31st Street and above). College kids and crowds tend to cluster along the strand from 20th to 30th streets. There are parking lots (arrive early) at 17th, 24th, and 31st streets.

Surfers. Ride the waves in the surfing zone between 4th and 6th streets.

SURFING AT SANDBRIDGE, VIRGINIA BEACH

Virginia Beach Convention & Visitors Bureau

Norfolk Botanical Garden (757-441-5830; www.norfolkbotanicalgarden.org), 6700 Azalea Garden Road. Open Apr.–Oct. Mon., Wed., and Thu. 4–7. Bring a bike a pedal along the paths through the petals.

Virginia Beach

Bike the Boardwalk. The 3-mile long, 28-foot-wide boardwalk has a separate bicycle lane. Many hotels and outfitters rent two-wheel bikes. We like to rent the four-wheel family bikes that have a fringed awning when traveling with kids and grandparents. Several places along the boardwalk rent these for about $15 per hour. Among the companies offering a range of bicycles to rent is **Cherie's Bike & Blade Rentals** (757-437-8888), 705 Atlantic Avenue and 12 other locations.

BIRDING

Virginia Beach

Back Bay National Wildlife Refuge (757-721-2412; backbay.fws.gov), 4005 Sandpiper Road. Visitor Center open Mon.–Fri. 8–4, Sat. and Sun. 9–4, At this 9,000-acre waterfowl refuge, nearly 300 species of birds have been observed. Egrets and herons can be spotted along the 9 miles of dikes built to separate the man-made freshwater impoundments from the saltwater of Chesapeake Bay. Approximately 10,000 snow geese and a large variety of ducks visit here during the peak of their migration, usually in December. $2 entrance fee walkers and bikers, $5 per car.

Chesapeake Bay-Bridge Tunnel affords birdwatchers a prime spot to view the September and May migrations. See "Bridges."

Seashore to Cypress Birding Trail. Contact the **Virginia Beach Convention and Visitors Bureau** (1-800-822-3224; www.vbfun.com), 2100 Parks Avenue, Suite 500. The trail links several of Virginia Beach's prime birding places, connecting 130,000 acres of natural area from First Landing State Park, the Chesapeake Bay Bridge-Tunnel, Back Bay National Wildlife Refuge, False Cape State Park, the Virginia Aquarium & Marine Science Center, and the Great Dismal Swamp National Wildlife Refuge.

BOAT EXCURSIONS

Hampton

Miss Hampton II (757-722-9102, 888-757-BOAT; www.misshamptoncruises .com), 710 Settlers Landing Road. Available Apr.–Oct. The two and a half to three-hour tours afford scenic views of area attractions, including Hampton University, Blackbeard's Point, Fort Monroe, and the Norfolk Naval Base. $23 adults, $12 ages 6–12.

Norfolk

American Rover Tall Ship Cruises (757-627-7425; www.americanrover.com), 333 Waterside Drive. Cruises available mid-April to October. Schedules vary. The ship, a three-masted topsail schooner carrying up to 149 passengers, offers 90-minute to two-hour narrated cruises. On board, if you want to help with the sails you can, or simply enjoy the sea breezes. 90-minute cruise $18 adults, $10 children.

VisitNorfolk

AMERICAN ROVER

Spirit of Norfolk Cruises (1-866-304-2469; www.spiritcitycruises.com), Otter Berth next to Waterside, Downtown Norfolk.) This 450-passenger ship offers lunch cruises as well as dinner and dancing outings. Children are welcome on lunch and dinner cruises (although the kids may be bored). On Club Norfolk Midnight Moonlight sailings, passengers must be at least 21 years old. Groups also book the ship for catered sailings. Prices vary with outings.

The *Victory Rover* (757-627-7406; www.navalbasecruises.com), docked at Nauticus, One Waterside Drive, Mar.–Dec. offers two-hour, narrated cruises of the of the Elizabeth River and the Hampton Harbor. The ship cruises by some of the navy's aircraft carriers, submarines, and guided missile cruisers. See **Norfolk Naval Station Tours** above.

Virginia Beach
Virginia Aquarium & Marine Science Center (757-385-0300; www.virginia aquarium.com) offers dolphin-watching cruises Apr.–Oct. $20 adults, $14 ages 4–11; humpback and fin whale cruises Dec.–Mar., $28 adults, $24, ages 4–11.

BRIDGES
Virginia Beach and Cape Charles
The Chesapeake Bay Bridge–Tunnel (757-331-2960; www.cbbt.com), Rte. 13, information 32386 Lankford Highway, Cape Charles. The 17.6-mile-long bridge tunnel, fun to cross, loops over and under the Chesapeake Bay,

connecting Virginia Beach to Cape Charles on Virginia's Eastern Shore. The structure is one of the world's longest bridge-tunnels. When there's little traffic, we enjoy the panoramic water views and the sea breezes. There's a fishing pier and restaurant on one of the man-made islands about 3½ miles from Virginia Beach. In September and early May, hundreds of birdwatchers come to observe the mid-Atlantic flyway for migratory sea birds.

Bill Conway

FISHING

Newport News

James River Bridge Fishing Pier (757-247-0364; www.nesport-news.org), 6701 River Road. Open Apr.–Nov. Wed.–Sat. 24 hours, Sun.–Tue. 9 AM–11 PM. From the 6/10-mile fishing pier, one East Coast's longest, try your luck catching striped bass, flounder, gray trout, and other seasonal fish.

King-Lincoln Park (757-886-7912; www.newport-news.org), 600 Jefferson Avenue. Open summer months. The park has a saltwater fishing pier in addition to tennis and basketball courts.

Norfolk

Ocean View Fishing Pier (757-583-6000; www.oceanviewfishingpier.com), 400 West Ocean View Avenue. Open Memorial Day–Labor Day 24/7. The fishing pier juts out 1,690 feet into the Chesapeake Bay. The location has bathrooms, a restaurant, and a bait house where you can also rent rods and reels. Four-hour fishing trips departing from the pier $20–30 adults, $20–25 children under 12. Pier admission $8 adults, $6 age 9 and younger.

Virginia Beach

Back Bay National Wildlife Refuge (757 721–2412; backbay.fws.gov), 4005 Sandpiper Road. Visitor Center open Mon.–Fri. 8–4, Sat. and Sun. 9–4. Allows surf and freshwater fishing. A fishing license is required.

Dockside Marina Fishing and Dolphin Watching (757-481-4545; www.fishingvabeach.com), 3311 Shore Drive. The outfitter offers fishing and dolphin-watching excursions. Prices vary with the excursion.

First Landing State Park (757-412-2300; 1-800-933-PARK; www.dcr.virginia.gov/state_parks), Hwy. 60 at Cape Henry, 2500 Shore Drive. The Narrows, between Broad Bay and Linkhorn Bay, is a popular fishing and crabbing spot. Parking $4–5.

Wild River Outfitters (757-431-8566; www.wildriveroutfitters.com), 3636 Virginia Beach Boulevard combines fishing with kayaking. Prices vary with the excursion.

GOLF

Hampton
Hamptons Golf Course (757-766-9148; wwww.hampton.va.us/thehamptons/), 320 Butler Farm Road. Open daylight hours year-round. The 27-hole public course offers gently rolling terrain. Weekdays $19, weekends $21.

Newport News
Newport News Golf Club at Deer Run (757-886-7925; www.nngolfclub .com), 901 Clubhouse Way. The public facility has two 18-hole courses. Weekdays $27–32, weekend $13–36.

Norfolk
Lamberts Point Golf (757-489-1677; www.lambertspointgolf.com), 4301 Powhatan Avenue. Open weather permitting Mon.–Fri. 7–7, Sat. and Sun. 6:30 AM–7 PM. Along with nine holes, this course has a 7,500-square-foot chipping area and a 10,000-square-foot putting green. 18 holes $18–19.

Ocean View Golf Course (757-480-2094; www.oceanviewgc.com), 9610 Norfolk Avenue. Open daylight hours, year-round, weather permitting. Located 20 minutes from both downtown Norfolk and Hampton, Ocean View offers 18 holes of golf. $21–42.

Virginia Beach
From among Virginia Beach's more than a dozen golf courses, we have listed the three municipal courses.

Bow Creek Municipal Golf Course (757-431-3763; www.vbgov.com, 3425 Club House Road. The 18-hole course is a par-70. $17–25.

Kempsville Greens Municipal Course (757-474-8441; www.vbgov.com), 4840 Princess Anne Road. The 18-hole course is a par-70. $17–25.

Red Wing Lake Municipal Golf Course (757-437-2037; www.redwinglake golf.com), 1144 Prosperity Road. The 18-hole course was recently renovated. $42–59.

HISTORIC DRIVES

Newport News
Founders' Trail, a brochure available from the Newport News Visitor Center (757-886-7777; 1-888-4-WE-R-FUN; www.newport-news.org), links 12 historic sites dating to the 17th century, including Mulberry Island, a peninsula named by Captain John Smith for its many mulberry trees; the 1649 Mathews Mill; and Warwicktown, the 1690 site of Warwick County's first town.

Passport to Newport News is an audio CD driving tour of 23 points of interest that provides historical background. Newport News Tourism Development

Office created the CD and it's available from the Newport News Visitor Center (757-886-7777; 1-888-4-WE-R-FUN; www.newport-news.org. $12.95.

Norfolk

Civil War Trails (757-441-1852; 1-800-368-3097; www.visitnorfolktoday.com), Norfolk Visitor Information Venter, I-64 exit 273.

WALKS

Hampton

iPod Walking Tours are available from the **Hampton Visitor Center** (757-727-12102; 1-800-800-2202; www.hamptoncvb.com), 120 Old Hampton Lane, Hampton. Open daily 9–5. Closed Thanksgiving, Dec. 25, and Jan. 1. A mix of historical fact, commentary, music, and images, the tours cover several routes, including the Virginia Air & Space Center, Fort Monroe, Hampton University Campus, Downtown Hampton, and Hampton's Historic Neighborhoods. Download of the tours is free. If you need an iPod, the Visitor Center rents them for $10.

Norfolk

Freemason Historic District (www.freemasonstreetassociation.com), Brambleton Avenue and Bosch Street is the heart of the district. On a stroll along the cobblestone streets of this historic district, part of the National Register of Historic Places, see Norfolk's largest collection of pre–Civil War buildings. Among them are the Moses Myers House, Norfolk History Museum at the Willoughby-Baylor House, and Freemason Abbey, now a restaurant.

Virginia Beach

Boardwalk. Stretching for three oceanfront miles, Virginia Beach's 28-foot-wide boardwalk lined with cafés and shops is a prime place to walk.

✳ Green Spaces

Hampton

Grandview Nature Preserve (757-825-4657, or call Buckroe Beach Park about programming 757-850-5134; www.hampton.gov/parks), State Park Drive. Open daily sunrise–sunset. Explore salt marshes, tidal creeks, and Chesapeake Bay beachfront at this 475-acre park, also a favorite for local birders.

Sandy Bottom Nature Park (757-825-4657; www.hampton.gov/sandybottom/), 1255 Big Bethel Road. Open May–Sept. daily 9–6, Oct.–Apr. daily 9–4:30. Reclaimed from a former garbage dump, this 456-acre park has a nature center and walking trails through woodlands and wetlands, as well as a lake with boat rentals and fishing. Free admission.

Newport News

Newport News Park (757-886-7912; 1-800-203-8322; www.nnparks.com), 13564 Jefferson Avenue. Its 8,000 acres make this one of the largest municipal parks in the United States. It offers hiking and mountain biking trails as well as canoeing and paddleboats on the lake, plus an archery range and a disc (Frisbee)

golf course. The Discovery Center has nature exhibits and in summer hosts
nature program on Friday nights.

Norfolk

& **Norfolk Botanical Garden** (757-441-5830; www.norfolkbotanicalgarden
.org), 6700 Azalea Garden Road. Open Apr.–Oct. 15 daily 9–7, Oct. 16–Mar.
daily 9–5. Closed Thanksgiving Day, Dec. 25, and Jan. 1. Tram tours Apr.–Oct.
15 daily, free with admission. Boat tours Apr.–Oct. 15, weather permitting. Pick
your favorite oasis from among 30 themed gardens blooming on 155 acres. The
rose garden comprises more than 3,000 plants, the rhododendron glade showcases more than 175 varieties, and more than 1,700 camellias flower along Mirror Lake and in the Hofheimer Camellia Garden. The World of Wonders
(WOW) Children's Garden, features dancing fountains and re-created diverse
environments as an Australian red rock desert, a Serengeti savannah, and an
Asian bamboo rainforest. $9 adults, $7 ages 3–18. Boat tours $5 adults, $3 ages
3–12. Special events include Bike Nights. See "Biking" in *To Do*.

Town Point Park (757-441-2345; www.festivals.org), 333 Waterside Drive. The
stretch of green along the waterfront is the site of many of Norfolk's festivals.
When not the venue for summertime free music or ticketed events such as wine
festivals, the strip is a pleasant place to stroll and sit.

Virginia Beach

& **First Landing State Park** (757-412-2300; www.dcr.virginia.gov/state_parks
/fir.shtml), Hwy. 60 at Cape Henry, 2500 Shore Drive. This 2,888-acre park, Virginia's most popular state park, offers boating, swimming, bicycling, fishing, and
nearly 20 miles of hiking trails. Paths lead you by freshwater ponds and through
thickets of large cypress trees draped with Spanish moss. The first mile of the

FIRST LANDING STATE PARK, VIRGINIA BEACH AREA

pcopros

Bald Cypress Trail crosses dunes and ponds, and is wheelchair accessible. The Chesapeake Bay Center, an environmental education facility, is located in the park. The park also has cabins and camp sites. Parking $4–5.

✍ **Mount Trashmore Park** (757-473-5237; www.vbgov.com/parks), 310 Edwin Drive. Open 7:30 AM. Closing times vary seasonally. An environmental success, the 165-acre park takes its name from the fact that it was created from a landfill of compacted solid waste and clean soil. The park features two man-made mountains, two lakes, two playgrounds, walking paths, and its jewel, a skateboarding park.

PORTSMOUTH

Although you can drive to Portsmouth, a great day trip from Norfolk, it's more fun to get the wind in your hair by taking the passenger ferry across the Elizabeth River. Scenic Olde Towne features prettily restored houses spanning a variety of architectural styles from Federal to Victorian. The following are some of the city's highlights.

CRUISES The Spirit of Independence (757-971-1865; www.spiritof independence.net), a schooner, sails on scenic cruises three times daily—11, 3, and 6—in season. You can also book a cabin for a Boat and Breakfast overnight.

MUSEUMS AND HISTORIC ATTRACTIONS Fresnel Lens, near the Portsmouth Seawall south of High Street Landing, is 10 feet tall, weighs 2,500 pounds, and has 250 prisms of optical glass, the better to magnify a beam of light. In 1896, this lens served as a part of the Hog Island Light off the Great Machipongo Inlet on the Eastern Shore.

Jeffrey Greenberg, Virginia Tourism Corporation

A CHURCH STEEPLE IN PORTSMOUTH

Lightship Portsmouth Museum (757-393-8741; www.portsnavalmuseums .com), London Street at the waterfront, Historic Olde Towne, Portsmouth.

❋ Lodging

HOTELS, RESORTS, AND LODGES

Hampton

& ⟨ᵖ⟩ **Crowne Plaza Hampton Marina Hotel** (757-727-9700; 1-866-727-9900; www.hamptonmarinahotel.com),700 Settlers Landing Road.

This hotel has 172 rooms and suites, many with waterfront views, as well as an on-site restaurant and an outdoor pool. $90–260.

& **Embassy Suites Hampton Roads Hotel, Spa and Convention Center** (757-827-8200: embassysuites1 .hilton.com), 1700 Coliseum Drive. Each of these 295 suites has a living

---

Open Fri. and Sat. 10–5, Sun. 1–5. Lightships—vessels with lights atop their masts—functioned as portable lighthouses. Built in 1915, the Portsmouth served for 48 years, helping to provide safe passage to vessels off the coast of Virginia, Delaware, and Massachusetts. The ship is part of the collection of Portsmouth's Naval Shipyard Museum. Admission to both the Portsmouth Naval Shipyard Museum and the lightship, $3 adults, $1 ages 2–17.

Portsmouth Naval Shipyard Museum (757-393-8591; www.portsnavalmuseums .com), 2 High Street. Open Memorial Day–Labor Day Mon.–Sat. 10–5, Sun. 1–5; September–May Tue.–Sat. 10–5. The museum traces Portsmouth's naval presence from colonial times to the Civil War and beyond. Peruse uniforms, ship models, and other artifacts. Admission to both the Portsmouth Naval Shipyard Museum and the lightship, $3 adults, $1 ages 2–17.

WALKS The **Olde Towne Lantern Tour**'s (757-393-5111) walk past some of Portsmouth's prime places as the guide relates facts and legends about the city. Tours June–Sept., Tue. and Sat. nights. Call ahead.

The Path of History Walking Tour leads you to 45 sites in a mile-long route between two parks. A brochure is available from the Visitor Information Center.

LODGING **The Glencoe Inn** (757-397-8128; www.glencoeinn.com), 222 North Street. Built in 1890, Glencoe, a Victorian bed-and-breakfast inn located in Olde Towne, overlooks the Elizabeth River.

WHERE TO EAT **High Street**, the historic main street, offers a range of cafés and restaurants, including pizzerias, sub shops, and the sports bar Roger Brown's (757-399-5377), 319 High Street. For meals with a bit more flare, consider the Mediterranean fare at **Café Europa** (757-399-6652), 319 High Street. Off High Street, try **Stove, the Restaurant** (757-397-0900; www.stoverestaurant.com), 2622 Detroit Street, an award-winning eatery with folk art–like paintings, which serves what Chef Sydney Meers calls a "neo-Southern style of cookin'."

area with a television, plus a refrigerator and microwave. Some two-bedroom suites are available. The property has an indoor pool and also offers a hot breakfast. $110–400.

(𝗐) **Hilton Garden Inn Hampton Coliseum Central** (757-310-6323; 1-877-STAYHGI; http://hiltongarden inn1.hilton.com), 1999 Power Plant Parkway. This 149-room hotel in the Hilton chain has a restaurant serving breakfast and dinner, offers room service, and has an indoor pool and whirlpool. Free wireless high-speed Internet in guest rooms. $120–200.

Newport News

& **Newport News Marriott at City Center** (757-873-9299; 1-866-329-1758; www.), 740 Town Center Drive. All rooms at this 256-room Marriott property, located in City Center, come with complimentary Internet. The hotel has a gym and an indoor pool. $140–170.

🐾 (𝗐) **Point Plaza Suites at City Center** (757-599-4460; www.funinva .com), 950 J. Clyde Morris Boulevard. This 150-room hotel has rooms as well as suites. An indoor pool, gym, and restaurant are on site. $70–190.

Norfolk

& (𝗐) **Norfolk Waterside Marriott** (1-800-228-9290; www.marrriott .com), 235 East Main Street. This 24-story hotel has 405 rooms, some of which have water views. The hotel has an indoor pool and a branch of Don Shula's Steakhouse. $200–245.

🐾 & (𝗐) **Sheraton Norfolk Waterside Hotel** (1-800-325-3535; www .starwoodhotels.com/sheraton), 777 Waterside Drive. This 10-story hotel overlooks the Norfolk Harbor and is near Town Point Park. The hotel has an outdoor pool. $180–225.

🐾 (𝗐) **Tazewell Hotel & Suites** (757-623-6200; www.thetazewell .com), 245 Granby Street. In a 1906 building located in the heart of Granby Streets restaurants, this boutique hotel offers 55 rooms. $110–200.

Virginia Beach

(𝗐) **Barclay Towers Resort Hotel** (757-491-2700; 1-800-344-4473; www.vbhotels.com), 809 Atlantic Avenue. This older, oceanfront hotel offers suites with kitchenettes. The year-round property has an indoor pool. In June and July, the hotel prefers to book five- and seven-night packages. Off-season from $90 per night, June high season five nights from $900.

✎ **The Cavalier Hotel** (757-425-8555; 1-800-446-8199; www.cavalier hotel.com), 4201 Atlantic Avenue. This property on 18 acres is two hotels. The more modern, beachfront Cavalier on the Ocean is open year-round. The other, Cavalier on the Hill, built in 1927, opens for the summer only. We prefer the oceanfront property. In summer, it offers room service, bike rentals, an outdoor pool, a large kiddie pool, plus Camp Cavalier, an activities program for ages 4–12. Cavalier on the Ocean, $110–300.

& (𝗐) **Hilton Virginia Beach Oceanfront** (1-800-445-8667; www.hilton vb.com), 3001 Atlantic Ave, Virginia Beach. One of the area's most modern hotels, the beachfront property has an indoor as well as an outdoor pool, a kids' playground on the beach, room service and a good restaurant, Catch 31 see "To Eat " above

& (𝗐) **Wyndham Hotel & Resort** (757-428-7025; 1-877-999-3223), 5700 Atlantic Avenue. Open year-round.

This beachfront property is a good choice for those who want to stay in the quieter north end of town. The facility has an indoor/outdoor pool. $80–300.

BED & BREAKFAST INNS

Hampton
Lady Neptune Bed & Breakfast Inn (888-837-0206; www.bbonline.com/va/neptune) 507 North First Street. Situated near Buckroe Beach, the Lady Neptune, a house built in 1930, offers three bedrooms, two with private baths, plus one suite with a private bath. Rates include full breakfast $140–185.

Newport News
Boxwood Inn (757-888-8854; www.boxwood-inn.com), 10 Elmhurst Street. Located in historic Lee Hall Village, the home has a full-service restaurant and offers two rooms plus two suites, all with private bath. Rates include breakfast. $105–150.

Norfolk
Page House Inn (1-800-599-7659; www.pagehouseinn.com), 323 Fairfax Avenue. Located in the Ghent District near the Chrysler Museum of Art, the Page House Inn rates Four Diamonds from AAA and offers seven guest rooms furnished with four-poster beds and antiques. Bikes are available for guests. Rates include breakfast. $140–230.

Virginia Beach
Beach Spa Bed and Breakfast (757-422-2621; 1-888-422-2630; www.beachspabnb.com), 2420 Arctic Avenue. Open year-round. Rates include breakfast. Located three blocks from the beach, the eight-room property adds some spa elements. All rooms feature private bathrooms, some of which have steamer rainfall showers or jetted tubs, and massages are available to guests for an extra fee. $120–250.

✳ Where to Eat

Hampton
Grey Goose (757-723-7978; www.greygooserestaurant.com), 101-A West Queens Way. Open daily 7–3. This casual restaurant serves breakfast and lunch. Lunch features salads, soups, and sandwiches, some on croissants and some on flatbread. $7–10.

Jason's Deli (757-825-1501; www.jasonsdeli.com), 39 Coliseum Crossing. Open daily 10–10. A 30-foot salad bar and a trans-fat-free menu of poboys and Reubens plus other sandwiches are among the choices.

Marker 20 (757-726-9410; www.marker20.com/) 21 East Queens Way. Open Mon.–Sat. 11 AM–2 AM, Sun. 10–2. Dine on the deck or inside at this downtown seafood restaurant that also offers nearly a dozen beers on tap and about 30 types in bottles. The all-day menu includes soups, salads, wraps, and seafood platters. $8–20.

Surf Rider Bluewater (757-723-9366; www.surfridergroup.com/Blue%20Water.html) 1 Marina Road. This local favorite serves good crab cakes as well as burgers and pasta. $8–15.

Taphouse Grill (757-224-5829); 17 East Queens Way. Open daily 11 AM–2 AM. A good selection of beer, tasty burgers, cider mussels, and other fare plus a nice Sunday brunch makes this casual eatery a good choice. $10–18.

Newport News
99 Main (757-599-9885; www.99mainrestaurant.com), 99 Main Street.

Open Tue.–Thu. 5–9:30, Fri. and Sat. 5–10:30. This upmarket restaurant, located in Hilton Village area, serves an eclectic dinner menu with a European bent. $17–30.

Crab Shack on the James (757-245-2711; www.crabshackonthe james .com), 7601 River Road. Open Sun.–Thu. 11 AM–11:30 PM, Fri. and Sat. 11 AM–12:30 AM. Located along the James River at the fishing pier, this casual restaurant serves fresh-caught fish and a great view. $7–22.

Jamestown Pie Company (757-596-3888; www.buyapie.com), 11800 Mariner's Row, suite 100. Open Mon.–Thu. 10–9, Fri. and Sat. 10–10, Sun. noon–8. "Because round food is good" is the motto of this restaurant that started in the Williamsburg area. This location has take-out but also indoor seating. Fare ranges from dessert pies, potpies, and pizzas to wraps and sandwiches. $7–30.

Quaker Steak & Lube Restaurant (757-874-LUBE; www.quakerstate lube.com), 12832 Jefferson Avenue. Open Mon.–Thu. 11 AM–1 AM, Fri.–Sat. 11 AM–2 AM, Sun. 11 AM–midnight. This motorsports-themed family restaurant, a good place for moderately priced meals with kids, serves burgers, sandwiches, and steaks. $8–18.

Norfolk

456 Fish (757-625-4444; www.456 fish.com), 456 Granby Street. Open Sun.–Thu. 5–10, Fri. and Sat. 5–11. The restaurant serves good seafood. Try the potato chip–encrusted crab cakes, the house specialty she-crab soup, and the tuna. $16–30.

Bodega (757-662-8527; www.bodega ongranby.com), 442 Granby Street. Open Tue.–Thu. 5–11, Fri. and Sat.

5 PM–2 AM. Bodega, a casual eatery, serves a variety of tapas as well as a few large plates. $4-20.

Byrd & Baldwin Brothers Steak House (757-222-9191; www.byrd baldwin.com), 116 Brooke Avenue. Open Mon.–Thu. 5–10, Fri. and Sat. 5–11. The restaurant, a traditional steakhouse, serves only grain-fed all-natural Midwestern beef. $27–42.

Five Points Community Farmers' Market (757-640-0300; www.5Pts FarmMarket.org), 2500 Church Street. Open Wed.–Fri. 11–7, Sat. and Sun. 11–5; dinner Wed.–Fri. 4–7. Foodies who admire fresh vegetables will like this market's produce, straight from Virginia farms. You can also purchase specialty edibles from Virginia, such as Meadow Croft Farms old-fashioned pickled okra and Liz is Nuts roasted pecans. Also, depending on the season, there may be sweet potato, apple, or sugarplum cherry pie. During the day, the market sells salads, sandwiches, and soups to eat in or to go. The dinners of pork ribs, meat loaf, and chicken and dumplings at $12 for two might be some of the city's best deals. Sandwiches $4–7.

Todd Jurich's Bistro (757-622-3210; www.toddjurichsbistro.com), 150 Main Street. Open Mon.–Fri. lunch 11:30–2, Mon.–Sat. dinner 5–10. "Regional" and "seasonal" are by-words of this bistro. Among the signature items are the oyster stew, the Virginia sea bass, and the lump crab Norfolk. $22–30.

Virginia Beach

Catch 31 (757-213-3474; www.catch 31.com), 3001 Atlantic Avenue. Open daily breakfast 6:30–11, lunch 11–5, dinner Mon.–Thu. and Sun. 5–10,

Fri.–Sat. 5–11. This oceanview restaurant, located in the Hilton Virginia Beach Oceanfront, has an outdoor terrace and serves good seafood for lunch and dinner. The restaurant also prepares a traditional breakfast. At dinner, signature items include chilled seafood towers, Carolina grouper, cod, and other items. Pasta, steak, and chicken are also available. Dinner entrées $17–35.

The Jewish Mother (757-422-5430; www.jewishmother.com), 3108 Pacific Avenue. Open 9 AM–11 PM. Along with breakfast, which is served all day, the Jewish Mother serves lunch and dinner. Choose from deli sandwiches, salad platters, burgers, steak, fish, and barbecued chicken. Some evenings, there is live music. On selected dates, the restaurant hosts concerts in its parking lot. Dinner entrées $10–18.

The Raven (757-425-1200; www .theraven.com), 1200 Atlantic Avenue. Open daily noon–2 AM. Founded in 1968, the Raven is still serving good burgers, wings, sandwiches and seafood. $7-24.

There's Something About Mary's (757-428-1355; www.marys-restau rant.com), 616 Virginia Beach Boulevard. Open daily 6–3. A local favorite for more than 40 years, this restaurant, six blocks from the boardwalk, serves breakfast and sandwiches, salads, and soups for lunch. $6–9.

& **Town Center of Virginia Beach** (757-965-5452; www.vabeachtown center.com), 222 Central Park Avenue. Hours vary. Within this 17-block complex are a number of restaurants, including such chain eateries as Cheesecake Factory,

DOUMAR'S

Doumar's (757-627-4163; www.doumars.com), 1919 Monticello Avenue, Norfolk. Open Mon.–Thu. 8 AM–11 PM, Fri. and Sat. 8 AM–midnight. This restaurant is a legend, and not just in Norfolk. The Smithsonian credits a Doumar ancestor with inventing the ice-cream waffle cone. "Big Al" Doumar, the current head of the family, told us that his Uncle Abe first rolled a thin waffle into a cone for his customers at the 1904 Saint Louis Exposition. It was a big hit there, then in Coney Island, where his uncle opened a stand, and at other state fairs. At the 1907 Jamestown Exposition, Abe sold 23,000 cones in one day. Doumar's still makes its own waffle cones on the same four-waffle grill Abe used in Coney Island. Depending on demand, cones are made the old-fashioned way, typically between 9 and 10:30 AM, Monday through Saturday. The crispy cones have a slightly sweet taste. Yes, Doumar's fills them with ice cream. Doumar's is also known for its homemade shakes, ice-cream sodas, and limeade, and its pork barbecue sandwiches. Burger, hot dogs, and tuna sandwiches are also available. Eat at the counter or use the "curb service"—the wait staff takes orders from people in their cars. The place, the food, and even the prices seem a throwback to an earlier era. Sandwiches $2.50–5. Ice-cream cones $2.50–5.25.

McCormick & Schmick's Seafood, and Ruth's Chris Steak House.

✳ Entertainment

THEATER, CONCERTS, DANCE, AND OTHER PERFORMANCES

Hampton

♿**American Theatre** (757-722-2787; www.hamptonarts.net), 125 East Mellon Street. This renovated 1908 theater hosts plays as well as symphony, dance, and opera performances.

Newport News

♿ **Downing-Gross Cultural Art Center** (757-247-8950; www.down inggross.org), 2410 Wickham Avenue. The facility houses the **Ella Fitzgerald Theater**, named for the noted First Lady of Song born in Newport News in 1917, as well as the **Anderson Johnson Gallery**, named for a local artist.

♿ **Ferguson Center for the Arts** (757-594-7448; http://fergusoncenter .cnu.edu), 1 University Place, Christopher Newport University. The center hosts theater, symphony, and other performances.

Norfolk

♿ **Virginia Opera Association, Harrison Opera House** (757-282-2800; 1-866-673-7282; www.vaopera .org), 160 Virginia Beach Boulevard. Opera performances are held at this 1,632-seat venue.

Virginia Stage Company, Wells Theatre (757-627-6988; 757-627-1234; www.vastage.com)

This regional, professional theater company's plays run the gamut from *Romeo and Juliet* to *A Christmas Carol.*

Virginia Beach

♿ 🐾 ♿ **Beach Street USA** (757-491-7866; www.beacheventsfun.com),

Atlantic Avenue 17th–25th streets. Open Memorial Day–Labor Day Sun.–Thu. 8 PM–11:30 PM, Fri. and Sat. 8–midnight. Beach stage concerts and performances 6 PM–11 PM nightly. Enjoy the free street performances by magicians, puppeteers, bands, and jugglers on the sidewalks nightly during the summer. Then walk over to one of the beach stages—on 7th, 13th, 17th, or 25th street—for a free, live concert or theatrical performance.

♿ **Sandler Center for the Performing Arts** (757-385-2555; www .sandler.org), 201 Market Street, Town Center. The modern building, opened in 2007, hosts several resident companies. Under the aegis of the Virginia Musical Theatre, Broadway at the Center stages such musicals as *Annie, Man of La Mancha,* and *Oklahoma*; The Virginia Symphony Orchestra; Symphonicity, a volunteer local orchestra; the Ballet Virginia International; and the Virginia Beach Chorale

Virginia Beach Amphitheater (757-368-3000; www.livenation.com), 3550 Cellar Door Way. Open Apr.–Oct. The outdoor arena, seating 20,000, hosts 30–40 events each year, including country, jazz, oldies, and rock concerts.

PROFESSIONAL SPORTS

Hampton

Langley Speedway (757-865-7223; www.langley-speedway.com), 11 Dale Lemonds Drive. The speedway, an official NASCAR track, hosts races in season.

Norfolk

Norfolk Admirals (757-640-1212; www.norfolkadmirals.com), 201 East

Brambleton Avenue. Oct.–Apr., root for the city's American Hockey League franchise, a team affiliated with the Tampa Bay Lightening.

Norfolk Tides (757-622-2222; www .minorleaguebaseball.com), Harbor Park, 150 Park Avenue. Apr.–Sept., cheer for the Triple-A affiliate of the Baltimore Oriole's baseball team.

NIGHTLIFE: BARS, CLUBS, EATERIES

Hampton

Ⴤ **Saddle Ridge Rock and Country Saloon** (757-827-8100; www.saddle ridgeva.com), 1976 Power Plant Parkway. Open Mon.–Sat. 4 PM–late. There's country music at this nightclub, along with pool tables and 20 televisions. Try a shag dancing lesson on Mondays and a line dancing lesson on Tuesdays. The place also hosts bikini contests. The on-site Cheyenne Supper Club serves pub fare plus dinner entrées. Saddle Ridge is located in the Power Plant, a part of the Coliseum Central Business District situated halfway between Williamsburg and Virginia Beach. $10–19.

Newport News

Ⴤ **Bailey's Sports Grille** (757-881-9180; www.foxandhound.com), 12300 Jefferson Avenue, no. 110. Open daily 11 AM–2 AM. Trivia and singing contests, billiard tables, televisions, and a variety of beer selections make Bailey's a local favorite. $9–12.

Ⴤ **Cozzy's Comedy Club & Tavern** (757-595-2800; www.cozzysclub.com), 9700 Warwick Boulevard. Open Mon.–Fri. 11 AM–2 AM, Sat. 7 PM–2 AM, Sun. 11–10. Since 1991, this club has been hosting stand-up comedians. At Thursdays' open-mike nights, newcomers take to the stage. Profession-

als take over on Friday and Saturday. The club serves lunch, dinner, and Sunday brunch. $6–10.

Ⴤ **Manhattan's N.Y. Deli & Pub** (757-873-0555; www.manhattansdeli .com), 601 Thimble Shoals Boulevard. Open Mon.–Sat. 11 AM–2 AM, Sun. noon–2 AM. This combination sports bar and deli also offers live entertainment nightly. Some nights, watch or perform karaoke; on other nights, there are DJs or bands. Select from sandwiches, wraps, and burgers, as well as steak and chicken entrées. $9–16.

Ⴤ **Tribeca Night Club** (757-873-6664;), Omni Newport News, 1000 Omni Boulevard. Open Fri. and Sat. 7:30 PM–2 AM. Located in the Omni Hotel, the Tribeca's live music and dancing tends to attract those in their twenties and thirties. Cover fee $5.

Norfolk

Ⴤ **Baxter's: A Sports Lounge** (757-622-9837; baxterssportslounge.com), 500 Granby Street. Sept.–Mar. Mon.–Fri. 5 PM–2 AM, Sat. and Sun. 11 AM–2 AM; Apr.–Aug. Mon.–Sat. 5 PM–2 AM, closed Sun. More than 70 flat-screen televisions make this place one of Norfolk's most popular sports bars. The fare includes meatball subs, burgers, taco salad, and similar items. $4–7.

Ⴤ **Cogan's** (757-627-6428; www .coganspizza.com), 1901 Colonial Avenue. Open daily 11 AM–2 AM. During the day, Cogan's attracts everyone—families, workers, and students drawn to the great pizza, and for those 21-plus, the selection of more than 30 beers on tap. In the evening, Cogan's live music draws college students and others.

Ⴤ **Granby Theater** (757-961-7208;), 421 Granby Street. Open Fri. and Sat.

9 PM–2 AM. The largest nightclub in the Hampton Roads area, Granby's asks patrons to "dress to impress" to dance to the DJ-spun tunes. The nightclub has three levels, four bars, and several VIP areas.

Ỵ **O'Sullivan's Wharf** (757-434-3746;), 4300 Colley Avenue. Open daily 11 AM–2 AM. Specialties for dinner include crab cakes at this local bar whose deck overlooks the river. There's live entertainment on Tuesday nights.

Ỵ **Tap House** (757-627-9172; www .myspace.com/thetaphouse), 931 West 21st Street. Open daily 4 PM–2 AM. The pub grub includes good wings and there's live music on some nights.

Virginia Beach
Ỵ **Awful Arthur's Oyster Bar** (757-426-7300; awfuls.com), 1630 General Booth Boulevard. Open Mon. 4 PM–2 AM, Tue.–Sat. 11 AM–2 AM, Sun. noon–2 AM. In addition to the raw bar, Awful Arthur's serves sandwiches, wings, and seafood platters. Wednesday is karaoke night and there's live music on Saturday nights. $9-18.

Ỵ **Funny Bone Comedy Club & Restaurant** (757-213-5555; www .vbfunnybone.com), 217 Central Park Avenue. Evening showtimes vary: Tue. 7:30 and 8; Wed. and Thu. 8 and 10:15; Fri. and Sat. 8, 9:45, and 10:30; Sun.; 7, 9, and 9:30. Chicken tenders, salads, sandwiches, burgers, and pizza are served along with performances by stand-up comics. Tickets $20–25. Pub fare $4–16.

Ỵ **Sky Bar** (757-213-3473; www.sky bar.com), 3001 Atlantic Avenue, Hilton Virginia Beach Oceanfront. Open Wed.–Sun. 10 PM–1 AM. Take in the view from the bar on the 21st floor of a trendy hotel.

✱ Selective Shopping

Hampton
&. **Bass Pro Shops Outdoor World** (757-262-5200; www.basspro.com), 1972 Power Plant Parkway. Open Mon.–Sat. 9–9, Sun. 9–7, closed Dec. 25. To those who fish, hunt, camp, and boat, the Bass Pro shops are something of a fantasyland, but one with obtainable gear to make an outdoor dream experience come true. For those who can't see the beauty in a camouflage Windbreaker, a professional-grade casting rod, or a top-quality tent, the Bass Pro Shop can still be an experience. After all, the 105,000-square-foot store contains a 40-foot rock-climbing wall, a 19,000-gallon freshwater aquarium, an archery range, and lots of wildlife mounts (warn squeamish kids). Check the schedule for the store's fishing and hunting workshops.

Charles H. Taylor Arts Center (757-727-1490; www.hamptonarts .net), 4205 Victoria Boulevard. Along with workshops and classes, the center offers nine changing exhibits of art each year that cover glass, drawings, paintings, sculpture, and other mediums.

Norfolk
D'Art (757-625-4211; www.d-art center.org), 208 East Main Street. Open Tue.–Sat. 10–5, Sun. 1–5. Part gallery and part studio space, D'Art is a downtown visual arts center worth browsing. If the artists are creating in their studios, feel free to walk in and chat. That's part of the purpose of D'Art, whose resident painters, potters, jewelers, photographers, printmakers, and hot glass artists are there to engage with the public and to sell their wares. Free admission.

Futures Antiques (757-624-2050; www.futuresantiques.com), 3824 Granby Street. Browse here for art deco, midcentury modern, and other 20th-century finds from posters to toys, furnishings, jewelry, toasters, lamps, and other items.

✳ Special Events

Hampton

Find out more about these events and others by contacting the **Hampton Visitor Center** (757-727-12102; 1-800-800-2202; www.hamptoncvb .com).

April–August: **Saturday Night Street Fest Series**, a block party in downtown Hampton at the intersection of Kings and Queens way, features music, dancing, and food.

April–October: **NASCAR Whelen All-American Series Racing**. Langley Speedway blooms with Late Model, Legends, Super Trucks, UCARS, Pro Wing Champ Karts, and other vehicles.

July: **Annual Blackbeard Festival**, Mill Point Park, Queens Way, Carousel Park, and along the Hampton River (www.blackbeardpirate festival.com). Join the city in celebrating the demise of Edward Teach (Blackbeard the Pirate) with pirate skirmishes, battle reenactments, a ball, fireworks, food, and costumes.

June: **Hampton Jazz Festival** (www .hamptonjazzfestival.com) is a two-day celebration of jazz with up to 100 artists.

August: **Annual Hampton Cup Regatta** is North America's oldest continuously run hydroplane boat race.

September: **Hampton Bay Days** is the city's largest annual festival with live performances, food, and fireworks.

December: **Annual Lighted Boat Parade** has scores of boats draped with lights cruising along the waterfront.

Newport News

Find out more about these events and others by contacting the **Newport News Visitor Center** (757-886-7777; 1-888-493-7386; www.newport -news.org).

March: **Battle of Hampton Roads Weekend**, scheduled on a weekend close to the March 9 date of the battle, typically gives behind-the-scenes tours of the USS *Monitor* and other special events.

June: **Summer Celebration Wine Festival, Lee Hall Mansion**, brings together Virginia wines, crafts, and music.

November: **Oyster Point Oyster Roast** features seafood and often crafts and music.

December: **Christmas at Endview** showcases antebellum decoration at the 1861 plantation.

Norfolk

Contact **Visit Norfolk Today** (757-664-6620; 1-800-368-3097; www.visit norfolktoday.com), 232 East Main Street, Norfolk. Open Mon.–Fri. 8:30–5 for the latest information. Many events are held at Town Point Park (757-441-2345; www.festivals .org), 333 Waterside Drive.

April: **Virginia International Tattoo Virginia Arts Festival** (1-877-741-ARTS). More than 700 local and international artists are involved in performances of marching bands, pipes and drums, drill teams, choirs, and other performances.

May: Southeastern Virginia Arts Association sponsors **AFR'AM Fest** to promote African-American artists and arts organizations.

May and October: **Virginia Wine Festival** takes place in spring and fall in Town Point Park along the waterfront. More than 20 Virginia wineries participate.

June: The three-day **Bayou Boogaloo & Cajun Food Festival** celebrates New Orleans' spirit, culture, music, and cooking. **Harborfest** is five days of celebration, with a parade of sails, a pirate battle, a water ski show, and fireworks, plus music and food.

July: **Norfolk Jazz Festival** features local, regional, and national artists.

October: **Norfolk's Salute to Fleet Week Concert** includes concerts, performances, and special events. **The Virginia Wine Festival** takes place in fall and spring in Town Point Park along the waterfront. More than 20 Virginia wineries participate. Local and regional artists display paintings, pottery, fiber arts, and other works at the **Stockley Gardens Fall Arts Festival.**

November/December: **Holidays in the City** Six weeks of festivities start with Thanksgiving and include the Annual Grand Illumination Parade of floats, marching bands, giant balloons, dancers, and Santa.

Virginia Beach

Find out more about these events and others by contacting the **Virginia Beach Convention and Visitors Bureau** (1-800-822-3224; www.vbfun.com).

March: **Annual Virginia Beach Shamrock Sportfest** (757-412-1056) includes a marathon and children's races.

SAND CASTLE KING, VIRGINIA BEACH NEPTUNE FESTIVAL

Virginia Beach Convention & Visitors Bureau

May: **Memorial Day Weekend**. Live music along the boardwalk stages. **Annual Panorama Caribbean Music Festival** provides another chance to dance in the sand.

June: **Boardwalk Art Show and Festival** typically has hundreds of artists and craftspeople.

August: **East Coast Surfing Championships**. Watch the best catch waves.

September: **Annual Blues at the Beach Festival**, 17th Street Park.

Enjoy three days of free concerts on an outdoor stage. **Neptune Festival Boardwalk Weekend**, held the last weekend of September, is a grand finale to summer. Along with music and crafts, watch professionals create masterpieces in the North America Sandsculpting Competition.

October: **Brewfest** brings an Oktoberfest atmosphere to the beach, with samplings of beers, microbrews, and cider.

CHESAPEAKE BAY: NORTHERN NECK AND THE MIDDLE PENINSULA

Water—creeks, streams, ponds, rivers, and the bay—define Virginia's Northern Neck and its Middle Peninsula. The Northern Neck, bounded by the Potomac River on the north, the Rappahannock River on the south, and the Chesapeake Bay on the east offers more than 1,200 miles of tidal coastline as well as 6,500 acres of natural areas, including marshes, state parks, and preserves. There are also 18th-century plantations to tour, plus several wineries.

The Middle Peninsula has the Rappahannock River on the north and the York River on its south, as well as hundreds of miles of coastline.

For more than 400 years, people have been drawn to this region. Captain John Smith and his crew landed farther south on the Powhatan (James River) in 1607, establishing the settlement he named Jamestown, after his king. The next year, Smith and his crew explored the Chesapeake by oar and sail, traveling up the Potomac and the Rappahannock rivers and the latter's tributaries. You can walk in the footsteps of George Washington by strolling the farm site where he was born, as well as discover just how well the landed gentry lived on a tour of Stratford Hall Plantation. Completed in the 1740s, the mansion, one of the South's remaining early estates, was home to four generations of Lees. Robert E. Lee of Civil War fame lived at Stratford until nearly four years old.

The Northern Neck and the Middle Peninsula are also delights for boaters and eco-adventurers. At state parks and reserves you can hike trails through forests, marshes, and to the beach. Guides at Caledon Natural Area lead tours of one the East Coast's largest concentrations of eagles. Go local by renting a boat or taking a guided boat or kayak tour. Enjoy the breeze in your face and the sun glinting off the region's many creeks, rivers, and the wide Chesapeake Bay.

Despite the sale of some farms to developers who are constructing vacation or retirement homes, the essence of what Washington and Lee loved about the region remains: peaceful farms with sweeping lawns and fields rolling to the water. Ospreys arrive in March as the first harbingers of spring. In the morning, seagulls flutter like angels above the fields of soybeans, sorghum, and sweet

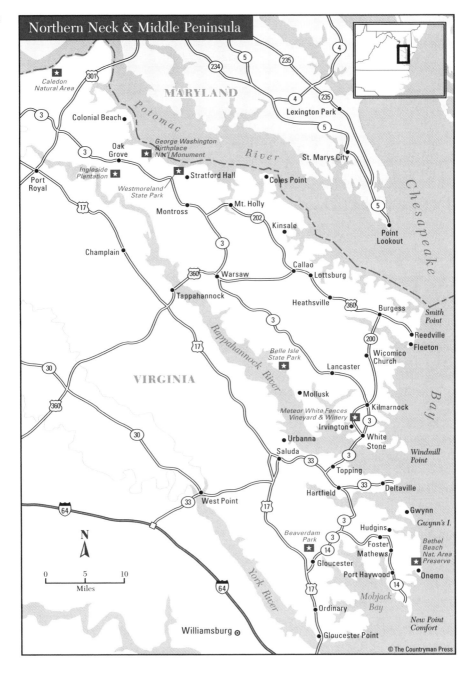

Northern Neck & Middle Peninsula

Caledon
Natural Area

MARYLAND

Colonial Beach

Lexington Park

Oak
Grove

George Washington
Birthplace
Nat'l Monument

St. Marys City

Ingleside
Plantation

Stratford Hall

Coles Point

Port
Royal

Westmoreland
State Park

Mt. Holly

Montross

Point
Lookout

Kinsale

Champlain

Callao

Warsaw

Lottsburg

Tappahannock

Heathsville

Burgess

Smith
Point

Reedville

Fleeton

Belle Isle
State Park

Wicomico
Church

Lancaster

VIRGINIA

Mollusk

Kilmarnock

Meteor White Fences
Vineyard & Winery

Irvington

White
Stone

Urbanna

Saluda

Windmill
Point

Topping

Bay

Hartfield

Deltaville

West Point

Gwynn

Gwynn's I.

Beaverdam
Park

Hudgins

Bethel
Beach
Nat. Area
Preserve

Foster

Mathews

Gloucester

Onemo

Port Haywood

Miles

Ordinary

Mobjack
Bay

New Point
Comfort

Williamsburg

Gloucester Point

York River

Rappahannock River

Potomac River

Chesapeake

© The Countryman Press

N

potatoes. At dusk, the setting sun falls gently on the rows or corn, turning the stalks to spun gold. In summer, roadside stands burst with tomatoes, cantaloupes, watermelons, and cherries. You can pick your own bushels of peaches, blackberries, raspberries, and strawberries at Westmoreland Berry Farm, Oak Grove, and buy jars of apple or hot pepper–raspberry preserves from their shop. Especially when compared with the urban East Coast, the Northern Neck and the Middle Peninsula are still country comfortable and as alluring as a bay breeze.

TOWNS AND COUNTIES Because of the rural nature of much of the Northern Neck and the Middle Peninsula, it makes sense to detail attractions by counties as well as by towns.

Middle Peninsula
Frequently promoted along with the Northern Neck's attractions, **Essex County**, whose major town is **Tappahannock**, is physically located on the Middle Peninsula across the Rappahannock River from the Northern Neck. The Middle Peninsula's other five counties are **King and Queen**, **King William**, **Mathews**, **Gloucester**, and **Middlesex**, this last home to **Urbanna**. From Gloucester Point, Gloucester County, it's easy to cross the York River and be near the Colonial Parkway that leads to Williamsburg or to travel to the Hampton Roads region.

Northern Neck
The most northern county in the Chesapeake Bay region, **King George County**, serves as the gateway to the Northern Neck. Major towns include King

TAPPAHANNOCK

Tony Hall, Virginia Tourism Corporation

George. A major preserve is the **Caledon Natural Area**, which shelters one of the East Coast's largest nesting areas for bald eagles.

Lancaster County draws many of Northern Neck's visitors. Situated on the southern part of the Northern Neck, **Irvington**, with a population under 1,000, is both historic and trendy. The small town is home to Christ's Church, which dates back to 1735, and to popular lodging, including the Tides Inn resort and the bed-and-breakfast inn Hope and Glory. Nearby and larger **Kilmarnock** straddles both Lancaster and Northumberland counties.

Northumberland County includes **Reedville**, home to the Reedville Fishermen's Museum.

Westmoreland County has miles of shore along the Potomac River, rich farmlands, wineries, state parks, and two important historic plantations, **Stratford Hall Plantation**, home to several generations of the prominent Lee family, as well as **George Washington Birthplace National Monument** (Popes Creek Plantation). Towns include Colonial Beach, Stratford, Oak Grove, and Montross.

In **Richmond Country**, which lies between Westmorland County and the Rappahannock River, Warsaw is a major town.

GUIDANCE Northern Neck Tourism Commission (804-333-1919; 1-800-393-6180; www.northernneck.org), P.O. Box 1707, Warsaw. Also check with the tourism offices of the Northern Neck's major counties:

Essex County and the Town of Tappahannock (804-443-4331; www.essex-virginia.org), 205 Cross Street, Tappahannock. Open Mon.–Fri. 10–4. While often promoted along with the Northern Neck, these areas are physically located across the Rappahannock River on Virginia's Middle Peninsula, bounded by the Rappahannock River on the north and the York River on the south.

King George County Parks and Recreation (540-775-4386), P.O. Box 71, King George. Open Mon.–Fri. 10–4.

Lancaster by the Bay Chamber (Irvington, Kilmarnock) (804-435-6092; www.lancasterva.com), 506 Main Street, P.O. Box 1868, Kilmarnock. Open Mon.–Thu. 8:30–4:30. A **Visitor Center** is also housed in the Kilmarnock Antique Gallery, 144 School Street, Kilmarnock. Open daily 10–5.

Northumberland County Chamber of Commerce and Visitor Center (804-529-5031; www.northumberlandcoc.org), 410 Northumberland Highway, Callao. Open Thu.–Sat. 9–1.

Westmoreland County Visitor Center (804-493-8440), 43 Courthouse Square, Montross. Open Mon.–Sat. 10–4.

GETTING THERE *By air:* **Richmond International Airport** (804-226-3052), off I-64, I-295 and US 60, Richmond, is approximately 47 miles (1½ hours) from the Northern Neck. **Newport News/Williamsburg International Airport** (757-877-0221), 900 Bland Blvd, off I-64 exit 255B, is 63 miles (2½ hours) from the Northern Neck. **Tappahannock-Essex County Airport** (804-443-5885), 140 Aviation Rd., Tappahannock, services the Northern Neck.

By bus: There is no public bus service on the Northern Neck or the Middle Peninsula.

By car: From Washington and Baltimore, take I-95 to Fredericksburg to US 17 to Rte. 3 east. From Richmond, take US 360 to Rte. 3. From Norfolk/Hampton Roads, take I-64 west to US 17 to Rte. 3. Washington, D.C., Richmond, and Norfolk are all within a 2½-hour or less drive to Irvington.

By ferry: The **Chesapeake Breeze**, the ferry to Tangier Island, part of Virginia's Eastern Shore, operates daily May through October.

By private boat: For details about moorings, contact **Virginia Tourism Corporation** (804-545-5500).

By train: **Amtrak** (1-800-872-7245) services Fredericksburg as well as Richmond, about 47 miles from the Northern Neck.

GETTING AROUND A car is a necessity. Boaters can get many places by boat.

WHEN TO COME Summer is high season, when boaters dot the region's rivers and the bay. Spring and fall bring nice walking weather and fewer crowds.

✷ To See

HISTORIC LANDMARKS, PLACES, AND SITES
MIDDLE PENINSULA
Urbanna
Old Tobacco Warehouse contains the **Urbanna Visitor Center** (804-758-8181; www.urbanna.com), 130 Virginia Street. Open Thu.–Sun. 10–4. Urbanna dates its history to 1680, when the Jamestown Assembly authorized the creation of 20 port towns, each of which was to be 50 acres. Built for the transportation of tobacco, only four of these colonial towns remain. The Old Tobacco Warehouse, now the Visitor Center, sits atop a hill about two blocks from the harbor. The hilltop location made it easy to roll the tobacco hogsheads, the large barrels in which tobacco was stored, down the hill to the harbor. The Visitor Center has some interesting information about the town during tobacco's heyday, as well as a walking brochure of town that leads past several 18th- and 19th-century buildings. In season, **Moo's River Edge Eatery** (See *Where to Eat*) serves ice cream. Urbanna's big blast is its annual November oyster festival, a weekend celebration of oysters, seafood, music, and crafts (See *Special Events*).

NORTHERN NECK
Lancaster County: Irvington area
♿ **Historic Christ Church** (804-438-6855; www.christchurch1735.org), Rte. 646, off Rte. 200, between Kilmarnock and White Stone. Open year-round Mon.–Fri. 8:30–4:30; Apr.–Nov. Sat. 10–4, Sun. 2–5. Closed weekends Dec. 1–Mar. 31, Thanksgiving Thu. and Fri. Dec. 24 and 25, Dec. 31, and Jan. 1. Carter Reception Center open Apr.–Nov. Mon.–Sat. 10–4, Sun. 2–5. For lovers of both colonial history and old buildings, Christ Church is a find. It's the best

preserved of colonial Virginia's Anglican parish churches and a National Historic Landmark. Built by Robert "King" Carter, one of the richest men in the colonies, the church, completed in 1735, was designed to be impressive. It still is for its authoritative simplicity. An outstanding example of early colonial religious architecture, the brick building features vaulted ceilings, a walnut altarpiece, a triple-decker pulpit, and high-backed pews. The historian who led our tour pointed out that from every pew one can see the pulpit but not the altar. The design emphasizes the fact that in the post-Reformation Church, the spoken word is what's most important. The biggest pew opposite the pulpit belonged to Carter and his family. John Carter, Robert's father, and several of his wives are entombed in the church, while Robert Carter is buried outside.

C. Stapen

HISTORIC CHRIST CHURCH

The small museum has artifacts from Carter's estate. Suggested donation $5.

Northumberland County: Reedville

Reedville Fishermen's Museum (540-453-6529; www.rfmuseum.org), 504 Main Street. Open May 1–Nov. daily 1 10:30–4:30; Nov. 1–Dec. 20 Fri.–Sun. 10:30–4:30, mid-Mar.–Apr. 30 Sat. and Sun. 10:30–4:30. Exhibits in the museum's two buildings pay homage to the town's longtime main industry, menhaden fishing. Among the facility's historic craft, docked on the nearby creek, are the 1911 skipjack *Claudia W. Somers,* and the *Elva C.,* a deck boat. On selected Saturdays, the museum offers two-and-a-half-hour sails on the historic skipjack. While cruising Cockrell's Creek to the Great Wicomico River and Chesapeake Bay, learn about Reedville's oystering and fishing. Sails $25 per person; museum $5 adults, free for under age 12.

Westmoreland County

&. **George Washington Birthplace National Monument** (804-224-1732; www.nps.gov/gewa), 1732 Popes Creek Road, Colonial Beach. Open daily 9–5. Originally named Popes Creek Plantation, this is where the Father of Our Country was born on February 22, 1732. Even though only the footprint of the original Washington home remains, you do gain insight into what early life was like for little Georgie. You hear the same lapping of the creek that soothed our first president. An informative film using excerpts of Washington's own diaries sets the tone about life on a tobacco farm. The living history farm located on this site raises animals of the period. You can also tour a reconstructed 18th-century

C. Stapen

GEORGE WASHINGTON BIRTHPLACE NATIONAL MONUMENT

upper-class plantation house—albeit not a replica of the one George inhabited. $4 adults, free for age 16 and younger.

&. **Stratford Hall Plantation** (804-493-8038; www.stratfordhall.org), 483 Great House Road, on Rte. 214 off Rte. 3, Stratford. Open daily 9:30–4; tours on the hour 10–4; dining room open 11:30–3. The stately great house, completed in the 1740s and surrounded by nearly 1,600 acres, was the family home of the Lees of Virginia. In the Great Hall, an impressive Georgian-style reception area hung with family portraits, the Lees received the other landed gentry of the era. Richard Henry Lee and Francis Lightfoot Lee, both signers of the Declaration of Independence, grew up at the plantation whose green lawns roll toward the Potomac River. Robert Edward Lee, born in the residence on January 19, 1807, resided here until he was almost four years-old, spending much of his time in the nursery. Legend has it that

REEDVILLE FISHERMEN'S MUSEUM

Tony Hall, Virginia Tourism Corporation

when the carriages were packed and the family about to depart, no one could find young Robert. He was discovered in the nursery saying goodbye to "his angels," a pair of still visible winged guardians sculpted into the back of the nursery fireplace. Along with the mansion, see the carriage house, the "Negro cabins," and the kitchen and stroll the gardens. Check the schedule of special events, including hands-on history activities for children. The plantation has overnight accommodations (see *Lodging*). $10 adults, $5 ages 6–11.

✳ To Do

BEACHES Colonial Beach (804-224-7181; www.colonialbeachva.net), Visitor Center, 18 North Irving Avenue. In the 19th century, Colonial Beach's mile-long swath of brown sand hugging the Potomac River gave the town the nickname "Playground on the Potomac." Among the residents who summered here in the beach's fashionable Victorian homes was Alexander Graham Bell. The town's fortunes declined with the rise of automobiles as drivers headed to the region's ocean beaches. Colonial Beach attracts boaters to its deep water harbors, as well as people looking for a small town getaway.

BICYCLING

NORTHERN NECK

Northern Neck Heritage Trail Bicycle Route Network, contact the Northern Neck Tourism Council (1-800-393-6180; www.northernneck.org). Weaving

BETHEL BEACH

John Gresham, Virginia Department of Conservation & Recreation

through many of the Northern Neck's counties, the seven paved bicycle trails connect in several places with the Potomac Heritage National Scenic Trail, a developing system for cyclists that follows the Potomac River. The local loops pedal you to regional highlights such as Colonial Beach, Westmoreland State Park, Stratford Hall, Belle Isle State Park, and Christ Church.

BIRDING

NORTHERN NECK

King George

Caledon Natural Area (540-663-3861; www.dcr.virginia.gov/state_parks/cal), 11617 Caledon Rd., King George. Open daily. Reserve ahead to tour one of the East Coast's largest colonies of bald eagles. More than 60 of these majestic birds roost on the park's cliffs from April to September. Limited guided tours are available mid-June through August. The park also has hiking trails, some of which close during eagle season so as not to disturb the fledglings. The 2,579-acre park is also a good place from which to spot flocks of migrating birds. Guided tours $6.

BOATING

MIDDLE PENINSULA

Rappahannock River Cruises (804-453-2628; www.tangiercruise.com), main office 468 Buzzard Point Road, Reedville. May–Oct. cruises depart from Hoskins Creek, Tappahannock, Wed.–Sun. at 10 AM and return at 4:30 PM. Bring binoculars, as you're likely to spot some of the 50 resident bald eagles that nest in the trees along the Rappahannock River. The boat cruises 18 miles upriver to Ingleside Winery for lunch (optional) and a winery tour and tasting. Cruise $25 adults, $13 children; lunch $11 adults, $8 children. The company's cruises to Tangier Island on the Eastern shore depart from Buzzard's Point Marina at 10 AM and return at 4 PM. On Tangier, there's time for a stroll and lunch. Bring a picnic or dine at the Chesapeake House or other island restaurants. Cruise $25 adults, $13 children; lunch additional.

NORTHERN NECK

Northumberland

Smith Island and Chesapeake Bay Cruises (804-453-3430; www.cruiseto smithisland.com), Chesapeake Bay Camp Resort, 382 Campground Road, Reedville. Cruises operate May–Oct., departing at 10 AM and returning at 3:45 PM. Cruise 13½ miles (90 minutes) across the Chesapeake Bay from Reedville to Smith Island, MD, passing Smith Point, famous for its lighthouse and for the confluence of the Potomac River and the Chesapeake Bay. Upon arrival at Smith Island, the self-proclaimed "Softshell Crab Capital of the World," there's time to explore Ewell, one of the island's three fishing villages, as well as have lunch in town (or bring a picnic lunch) before the return cruise back to Reedville. $25 adults, $12.50 ages 3–12.

CANOEING, KAYAKING, PADDLING, ROWING Three rivers—the Potomac, the Rappahannock, and the York—border the Northern Neck and the Middle Peninsula, creating miles of shoreline and creeks well-suited to paddlers.

MIDDLE NECK

Gloucester County

Bay Trail Outfitters (804-725-0626; www.baytrails.com), 2221 Bethel Beach Road, Rte. 609, Onemo. Tours mid-May–Oct. Reserve ahead. The three-hour guided tours include a treasure hunt using a GPS unit, a paddle to Jamestown Island, an Island Breezes trip to sheltered coves, a "Poddery" paddle along the East River to a pottery, and more. Prices vary.

King William County

Mattaponi Canoe & Kayak (1-800-769-3545; www.mattaponi.com), Aylett. Paddle on your own or go on a guided natural history canoe or kayak tours. Explore remote stretches of the Mattaponi River or try a sunset tour of the Pamunkey River that cuts through the Pamunkey Indian Reservation. Tours $20–50 per person; day rentals, $45 canoes and $25 kayaks.

NORTHERN NECK

Lancaster County

Belle Isle State Park (804-462-5030; www.dcr.virginia.gov/state_parks/bel), 1632 Belle Isle Road, Rte. 683, Lancaster. Open daily. Explore some of the 7½ miles of Rappahannock River shoreline on a guided canoe or kayak trip. Bring your oak equipment or rent a canoe, kayak, or even a motorboat. Modest rental fees; vehicle entrance fee $2–3.

Calm Waters Rowing (1-800-238-5578; www.calmwatersrowing.com), 10155 Mary Ball Road, Lancaster. Calm Waters Rowing is a sculling camp set in a lovely bed-and-breakfast. Although the programs are primarily designed for master rowers, the coaches will design a program suitable for a beginner or recreational rower. The Inn at Levelfields, dating to 1857, is set on 54 acres of woods and lawn. For longtime rowers, the owners have created three-day (Thu.–Sun.) and four-day (Sun.–Thu.) sculling camps. Off-season (July, Au., Nov.) rates for three-day program $665–790, mid-peak season (Mar., Sept.–Oct.) $700–835, peak season (Apr.–June) three-day program, $745–880.

NORTHERN NECK AND MIDDLE PENINSULA

Captain John Smith Chesapeake National Historic Trail, National Park Service Chesapeake Bay Office, 410 Severn Avenue, Annapolis, MD. For additional information, contact www.smithtrail.net). America's first national water trail, this 3,000-mile route takes paddlers along waterways explored by Captain John Smith in the 17th century as he sailed the Chesapeake Bay, Northern Neck, and Middle Peninsula rivers and their tributaries in Virginia and Maryland. Virginia has three of the trails six "smart buoys." These relay weather, water quality, and other information. Simply put down your paddle and input www

.buoybay.org/m on your mobile phone; from your computer, check www.buoy
bay.org; to find out what the Chesapeake was like in that area during Smith's
time, call 1-877-BUOYBAY.

FARMERS' MARKETS
NORTHERN NECK

Lancaster County
Irvington Farmers Market (www.irvingtonva.org), Irvington Commons, King
Carter Drive. Held the first Saturday of every month, May–Nov., 9 AM–1 PM.

Kilmarnock Farmers Market (www.kilmarnockvirginia.org), North Main
Street. Held the fourth Saturday of every month, May–Oct. 9 AM–1 PM.

Westmoreland County
♪ **Westmoreland Berry Farm & Orchard** (804-224-9171; 1-800-997-
BERRY; www.westmorelandberryfarm.com), 1235 Berry Farm Lane, Oak
Grove. Apr.–Oct. Pick your own bushels of peaches, blackberries, raspberries,
or strawberries—whatever is in season. Purchase jars of apple or pumpkin butter
as well as hot pepper–raspberry preserves. Put a coin in the feed dispenser and
watch the farm goat walk ramps and platforms 20 feet high to get his reward.
Yours can be an ice-cream sundae topped with fruit just off the trees.

FISHING Several outfitters offer fishing charters on the Northern Neck and
Middle Peninsula.

Northumberland County
Bayfish Sport Fishing Charters (888-BAY-FISH; www.bayfish.net), 579 Buzzard Point Road, Reedville. May–Dec. Bayfish offers full and half-day chartered
fishing excursions on the Chesapeake Bay for up to six anglers. Half-day from
$360, full day from $600.

Captain Billy's Charters (804-580-7292; www.captainbillyscharters.com), 545
Harvey's Neck Road, Heathsville. Captain Billy offers morning, afternoon, and
evening fishing excursions on the Chesapeake Bay and on the Atlantic Ocean
along Virginia Beach. Also available are creek tours and sunset cruises. Prices
vary with the trip. Day trip $650 for six passengers.

Fisher's Bay Charters (804-580-2548; www.fishersbaycharters.com), 1051
Presley Creek Drive, Heathsville. Aboard the *Heritage* with Captain David Fisher, you'll try your luck catching striped bass, bluefish, Spanish mackerel, and red
drum. $570 for six passengers.

SAILING **Premier Sailing School** (804-438-9300; www.premiersailing.com),
Tides Inn, 480 King Carter Drive, Irvington. Apr.–Oct. Even if you don't know
your aft from your rudder, you can learn to sail during daily or weekly classes.
Sailors who know the basics can perfect techniques with private lessons. Conveniently located at the Tides Inn (see *Lodging*), Premier offers a variety of classes
for kids, teens, and adults.

VIRGINIA WINERIES: THE CHESAPEAKE BAY WINE TRAIL

Because the soil and climate along the Chesapeake Bay prove conducive to growing grapes, the region has a burgeoning business in commercial vineyards. **Ingleside**, the largest winery on the Chesapeake Bay Wine Trail, as well as the several boutique vineyards are fun to visit. Enjoy tastings, tours, and often sweeping views of vineyards and water. The **Chesapeake Bay Wine Trail** (www.chesapeakebaywinetrail.com) leads to nine wineries. **White Fences Vineyard & Winery**, Irvington, a popular but small operation, closed in 2011. If you intend to tour several wineries, consider signing up for the Passport Program: After visiting six regional wineries, receive a 10 percent discount on purchases for one year.

The **Potomac Point Vineyard & Winery** (540-446-2266), 275 Decatur Road, Stafford. Open Sun., Mon., Wed., and Thu. 11–6; Fri. and Sat. 11–9. Bistro on property. Too far south to be considered part of northern Virginia and too far north to be officially a part of the Northern Neck, Potomac Point Vineyard, situated in the northern part of Stafford County, borders the Potomac River. In the 2010 Decanter World Wine Awards, this relatively new winery won a Silver Medal for its 2009 Viognier Reserve. Sat. and Sun. tours 10-person minimum) $10–15 per person.

Although listed on the Chesapeake Bay Wine Trail, the **New Kent Winery** (804-932-8240; www.newkentwinery.com, 8400 Old Church Road, New Kent) is located between Richmond and Williamsburg (see chapter 4: Central Virginia). Open Tue.–Sun. 10–6.

The Northern Neck features six wineries. King George County is the home of **Oak Crest Vineyard & Winery** (540-663-2813; www.oakcrestwinery.com), 8215 Oak Crest Drive, 3 miles from Rte. 301, King George. Open Apr. 1–Dec. 23 Wed.–Sun. 10-5. Opened in 2002, the winery offers free tastings of their available wines and you may bring a picnic to enjoy on their property. **Athena Vineyards & Winery** (804-580-4944; 804-580-7327; www.athenavineyards.com), 3138 Jessie Dupont Memorial Highway, Heathsville, in Northumberland County. Open Jan.–May Sat. noon–6, June–Dec. Wed.–Sun. noon–6. This winery grows more than 20 varieties of grapes in its 15 acres of vineyards that overlook the Great Wicomico River.

Richmond County's **Belle Mount Vineyards** (804-333-4700; www.bellemount .com), 2570 Newland Road, Warsaw. Open Wed.–Sun. 11–5 for complimentary tours and tastings. Belle Mount Vineyards is an interesting hybrid. Its 243 acres support both the winery and a cabin rental resort, **Heritage Park Resort** (see *Lodging*). Chardonnay, Merlot, and picnic wines are among those produced.

Four of the Chesapeake's wineries are in Westmoreland County. **General Ridge's Vineyard** (804-493-0226; 703-313-9742; www.generalsridgevineyard.com), 1618 Weldons Drive, Hague, grows grapes on its 100-acre farm. Enjoy the vineyard views and guest rooms for getaways (see *Lodging*).

A small, family winery, **The Hague Winery** (804-472-5283; www.thehaguewinery .com), 8268 Cople Highway, Hague. Open Apr.–Nov. daily 11–5, is part of Buena Vista Plantation. The main house was built in 1830s, but some of the outbuildings date back to the 1700s. The current owners purchased the 139-acre property in 2000, spent eight years restoring it, and sold their first crop of grapes in 2007. A custom crush facility near Charlottesville processes the grapes. The winery released its Meritage Reserve, a Bordeaux-style blend, in February 2010.

Ingleside Plantation Vineyards (804-224-8687; www.inglesidevineyards.com), 5872 Leedstown Road, Oak Grove. Open summer Mon.–Sat. 10–6, Sun. noon–6; remainder of the year Mon.–Sat. 10–5, Sun. noon–5. Established in 1980, the largest winery in the Northern Neck, produces 18 varieties of wine from its 60 acres of vineyards. Ingleside's wines have won many awards in its 30 years. The reserve's Virginia Brut is a sparkling wine and the Blue Crab Blanc, an Ingleside favorite, features a distinctive blue crab label. The winery hosts monthly evening concerts in summer. June features oldies rock and roll, July is a barbecue with bluegrass, and September is jazz. Tours are free, but tastings cost $5–10. The winery has overnight accommodations (see *Lodging*).

Vault Field Vineyards (804-472-4430; www.vaultfield.com), 2953 Kings Mill Road, Rtes. 601 and 602, Kinsale. Feb. 13–Dec. Thu.–Sat. 11–5, Sun. noon–5; summer Thu.–Sat. 11–6, Sun. noon–6; Jan.–Feb. 12 Fri.–Sun. 11–5. Vault Fields medals include two gold, a silver, and a bronze won in the 2009 Virginia Wine Lovers' Classic.

NORTHERN NECK

King George County

Caledon Natural Area, an oasis for birders, has six well-marked trails that cut through forest, fields, and shore. You don't have to be a birder to enjoy hiking through the 2,579-acre park. (See "Birding.")

Lancaster County

♿ **Belle Isle State Park** (804-462-5030; www.dcr.virginia.gov/state_parks/bel), 1632 Belle Isle Road, Rte. 683, Lancaster. Open daily. Explore some of the 7½ miles of Rappahannock River shoreline on a guided canoe or kayak trip (see "Canoeing"). The 739-acre park has picnic shelters and a 1,000-foot accessible boardwalk. Vehicle entrance fee $2–3.

Westmoreland County

♿ **Westmoreland State Park** (804-493-8821; 1-800-933-PARK; www.dcr.virginia .gov/state_parks/wes.shtml). This park lies within Westmoreland County and extends about 1½ miles along the Potomac River; its 1,311 acres neighbor the former homes of both George Washington and Robert E. Lee. The park's Horse-head Cliff provide visitors with a view of the Potomac River. In addition, there is hiking, camping, cabins, fishing, boating and swimming. Visitors can enjoy the park's vacation cabins as well.

WESTMORELAND STATE PARK

pcopros

✳ Lodging

HOTELS, RESORTS, AND LODGES

MIDDLE PENINSULA

Essex County

& (꜡) **Holiday Inn Express** (804-445-1200; 1-800-423-0908; www.hiexpress.com), 1648 Tappahannock Boulevard, Tappahannock. The hotel offers 63 standard rooms plus an indoor heated pool. $100–150.

NORTHERN NECK

Lancaster County

🐾 🦀 ♂ & **Tides Inn** (804-438-5000; 1-800-843-3726; www.tidesinn.com), 480 King Carter Drive, Irvington. Closed after New Year's Day until early Mar. The waterfront, 106-room, AAA Four Diamond property sprawls on a peninsula on Carters Creek. Enjoy the complimentary kayaks, canoes, and paddleboats; play golf;

swim in the pool; and learn to sail at the on-site Premier Sailing School. There's a 60-slip marina, too. The 18-hole Golden Eagle course is 1 mile away and you can teach kids the game on the front lawn's complimentary par-3 course. Guest rooms, renovated in 2002, feature a British Colonial décor of ceiling fans and wooden plantation shutters accented with beige fabrics. Cottage rooms tend to be larger than those in the main building. Dogs 75 pounds or smaller are welcome in the pet-friendly Garden Wing rooms ($25 nightly fee). All rooms have high-speed Internet access. At Crab Net Kids, ages 4–12 keep busy with kite making, tag, swimming in the pool, and other activities 9:30 to 3:30 daily, and from Memorial Day to Labor Day and during Easter and other holidays, on Fridays as Saturdays from 5 to 8 (dinner included). The Chesapeake Club, the

TIDES INN

C. Stapen

resort's signature dining room, is divided into two areas. The Club Lounge offers lighter fare and the East Room is the more formal area. Popular dishes include crab cakes and pan-roasted rockfish. Entrées $25–38. In season (June–Sept.) $265–395.

Richmond County
Heritage Park Resort, on the grounds of **Belle Mount Vineyards** (804-333-4700; www.bellemount .com), 2570 Newland Road, Warsaw. Open year-round. The resort shares its 243 acres with Belle Mount Vineyards (see "Wineries"). Each of the five simply but comfortably furnished one- or two-bedroom cabins come with a private bath, kitchen, and air-conditioning and heating. Hike the trails, tour the winery, and from Memorial Day–Labor Day, cool off in the swimming pool. Cabins $95–125.

Westmoreland County
占 **Stratford Hall Plantation** (804-493-8038; www.stratfordhall.org), 483

Great House Road, on Rte. 214 off Rte. 3, Stratford, is an impressive and important Southern plantation house (see "Historic Sites"). Although lodging isn't available in the mansion, choose from three types of accommodations on property. Geared toward groups, the **Cheek House** has a parlor plus 15 guest rooms. To stay overnight, at minimum you must reserve at least five rooms. **Astor Guest House** has six rooms with private baths plus a parlor. Occasionally, some of the property's log cabins become available for rent. From $125.

BED & BREAKFAST INNS AND CABINS

MIDDLE PENINSULA

Essex County
☀ (ꝏ) **Essex Inn** (1-866-ESSEX-VA; www.essexinnva.com), 203 Duke Street, Tappahannock. Located in town, this inn, decorated with

STRATFORD HALL

C. Stapen

antiques, dates to 1705. The main house has four rooms and the Quarters, formerly the servant's quarters, offers four suites, each with a bedroom and kitchen. Rates include full breakfast. $165–210.

♂ **Linden House Plantation** (804-443-1170, 804-445-4526; www.linden plantation.com), 11770 Tidewater Trail, Rte. 17 South, Champlain. Seven rooms with private baths. Dating to 1750, Linden House, a brick manor house, has been restored and decorated with 19th-century antiques and period pieces. The owners also built a carriage house and ballroom and planted 650 trees. Rates include full breakfast. $120–185.

Gloucester County
☀ ♂ **Warner Hall** (804-695-9565; 1-800-331-2720; www.warnerhall .com), 4750 Warner Hall Road. 11 guest rooms with private baths. The original 600-acres of land on the Severn River was granted to Augustine Warner in 1642 as payment for bringing 12 settlers from Britain across the ocean to Jamestown Settlement. Descendants of Warner include George Washington, Captain Meriwether Lewis, the explorer, and Queen Elizabeth II, who visited Warner Hall in 1957. Warner Hall, now consists of 38 acres, with a Colonial Revival–style manor house built in 1900 and an 18th-century stable, smokehouse, and dairy barn. The house and guest rooms mix antiques and reproductions. Rates include full breakfast. $190–275. The inn offers dinner Fri. and Sat., picnic baskets, and box lunches.

Mathews County
♂ **Kingston Plantation** (804-725-8582; www.kingston-inn.com), P.O.

Box 190, North River. The home, situated on 200 acres fronting the North River in Mathews County, near the tip of the Middle Peninsula, offers three suites and two rooms for guests as well as a separate carriage house with a kitchen and bedroom. $150–250.

NORTHERN NECK
Lancaster County
✎ ♂ **Hope and Glory Inn** (804-438-6053; 1-800-497-8228; www .hopeandglory.com), 65 Tavern Road, Irvington. Open year-round. Seven rooms, 13 cottages. The owners describe the décor as "shabby-chic." Add " with a sense of humor" to describe the whimsical mix of slipcovered couches, white wicker, and painted furniture with folk art and found objects that characterize the 1890 schoolhouse turned B&B. A tic-tac-toe board using yellow and white chickens for markers and a Victorian birdcage filled with flowers adorn parlor tables. Some of the seven rooms in the main building feature white wooden headboards carved by a local artist. Our favorite headboard has silhouettes of church steeples. The 13 cottages offer more space and privacy than do the inn's rooms. Six one-bedroom units are behind the inn in the garden, whose highlight is an outdoor clawfoot tub that is screened from the view of other cabins, making a moonlight soak possible. In a nearby vineyard, seven Carpenter Gothic cottages, confusingly called "tents," have three bedrooms and three baths plus a kitchen and living/dining area. These units rent by the night or the week. Kids are welcome in the cottages, some of which also accept pets. The vineyard has an outdoor pool. In

season, the inn serves a chef's table dinner on Saturday night and offers boat outings on Carters Creek. All inn rooms and garden cottages come with private baths and full breakfast. Inn rooms $175–290; garden cottages $255–345; vineyard cottages, one-bedroom $310–385, two-bedroom $460–545, three-bedroom $610–695. Contact the inn for weekly rates.

Northumberland County

The Gables (804-453-5209; www .thegablesbb.com), Main Street, Rte. 360. A four-story, Queen Anne–style brick house named for its gables, this grande dame was completed in 1914 for wealthy Captain Fisher. The Gables offers one room in the mansion, four rooms in the Coach House, plus two suites in the Waterside Cottage. Rates include breakfast. $90–240.

Westmoreland County

Bell House Bed and Breakfast (804-224-7000; www.thebellhouse .com), 821 Irving Avenue, Colonial Beach. Four rooms, each with private bath. Alexander Graham Bell, the inventor, summered at this 1883 home on the Potomac River. Rates include wine and cheese in the late afternoon and a full breakfast. $145.

General Ridge's Vineyard (804-493-0226, 703-313-9742; www.gen eralsridgevineyard.com), 1618 Weldons Drive, Hague, grows grapes on its 100-acre farm and offers guest rooms in two facilities. The Manor House has three bedrooms, sitting rooms, and a porch; Vineyard Views has two bedrooms, a sitting room, and a porch. A conference center is also on property. Rooms from $159 per night.

Ingleside Plantation Vineyards (804-224-8687; www.inglesidevine

yards.com), 5872 Leedstown Road, Oak Grove, offers two separate lodgings. Located along the Rappahannock River, the **Pointe at Liberty Farm**, a contemporary home, offers one main bedroom and bath plus a loft bedroom, kitchen, and deck. $175 per night, two-night minimum. Also **Summerton at Roxbury Pond**, overlooking a pond, has a bedroom, bath, and an additional loft bedroom, and comes with dishes, a microwave, a refrigerator, and an outdoor gas grill. $150 per night, two-night minimum.

✳ Where to Eat

MIDDLE PENINSULA

Essex County

Lowery's Seafood (804-443-4314; www.lowerysrestaurant.com), 528 Church Lane, Tappahannock. Open Mon.–Thu. 11–9, Fri. 11–9:30, Sat. 8 AM–9:30 PM, Sun. 8–8. Since 1938, Lowery's has been luring locals and visitors with its fresh seafood. Signature items include its crab cakes and rockfish. Dinner entrées $20–30.

Middlesex County

Café Mojo (804-758-4141; www.cafe -mojo.com), 230 Virginia Street, Urbanna. Open Tue.–Sat. 4–10, Sun. 11–3. The eclectic seafood dishes here mix Caribbean, Japanese, and Italian influences. $12–25.

🎣 **Moo's River Edge Eatery** (804-758-1447; www.localicecreamshop .com), 217 Virginia Street, Urbanna. Open seasonally.

NORTHERN NECK

Lancaster County

Lancaster Tavern Bed &Breakfast (804-462-0080; www.lancastertav ern.com), 8373 Mary Ball Road, Lancaster. Wed.–Sun. breakfast, lunch, and dinner; Mon. and Tue. dinner only. The tavern has been serving meals for the last 200 years. The menu includes meat loaf, chicken potpie, fried oysters, crab cakes, and filet mignon. Dinner $12–27.

Nate's Trick Dog Café (804-438-6363; www.trickdogcafe.com), 4357 Irvington Road, Irvington. Open for dinner winter Tue.–Sat. 5–closing (reservations recommended), summer Mon.–Sat. 5-closing. Tiles on the roof outline a dog bone, a statue of a terrier (a pet for good luck) is inside the door, and the wait staff wear T-shirts with such doggie-related sayings as "Sit and stay" and "Beg." The shirts are available for purchase. The menu includes roast chicken, filet mignon, glazed duck, shrimp and linguine, and crab cakes. $18–33.

🍴 **Willaby's Café** (804-435-0044; www.willabys.com), 435 Rappahannock Dr., White Stone. Open Mon.–Sat. 11–3. Known locally for its burgers, this casual eatery with black-and-white checked tablecloths also serves crab cakes, tuna melts, grilled cheese, and other sandwiches for lunch. $5–10.

Northumberland County
Crazy Crab at the Reedville Marina (804-453-6789), 902 Main Street, Reedville. Open mid-May–mid-Dec., Tue.–Sun. 11:30–9 PM. Popular with locals, the restaurant serves hardshell crabs and homemade specialties. Enjoy the indoor dining with large windows or outdoor seating that allow you to watch the boats on Cockrell's Creek. $10–22.

Tommy's Seafood & Steaks Restaurant (804-453-4666; www.tommysrestaurant.net), 729 Main Street, Reedville. Tommy's serves steaks and seafood. $14–30.

Richmond County
Northern Neck Gourmet (804-333-3012; www.northernneckgourmet .com), 115 Main Street, Open Tue.–Sat. 10–5, summer also Fri. and Sat. 6–9 PM. This gourmet deli offers a wide selection of sandwiches as well as wines to eat in or take out. In summer on weekend nights, tapas and wine are served. Lunch $6.50–12.

✳ Entertainment

For entertainment, check out the special events hosted by the region's wineries, churches, museums, and civic organizations. See also *Special Events*.

✳ Selective Shopping

MIDDLE PENINSULA

Essex County
Tappahannock has several shops that sell antiques and collectibles.

Among the stores are **Nadji Nook Antiques** (804-443-3298), 303 Queen Street. Open Mon. and Thu.–Sat. 10–5. Browse for oyster plates, estate jewelry, Victorian furniture, and more at this 10,000-square-foot shop.

NORTHERN NECK

Lancaster County
Kilmarnock Antique Gallery (804-435-1207; 1-800-497-0083; www .virginia-antiques.com), 144 School Street, Kilmarnock. Open daily 10–5. Browse the collection of oyster plates, tall case clocks, desks, and sideboards at this multiple-dealer gallery.

Westmoreland County
Ingleside Plantation Vineyards (804-224-8687; www.inglesidevineyards.com), 5872 Leedstown Road,

Oak Grove. Open Mon.–Sat. 10–5, Sun. 12–5, summer until 6. The reserve's Virginia Brut is a sparkling wine and the Blue Crab Blanc, an Ingleside favorite, comes with a distinctive blue crab label.

☙ **Westmoreland Berry Farm & Orchard** (804-224-9171; 1-800-997-BERRY; www.westmorelandberry farm.com), 1235 Berry Farm Lane., Oak Grove. Open Apr.–Oct. Pick your own bushels of peaches, blackberries, raspberries, or strawberries— whatever is in season. Purchase jars of apple or pumpkin butter as well as hot pepper–raspberry preserves. Enjoy ice-cream sundaes topped with fresh fruit.

✳ Special Events

June: **Stratford Hall Plantation** (804-493-8038; www.stratfordhall .org), Stratford. In early June, a Revolutionary Army encampment and evening concert commemorate Richard Henry Lee's motion for independence from England.

September: ☙ **Irvington Stomp** (804-438-5559), White Fences Vineyard and Winery, Irvington. In early September, celebrate the harvest by stomping on grapes with your bare feet. (Your purple footprint makes a great T-shirt souvenir). Enjoy hayrides, face painting, kite demonstrations, and a rock-and-roll performance. Also in September, show up for the **Annual Chesapeake Bay Seafood Festival** (804-462-5030; 1-800-933-7275), Belle Isle State Park, Lancaster. mid-September. Reserve ahead for this fundraiser and traditional feast of scallops, oysters, softshell crabs, crab cakes, and steamed shrimp. Sample the region's wines at the **Chesapeake Bay Wine Festival** in late September.

November: Since 1958, Urbanna has been hosting the **Urbanna Oyster Festival**, a weekend festival filled with seafood, especially oysters, and music, as well as an oyster-shucking contest. If planning to stay in or near Urbanna, reserve rooms early, as more than 80,000 people descend on the historic town.

Virginia's Eastern Shore

VIRGINIA'S EASTERN SHORE

T wenty-two miles across at its widest, 70 miles from end to end, this strip of land is flanked by the Chesapeake Bay on the west and the Atlantic Ocean on the east. It takes just a couple of hours to drive the entire length of the Eastern Shore of Virginia, but its size belies an enormous presence: immensely fertile land and water, a rich history, and indelible, sometimes quirky charm. Visitors could explore for a lifetime and still not discover all the Eastern Shore's secrets.

Fortunately, it doesn't take long to discover a few of them, right on the surface at US 13, the main artery where fish shacks, antique sheds, and wine-tasting rooms begin to hint at what lies on the back roads behind them. Get beyond the highway—as any serious shore visitor must—and you'll find quaint villages with rows of restored Victorian homes and Federalist halls, fishing communities with piles of crab traps and workboats and lines of offshore game-fishing vessels, and pristine beaches and barrier islands with rolling dunes and flocks of shorebirds floating their songs across the water. Country roads unwind past fields of sweet corn and tomatoes and produce stands with ripe cantaloupe and watermelon piled so high they look as if they're ready to roll away. Vineyards boast grapes for locally made wine, with a taste made distinctive by the sandy loam and salty air.

Virginia's Eastern Shore has long been known for its abundance, as far back as when Native Americans harvested mounds of shellfish thousands of years ago and first named the bay Chesepiooc, meaning "great shellfish bay." The shore's shell middens—discarded oyster shells—are evidence of early locals' penchant for shellfish, and ancient arrowheads can still be found, at least in local museums.

Agriculture is another historical marker; the Native Americans also cultivated corn. During colonial times, tobacco was king, and by the 18th and 19th centuries, livestock grazed on the barrier islands—natural pastures where water made fences unnecessary.

Those islands, which protect the Atlantic coast from storms, continue to provide a rich environment for fish and shellfish, a fact that still shapes the area's economy. Although oysters are struggling to survive overharvesting and disease, crabs, scallops, shrimp, and fish continue to lure local watermen—and visitors—to get back out on the water and set their traps, cast their nets, and bait their fishing lines. Now clam aquaculture has begun to supplement the wild harvest,

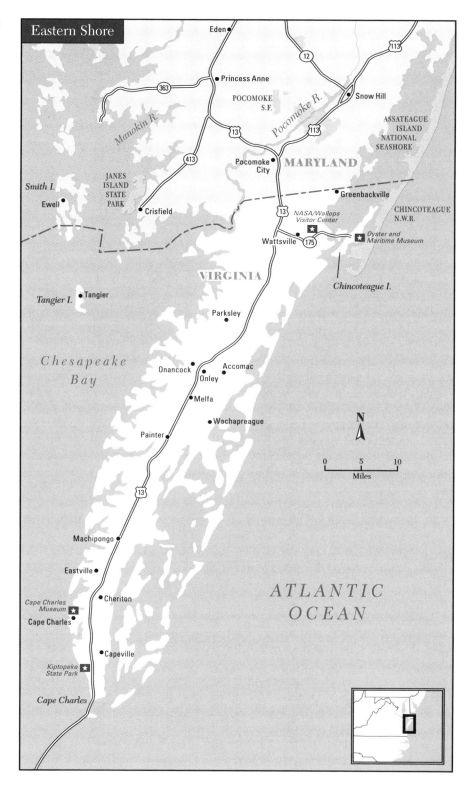

Eastern Shore

Eden

Princess Anne

POCOMOKE
S.F.

Snow Hill

Pocomoke R.

ASSATEAGUE
ISLAND
NATIONAL
SEASHORE

Manokin R.

MARYLAND

Pocomoke
City

JANES
ISLAND
STATE
PARK

Smith I.

Greenbackville

Ewell

Crisfield

NASA/Wallops
Visitor Center

CHINCOTEAGUE
N.W.R.

Wattsville

Oyster and
Maritime Museum

VIRGINIA

Chincoteague I.

Tangier

Tangier I.

Parksley

Chesapeake
Bay

Onancock

Accomac

Onley

Melfa

Wachapreague

Painter

N

0   5   10
Miles

Machipongo

Eastville

ATLANTIC
OCEAN

Cheriton

Cape Charles
Museum

Cape Charles

Capeville

Kiptopeke
State Park

Cape Charles

with profitable facilities in Willis Wharf, Chincoteague, and Cherrystone Creek,
home to the famous cherrystone clam. All of this supplies local restaurants, especially good news for those who want to sample local fare: Seafood is everywhere,
and it's as fresh as it can possibly be.

Even tourism is nothing new: In the late 19th and early 20th centuries,
wealthy families came here to enjoy the seaside, the ladies in their bathing costumes cavorting in the waves off grand hotels on the barrier islands, the men
fishing and hunting the abundant game, especially waterfowl. Lodges, hotels,
and hunt clubs peppered the islands and the main shore until hurricanes
scoured the low beaches and property owners reconsidered the wisdom of building on the shifting stands of the dunes. Now the deserted islands have become
an ecotourism destination, with kayakers paddling the marshes and small tour
boat operators explaining the barrier islands' history between lessons on the
ecosystem and area wildlife.

Active visitors have many ways to
explore the Shore: Bicycling is easy
on the flat roads and the pedaling
pace makes it simple to stop in at a
general store or take a quick stroll
down an inviting dock for a bayside
sunset. Kayaking and boating bring
you face to face with the wildlife on
the water. You can also swim, surf,
and fish at the ocean beach at
Assateague, as well as swim and fish
at the bay beaches in Cape Charles
and Kiptopeke. Lots of people come
here to the Eastern Shore for the
birding, to add species such as the
gull-billed tern and piping plover to
their life lists.

CAPE CHARLES PIER

Virginia Myers

All this natural beauty has attracted
a substantial community of artists
whose work is available in galleries in
Chincoteague, Onancock, and Cape
Charles. These artists and other
urban transplants have added a
sophisticated element to the otherwise country flavor of the shore,
bringing not only an artistic aesthetic
but chef-owned restaurants and high-
end B&Bs and inns.

Architecture also tells the social
history of the area. You'll see every
era here: colonial courthouse commons in Eastville and Accomac; classical revival homes from the 1830s

Virginia Myers

VICTORIAN HOMES IN CAPE CHARLES

and '40s in Onanocock, along with the Federal-style brick manse, Ker Place; an 18th-century almshouse in Exmore; Victorian gingerbread from the late 1800s in Cape Charles; and retro, 1950s-style motels and diners sprinkled near the highway. Many of the properties have been restored.

Along with appreciating the area's natural beauty, many visitors remark on the slower pace of shore life. It's true: Locals accustomed to driving behind a farm vehicle, or waiting for the fish to bite, have learned not to rush. In this geographically small area, that's a big lesson worth learning.

TOWNS Cape Charles. Once a bustling railroad town, Cape Charles was one of the most affluent towns on the shore. Today, it is still lined with picture-perfect Victorian homes, many of them restored. Cape Charles is experiencing a bit of a renaissance as a summer resort, with two golf courses and a sweep of beach along the bay. A bit of an urban aesthetic has crept onto the Mayberry-like Main Street, with an artsy coffee shop and new loft apartments, but what really attracts visitors is the down-home friendliness of the place.

Chincoteague. The biggest town on Virginia's Eastern Shore, Chincoteague swells each summer with visitors who return year after year and feel like the next best thing to locals. While there are plenty of "Misty" T-shirts, fried seafood joints, and even a couple of miniature golf amusement parks, they're balanced with the wild seashore and an artistic attitude that keeps things from getting too honky-tonk. Off season, hunters and nature lovers come for the wildlife and quiet.

Onancock. Onancock still has a hardware store where the men gather to play cards around the woodstove, but along with country charm it's developed a sophistication thanks in part to "come heres," people who have moved from more urban areas and started over as innkeepers, artists, gallery owners, and restaurateurs. Situated on Onancock Creek, the town is water-oriented toward the bay, so there are no beach-themed bars, just quiet streets lined with historic homes and some of the best dining on the shore.

GUIDANCE **Chincoteague Chamber of Commerce** (757-336-6161; chincoteaguechamber.com), 6733 Maddox Boulevard, the road leading to the beach. Open Mon.–Sat. 9–4:30. The office has a plethora of information on accommodations, eateries, events and attractions in Chincoteague.

Eastern Shore of Virginia Tourism Commission (757-787-8268; www.esva tourism.org) covers several small towns on the shore, along with wildlife preserves and natural attractions. Publications and brochures detail area festivals, art, nature, historic sites, and bike and kayak tours, plus accommodations and dining options. Two visitor information centers disseminate racks of information: The **New Church Welcome Center** (757-824-5000; newchurchtour@virginia .org), 1 mile south of the Virginia/Maryland state line on US 13, the main drag on the Eastern Shore); open daily 8:30–5; and the **Eastern Shore of Virginia Welcome Center** at the Chesapeake Bay Bridge Tunnel northern entrance, open daily 8:30–4:30 (call ahead in winter), which has revolving exhibits on local art as well as regional food and wine.

Onancock Business & Civic Association (757-302-0388; www.onancock.org) has a useful Web site with details on accommodations, activities, restaurants, attractions, events and more.

GETTING THERE *By air:* Private planes can fly into the **Accomack County Airport** (757-787-4600; www.co.accomack.va.us/airport), 29194 Parkway North, Melfa.

By car: From the north, after crossing the Delaware Memorial Bridge on I-295, continue on to I-95 (Delaware Turnpike) to exit 4A for US 1 South (this is much better than taking US 13 direct from I-295). Rte. 1 is expressway most of the way. Continue to exit 97, which is an expressway connection to US 13—turn south. Continue on US 13 to the Eastern Shore. From the south, take US 13 North and cross the Chesapeake Bay Bridge Tunnel from the Norfolk–Virginia Beach area. The Chesapeake Bay Bridge Tunnel connects US 13 in Virginia Beach to US 13 on the Eastern Shore.

GETTING AROUND Most locals drive just about everywhere, and some bike, but there's no everyday public transportation. Whatever way you travel, be sure to get off US 13 for a wander on back roads and past the small communities off the main highway—this is the heart of the Eastern Shore.

WHEN TO COME The Eastern Shore is most popular during the summer months. This is especially true of Chincoteague, the town closest to Assateague

Island (which includes the area's only ocean beach accessible without a boat), so it's wise to book accommodations in advance. Be aware that throngs of visitors create a backup at the Assateague Island beach parking lot on summer weekends. Go early in the morning or late in the afternoon to avoid the crowds. Throughout the Eastern Shore, museums, nature centers, shops, restaurants, and features are lively and ready for tourists during "season"; their hours can be hit-or-miss the rest of the year, so call ahead. Off-season is a lovely time to visit; migratory birds are at their best in the fall, but there's plenty of wildlife and open space to enjoy through winter and spring as well.

✳ To See

Chincoteague

✒ **Assateague Lighthouse, Assateague Island National Seashore** (757-336-3696; www.assateagueisland.com), just off the only road leading to the beach on Assateague Island. Open June 18–Sept. 28 Thu.–Mon.; Oct. 1–Nov. 29 Fri.–Sun. Ages 2–12 must be accompanied by adult; visitors must be at least 18 years old to climb unaccompanied. $4 adults, $2 children, free for under age 2.

NASA/Wallops Visitor Center (757-824-1344; www.wff.nasa.gov/vc), Hwy. 175, 5 miles west of Chincoteague. Open July–Aug. daily, Mar.–June and Sept.–Nov. Thu.–Mon., Dec.–Feb. Sat. and Sun. "Wallops Island," as it is locally known, is an active research facility that includes exhibits such as life-size plane and rocket models. Monthly model rocket and living-in-space demonstrations are especially popular with children, as are children's programs in the summer. Free admission.

ASSATEAGUE LIGHTHOUSE

Bill Conway

Oyster and Maritime Museum (757-336-5800; www.chincoteague chamber.com/oyster), 7125 Maddox Boulevard. Open daily in summer, weekends in spring and fall. Closed winter. Features displays illustrating oyster harvesting, the lives of watermen, the once-upon-a-time community on Assateague Island, Native American artifacts, and other local history. $2 age 13 and over, free for under age 13.

Onancock

♿ **Ker Place** (757-787-8012; http://kerplace.org), 69 Market Street. Open Mar.–mid-Dec. Tue.–Sat. 11–4. Ker Place was built in 1799 by wealthy merchant John Ker, and the first floor features furniture and artifacts reflective of the time when he lived there in the early 1800s. Upstairs exhibits chronicle local history, including the arrival of the first settlers in the 1620s and participation in the Revolutionary War by the Accomack County Minutemen. The Eastern Shore of Virginia Historical Society is headquartered here, and hosts workshops in the old traditions, including quilt making and building Windsor chairs, as well as presents lectures and demonstrations. $5 adults, $2 students.

Walking Tour of Onancock (757-787-3363), map available at town office, 15 North Street. A neatly written guide to numerous 19th-century homes sets visitors to dreaming of life in a gingerbread Victorian complete with wraparound porch and water view.

Cape Charles

Cape Charles Museum (757-331-1008; www.smallmuseum.org/capechas.htm), 814 Randolph Ave. Open weekdays mid-Apr.–Nov. 10–2, Sat. 10–5, Sun. 1–5. Local history and artifacts describe Eastern Shore houses, schools, commercial enterprises, and railroads, as well as some geological history, in what was once the town power plant. Free admission.

Outside town limits

✎ **Barrier Island Center** (757-678-5550; http://barrierislandscenter.com), US 13 between Nassawadox and Exmore. The center is a restored almshouse—the "poorhouse" or "workhouse," where destitute people lived and worked for the county in the 18th and 19th centuries. Now it is home to numerous exhibits about the barrier islands, describing the rich history of moneyed gentry who

BARRIER ISLAND CENTER

Virginia Myers

TANGIER ISLAND

Twelve miles out in the Chesapeake Bay, Tangier Island sits like a world unto itself. About 500 people live on the 3 by 1½-mile spit of land. Tangier is a tiny community of watermen and their wives, merchants who run the handful of businesses, and those who cater to the tourists who arrive by ferry for two- or three-hour tours (www.tangierisland-va.com).

Visiting Tangier isn't for everyone. For some people, two hours are more than enough to see the little island's one main street, modestly charming homes, and small strip of beach. But for those enchanted by thick, salty air; the smell of low tide; and the slow pace on an island where the only traffic jams are created by teenagers on Vespas, fishermen in golf carts, or the one police car parked at the ice-cream shop, it could take weeks to really breathe in the essence of the place. But even two-hour tourists can take in one of the island's best assets: its seafood. Famous for their softshell crabs, islanders cultivate them in little crab shanties built on stilts out in the shallow water of the harbor, then serve them up in Tangier's restaurants, fried lightly so the taste of the bay remains. They are the best softshells you'll ever have. (**The Fisherman's Corner**, 757-891-2900, Longbridge and Main Street; or **Hilda Crockett's Chesapeake House**, 757-891-2331, 16243 Main Street).

If you take the time to stay overnight on the island, pedaling one of the old-fashioned bikes provided by your hotel is a great way to explore. You

came for hunting trips and summer pleasures, built opulent homes, and experienced the fury of hurricanes and shipwrecks as well. Guide Jerry Doughty, whose family goes back to those who once lived on now-deserted Cobb Island, infuses his tours with personal connections to the past: his great-grandfather was arrested for blockade-running during the Civil War, and was later reported missing during the Great Hurricane of 1933 (though he eventually was found). An impressive collection of vintage photographs and archival items such as a "breeches buoy" lifesaving ring, like a man's pants with a life ring attached; ship's wheels; model boats and charts; a child's crib compete with antique dolls (which helps visitors imagine the families that might have lived in the almshouse); and hunting paraphernalia (including strings of wooden duck decoys) describe life on individual islands as well as the area in general. During the center's days as an almshouse, caretakers inhabited the main building; outbuildings include a surviving 1700s-era house for the poor, with original handmade bricks. A gift shop carries only locally produced, locally connected items, including many from area artists. In addition to functioning as a museum, the Barrier Island Center has become a community gathering spot for music festivals, art shows, and summer camps. Free admission.

can catch the sunset on the west end of the island, where you might also see manta rays churning up the water as they mate. You can also sign up for an hour-and-a-half boat tour with a local waterman who will show you the crab shanties, haul up a trap so you can see how the critters are caught, and fill you in on the natural history of the area.

Tangier History Museum (302-234-1660; http:/tangierhistorymuseum.org), 16215 Main Ridge. At this museum, you'll learn how Tangier families have made their living off the water for centuries, and you'll get to sit down on a picking bench to see what it might be like to pick crabs for hours on end—or, you can listen to oral histories at the press of a button. Visitors can sit on the museum porch and play checkers with shells as the pieces, or use the kayaks out back to paddle around the entire island; you might encounter children swimming off the small bridges that knit the island together over creeks and marshes studded with crab traps and dinghies.

LODGING Hilda Crockett's Chesapeake House (above), in two historic houses, offers homey accommodations with bathrooms down the hall, breakfast and lunch or dinner included, $90–145. **Bay View Inn** (757-891-2396; http://tangier island.net/home, 16408 West Ridge) provides modern hotel rooms facing a common green behind a historic home, plus a country-style breakfast, $120–215.

✳ To Do

AMUSEMENTS ✍ **Chincoteague Fireman's Carnival Grounds**, off Main Street, south of the bridge to the mainland. Every Fri. and Sat. of July and the last full week of July, 7 PM. Old-fashioned fun, with a Ferris wheel, games of chance, music, and food that includes fried oysters, clams, and crabs cooked up by locals to raise money for the volunteer fire department.

✍ **Refuge Golf and Bumper Boats** (757-336-5420), 6528 Maddox Boulevard, Chincoteague. Open May–Oct. daily 9–6. Mini-golf, bumper boats with spray jets, rock wall, arcade, and go-cart track.

✍ **Surfside Golf** (757-336-GOLF; Chincoteague.com/surfside), 6557 Maddox Boulevard, Chincoteague. Open Memorial Day–Labor Day daily 10 AM–11 PM. Spray mists and soft-serve ice cream keep players cool over 18 holes.

✍ **Wachapreague Carnival** (757-787-7818), Atlantic Avenue, Wachapreague. Three and a half weeks in late June/early July, weekdays 7:30–10:30 PM; food and bingo begin at 7. Since 1952, this small-town carnival has offered to townies and visitors alike a handful of rides, including a Ferris wheel and carousel, plus open-air bingo and other games of chance. The food, prepared from scratch, includes clam fritters and hand-cut French fries. Proceeds support the volunteer fire department.

BICYCLING Miles of flat roads, water views, and small-town life on the Eastern Shore attract leisurely cyclists as well as serious athletes. Seaside Road, or State Road 600, is a country-road alternative to the more commercial US 13. Bike routes wind past the general stores and bait shops, historic homes, and small farms of quaint bay and seaside communities. In Chincoteague, bikes are a great way to get around to explore the island, and kids love to pedal over to the ice-cream shops on their own. Bike rentals are available on Chincoteague at **Jus' Bikes** (757-336-6700), 6527 Maddox Boulevard, and **The Bike Depot** (757-336-5511), 7058 Maddox Boulevard.

Bay Creek Resort & Club (757-331-8640), Cape Charles. Cape Charles is another small town made for biking: a few rentals are available at (guests of the resort get first pick).

Citizens for a Better Eastern Shore (757-678-7157; www.cbes.org) suggests bike routes and organizes an annual bike tour each October. The Between the Waters Bike Tour gives riders 100-mile, 60-mile, 35- to 40-mile, and 25-mile alternatives with sag wagon and lunch stop, plus an oyster roast to celebrate completing the route. The tour begins and ends Onancock, exploring back roads and scenic rest stops along the Atlantic and the Chesapeake Bay. $50 adults, $20 ages 7–12, free for under age 6 (but registration required); discounts for early registration. Oyster roast, $35.

✍ **Wildlife Loop**, Assateague Island. Biking this loop is a great way to spot wild ponies and sika elk, and gives you a close-up view of the egrets and other shore birds that like to perch in the marshes along the road to the beach.

BOAT EXCURSIONS AND RENTALS Life on the Eastern Shore revolves around its waterways, so getting out on a boat is one of the best ways to immerse yourself in the heartbeat of the community. Plus, there's no other way to reach the remote barrier islands, where you'll find majestic blue herons and egrets, bright oyster catchers, and water teeming with sea life; abandoned communities and lighthouses drown in shifting sands; and deserted beaches to comb for shells. Tour guides, sometimes longtime locals, will customize your trip, which could include birding, clamming, fishing, or a gourmet picnic on the beach. Among the options: two- or three-hour tours, and sunset and sunrise tours.

Broadwater Bay Ecotours (757-442-4363; www.broadwaterbayecotour.com). **Captain Rick Kellam**, a fifth-generation waterman and certified ecotour guide whose family once lived on the now-deserted Hog Island, runs Broadwater Bay Ecotours, which takes visitors to the barrier islands. Kellam, who has coauthored two books about these now pristine, protected islands and waters, spins stories of Spanish treasure, wild hurricanes, and abandoned communities. His knowledge of the natural environment, from years spent on the water and recent experience guiding scientists and conservationists on research expeditions, gets hands-on with surf and fly-fishing, dolphin watching, and shell collecting, and can include

Virginia Myers

BROADWATER BAY ECOTOURS BOAT

beach picnics or wine and cheese tastings—each trip is planned according to guests' requests.

Capt. Zed's Bait & Shop and Marina (757-789-3222, captainzeds@verizon .net). If you really understand how to operate a boat and navigate tricky tides and shallow waters yourself, rent a runabout in Wachapreague and explore on your own. 16-foot Carolina skiff, carrying a maximum of four people, $99 per day.

WACHAPREAGUE'S CAPT. ZED'S

Virginia Myers

Chincoteague Cruises (757-336-5731; 757-894-8149; http://chinco taguecruises.com). In Chincoteague, native son and certified ecotour guide Charlie Birch takes up to six visitors at a time out to find the wild ponies and learn about the environment near Assateague on his boat.

Eastern Shore Adventures (757-615-2598; www.easternshoreadven tures.com) offers barrier island eco-tours with Captain Buddy Vaughan.

BROADWATER BAY ECOTOURS

Captain Rick Kellam is proud of being a native son, so it pains him to admit that he was actually born on the mainland. And so it goes when you are from the Eastern Shore: The fishing jobs shift, your family winds up in a mainland port, you move back to the shore, you spend time on the barrier islands. It's a fluid existence.

But Kellam, who says saltwater runs in his veins, has always flowed around the Eastern Shore. He is the fifth generation of a family that once lived on one of the now-deserted barrier islands. He has been a guide, a naturalist, an author, a historian, a member of the Virginia State Marine Police, and a waterman. He holds a master captain's license from the U.S. Coast Guard, is a certified master diver, and is also certified in first aid and CPR.

Plus, he's a friendly guy with no pretenses—just a lot of knowledge to share. Kellam is the perfect ecotour guide. His **Broadwater Bay Ecotours** has hosted Nature Conservancy officials, research scientists, and even treasure hunters, as well as tourists just interested in a pleasant outing. The shallow draft of his 24-foot, open-cockpit boat—and his knowledge of the local waters—allows wide access to the shallow waters around the barrier islands that line the Atlantic side of the Eastern Shore.

A typical tour may start at Wachapreague, a fisherman's haven where the docks are lined with boats outfitted for offshore fishing. Set off from the dock and birds wheel overhead—Kellam can tell you what species they are. Life listers—people checking off the birds they haven't yet seen—often tally

FISHING NEAR THE LIGHTHOUSE, VIRGINIA BEACH

Virginia Beach Convention & Visitors Bureau

FISHING The Eastern Shore is a mecca for in-shore and off-shore fishing, crabbing, and clamming. Some of the big catches include tuna and marlin; there's also rockfish, sea bass, king mackerel, wahoo, dolphin, shark, and more.

On Assateague Island, many visitors opt for surf casting—the best spot is on the southern tip of the island, just past the public beach. No permit is required; ditto for crabbing and clamming along the marshy banks of the bay.

Capt. Zed's Tackle Shop & Marina (757-789-3222), Wachapreague dock

a few more when they go out with Kellam. In the water, the captain will point out turtles swimming just ahead of the boat, and crab pots dotting the channels. He knows where the bald eagles nest and where the egrets roost, and will show you the difference between gull-billed and royal terns.

Out on the islands, you'll feel as though you're the last person in the world. There are few structures and only a handful of inhabited homes across miles and miles and sand. Broadwater Bay tours are tailored to Kellam's guests. Some want to comb the beaches to find whole sand dollars and giant whelk shells. Others like a romantic picnic on the beach, complete with tablecloth and a bottle of wine. Some want to learn more about crabbing, and Kellam will pull up a trap to show them how these Eastern Shore treasures are caught. Guests can learn to surf fish or fly-fish; they can go for a lighthouse tour, visit crab and clam aquaculture farms, or even stick to the mainland for a tour of art studios.

Kellam is as much teacher as he is skipper. The coauthor of two books—The Barrier Islands: A Photographic History of Life on Hog, Cobb, Smith, Cedar, Parramore, Metompkin, and Assateague and Cobb's Island, Virginia: Recollections, Traditions, and Transformations, he is a walking encyclopedia of history. You will hear about the hurricanes that scoured the islands and chased inhabitants back to the mainland—and get a wry account of a more recent story about a developer who built on Cedar Island, only to have the houses drown in the shifting tides.

And then you'll head back to the dock, windblown but with a new appreciation of the rich natural life of the Eastern Shore.

near 17 Atlantic Ave. Wachpreague is known as the "Flounder Capital of the World." Captain Zed will help you arrange a fishing trip on one of the many local charter boats docked in long rows at the marina.

Chincoteague Island Charterboat Association (www.chincoteague.com/char terboats). For in-shore and off-shore fishing charters, this organization can help you sort through almost two dozen charter outfits in the area.

Fish N'Finn Charters (757-787-3399), Onancock, operates from the town dock.

James Gang Sportfishing (757-787-1226) 4 Frances Street, Chincoteague, also can arrange fishing expeditions.

GOLF **Bay Creek Resort and Club** (757-331-8620; www.baycreekresort.com /golf), One Clubhouse Way, Cape Charles. Open year-round, 7 AM–dark, 8 AM in winter. Two 18-hole courses. An Arnold Palmer Signature Golf Course and a Jack Nicklaus Signature Course overlap across reclaimed marshland dotted with watery inlets and sweeping bayside views.

Virginia Beach Convention & Visitors Bureau

NICKLAUS COURSE AT BAY CREEK RESORT

Captain's Cove Golf & Yacht Club (757-824-3465; http://captscove.com), 3370 Captains Corridor, Greenbackville. Nine holes. Remodeled in 2007, this is a challenging course with plenty of water and sand—appropriate for its location just 20 minutes from Chincoteague.

KAYAKING Individual rentals or guided tours on the flat waters of the bays and inlets bring you as close as you can get to the natural beauty of this area. Tours are usually led by locals who share cultural and natural history during their guided outings.

Assateague Explorer (757-336-5956 or 1-866-PONY-SWIM; www.assateague island.com/kayaktours.htm), based in Chincoteague, open May–Oct., conducts three- to six-hour tours, and will arrange sunset outings by request.

East Side Rentals and Marina (757-336-5555), 7462 East Side Road, Chincoteague, rents kayaks by the hour, half day, or full day.

SouthEast Expeditions (877-22KAYAK; www.southeastexpeditions.net), 32218 Lankford Highway, Cape Charles, covers the entire shore for beginners or adventure kayakers, with half-day or full-day specialty tours such as a kayak-winery tour, or kayaking with clamming. They'll also rent kayaks by the hour, half day, full day, or week, and offer kiteboarding for those up for a new sort of adventure (1-877-9-GET LIT; http://gogetlit.com).

Up a Creek with a Paddle (757-693-1200; www.upacreektours.com), 27369 Phillips Drive, Melfa, features Virginia Ecotour guides and instructors during its sunrise, sunset, half-day, or full-day tours, and will rent kayaks by the day or week.

KITEBOARDING ✍ **Memorial Park**, west end of East Side Drive in Chincoteague. Hit the half-pipes at Memorial Park. The park is free and unsupervised; helmets, knee pads, and elbow pads are required and local police stop by to be sure the rules are respected.

SouthEast Expeditions Kiteboarding School (877-9-GET LIT; www.goget lit.com), based in Cape Charles, takes on beginners and experienced boarders, and shows them the best spots on the miles of flat water around the bays and inlets.

SURFING You can surf on Assateague Island; summer waves tend toward small, but that makes it easier for beginners.

Assateague Island Surf Station (757-336-1305), inside Saltwater Trading Company on the traffic circle, Maddox Boulevard, rents surfboards by the day or week.

WALKING TOURS Holiday Progressive Tour (757-331-0059; www.north amptoncountychamber.com). Each winter, Northampton County hosts a progressive dinner featuring visits to historic sites and restored homes, with food from local restaurants served at each tour stop. For 14 years, the event has showcased Cape Charles, but in 2010 it branched out to Eastville, with its colonial architecture and its claim to holding the nation's oldest court records, dating back to 1623.

Onancock Walking Tour (757-787-8012), 69 Market Street. A self-guided tour of Onancock's eclectic architecture and centuries-old history is available on a town map that includes descriptions of 34 historic buildings, available at Ker Place year-round.

WINERIES Bloxom Winery (757-665-5670; http://bloxomwinery.com), Mason Road (State Road 681), Bloxom. Fri.–Sun. noon–5. Six acres of Chardonnay, Merlot, Cabernet Franc, and Sauvignon first planted in 2000, produce "estate-bottled wines." You can drink them on the open patio shaded with vines and flowers, or go into the café for wood-fired pizza (Saturdays) or homemade pasta (Fridays).

Chatham Vineyards (757-678-5588; http://chathamvineyards.com), 9232 Chatham Road, Machipongo. Free tastings, Thu.–Mon. 10–5, Sun. noon–5. Second-generation vintner Jon Wehner grows all his own grapes to make seven distinctive (and award-winning) Eastern Shore wines shaped by the sandy loam and moderate maritime climate. The vineyard is located on historic Chatham Farm overlooking Church Creek; it has been a working farm for four centuries. (See sidebar.)

Holly Grove Vineyards (757-442-9090 tasting room; 757-442-2844 winery; www.hollygrovevineyards.com), "Off the Vine" tasting room, 4220 Lankford Highway/US 13, Exmore, Mon.–Thu. 11–5, Fri. and Sat. 10–6, Sun. 11–5; winery, 6404 Holly Bluff Drive, Franktown, open by appointment only. This family-owned farm winery utilizes locally grown grapes, including its own, to craft six varietals, and has won several awards.

✸ Green Spaces

✐ **Assateague Lighthouse** (757-336-3696; assateagueisland.com/lighthouse/lighthouse_info.htm). For bird's-eye view, you can climb the lighthouse.

♿ **Chincoteague National Wildlife Refuge/Assateague Island** (757-336-6122; www.chinco.fws.gov), 8231 Beach Road, Chincoteague, open May–Sept. daily 5 AM–10 PM, Nov.–Mar. 6–6, Mar.–Apr. and Oct. 6 AM–8 PM. Herbert H. Bateman Educational and Administrative Center open daily 9–4, summer 9–5. Closed Christmas and New Year's Day.

Chincoteague is the Virginia portion of Assateague Island, a barrier island that

VINTAGE: EASTERN SHORE

It's no secret that Virginia's wine industry has grown enormously in the last 20 years. There are now nearly 160 wineries in the state, and six nationally recognized American Viticultural Areas (AVAs) within its boundaries.

One of the most distinctive is the Eastern Shore AVA. With five vineyards and three wineries, the shore produces a variety of grapes, including Chardonnay, Merlot, Cabernet Franc, Cabernet Sauvignon, and Petit Verdot. Along with vintner decisions about when to harvest and how to prune, the maritime climate, with its long growing season and salty breezes blowing from the Atlantic Ocean on one side and the Chesapeake Bay on the other, influences the way the grapes grow and how they taste. Also important is the well-drained, sandy loam of the shore, which allows heavy rains from the occasional nor'easter to drain away.

"We try to produce wines that are site expressive, that express the land here," says Jon Wehner, who runs Chatham Vineyards with his wife and three small children. It's that whole concept of *terroir,* he explains—"the fingerprint of your place."

Chatham's land was first claimed by settlers in 1640. Wehner, a second-generation vintner whose father had a hobby farm for 30 years in Great Falls, VA, began planting French *Vitis vinifera* varietals at Chatham in 1999. But the land has been worked since at least 1818, when the farmhouse was built. That house still stands, and visitors driving past rows of grapes growing neatly up their arbors will see, at the end of a long, straight driveway, the grand, Federal-style building perched above Church Creek.

Wehner grows all the grapes for his wines, and each year sells about 30 tons of the fruit to other wineries, primarily in Virginia. His wine, he says,

stretches across the Virginia/Maryland border. The U.S. Fish and Wildlife Service and National Park Service share management of more than 14,000 acres of pristine ocean beaches and protected dunes, marsh and maritime forests full of migratory birds, white-tailed deer, sika elk, and a rich estuary for fish and shellfish. Fifteen miles of trails wind through the refuge, including a 3.2-mile paved Wildlife Loop open to vehicles after 3 PM; and Swans Cove Trail, which leads to the beach. Lifeguards patrol the central beach from Memorial Day to Labor Day, but the areas away from the crowds—and guards—are more pleasant.

The **Eastern Shore of Virginia National Wildlife Refuge** (757-331-2760; www.fws.gov/northeast/easternshore), off US 13 near the terminus of the Chesapeake Bay Bridge Tunnel, the refuge provides a good introduction to the Eastern Shore if you're entering from Virginia. The few trails are less impressive than the well-appointed interpretive center, where visitors can look through an

is flavored by the Chatham farmland that produces the grapes: Merlot, Chardonnay, Cabernet Franc, Cabernet Sauvignon, and Petit Verdot.

The wines are true to their varietals, but the land adds something extra. The Chardonnay takes on a tropical fruit flavor, he says, with a crisp acidity. The red wines—a Merlot he describes as having dark cherry and rich black currant flavors, and a Cabernet with flavors of ripe raspberry, a note of violet, and a hint of pepper, also take a "certain brown spice" he is sure comes from the land itself.

A late harvest dessert wine is especially distinctive. Produced when there is a hot, dry summer and fall, it is created by dehydrating the grapes while they still hang on the vines. Wehner harvests them just before they turn into raisins; three tons of grapes dehydrate down to a quarter-ton, he says, and each grape produces one drop of juice. The process dramatically reduces the skin-to-grape ratio, so, as Wehner describes it, the resulting wine "has a nice thick viscosity. It's very earthy and spicy, and it's a nice after dinner wine with cheese."

Other wineries on the shore offer similarly distinctive bottles as well as perks. At **Bloxom Vineyard**, an airy patio encourages lingering over bottles of estate-produced Chardonnay, Merlot, Cabernet Franc and Sauvignon. On select nights, wood-fired pizza and homemade pasta accompany the wine. **Holly Grove** recently opened a tasting room right on the main highway, US 13, for its handcrafted Chardonnay, Merlot, rosé, and Traminette. All three wineries host festivals and special tastings.

And at Chatham, a partnership with **SouthEast Expeditions** has created a kayak and wine tour: visitors paddle up to the Chatham farmhouse, walk over to the winery for a tasting, and paddle back.

expanse of windows out onto the marsh, using handy binoculars and ID displays to observe and identify some of the thousands of bird species on the 1,393-acre refuge. Interpretive displays and hands-on exhibits appeal to kids of all ages.

& **Kiptopeke State Park** (757-331-2267; www.dcr.virginia.gov/state_parks/kip .shtml), 3540 Kiptopeke Drive, Cape Charles, was a ferry terminal until 1949 and has since been transformed into a 562-acre recreational and natural state park with camping and beaches. Located on the bay with a view of the Chesa-peake Bay Bridge Tunnel, the north swimming beach is lively in summer, despite the rather grim view of concrete ships intentionally sunk off the waterfront as a breakfront. The wrecks make for great fishing, and a 1,000-foot pier supple-ments opportunities to catch dinner. The south beach is quieter, great for beach-combing and surf casting. Birding is especially popular here; there is a hawk observatory, where about a dozen different birds of prey have been sighted, and volunteers have banded more than 300,000 migratory birds here as part of ongo-ing studies. Interpretive programs include canoeing, crabbing, fishing, campfires, and junior ranger activities.

✋ **Wild Ponies.** Chincoteague is famous for its wild ponies, which are herded each summer to the small channel between Assateague and Chincoteague islands. There, they swim across under the watchful supervision of "saltwater cowboys" and are auctioned off; proceeds go to keep the local fire department running. The children's book *Misty of Chincoteague* (see sidebar) cemented this tradition in the imagination of countless girls and boys and spawned great crowds during Pony Penning Week (see sidebar), along with a plethora of

SHELL-DECORATED DRIFTWOOD AT CHINCOTEAGUE

Virginia Myers

Virginia Myers

KIPTOPEKE DUNES

"Misty" T-shirts and memorabilia. In the refuge, however, they can be seen grazing peacefully on seaweed and marsh grass, unaware of the hoopla and utterly unconcerned with the people snapping photos along the sides of the road.

To learn more about the natural environment of the refuge, the sustainably designed Bateman Center offers outstanding, hands-on displays and opportunities for kids to become "junior refuge managers" and "junior birders" by completing intelligently designed activity books.

✴ Lodging

Cape Charles
Bay Creek Resort & Club (57-331-8750 or 888-422-9275; www.baycreek resort.com), Cape Charles. The company rents upscale homes, condos, suites, and villas in a high-end golfing/boating community. Playfully labeled "the jelly bean factory" by at least one local, Bay Creek Resort sprawls on the edges of Cape Charles, with brightly colored buildings reminiscent of the Caribbean, all surrounded by water views, two award-winning golf courses, a luxurious marina, and two fine restaurants. Rentals run the gamut from one-bedroom suites to a five-bedroom duplex.

Cape Charles House Bed and Breakfast (757-331-4920; www.cape charleshouse.com), 645 Tazewell Avenue. Five rooms. This is the finest place to stay in Cape Charles. Innkeepers Bruce and Carol Evans, the third owners of the grand 1912 home, have been hosting guests here for more than a decade and sharing

✍ PONYING UP IN CHINCOTEAGUE

Every year, at the end of July, Chincoteague rounds up its ponies—and its tourists—for the biggest event of the year: Pony Penning Week. Some annual visitors avoid this time because of the noisy crowds of sunburned pony lovers buying up souvenir T-shirts and "pony tracks" ice cream, dishing out fees for pony rides, and flocking to the 1945 Roxy Movie Theater to see *Misty of Chincoteague*.

But despite the crowds—and partly because of them—pony-penning week is worth experiencing at least once. There's a reason it's so popular: Visitors get an up-close look at mysteriously wild ponies that live in charming little family groups all over Assateague Island, where they graze peacefully on seaweed and marsh grass. During pony penning, dashing "saltwater cowboys" mount their horses and herd the ponies across the channel between the wildlife preserve on Assateague Island, where they live, and Chincoteague Island, where the foals are sold to families eager to own a cute little piece of history.

Who knows, these babies could be related to the famous "Misty," the pony that was the object of youthful desire in Marguerite Henry's classic book. The novel has charmed generations of children and their parents with the romance of wild herds on windswept dunes, the ambition and passion of youth, and the innocence of a simpler time in a country town full of lovable characters.

BAY CREEK RESORT

Virginia Myers

the history of its previous families and neighbors with historic photographs and memorabilia tastefully infused in the décor. Antiques and unusual collectibles, such as the framed cross-stitched works in the second parlor, make wandering through the house especially engaging. Accommodations are luxurious—some of the five rooms include spa-style baths and the antiques, many of which have personal stories behind them, are lovingly maintained. In addition to a fine breakfast, wine and cheese and tea and sweets are served in the afternoon/evening. The Evanses, who are more than happy to share their local

147

VIRGINIA'S EASTERN SHORE

Today, ponies (shipwreck survivors per legend, but more likely left over from when locals grazed their livestock on Assateague) are first roped in, rounded up and brought to a holding area on Assateague Island. On pony-penning day, the cowboys lead them to the channel and monitor them closely as they swim across, landing near Memorial Park on Chincoteague. There, people line the banks of the channel, stand in the marshy water and even climb trees for a better view (get there early for a good spot, and be prepared to wait as the sun gets hotter and hotter—sunscreen and hats are a must). In the water, people in kayaks and small boats get a closer look at the ponies swimming together, a curious sight that is recorded endlessly in photographs and paintings in shops all over the island.

Once the ponies land, they are taken to a corral and eventually sold. Visitors can see the ponies as they await auction, in stables, on the fairgrounds. Proceeds from the sales go to the local volunteer fire department. About a week later, the rest of the herd—the adults—are herded back home to Assateague.

The excitement generated by this event is infectious, and so hard to contain that the fire department has established a carnival leading up to pony penning. The carnival's a homegrown affair, staffed primarily by locals who fry up oyster sandwiches and French fries in the food hall and run games of chance along with the usual small-town thrill rides. Carnival is open on weekends for the month of July, and during the entire week of pony penning.

Chincoteague Chamber of Commerce (757-336-6161; www.chincoteague chamber.com), at the traffic circle on Maddox Boulevard has more information.

knowledge and enthusiasm for the area, are active on the town council and tourism board and will guide you to local restaurants and shops, and fill in the details of Cape Charles's evolution from turn-of-the-century holiday town to teetering backwater and on to its miniature renaissance as a hidden resort community. $120–200.

Rittenhouse Motor Lodge (757-331-2768; www.rittenhousemotor lodge.com), 23054 Lankford Highway. (US 13), just outside of Cape Charles. The place is still run by octogenarian Robert Rittenhouse, who built the now-retro motel in 1951 and still lives in an apartment in the building. Rit-

tenhouse takes justified pride in the grounds, landscaped with winding paths through thick azaleas, ferns, old loblolly pines, and gardenias planted near the shady porch. If you're expecting modern facilities, the rooms may not be for you, but they are clean and sufficient; more important, the hospitality is genuine, authentic Eastern Shore. $75–125.

Sea Gate B&B (757-331-2206; http://seagatebb.com), 9 Tazewell Avenue. Four rooms. Just a block or so from the beach, the B&B features a stately wraparound porch tucked into a lush yard draped in trees and flowering shrubs. A Florida Room and a second-floor porch echo the theme. Inside, the cozy common areas are furnished with antiques. $120–130.

Chincoteague
If you're going to be at the beach for a week or more, renting a house from one of the agencies on the island is a good idea—you can cook for yourself, for one thing, which saves money and allows you to try some of the freshest seafood and produce from roadside stands. Most of the restaurants are nothing to write home about, anyway. There are lots of bed-and-breakfasts from which to choose, and conventional hotels from Best Western and Hampton Inn to locally owned inns. The Chamber of Commerce hosts a comprehensive list at www.chinco teaguechamber.com.

1848 Island Manor House B&B (757-336-5436; 1-800-852-1505; http://islandmanor.com), 4160 Main Street, Closed winter. Split in two to accommodate two 19th-century families, then knit back together in the 1980s through the creative use of a brick courtyard and garden room, this B&B has undergone significant restoration and now includes eight rooms with private baths, though some are outside the rooms. $125–215.

Anchor Inn Motel (757-336-6313; 1-800-887-5486; www.chincoteague .com/anchor), 3791 South Main Street. Open year-round. The motel faces west toward Chincoteague Channel, where you can watch the sunset—even though you're on the east coast. Fishermen can pull their boats in to the motel's dock, so they don't have to launch every day. Continental breakfast and pool are included. $85-159 rooms, $98-151 efficiencies.

☙ **Channel Bass Inn B&B** (757-336-6148; 1-800-249-0818; www .channelbassinn.com), 6228 Church Street. Closed winter. Well known for its generous afternoon tea and lush garden as it is for its accommodations, the structure, built in 1892 by a former Chincoteague mayor, has been an inn since the 1920s. It offers seven rooms and features an enormous breakfast. $125-225.

Harbour Rentals (1-800-221-5059; www.harbourrentals.net), 6455 Maddox Boulevard, has more than 100 single-family homes and condos to rent all over the island. **Island Properties** (1-800-346-2559; http://island prop.com), 6426 Maddox Boulevard, has a similar number of properties and has been in business nearly 40 years. Both companies are run by realtors.

🐾 **Maddox Family Campground** (757-336-3111; www.chincoteague .com/maddox), 6742 Maddox Boulevard. Open Mar. 1–Nov. 30. This has beautiful views across the water, and is close to town as well. A pool, playground, horseshoes, shuffleboard, and an arcade supplement the usual beach activities. $41–50.

🐾 **Refuge Inn** (757-336-5511; 1-888-257-0034; www.refugeinn.com), 7058 Maddox Boulevard. Open year-round except February. This is a family-run inn overlooking the wildlife refuge and near the road to the beach. Complimentary breakfast, indoor/outdoor pool, and Chincoteague ponies on site. Rooms $89–190, suites $179–320.

🐾 **Tom's Cove Family Campground** (757-336-6498; www.toms covepark.com), 8128 Beebe Road. Open Mar.–Nov. 30. This campground is oriented toward the water, with waterfront camping, boat ramp and marina, pool, playground, and fishing and crabbing piers. $32–40.

Onancock

Ψ ₺ (¶) **Charlotte Hotel & Restaurant** (757-787-7400; www.thechar lottehotel.com), 7 North Street. Open year-round. This eight-room boutique hotel was renovated with an artist's touch by Gary Cochran and his artist wife, Charlotte Heath, for whom the property is named. You'll often find them at the chef-driven restaurant, greeting locals as well as visitors at a closet-size bar that manages to feel sophisticated despite its diminutive size. No children under age 10. $110–180.

✔ ✿ ₺ **Colonial Manor Inn B&B** (757-787-3521; http://colonialmanor inn.com, 84 Market Street. Open year-round. Six rooms. The great, rambling inn was built in 1882, but you may find the hosts' history just as interesting: the mother-daughter pair have traveled the world, and have the knickknacks and art to prove it. Children welcome, pets allowed in some rooms. $99–139.

(¶) **The Inn at Onancock** (757-789-7711; 1-866-792-7466; www.innat onancock.com), 30 North Street. Open year-round. Five rooms. This B&B features such amenities as featherbeds, spa-type baths, towel warmers, and two rooms with gas fireplaces. Hosts Lisa and Kris LaMontagne are active members of the Onancock community who are just as likely to host a local poetry reading as they are to cook up a gourmet breakfast (Lisa is a professionally trained chef), and their enthusiasm for this artistic, historic town is contagious—plus, they give great advice for seeing the sights. No children under age 10. $185–215.

Outside town limits

Garrison Bed and Breakfast (757-442-9446; www.garrisonbandb.com), 34000 Seaside Road. (State Road 600), Painter. The picture-perfect B&B with a shady front porch, landscaped grounds, and a gazebo out back, is hosted by "Captain Cleo" and his wife, Barbara. They will take guests out to the barrier islands on their 24-foot Carolina skiff, for fishing, beachcombing, or just exploring the waters. In addition to breakfast, this B&B provides dessert each evening, and the option of dinner in a dining room often used for catered events. No children under age 6. $75–135.

Shore Stay Suites (757-331-4090; www.shorestaysuites.com), 26406 Lankford Highway (US 13), just south of Cape Charles, offers motel-style suites with full kitchens. $89–199.

Wachapreague Inn (757-787-2105; www.wachapreagueinn.com), One Main Street, across the street from the marina. The inn posts which fishing boats caught what on a chalkboard outside the motel office door. Its motel-style rooms are spare but fishermen who are rising at 5 AM to catch the big one don't mind; they grab coffee and fruit in the office and return in the afternoon triumphant, with fish to barbecue out back. And if they come up empty-handed, they can eat locally caught flounder and tuna across the street at the venerable Island House Restaurant. Upcoming renovations promise improved facilities, and a nearby property offers two-bedroom apartments and a five-suite house with shared kitchen for larger groups. Rooms $65–94, efficiencies $75–110, apartments $139–170, suites $99–120.

❋ Where to Eat

Cape Charles

Ɏ ὅ **Aqua** (757-331-8660; www.bay creekresort.com/dining/aqua.asp), 900 Marina Village Circle. Enjoy sunset views over the Chesapeake Bay from the spacious deck where guests gather for drinks. Upscale but not stuffy, Aqua is popular among locals and is a center of activity in the relatively new Bay Creek development. Its chef-driven menu uses locally grown produce and honors local seafood with fun presentations such as crab lollipops with mango chutney and chipotle aioli, and Thai fried shrimp with sweet chili sauce, lime, and cilantro, along with fried clam cakes, an Eastern Shore specialty. $14–27.

The Cape Charles Coffee House (757-331-1880; www.capecharles coffeehouse.com), 241 Mason Avenue. At one time, this abandoned 1910 building had trees growing inside it. After restoration, the place became a two-story gathering spot for locals and visitors alike. An art gallery upstairs showcases regional artists and features renovated tin ceilings. Breakfast includes in-house sweets by baker Roberta Romeo—get there early for her scones, as they'll sell out, and return for really quality cakes with such trimmings as Italian butter-cream. Lunch offerings, which they'll pack picnic style if you like, include sandwiches, salads, and soups. $3–14.

Rayfield's Pharmacy (757-331-1212), 2 Fig Street, is part pharmacy, part diner, and you're just as likely to hear local gossip at the counter as you are to get two eggs over easy.

Chincoteague

Bill's Prime Seafood and Steaks (757-336-5831; www.billsseafood restaurant.com 4040 Main Street.

WELK SHELLS ON CEDAR ISLAND

Virginia Myers

Open year-round for breakfast, lunch, and dinner. This cozy, comfortable spot overlooks downtown Chincoteague. The extensive menu of local seafood, steaks, and pasta also includes homemade desserts. $18–32.

✔ **The Island Creamery** (757-336-6236; www.islandcreamery.net), 6243 Maddox Boulevard. A great place for ice cream, the Island Creamery serves fresh-baked waffle cones. The eatery has an expansive porch overlooking the road to the beach.

Main Street Shop and Coffeehouse (757-336-6782), 4288 Main Street. Open daily in summer, weekends in fall and spring. Closed winter. The café mixes fair trade, shade-grown coffee and sweets with art and fine housewares in a converted Arts and Crafts home. The glassed-in porch and outside patio are especially pleasant, but so is wandering through rooms of local paintings, photography, and pottery, artful clothing, kitchen gadgets, tea towels, and the like. Food $2–8.

✔ **Mr. Whippy** (757-336-5122), 6201 Maddox Boulevard, serves classic soft-style ice cream.

✔ **Muller's Ice Cream Parlour** (757-336-5894; www.chincoteague chamber.com, 4032 Main Street. The place scoops up homemade ice cream in myriad combinations, including signature Belgian waffles with peaches and ice cream, in a historic Victorian home that may or may not host a resident ghost. You can sit in the classic ice-cream parlor and take in historic displays, or hang out on the porch where you might see resident chickens scrabble under the shrubs.

🦞 **Sea Star Gourmet Carryout** (757-336-5442), 4121 Main Street.

Open July 4–Labor Day daily, the rest of the year Thu.–Mon. Come here for healthy, hearty sandwiches bursting with sprouts, fresh veggies, and cheese or deli meat combos stuffed into multigrain breads or baguettes. $6–10.

Steamer's (757-336-5300; www.steam ersallyoucaneat.com), 6251 Maddox Boulevard. Open Memorial Day–Labor Day daily 4:30–9:30. Summer crowds flock here for all-you-can-eat crabs, shrimp, fried chicken, or combinations of these and more, plus accompanying sides such as sweet potato biscuits, corn on the cob, clam strips, popcorn shrimp, and corn chowder. If you're not up for all that quantity, you can get combo plates or individual entrées including all manner of seafood, beef, chicken, and pasta and cut-rate kids' portions, and still leave stuffed to the gills. Entrées $10, "market price" $28–40.

The Village (757-336-5120), 6576 Maddox Boulevard. Open year-round except a few weeks in winter; call ahead. This family-run restaurant is owned by a former waterman who has connections to the freshest seafood on the island. The seafood-stuffed tomato with crab imperial, shrimp, scallops, and cheese is especially popular, and the restaurant specializes in Chincoteague oysters; there's also steak, chicken, and veal. The tables with views over Eel Creek are most pleasant. $18–25.

🦞 **Woody's Beach BBQ** (www.woodys beachbbq.com), 6700 Maddox Boulevard at the traffic circle. Open summer. The eatery serves up generous, creative sandwiches, ribs, smoked chicken, and more, incorporating a retro-but-hip barbecue theme from a food wagon set in a retro-surf camp-style parking lot/park. You can go for such combinations as chicken with pulled pork, bacon jam, and coleslaw; pulled pork topped with onion rings; seafood such as the crab roll, fashioned after New England's lobster roll but made locally; or more conventional buckets of really good fried chicken or racks of ribs with unusual sides (cheddar-bacon mashed potatoes, gingered applesauce, sweet potato fries). While you're waiting, you can play tetherball, hang out on benches made from surfboards, or admire the funky driftwood art. $6–10.

Onancock

♀ **Bizzotto's Gallery-Caffe** (757-787-3103; http://bizzottos.esva.net), 41 Market Street. This sophisticated, artsy bar and restaurant is run by the creative Miguel Bizzotto, one of the first artists to discover Onancock's charms in the 1980s. Along with a full menu of everything from crab cakes with roasted sweet potatoes and chipotle aioli and scallops with risotto, to rack of lamb and duck, the place displays Bizzotto's fine leather bags and work from other local artists. $18–25.

♀ **The Blarney Stone Pub** (757-302-0300; www.blarneystonepubon ancock.com), 10 North Street. The pub combines an Irish menu with bangers and mash or shepherd's pie with bar food, 12 beers on tap, and live Irish dancing and music. $8–24.

Mallards at the Wharf (757-787-8558; http://mallardsllc.com), 2 Market Street. Open for lunch 11:30–4, dinner 5–late. The restaurant combines waterfront views with an upbeat approach to dining from professionally trained chef Johnny Mo. The menu covers seafood such as sushi-grade

tuna, crab-stuffed grouper, and sea scallops, as well as chicken, beef, and lamb, and salads and sandwiches at lunch. You can eat on the deck in summer and the chef may come out of the kitchen to join the band for live music on weekends. Entrées $22–28.

Outside town limits

Eastville Inn (757-678-5745; www .eastvilleinn.com), 16422 Courthouse Road, Eastville. Blessedly off-the-beaten-path in tiny Eastville, a historic town dating back to the 1600s, this inn's chef honors the locally grown tradition. That includes local wines, locally roasted coffee, and organic Mattawoman produce. Specials are labeled by farm: Shockley Farms sweet corn, H. M. Arnold softshell crabs, and Pickett's Harbor Farm petite summer squash and zucchini; the menu emphasizes seafood such as oysters, scallops, and crab. $14–25.

Exmore Diner (757-442-2313; http://exmorediner.com), 4264 Main Street, This eatery is a blast from the past, with an old-fashioned diner menu, bottomless coffee mugs, and friendly regulars chatting it up at the counter. Transported to tiny Exmore in 1954, it's still run by locals, and the son of its original owner is among the customers at the counter. $5–15.

Great Machipongo Clam Shack (757-442-3800; www.greatclams.com), 6468 Lankford Highway (US 13), Nassawadox. Come for the great selection of local seafood, especially the incredibly tasty clam chowder, Eastern Shore style—in a clear broth that brings out the flavor of the shallow waters around the shore. The specialty is a twist on crab cakes that combines crab, fish, shrimp, and scallops; sweet potato fries are sprinkled with cinnamon and sugar; and the hush puppies are especially delicious. Everything is served in plastic baskets lined with paper, so don't expect a lot of sophisticated sauces and presentations. Vintage photos and fishermen and boats, fish identification charts, boat builder drawings, and locally influenced bumper stickers ("We're rural, not stupid" is a favorite) keep the place grounded with a sense of place. The seafood market in the back features rows of freezers full of everything from alligator tail and crawfish to sea scallops and clam strips, plus prepared fish fillets and chowders ready to cook or reheat. $10–25.

Island House Restaurant (757-787-4242; www.wachapreague.com /islandhouse/index.html), 17 Atlantic Avenue, Wachapreague. Open Apr.– May 31 Tue.–Sun. 11–9, June–Aug. 31 daily 11–9. The restaurant has the best view of the barrier islands. The original Island House Hotel was located on one of the biggest, Cedar Island. The current restaurant was modeled after the Parramore Island Lifesaving Station, with a post-and-beam construction and a lookout tower. On the walls and hanging from the ceiling you'll see not the ubiquitous fishing nets of other seafood restaurants, but small boat hulls and strings of antique duck decoys. The best-known restaurant in Wachapreague, "Flounder Capital of the World," the Island House caters to fishermen and will cook your own catch three different ways, if you like. The steamed clams are heavenly, and the tuna steaks come highly recommended, cooked rare. $10–20.

Machipongo Trading Company (757-678-0005; http://esvamtc.com), across from the Barrier Island Center in Machipongo. This fun and funky shop focuses on selling locally produced goods such as Eastern

EXMORE DINER

Virginia Myers

Shore wines and coffee roasted by parent company Eastern Shore Coastal Roasting Company, and serving up breakfast and lunch with bagels, pastries, sandwiches, wraps, and baked goods. You'll find local art here, too. $4–12.

Sting-Ray's Restaurant (757-331-2505; http://cape-center.com), 26507 Lankford Highway (US 13), Cape Charles. The place looks like a conventional gas station, but hidden behind the tchochkes in the gift shop is a full restaurant serving breakfast, lunch, and dinner to locals and travelers in the know. You can have such diner fare as "hamburger steak, well-done" with fried onions and gravy, pulled pork with Sting-Ray's signature sauce, or shore specialties such as deep-fried crab cakes and flounder. Desserts are especially tempting:

sweet potato pie with local potatoes and damson plum sauce, Southern pecan pie, and apple dumpling with caramel sauce among them. Dinner entrées $8–27.

✳ Entertainment

North Street Playhouse (757-787-2050; 1-866-70-DRAMA; www.north streetplayhouse.org), 34 Market Street, Onancock. The Eastern Shore's only regularly producing theater company offers locally acted, directed, and produced classic comedies, drama, staged readings, and workshop productions.

The Palace Theater (757-331-2787; www.artsentercapecharles.org), 305 Mason Avenue, Cape Charles. The theater stages locally produced and touring plays as well as dance and music performances in a historic 1941

CRAB TRAPS

Virginia Myers

art deco building that doubles as a community art center. Exhibits are ongoing, and arts education—dance classes, lectures, and watercolor workshops—keeps the building busy.

✳ Selective Shopping

Blue Crab Bay Company (1-800-221-2722; www.bluecrabbay.com), 29368 Atlantic Drive, Melfa. The company specializes in regional gifts of food, art, and interesting housewares, and has hit a niche with baskets of signature products such as seafood seasoning, spiced peanuts, bloody mary mix, and crab soup. Mail order is a big part of the business as well.

Blue Crow Antique Mall (757-442-4150), 32124 Lankford Highway (US 13), Keller. Open Mon.–Sat. 10–5, Sun. 12–5. More than 250 antique dealers share 35,000 square feet of space, selling collectibles, furniture, china, and jewelry.

Crockett Gallery (757-787-2288; www.williecrockett.com), 39 Market Street, Onancock. This gallery showcases the paintings of Tangier Island native Willie Crockett, who captures the natural allure of the area beautifully in seaside landscapes.

Egret Moon Artworks (757-336-5775), 4044 Main Street, Chincoteague, stands out among the many good art shops and galleries in Chincoteague as a quirky, fun, fantasy spot steeped in mermaid energy by owner/artist Megan McCook. The pottery, jewelry, paintings, woodwork, fabric, and knickknacks for sale here are quirky, beautiful, and fun. During the Second Saturdays Art Strolls, McCook will help you can create a

crown so you can play queen for the day.

Red Queen Gallery Onancock (757-787-4040; www.redqueen gallery.com), 57 Market Street, Onancock, features an eclectic, sometimes funky collection of local art.

gardenART on King Street (757-787-8818; www.gardenartonking .com), 44 King Street, Onancock. Open Apr.—Sept. 10–5:30 Tue.–Sat., Sun. 12–4. The shop mixes local art with home accents and gifts, garden supplies, and inspiration, including a courtyard of bedding plants, trees, shrubs, and specialty orchids. Owner Joani Donohoe was a professional gardener for years, and now enjoys greeting guests with the shop's mascot, Lulu, a friendly Portuguese water dog, especially during "yappy hour," when well-behaved pups are welcomed, each second Friday.

((ᵍ)) **Sundial Books** (757-336-5825; www.sundialbooks.net), 4065 Main Street, Chincoteague. A cultural center for this little town, this shop sells new and used books as well as music CDs and art. There's space to sit and read or use free Wi-Fi. You can sip a cup of coffee while you browse. Live music and book signings are scheduled regularly.

Windsor House (757-331-4848; http://lewinwindsorhouse.com), US 13 and Capeville Road, Capeville. Open Thu.–Mon. This restored Victorian home is filled with antique furniture and other items, plus local folk art like decoys and handwoven baskets. The place also houses the workshop where Kurt and Sally Lewin craft Windsor chairs.

Virginia Myers

BARRIER ISLAND DUNES

✳ Special Events

April–December: Every second Saturday, **Art Stroll** showcases artsy shops and galleries and features live music, book signings, wine tastings, and other activities throughout downtown Chincoteague.

May–December: **Second Fridays** mix local art openings with craft demonstrations, wine tastings, restaurant discounts, and a generally festive mood every second Friday of the month in historic Onancock.

July: **Pony Swim and Auction** occurs in Chincoteague the last consecutive Wednesday and Thursday of July, when wild ponies from

Assateague Island are herded across the channel by "saltwater cowboys" who then auction off the foals to benefit the volunteer fire department. Spectators line up along the shore and in kayaks and boats in the water to watch the spectacle. The **Chincoteague Volunteer Fireman's Carnival** precedes the event for the entire month of July on weekends, with carnival rides and a food hall with fried oyster sandwiches among other fresh-prepared items. (See "Ponying Up in Chincoteague" sidebar.)

August: **Annual Fish Fry** in Wachapreague in late August features the town's best asset: seafood. The **Annual Tuna Tournament** is also in August.

October: **Oyster Festival** brings crowds back to Chincoteague on the Saturday of Columbus Day weekend for oysters cooked every which way, along with crabs, clam fritters, and hot dogs. Tickets are available through the Chincoteague Chamber of Commerce. **The Eastern Shore Harvest Fest**, on the first Wednesday in October in Cape Charles, serves up regional specialties such as seafood, Hayman sweet potatoes, crab, and chicken.

November: **Waterfowl Weekend** in Chincoteague celebrates migratory birds, opening all 7 miles of the wildlife refuge to vehicles and hosting guided walks.

Northern Virginia 3

NORTHERN VIRGINIA

While northern Virginia is shaped by its proximity to Washington, D.C., and the rich history of the nation's capital, it is also a distinct area, with unique ethnic communities, urban villages of young professionals, and in its farther reaches, rolling countryside with vineyards and horse farms and views of the not-so-distant Blue Ridge Mountains.

Close to the city, such communities as Arlington, Alexandria, and Fairfax County are most influenced by the urban population that works and plays in Washington and its suburbs. Farther out, towns such as McLean and Vienna, in many ways bedroom communities for Washington, have a bit more of a country feel. By the time you get to Manassas, Culpeper, and certainly Fredericksburg, the urban flavor begins to drop away, but not entirely—these communities still house many commuters, and cater to city dwellers on mini-holiday, anxious for a breath of fresh air away from Washington's beltway.

Perhaps D.C.'s influence is felt most significantly in Arlington, where the monuments of the Capital spill over the river at such moving sites as Arlington National Cemetery, the Women in Military Service for America Memorial, and the Iwo Jima Memorial. An entire island in the Potomac River is devoted to Theodore Roosevelt's legacy of national parks, with trails and a plaza that features an oversize statue of the former president; the more recent Pentagon Memorial is a moving tribute to those who lost their lives on September 11, 2001. And for visitors focused on Washington, D.C., the views of the city from some Arlington hotels can be spectacular.

The region's rich colonial history is evident in Alexandria, also close to D.C. Its cobblestone and brick streets and sidewalks are lined with historic homes and shops dating back to the days when this country's founding fathers danced in its taverns and prayed in its churches. Tours can illuminate some of the most outstanding properties, but just strolling the streets is enough to conjure up the white wigs, rustling petticoats, and buckled shoes of the 18th century. Costumed guides in many museums, and the opportunity to dance at Gadsby's Tavern or dine on colonial fare, lend more life to the area. And at Mount Vernon, George Washington's beloved estate, visitors can see demonstrations of colonial farm crafts, or visit the well-tended gardens for a close-up glimpse of what life in the 1700s might have been like on a day-to-day basis.

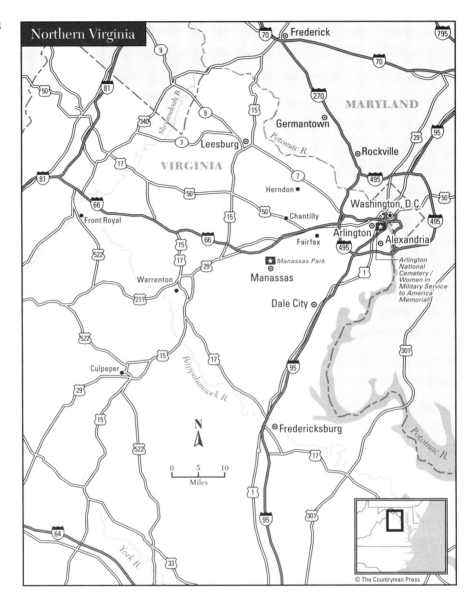

The waterfront still recalls colonial commerce, but also shows more recent history at the Torpedo Factory: Once used to build World War II munitions, it was revived in the 1970s as an artists' colony, renovated in the 1980s, and currently houses studios and galleries plus classroom space—and a remnant torpedo.

History extends itself further into northern Virginia in those areas that saw heavy fighting during the Civil War beginning, quite literally, with the war's first battle, the Battle of Bull Run, in Manassas. Here, an entire park is devoted to

Civil War history. Culpeper, farther south and west, has no fewer than 20 Civil War sites to visit, along with its museum. Fredericksburg and Spotsylvania County are full of battlefields with visitor centers and museums displaying collections of artifacts from the soldiers who fought for both the Blue and the Gray. Civil War walking and driving tours are outlined throughout this region of the state.

Although not quite an urban hub, northern Virginia is heavily influenced by the sophistication of the city, evident in its selection of accommodations and restaurants, art galleries, and shopping options, especially in Arlington and Alexandria. A significant population of immigrants and other residents from abroad, including diplomats serving in embassies, flavor of the area with authentic ethnic cuisine in area restaurants, from Salvadoran to Vietnamese, Pakistani to Burmese. These international transplants have created a thriving arts community that is shared by American artists to create a broad palette of styles. In Arlington, the Signature Theatre has garnered national attention for the performing arts; Wolf Trap National Park for the Performing Arts in Vienna hosts national and international musicians, actors, and dancers in a spacious outdoor amphitheater as well as its smaller, indoor "Barns." Smaller companies such as the highly innovative Synetic Theater, Teatro de la Luna, the Hesperus collective for historic music, and modern dance companies Jane Franklin Dance and Bowen McCauley, give notice that northern Virginia is very much a living community of performing artists responding to modern challenges and themes.

OLD TOWN FREDERICKSBURG
Fredericksburg Area Tourism

For outdoor enthusiasts, there are opportunities to explore right on the Potomac River at Great Falls Park, a popular rock-climbing destination. Easy hiking trails afford breathtaking views of the rugged falls for those who prefer horizontal treks to vertical challenges. For whitewater adventure, kayakers paddle the Potomac and, farther south, the Rappahannock.

As visitors travel south and west in northern Virginia, the countryside opens up first to Piedmont, then mountains. More than 50 wineries dot the landscape here, and most of them are open to visitors for tastings, tours, and festivals. Quaint towns such as Lees-burg and Middleburg and, on the southern end of this region, Fredericksburg, offer historic sites, antique shops, small restaurants, and big country vistas.

GUIDANCE Information is listed by area:

Alexandria Visitor Center (703-746-3301; 1-800-388-9119; htp://visitalexandria va.com), 221 King Street, is located in the historic Ramsay House, built in 1724 and named for one of the city's founding fathers. Scores of brochures for muse-ums and historical sites are available, and the staff is knowledgeable, as most of them have lived in the area for years. Out-of-town visitors can get free parking "proclamations" good for 24 hours, a boon in the tight Old Town area where parking is otherwise limited.

Arlington Convention and Visitors Service (1-800-677-6267; www.stayarling ton.com) will guide you to Arlington's monuments as well as its eight "urban vil-lages," where restaurants and shops mix with residential buildings.

Culpeper County Chamber of Commerce and Visitor Center (540-825-8628; 1-888-285-7373; www.culpepervachamber.com), 109 South Commerce Street.

Fairfax County Visitors Centers (703-550-2450; 1-800-7-FAIRFAX; www.fxva .com), Lorton off I-95 or inside Tysons Corner Center.

Fredericksburg Visitor Center (540-373-1776; 1-800-678-4748; www.visitfred .com), 706 Caroline Street, offers several walking tours, including historic neigh-borhoods and African American sites.

Manassas Visitor Center (703-361-6599; www.visitmanassas.org), 9431 West Street, Manassas, in a historic 1914 train depot.

Prince William County Visitor Center (703-491-4045; www.visitpwc.com), 200 Mill Street, Occoquan; or Prince William County/Manassas Convention and Visitors Bureau (703-396-7130; 1-800-432-1792), 10611 Balls Ford Road, Man-assas.

Spotsylvania County Visitor Center (540-891-8687; 1-877-515-6197; www .spotsylvania.org), 4704 Southpoint Parkway, Fredericksburg, is worth a stop for maps as well as brochures and discount touring tickets.

GETTING THERE *By air:* Northern Virginia is considered part of the Wash-ington Metro area, and is served by two major airports: **Reagan National** (703-417-8000; www.metwashairports.com), which is closest to Washington, Alexandria, and Arlington; and **Dulles International** (703-572-2700; www .metwashairports.com), in Chantilly, 26 miles from Washington. **Baltimore Washington International Thurgood Marshall Airport** (1-800-I-FLY-BWI; www.bwiairport.com) is also used for the area.

By bus: **Greyhound buses** (1-800-231-2222; www.greyhound.com) serve Wash-ington, D.C., just across the Potomac River from northern Virginia, and a num-ber of New York–to–Washington buses provide cheap transport between the two cities, such as **Vamoose** (212-695-6766; 301-718-0036; wwwvamoosebus.com) and **Bolt Bus** (1-877-BOLTBUS; 1-877-265-8287; www.boltbus.com),

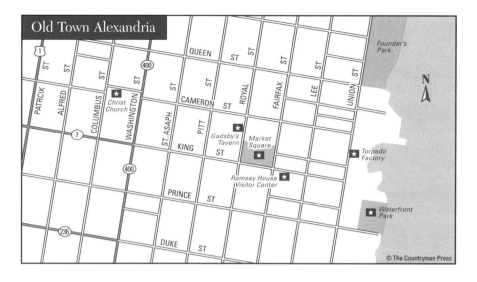

By car: Northern Virginia lies along the I-95 corridor and west; if you are visiting Arlington, Alexandria, Great Falls, Falls Church, or Fairfax, you'll probably also be near the Capital Beltway (I-495, which encircles Washington, D.C.). If you're moving west, the major routes include I-66 and US 29.

GETTING AROUND In Arlington, Alexandria, and as far out as Falls Church and Vienna, Metro subway trains and buses are generally the best way to go. The monuments (Arlington Cemetery, the Pentagon Memorial, and so on) are right near Metro train stops, as are Arlington neighborhoods; Alexandria has four Metro stops and the free King Street Trolley that runs the mile and a half from the Metro station through Old Town to the waterfront, with frequent stops. The Alexandria Convention and Visitors Association (703-746-3301; 1-800-388-9119; www.visitalexandriava.com) has complete information on transportation, or visit the Washington Metropolitan Area Transit Authority's virtual trip planner (www.wmata.com).

PARKING can be tight in Arlington and Alexandria; be prepared with quarters to pay meters on the street, or look for a parking garage. Meter rates and parking garages vary. In other towns in northern Virginia, parking is not as much of an issue.

WHEN TO COME The areas of northern Virginia closest to Washington, D.C., follow the tourist schedule there: Spring and summer are the most popular times to visit, and the most crowded. Outdoor concerts are numerous, and street musicians playing at Metro stations and along the waterfront in Alexandria are warm-weather treats. But attractions are generally open year-round, and there are plenty of cozy pubs and restaurants to visit the rest of the year. The December holidays are especially bright in Alexandria and at Mount Vernon, George Washington's estate: both are gussied up with decorations and there are candlelight tours as well.

✳ To See

MUSEUMS

Alexandria and Arlington

& **Alexandria Archeology Museum** (703-838-4399; http://oha.alexandriava .gov/archaeology), 105 North Union Street, in the Torpedo Factory, Alexandria. Open Tue.–Fri. 10–3, Sat. 10–5, Sun. 1–5. Closed major holidays. This living museum features archaeologists still at work unearthing Alexandria's considerable history, which includes not only the colonial period and 19th century but also pre-Columbian Native American culture. Call to find out when archaeologists will be working, or for information about hands-on activities. Free.

& **Carlyle House** (703-549-2997; www.nvrpa.org), 121 North Fairfax Street, Alexandria. Open for tours only, with guided tours on the hour Tue.–Sat. 10–4, Sun. 12–4. The only 18th-century Palladian-style stone house remaining in Alexandria was built in 1753 by a British merchant, John Carlyle, considered one of the city's founding fathers. Visitors are led through rooms where pre–Revolutionary War life is re-created, and you can see original nails, plaster, and stone where construction is exposed. One room tells the story of British general Braddock's meeting with colonial governors to plan the French and Indian War. $5.

& **Drug Enforcement Administration Museum and Visitor Center** (202-307-3463; www.deamuseum.org), 700 Army Navy Drive, Arlington. Open Tue.–Fri. 10–4. Starting with the opium dens of the late 19th century, and taking visitors through early drug regulation, the resurgence of drug use in the 1960s, the rise of cocaine and crack, and the abuse of prescription drugs, this museum covers the history of drug use and enforcement with interactive exhibits and displays of everything from vintage pharmaceuticals to weapons used by DEA agents and vivid depictions of individuals lost to drug abuse. Free admission.

& **Gadsby's Tavern Museum** (703-838-4242; www.gadsbystavern.org), 134 North Royal Street, Alexandria. Open Apr.–Oct. Tue.–Sat. 10–5, Sun.–Mon. 1–5; Nov.–Mar. Wed.–Sat. 11–4, Sun. 1–4. Guided tours at quarter before and quarter past the hour; last tours 4:45 in summer, 3:45 in winter. Although there were once some 50 taverns in 18th-century Alexandria, Gadsby's is the only one still reflective of its original use. Rooms are re-created to show where visitors would have eaten (and what—tables are spread with duck and oysters and other typical fare), where they would have gathered for an indoor market (imagine such entertainments as tightrope walking, and such services as those provided by a traveling dentist), and where they would have danced and slept (several men to a mattress). The tavern hosted many of the country's founding fathers, including George Washington, and annual events include reenactments of Thomas Jefferson's inaugural celebration and George Washington's Birthnight Ball. A separate restaurant (www.gadsbystavernrestaurant.com), also in the historic building, serves colonial and modern American fare. Museum, $5 adults, $3 ages 5–12, free for under age 5 with a paying adult.

Lee-Fendall House Museum and Garden (703-548-1789; www.leefendall house.org), 614 Oronoco Street, Alexandria. Open Wed.–Sat. 10–4, Sun. 1–4; call ahead, as the house is sometimes closed for private events. Guided tours begin on the hour, last tour begins at 3. Built in the late 18th century, this was home to the Lee family for more than 100 years: That would the family of Revolutionary War general "Light-Horse Harry" Lee, father of Confederate general Robert E. Lee. Now restored to the Victorian era, it is a study in 19th-century family life, with Lee family heirlooms and furniture created in the style of the 1850–70 period. $5 adults, $3 students 11–17, free age 11 or under.

& **The Lyceum, Alexandria's History Museum** (703-838-4994; http://oha .alexandriava.gov/lyceum), 201 South Washington Street, Alexandria. Open Mon.–Sat. 10–5, Sun. 1–5. Closed major holidays. Built in 1839 as a community center and library, the impressive columns of this Greek Revival building tower over the entrance to a chronological tribute to the City of Alexandria, from Paleo-Indians to Captain John Smith's first visit through colonial times, the Civil War, and up to the present day. The collection includes old photographs, artifacts such as the Jones Point Lighthouse lens, war uniforms and a musket, and a reproduction of a Georgian-style parlor. The building still serves the community with school programs, lectures, and concerts. $2.

GADSBY'S TAVERN MUSEUM

Virginia Myers

Manassas area

Freedom Museum (703-393-0660; http://freedommuseum.org), 10400 Terminal Road, at the Manassas Regional Airport. Open 10–4 daily. An outdoor display of military vehicles supplements a collection of memorabilia, photography, artifacts, and interactive displays illustrating the wars of the 20th century.

Manassas Museum (703-368-1873; http://manassasmuseum.org), 9101 Prince William Street, Manassas. Open Tue.–Sun. 10–5, Artifacts, exhibits, documents, photographs, and videos describe the area's history, focusing not only on the Civil War but also on daily life. Visitors will see weapons and uniforms, as well as 19th- and 20th-century toys and clothing, quilts, furniture, and store signs. $5 adults, $4 seniors and children, free for children under 6.

& **National Museum of the Marine Corps** (877-635-1775; www.usmcmuseum .org), 18900 Jefferson Davis Highway, Triangle. Open daily 9–5. Interactive exhibits and two centuries' worth of artifacts, from uniforms to medals, weapons, vehicles and aircraft to works of art, bring to life the marine experience. Especially moving is the flag raised at Iwo Jima and memorialized in the famous AP photograph, then in a memorial statue in Arlington. Separate galleries explore the two world wars, Korean War, and Vietnam War, and the temporary exhibits cover more recent warfare. Free admission.

Fredericksburg and Spotsylvania County

Fredericksburg Area Museum (540-371-3037; www.famcc.org), 907 Princess Anne Street. Open daily noon–5. The 1927 Planter's Bank Building and the 1816 Town Hall combine to offer permanent and temporary exhibits highlighting 18th- and 19th-century arts and crafts (e.g., masonry, carpentry, cabinetry, ironwork, and silver smithing); items from George Washington's life; personalized objects such as diaries, letters, and uniforms from the Revolutionary, Civil, and world wars; and accounts of Fredericksburg's Algonquian Indian history, the town's early reliance on the Rappahannock River, and the influence of railways. Every second Saturday of the month from 1 to 3 PM, family programs offer hands-on activities and make-and-take crafts, with varying themes. $7 adults, $2 students with ID, free for age 6 and under.

& **James Monroe Museum and Memorial Library** (540-654-1043; www .umw.edu/jamesmonroemuseum), 908 Charles Street. Open Mon.–Sat. 10–5, Sun. 1–5, Dec.–Feb. closes at 4 PM. James Monroe, the fifth president of the United States, practiced law in Fredericksburg for many years. This museum, renovated in 2009, showcases his life with some 1,600 items, including furnishings, personal items, costumes, and memorabilia. Of particular interest is the desk at which Monroe wrote the Monroe Doctrine; the jewels that belonged to his wife, Elizabeth, are also on display. The associated archives boast more than 10,000 documents, and the library holds more than 3,000 volumes of rare and historic books. $5 adults, $1 children.

White Oak Civil War Museum and Research Center (540-371-4234), 985 White Oak Road, Falmouth. Open Wed.–Sun. 10–5. You can imagine life as a Civil War soldier when you see the hand-dug replicas of the huts they built for themselves in winter, along with thousands of artifacts left behind by Union and Confederate soldiers, and later found in the area. $4 adults, $2 seniors and students, free for children under 7.

HISTORIC SITES

Alexandria

✿ ❀ **Alexandria Waterfront** The historic center of commercial activity for this seaport town, Alexandria's Potomac River waterfront now includes a number of parks. At the City Marina, a public plaza faces docks populated by private and tour boats, with the Pyramid Atlantic art center and food court plus the Chart House seafood restaurant nearby. Founders Park, a short stroll away, is a grassy expanse where dog walkers tend to gather. Other nearby green spots along the water are King Street Park and Waterfront Park, Point Lumley, Shipyard Park, and the 65-acre Jones Point Park, which includes a community garden and the historic Jones Point Lighthouse.

Christ Church (703-549-1450; www.historicchristchurch.org), 118 North Washington Street. Open daily. Built by John Carlyle in 1773, this Georgian-style building was the first Episcopal church in Alexandria, and was frequented by George Washington and Robert E. Lee, among other historical figures. It is an active parish that combines current worship and ministry with a reverence for the church's history; trained docents from the congregation lead tours three days a week, and services are held every Sunday. Call for times.

Market Square 301 King Street, a wide-open space for outdoor concerts, festivals, demonstrations, and public addresses, is thought to be the site of the oldest farmers' market in the country. Situated outside City Hall, it is a gathering place for locals and tourists alike. The Farmers' Market—which once included produce from George Washington's Mount Vernon farm—now runs every Saturday morning, year-round, 5 AM–10:30 AM. Free parking in the Market Square garage during market hours.

& **Torpedo Factory** (703-838-4565; www.torpedofactory.org), 105 North Union Street. Open daily 10–6; second Thu. of every month, 10–9; closes an hour early when rented for a private event, so check the Web site before your visit. From the time it was built in 1918, the Torpedo Factory manufactured and maintained torpedoes and stored munitions, at one point during World War II men and women worked there round the clock to produce submarine torpedoes. A Mark XIV torpedo, built in 1945, is displayed in the main hall—it is bright green so navy soldiers could find it after it was tested. An exhibit case tells the story of its history, and in the back hall a silver torpedo provides an example of torpedoes that were dropped from planes. After 1945, factory activity screeched to a halt and the factory became a storage facility for everything from Smithsonian dinosaur bones to government documents and German war films. The warehouse-like building was turned into an art center in the 1970s and renovated in

TORPEDO FACTORY, ALEXANDRIA
Courtesy of the Torpedo Factory Art Center

the 1980s; it currently hosts 160 artists in a beehive of studios and galleries. A comprehensive schedule of art classes is open to the public.

Arlington

& **Air Force Memorial** (703-979-0674; www.airforcememorial.org), One Air Force Drive, off Columbia Pike near Hwy. 244. Three simple spires rise elegantly, 270 feet into the sky, to evoke a feeling of flight and to honor those air force soldiers who died in combat.

& **Arlington National Cemetery** (703-607-8000; arlingtoncemetery.mil/), at the end of Memorial Drive. Open Apr.–1—Sept. 30 daily 8–7, Oct. 1–Mar. 31 daily 8–5. Rows of gravestones stitch themselves across rolling green lawns for 200 acres, where more than 300,000 people are buried. The cemetery embraces soldiers from every U.S. military conflict, from the Revolutionary War to the Civil War, the two world wars, Iraq, and Afghanistan. For such a vast expanse, the cemetery instills a great sense of reverence and solemnity for each individual represented here; inspirational words are carved in various stone memorials and even the most reluctant patriot will stir when the strains of "America" come across the property, or guns are shot to mark the most recent funeral. This is very much a place of the present as well as the past; funerals are held every weekday, and average 28 per day.

Special spots to visit include the **Tomb of the Unknown Soldier**, a moving tribute to the many soldiers who died unidentified. Despite crowds of onlookers, the only sound here is the click of the guard's spit-polished shoes as he turns at the end of his short march along the length of the tomb, which holds the

ARLINGTON NATIONAL CEMETERY

Virginia Myers

remains of three unknown soldiers but represents so much more. The tomb is guarded 24/7. You can also see the burial spot of **John F. Kennedy**, with its eternal flame, and the simple white crosses marking the graves of his brothers, Robert and Edward. There is a grave for the remains of the seven astronauts who died aboard the space shuttle *Challenger,* and the graves of explorer Rear Admiral Robert E. Peary, boxer Joe Louis, and other U.S. luminaries such as William Howard Taft, William Jennings Bryan, and Oliver Wendell Holmes. Free admission to the Visitor's Center and cemetery; audio tours available. Parking costs $1.75/hour for the first three hours, $3.50/hour each hour thereafter. A 40-minute tour bus trip costs $7.50 and stops at major sites along the way.

& **Marine Corps War Memorial/Iwo Jima Memorial** (703-289-2500; www .nps.gov), Marshall Drive between US 50 and Arlington National Cemetery. The iconic depiction of the capture of Iwo Jima during World War II, with its five marines and one navy corpsman raising the flag, has become an American landmark. Sculpted by Felix W. de Weldon after a photo by newsman Joe Rosenthal, it honors not just World War II veterans, but all marines. On Tuesdays from June through mid-August, the U.S. Marine Drum and Bugle Corps and the Marine Corps Silent Drill Platoon present an hourlong sunset parade at 7 PM.

& **Pentagon Memorial** (www.pentagonmemorial.net), 1 Rotary Road, on the Pentagon Reservation. Limited parking; take Metro to Pentagon Metro Stop. Open 24/7. This elegant memorial, just outside the Pentagon itself, honors the 184 people who died here when terrorists crashed an airplane into the building on September 11, 2001. You can still see where the plane hit, as the stone that repaired the damage is a slight differently color than the original. The memorial is a collection of simple cantilevered benches, one for each victim, rising from the gravel surface. Those facing the Pentagon represent the people who died on the plane (so that viewers will read their names on the end of the bench and look beyond to the sky); those facing away, the people working in the building. Lighted fountains run under each bench, creating a contemplative mood, and trees are planted as if to signify ongoing life. "We claim this ground in remembrance of the events of September 11, 2001," states the engraved proclamation. "We will never forget." Indeed, anyone alive on that day will come here, see these individual commemorations, hear planes that still fly overhead, and remember with a chill.

& **Women in Military Service for America Memorial** (703-533-1155; www.womensmemorial.org), near Arlington National Cemetery, at the end of Memorial Drive. Open Oct. 1–Mar. 31 daily 8–5, Apr. 1–Sept. 30 daily 8–7. Dedicated in 1997, this moving memorial pays tribute to all women who have served in the military, from as far back as the Revolutionary War–era women who disguised themselves as men to be able to go to war, all the way through Civil War heroines and World War II Fly Girls, to modern women balancing military duty in Iraq and Afghanistan with motherhood and family at home. The building itself is a monument, a curve of stone carved with inspirational quotes, and a glass roof etched with more. Beneath the roof is a slim display area—narrow to preserve the Arlington Cemetery graves just behind the monument—with permanent and changing exhibits including oral histories on video and an

NORTHERN VIRGINIA'S CIVIL WAR SITES

Arlington House, The Robert E. Lee Memorial (703-235-1530; www.nps.org /arho), in Arlington National Cemetery, at the end of Memorial Drive. Open daily 9:30–4:30, and until 5:30 in summer. Even while undergoing restoration, the Arlington House offers a window on the Lee family's life before the Civil War and during the wrenching time when they were forced to leave their family home. You can see the parlor where Lee proposed to Mary Custis in 1830, and the bedroom where six of their seven children were born. There's also Union soldier graffiti on the top floor. Interestingly, Arlington House was built by George Washington Parke Custis, grandson of Martha Dandridge Custis—who later became Martha Washington. The property was originally Martha's, and her grandson first named the estate Mount Washington after his grandfather; it housed his "Washington treasures"—mementos from George Washington's life. It was Custis's daughter, Mary Anna Randolph Custis, who married Lt. Robert E. Lee. Guided tours include the grounds, with a kitchen garden, flower garden, and slave quarters. By spring 2011, the house should again be furnished in the style of the period. Free admission.

&. **Fredericksburg/Spotsylvania National Military Park** (540-373-6122; www.nps.gov/frsp), Fredericksburg Battlefield Visitor Center, 1013 Lafayette Boulevard; (540-786-2880; www.nps.gov/frsp) Chancellorsville Battlefield Visitor Center, Hwy. 3 West. Open daily 9–5. The Civil War raged through this area and there are four major battlefields to see—Fredericksburg, Chancellorsville, Wilderness, and Spotsylvania Court House. To cover it all, this park stretches more than 8,300 acres. Driving from battlefield to battlefield will put 75 miles on your odometer. You'll learn the most if you take an audiotape driving tour (available at the visitor centers). A good starting point is one of the visitor centers, which offer maps, brochures, and films that help orient you to the history of the region. If you'd rather poke around on your own, there are plenty of interpretive trails, maps, and monuments to discover.

opportunity to register with the memorial, if you are a woman who is or has been a member of the U.S. military. Free admission.

Fredericksburg and Spotsylvania County

Hugh Mercer Apothecary Shop (540-373-3362; www.apva.org/hughmercer apothecary), 1020 Caroline Street. Open Mar.–Oct. Mon.–Sat. 9–4, Sun. noon–4; Nov.–Feb. Mon.–Sat. 10–3, Sun. noon–4. Mary Washington came to Dr. Mercer's Apothecary for remedies that might have included the use of such 18th-century standards as leeches, lancets, snakeroot, crab claws, and silver-plated

Among the highlights: at Chancellorsville, where Robert E. Lee and Stonewall Jackson battled it out against General Joseph Hooker, you'll see where Jackson was mistakenly shot by his own troops (he later died of his wounds). Jackson also made his mark at the Wilderness Battlefield, where his arm was amputated after a wound, then buried.

Historic homes further illuminate Civil War story: **Chatham** (540-654-5121; nps.gov/frsp/chatham.htm), 120 Chatham Lane, Falmouth, open daily 9–4:30, at the Fredericksburg Battlefield, served as Union headquarters and its exhibit includes a pontoon boat like the ones used to cross the Rappahannock during the battle, as well as a film showing the impact the war had on area residents. Free admission. **Ellwood**, at the Wilderness Battlefield, is open on summer weekends.

& **Manassas National Battlefield Park** (703-361-1339; nps.gov/mana), 12521 Lee Highway, Manassas. Visitor Center open daily 8:30–5. This is where the Civil War began: The war's first major battle, known as First Manassas or the Battle of Bull Run, erupted here on July 21, 1861. A mile-long walking tour leads visitors along important sites, describing events on recorded tapes and interpretive signs. You'll see the spot where General Thomas J. Jackson got his nickname, "Stonewall," and where, by battle's end, the rebels routed the entire Union army. More than 900 soldiers died that day. The Battle of Second Manassas, a three-day bloodbath, left 3,300 dead and allowed the Confederacy to take a clear lead in the war. This battle spanned 16 miles; today visitors take a driving tour to see the spots where fighting was most fierce or most strategic. You can see the Stone House, which served as a field hospital; the L. Dogan House, from the old village of Groveton; the Groveton Confederate Cemetery, with its more than 260 soldiers; and memorials to New York regiments. The Visitor Center has a small museum, orientation film, and battle map. The park is open during daylight hours only. Free admission.

pills. Displays also include a rose water "still" and handblown glass apothecary jars. $5 adults, $2 children, free for under age 6.

Kenmore (540-373-3381; http://kenmore.org), 1201 Washington Avenue. Open Mar.–Oct. daily 10–5; Nov.–Dec. 10–4. George Washington's sister, Betty, lived here with her husband, Fielding Lewis, and the home displays an elegant colonial lifestyle, with elaborate plasterwork (by the same craftsman who plastered Mount Vernon) and colorful, patterned wallpapers and paint. Fielding lost his merchant's fortune to the war, but the house remains a testament to fine living in early America. $8 adults, $4 students, free for under age 6.

Mary Washington House (540-373-1569; www.apva.org/marywashingtonhouse), 1200 Charles Street. Open Mar.—Oct. Mon.–Sat. 11–5 and Sun. noon–4; Nov.–Feb. Mon.–Sat. 11–4 and Sun.noon–4. George Washington bought this wood-frame home for his mother, Mary, and she lived here, just down the street from her daughter, Betty, at Kenmore, for 17 years. It is restored with period decorations, including Mary Washington's "best dressing glass" and her sundial, still keeping time in the garden. $5 adults, $2 children, free for under age 6.

Rising Sun Tavern (540-371-1494; www.apva.org/risingsuntavern), 1304 Caroline Street. Open Mar.–Oct. Mon.–Sat. 10–5 and Sun. noon–4; Nov.–Feb. Mon.–Sat. 11–4, Sun. noon–4. Charles Washington, the youngest brother of George, built this tavern around 1760 as his home; in 1792, it became a tavern for Fredericksburg citizens of the late 18th century. Restoration, done in the 1930s, kept the original woodwork, and there's a reconstructed bar cage along with a collection of early American pewter and period furnishings to give the place that tavern feel. Costumed "tavern wenches" complete the lively picture. $5 adults, $2 children, free for under age 6.

Woodlawn Plantation (703-780-4000; http://woodlawn1805.org), 9000 Richmond Highway at the intersection of US 1 and Hwy 235. Open Apr.–Dec. Thu.–Mon. 10–5; last tour begins at 4. Guided tours only. An extension of George Washington's world, and originally part of the Mount Vernon Estate, this was the home he gifted to his step-granddaughter, Eleanor "Nelly" Parke Custis, whom he raised with his wife, Martha; and her husband, Washington's nephew, Lawrence Lewis. A tour includes Washington and Lewis heirlooms, paintings from the Federal period, and a garden planted with 19th-century roses. After Woodlawn was sold, in 1846, Quaker families established a free colony of black

RISING SUN TAVERN WENCH, FREDERICKSBURG

Fredericksburg Area Tourism

and white farmers, a sort of social experiment to prove that slavery was not a requirement for a successful plantation economy. It fell into disrepair until the early 1900s, when it was restored to become the first historic site owned by the National Trust for Historic Preservation. $8.50 adults, $4 ages K–12, discounts for groups of 15 or more, or for combining admission with the Pope-Leighey House.

Mount Vernon area

Frank Lloyd Wright's Pope-Leighey House (703-780-4000; http://pope leighey1940.org), 9000 Richmond Highway at the Woodlawn Plantation (q.v.). Open Apr.–Dec. Thu.–Mon. 10–5, last tour begins at 4. Guided tours only. A classic example of Wright's "Usonian" house, a design approach that eschewed traditional architectural styles in favor of a new respect for environment and an intention to create affordable housing for families. The house was originally built in Falls Church, but was scheduled for demolition when US 66 came through. It was relocated to Woodlawn in1965. $8.50 adults, $4 ages K–12; discounts for groups or combination admission to Woodlawn.

Gari Melchers Home and Studio at Belmont (540-654-1015; www.umw.edu /gari_melchers), 224 Washington Street, Falmouth. Open Thu.–Tue. 10–5. Gary Melchers, a renowned impressionist painter, bought this house in the early 1900s and used it as a working studio and country home. It is restored to how it would have appeared in the 1920s, and includes exhibitions of art from Melcher as well as his contemporaries. The extensive grounds include wooded walking trails and formal gardens. $10 adults, free for students 18 and younger with accompanying, paying adult (limit two; additional students $5 each).

George Washington's Ferry Farm (540-373-3381; http://kenmore.org), 268 Kings Highway, Hwy. 3 at Ferry Road. Open Mar.–Oct. daily 10–5, Nov.–Dec. daily 10–4. George Washington's boyhood home is a sprawling estate where you can see the old icehouse and surveyor's shack, and wander the woods where he learned his first trade. Washington lived here from age six to almost 20, and exhibits at the archaeology lab in the Visitors Center show the process of uncovering his family's history through excavation and interpretation. There are also displays about the farm's role during the Civil War, when Union troops camped here, and exhibits describing Washington's young life (did he really cut down that cherry tree?). $5 adults, $3 students, free for under age 6.

George Washington's Gristmill and Whiskey Distillery (703-780-2000; www.mountvernon.org), 5514 Mount Vernon Memorial Highway, 3 miles west of Mount Vernon Estate. Open Apr.–Oct. 10–5. Built on the site of the original gristmill and distillery, these reproductions show in detail the mechanics of grinding wheat and corn, and making whiskey, providing a fascinating look at Washington's entrepreneurial endeavors. The mill, still driven by the water of a nearby creek, is all wooden gears and enormous mill stones. Costumed interpreters demonstrate its mechanics, and visitors can buy mill-ground cornmeal in the gift shop. The distillery, with its enormous barrels and five copper stills, was once the largest distillery in the United States, producing 11,000 gallons in 1799. $4 adults and seniors, $2 ages 6–11, free for under age 5.

Virginia Myers

GEORGE WASHINGTON'S GRISTMILL

&. **George Washington's Mount Vernon Estate and Gardens** (703-780-2000; www.mountvernon.org), 3200 Mount Vernon Memorial Highway, at the south end of George Washington Memorial Parkway. Mount Vernon open 8 or 9–4 or 5 depending on the season; Donald W. Reynolds Museum and Education Center open 8 or 9–5 or 6. This beautifully run facility is the place to come to understand colonial times and, specifically, the life of the first U.S. president. Of all the colonial homes restored and furnished in the style of the period, this one is especially intriguing, with paint colors matching the then-fashionable verdigris the Washingtons used, the harpsichord granddaughter Nelly played, and intriguing views of the Potomac River from the cupola. Costumed guides tell the stories behind the rooms: where the Marquis de Lafayette stayed, how 677 guests stayed in the house the first year, and how, when George died, Martha left the bedroom she shared with George and kept to the garret.

The **Donald W. Reynolds Museum and Education Center** uses state-of-the-art exhibits in 23 galleries to reveal Washington's life from his early boyhood to his death. Displays take visitors through his years as a surveyor, military leader, farmer and husband; and life-size wax figures, based on modern-day forensic research, show him at different stages of his life. Exhibits are so detailed you'll hear soldiers coughing and moaning in the bunkers of the Revolutionary War. An 18-minute film, *We Fight to Be Free,* immerses visitors in the war with flashing lights, rumbling musket fire, and falling snow. Other films throughout the exhibit halls are produced by the History Channel and peopled with professional actors depicting the many historical figures of the country's earliest years. A hands-on activity room for children presents myriad opportunities to try on colonial culture, with dress-up clothes, art projects, a table set for tea, and a dollhouse reproduction of Mount Vernon.

Washington thought of himself as a farmer first, a general and politician second, and the Mount Vernon Estate shows his commitment to the land. Outbuildings for spinning and laundry, food preparation, and blacksmithing often host demonstrations, and the four-acre Pioneer Farm includes domestic animals, demonstration crops, and a 16-sided treading barn for processing grain. The gardens are legendary, and comprise a pleasure garden, kitchen garden, fruit garden, nursery, and botanical garden where Washington experimented with plants. $15 adults, $14 age 62 and older, $7 ages 6–11, free for under age 5.

& **Gunston Hall** (703-550-9220; www.gunstonhall.org), 10709 Gunston Road (Hwy. 242), Mason Neck. Open daily 9:30–5 except major holidays; guided tours only, offered every half hour 9:30–4:30. Grounds close at 6. An outstanding example of Federal-style architecture, Gunston Hall once belonged to the influential George Mason IV, who ran the 5,500-acre tobacco and corn plantation during the 18th century. Mason was among the framers of the U.S. Constitution, but never signed it because it did not abolish slavery. Exhibits illuminate his life further, but the house is best known for its architectural detail, like the elaborate carvings in the Palladian Room. The grounds include reconstructed outbuildings that house a kitchen, dairy, smokehouse, and laundry. A garden south of the mansion was designed in keeping with the original plans, and includes a 150-year-old boxwood allée and enchanting vistas of Deer Park, along the Potomac

MOUNT VERNON ESTATE

Visit Fairfax

River. $9 adults, $8 age 60 and older, $5, ages 6–18, free for under age 6. $1 discount coupon on Web site.

Other areas of northern Virginia

Belmont Farm Distillery (540-825-3207; www.virginiawhiskey.com), 13490 Cedar Run Road, Culpeper. Open Apr. 1–Dec. 20 Tue.–Sat. 10–5. Watch as home-grown moonshine drips from copper kettles at this living museum. Using a family recipe and corn from their farm, distillers produce Virginia Lightning Whiskey and aged Kopper Kettle Whiskey. Tours begin every 15 minutes; a History Channel and National Geographic video plays in the "informational room," which also includes news articles and artifacts. Whiskey is available for purchase in the gift shop to those age 21 and older. $8.

✍ **Claude Moore Colonial Farm at Turkey Run** (703-442-7557; www.1771 .org), 6310 Georgetown Pike, McLean. Open Apr.–mid-Dec. Wed.–Sun. 10–4:30. Closed July 4 and Thanksgiving Day. An 18th-century tenant farm comes to life with period interpreters going about their chores, planting vegetables, cooking over an open fire, weeding, and harvesting tobacco. Visitors can pitch in to help costumed farmers hoe the fields, card wool, or make hoecake batter. Special events include colonial market fairs, when visitors can try spinning and dipping candles; and workshops in soap making, hearth cooking, and caring for farm animals like cows, pigs, chickens, and geese. $3 adults, $2 ages 3–12 and over 60, discounts for groups; during special events, $5 adults, $2.50 ages 3–12 and over age 60.

Colvin Run Mill Historic Site (703-759-2771; www.fairfaxcounty.gov/parks /crm), 10017 Colvin Run Road (Hwy. 7), Great Falls. Open year-round Wed.–Mon. 11–5; guided tours on the hour. The mill operates Sun. noon–3, conditions permitting. A historic crossroads, this 36-acre park includes a restored 18th-century mill that still grinds corn and wheat (for sale as cornmeal, grits, and whole wheat flour at the General Store). Free admission to park; tours $6 adults, $5 students age 16 and older, $4 under age 16 and over age64.

Graffiti House (540-727-7718; www.brandystationfoundation.com), 19484 Brandy Road, Brandy Station. Open Apr.–Oct. Fri.–Sun. and Mon. on major holidays 11–4; Nov.–Mar. Fri. and Sat. 11–4. Closed major holidays. Believed to have been used as a hospital by both Union and Confederate soldiers, this ca. 1858 building has more than 200 bits of graffiti left by the wounded and those just passing through, including names, drawings, and information recording their regiments. $3.

✍ ♿ **Smithsonian Air and Space Museum Steven F. Udvar-Hazy Center** (703-572-4118; www.nasm.si.edu/museum/udvarhazy), 14390 Air and Space Museum Parkway, Chantilly, at Dulles International Airport. Open daily 10–5:30, and Apr.–Labor Day until 7:30. Part of the largest collection of air and space artifacts in the world, the Udvar-Hazy Center houses the Smithsonian's biggest pieces: hangars full of historic airplanes, space ships, and other artifacts hanging from 10-story-high trusses. Elevated skywalks give visitors an up-close view of different aircraft, from early, experimental flying machines to the Lockheed SR-71 Blackbird, the fastest jet in the world; the famous Boeing B-29 Superfortress

Enola Gay; and the Space Shuttle *Enterprise.* Flight simulators are a fun way to get the feel of flying; equally realistic are the IMAX films, shown on a five-story screen with surround-sound, and the live air traffic at Dulles Airport, just outside the observation tower. Free; fees for films.

The Town of Culpeper is peppered with historic sites, including Civil War battlefields, the old courthouse, and two cemeteries, plus a revitalized Main Street with shops and restaurants. An informative "Driving Tour of Civil War Culpeper" brochure, with maps and historical information on two dozen sites in the area, is available through the Culpeper County Chamber of Commerce and Visitor Center (see "Guidance").

The Town of Manassas was a strategic site during the Civil War, as it was the only railroad connection between Washington, D.C., and the Confederate capital, Richmond. Whoever controlled Manassas, controlled northern Virginia's Piedmont and the rail link to the Shenandoah Valley. Historic markers throughout the city describe the key role it played during the war, and also highlight such buildings as the turn-of-the-century railroad depot, town hall, and opera house. Modern cafés, outdoor dining, antique shops, and art galleries fill the historic downtown area, which is also a designated arts and cultural district. The **Loy E. Harris Pavilion**, at the corner of West and Center streets (703-361-9800; http://harrispavilion.com) is the place for outdoor concerts and children's programs in summer, and ice skating in winter.

The Town of Occoquan (http://ccoquan.com) has a long history as a thriving riverfront town. Captain John Smith passed through in the 1600s, and by the 1700s a tobacco warehouse had been built. The Confederate army camped here, and after the Civil War, the town bustled with commerce and social activity (the first opera house in the area was built here). In the early 20th century, things

SPACE SHUTTLE *ENTERPRISE* AT UDVAR-HAZY CENTER

Visit Fairfax

went downhill: Fire destroyed much of the town in 1919, traffic was routed to US 1, the new railroad bypassed Occoquan, and Hurricane Agnes destroyed much of the town's infrastructure. Restoration has been remarkable, and is recorded on historic plaques throughout town; many old buildings still stand, and legend has it that a great number of them are haunted. Artists' cooperatives and galleries, gift shops, and cafés draw visitors, especially in summer. Crafts shows in spring and fall show off local jewelry, pottery, furniture, clothing, and more.

✳ To Do

BICYCLING Northern Virginia has an extensive network of bike trails, including one of our favorites, the 18-mile **Mount Vernon Trail**, which runs along the Potomac River from Theodore Roosevelt Island to Mount Vernon Estate. This trail passes by the Washington Sailing Marina, National Airport (you can watch planes take off from Gravelly Point), through Dyke Marsh Wildlife Preserve, on to Old Town Alexandria and finally to Mount Vernon Estate, where rolling lawns are a great spot to rest.

Another favorite is the **W&OD Trail**, also known as the Washington and Old Dominion Railroad Regional Park, with its 45 miles of paved bikeway along a flat railroad bed. In Fairfax, the 40-mile Cross County Trail cuts through stream valleys on a north–south route.

Virginia Department of Transportation Office of Public Affairs (804-786-2801; www.virginiadot.org) will send a map, "Bicycling in Virginia," which has an extensive section on northern Virginia. The **Washington Area Bicyclist Associ-**

BIKING IN ALEXANDRIA

Photo by Richard Nowitz

ation (202-518-0524; www.waba.org) offers a dozen different maps, including Arlington, Alexandria, Fairfax County, the Mount Vernon Trail, and Four Mile Run, plus information about riding the Metro, bike laws, and safety. Maps are available online or to order.

Bicycle tours and rentals are available in Alexandria at **Bike and Roll** (703-548-7655; www.bikethesites.com), One Wales Alley, open mid-Mar.–mid-Dec. Sun.–Fri. at 10 AM, Sat. at 9 AM, where you can also buy a tour of Old Town, or the popular Bike and Boat tour, during which visitors bike to Mount Vernon and take the river boat back to Alexandria. Rent for two hours, half day, full day, or overnight; prices for hybrids, cruisers, kids' bikes, tandems, or road or perform-ance bikes run from $10–30 for two hours to $35–80 for overnight. **Washington Sailing Marina** (703-548-9027; www.washingtonsailingmarina.com), One Marina Drive at Daingerfield Island, George Washington Memorial Parkway, Alexandria. Open daily 9–4 (call for winter hours). The marina rents single-speed cruisers right on the Mount Vernon Trail, $8 per hour, $25 per day.

Great Falls Park Mountain Biking (703-285-2965; www.nps.gov/grfa), 9200 Old Dominion Drive, McLean. Open daily 7–dark, Visitor Center and bookstore daily 10–5. Five miles of trails—some wide, dirt carriage roads and others steep, rocky, and narrow—run through this park. Trail maps showing which trails are available and which are off-limits to bikes can be obtained from the Visitors Cen-ter. $3 per person; annual passes available.

BOATING, KAYAKING, AND WATER PARKS For guided tours, **Potomac Paddle Sports** (301-881-2628; www.potomacpaddlesports.com) offers a four-hour flatwater trip setting off from the Virginia side of the river at Columbia Island Marina for a tour of Washington's monuments ($98). Its other tours and classes, flat water and whitewater, take off from the Maryland side of the river, easily accessible from Virginia.

Other tours and boat rentals are available across the river in Washington: **Jacks Boathouse** (202-337-9642), 3500 K Street NW, Georgetown, offers 90-minute tours around Roosevelt Island and near the monuments for $25 per person; rentals are $12 per person, per hour for canoes or kayaks. **Thompson Boat Center** (202-333-9543; www.thompsonboatcenter.com), 2900 Virginia Avenue NW, between Memorial and Key bridges and near the Kennedy Center, has no tours but rents kayaks, canoes, rowing shells, and Sunfish sailboats by the hour or day ($10, $12, $16, and $10/hour, respectively; double kayak $17/hour; double scull $26/hour; see Web site for larger sculls and day rates; Sunfish by the hour only). **Fletcher's Boathouse** (202-244-0461; www.fletcherscove.com), 4940 Canal Road, is nestled into the woods along the C&O Canal and rents kayaks, canoes, or rowboats, as well as bicycles and fishing licenses, tackle, and bait. Sin-gle kayaks are $10 per hour, $28 per day; doubles $17 per hour, $40 per day. Canoes, $12 per hour, $24 per day; rowboats, $12 per hour, $22 per day.

It's exciting to watch the kayaks and canoes from the overlooks at **Great Falls Park** (703-285-2965; www.nps.gov/grfa), 9200 Old Dominion Drive, McLean); and if you're an experienced boater, shooting the rapids here, where the Potomac River funnels through narrow passages, churning itself into challenging currents, standing waves, and hydraulics, can be a thrill. This section of the river ranges from Class II to Class VI, so you have to know the area before you put in. All boaters must enter the river below the falls in Fisherman's Eddy, between Overlooks 1 and 2, and in the AA Gorge. The river is closed to boating above the falls on the Virginia side; Maryland has easier access and offers some flat water for boaters as well.

⌀ **Potomac Riverboat Company** (703-684-0580; www.potomacriverboatco .com), Cameron and Union streets at the Alexandria City Marina. Operates Apr.–Oct., times vary. A variety of narrated cruises on the Potomac cover Alexandria Seaport, Washington Monuments by Water, and Mount Vernon. There is also a water taxi to National Harbor, across the Potomac in Maryland. Themed cruises include a Pirate Cruise and a Canine Cruise.

Rappahannock River Campground (540-399-1839; 1-800-784-PADL; http: //canoecamp.com), 33017 River Mill Road, Richardsville. Open Apr.–Oct. Canoe and kayak down the scenic Rappahanock, past Civil War battlefields, abandoned gold mines, and the ruins of a 19th-century canal. Trips can be 11 miles (Kelly's Ford to Rappahannock River Campground), done in five or six hours; or 3 miles (Snake Castle Rock to Rappahannock River Campground), taking two or three hours. Many visitors fish the river or the stocked pond at the campground, where there are 45 rustic campsites. Campground fees $9–11 per person. $30 per person includes boat or tube, shuttle, life jacket, safety instruction, and a

GREAT FALLS PARK, FAIRFAX COUNTY

river map; taxes extra. All river sports participants must be at least 6 years old and able to swim.

✍ **SplashDown Waterpark** (703-361-4451; www.splashdownwaterpark.com), 7500 Ben Lomond Park Drive, Manassas. Open late May–Labor Day, hours vary depending on month and day of the week. Thirteen acres of water features, from a 770-foot Lazy River to a 25-meter lap pool, two four-story waterslides, two slippery-fast cannonball slides, a log walk, lily pads, a beach, and fountains. $10.95 admission if under 48 inches in height, $14.95 if 48 inches and above.

Virginia Outdoor Center (540-371-5085; www.playva.com), 3219 Fall Hill Avenue, Fredericksburg. You can take your pick of canoeing, kayaking, or tubing down the Rappahannock with this outfitter, which also has a riverfront beach and campsites for outdoor enthusiasts. Trips vary from a few hours to up to five days. VOC also arranges rock-climbing sessions and guided hikes in Shenandoah National Park.

Washington Sailing Marina (703-548-9027; www.washingtonsailingmarina .com), 1 Marina Drive at Daingerfield Island, George Washington Memorial Parkway, Alexandria. Rentals 11–4, all boats must return by 5. Sailboat rentals near Old Town Alexandria include the 19-foot Flying Scot, which holds five people, or the little Aqua Finn, for two. By reservation only, on-the-water certification from a sailing school or written test required. Flying Scot $23 per hour or $80 for four hours; Aqua Finn $15 per hour or $40 for three hours.

FARM ✍ ♿ **Belvedere Plantation** (540-373-4478; www.belvedereplantation .com), 1601 Belvedere Drive, Fredericksburg. Open late Sept.–early Nov. weekends. A 645-acre farm first built in the 1760s, Belvedere is a working farm but has recently become a family playland as well. In addition to fields of corn, wheat, and soybeans, Belvedere features a corn maze, pumpkin-picking patches, hayrides, and bonfires, plus pedal tractors and pig races. Children can also visit a barnyard full of animals: pygmy goats, chickens, ducks, and calves; and on weekends in season, the market sells fresh-baked pies and farm produce, plus crafts.

GOLF *Golf Guide*, **Prince William County and Manassas**, Prince William County/Manassas Convention and Visitors Bureau (703-396-7130; 1-800-432-1792; www.visitpwc.com). Eleven courses are described in detail with hours of operation, fees, dress codes, weather policies, directions, and contact information for tee times. Free brochure.

Virginia Golf Guide, Virginia Tourism Corporation (804-545-5500; www .virginia.org). Forty-eight golf courses are outlined in the northern Virginia section of this comprehensive guide. Many, like Bull Run Golf Club, Cannon Ridge Golf Club, General's Ridge Golf Course, and Lee's Hill Golfer's Club, are set on historic countryside, where Civil War soldiers once marched. Others are on reclaimed land: the nine-hole Hilltop Golf Course in Alexandria was fashioned on top of a hilly landfill of construction debris, and now offers spectacular views of Mount Vernon and the Potomac River. Laurel Hill Golf Club's 18-hole, Bill Love–designed course was built over what was once the Lorton Correctional Facility, where some of Washington, D.C.'s most serious criminals

VINTAGE: VIRGINIA

Compared to California, Virginia seems to be a newcomer to winemaking, but its history with the fruit of the vine goes back to Jamestown's very first settlers. In 1607, when these pioneers arrived, part of their mission was to create a thriving wine industry, and each household was required to grow at least 10 grapevines. A visit to Monticello, Thomas Jefferson's home in Charlottesville, illustrates the grand effort he put forth in creating fine wines on his estate—though he was never successful, due to disease among his vines. Finally, in the 19th century, Virginia vineyards began to flourish. The native Norton grape and others were cultivated, and the industry began to grow. A wine made from Norton grapes won "best red wine of all nations" at the Vienna World's Fair in 1873.

Then came Prohibition. It took decades to recover from that early 20th-century ban on all alcohol, but finally winemaking in Virginia began to creep back in the 1970s. Now there are almost170 wineries in the state, and more than 50 of them are in Northern Virginia. The state's vintners compete with the best in the country, winning national and international awards, and the industry is considered up and coming by some wine connoisseurs.

Virginia wines are typically styled after old-world vintages, as the climate in Virginia mirrors that of much of Europe. Especially distinctive are

were imprisoned. Locations vary from inside the Capital Beltway—that is, close to Washington, D.C.—to rural Piedmont and historic Fredericksburg. Free guide.

ROCK CLIMBING **Great Falls Park** (703-285-2965; www.nps.gov/grfa), 9200 Old Dominion Drive, McLean. Open daily 7–dark, Visitor Center and bookstore daily 10–5. The rock faces towering over the Potomac River in Great Falls are often dotted with climbers hanging from ropes over the whitewater below. Climbing sites are found along the River Trail and shown on a map available at the Visitor Center. Routes are rated 5.0 to 5.14 in difficulty, with most between 5.5 and 5.9; they range from 25 to 75 feet in length, and all routes are top-rope, with no anchors drilled into the rock. James Eakin's book *Climber's Guide to the Great Falls of the Potomac* has detailed information about maps, approach, conditions, and safety and is available at the park bookstore or online through the Potomac Appalachian Trail Club (www.patc.net). For guided climbs, private instruction is available through **Adventure School Rock Climbing** (703-923-9700; www.adventureschool.com). Entrance to the park, $3 per person, $5 per vehicle; $20 for annual pass.

the Virginia Viognier, a dry white wine, along with Cabernets and Merlots. The state's small vineyards, usually run by the same families that first established them, are also reminiscent of the European approach to winemaking.

The Virginia Wine Board has created a dozen wine trails across the state; a map of wineries with detailed directions, information about hours of operation, and contact information (including Web sites) is available through most tourist bureaus (see "Guidance") or directly from the Wine Board (www .virginiawine.org). Almost all the wineries welcome visitors with tasting rooms and tours, and many provide picnic areas and/or have food available for purchase.

HARTWOOD WINERY, FREDERICKSBURG

WALKING AND DRIVING TOURS **Alexandria Colonial Tours** (703-519-1749; http://alexcolonialtours.com), beginning at Ramsay House, 221 King Street, Alexandria. Costumed guides (including a few veterans of the two-decade-old company) lead visitors on walking tours through the narrow alleys and cobblestone streets of Old Town, regaling them with historical tales both entertaining and educational. Themed, hour to hour-and-a-half tours concern colonial history, ghosts and graveyards (for ages 9 and up), and African American history. A Christmas driving tour of Washington and Alexandria is held each December. Both public and private tours available; some tours by prior arrangement only. A self-guided Scavenger Hunt designed for children ages 8 to 11 leads visitors to clues about George Washington's history in Old Town. Tours, $5–10 per person; Scavenger Hunt maps $4, available at **The Christmas Attic**, 125 South Union Street on the corner of Union and Prince streets.

Civil War Heritage Trail, Manassas Visitor Center, 1914 Train Depot, 9431 West Street, Manassas. A brochure includes a brief history and timeline with a complete map of Civil War sites and trails in Virginia and Maryland.

Civil War Walking Tours (540-825-9147; http://marchingthroughculpeper .com), Culpeper. Two-hour tours of Civil War sites in downtown Culpeper, led by author Virginia Morton, who wrote the novel *Marching Through Culpeper.* Tours are peppered with characters from the past, such as "Extra Billy" Smith, and General J. E. B. Stuart, two-time governor of Virginia. Morton also gives tours of Brandy Station and Cedar Mountain Battlefields.

Piedmont Pathways Driving Tours (www.visitculpeperva.com). Subtitled "Day Rides and Sunday Drives from Culpeper," these four routes wind through countryside to explore Skyline Drive, Civil War sites, historic homes, vineyards, and scenic back roads. Brochure with the four routes available through the Culpeper County Chamber of Commerce and Visitor Center (see "Guidance").

GREEN SPACES ♂ ☻ **Great Falls Park** (703-285-2965; www.nps.gov /grfa), 9200 Old Dominion Drive, McLean. Open daily 7–dark, Visitor Center and bookstore daily 10–5. This 800-acre park has hiking trails with spectacular views of Great Falls, where the Potomac River is funneled into narrow, rocky passageways and foams and churns its way into Washington, D.C. Five miles of mountain biking trails as well as horse trails supplement hiking and boulder climbing. Trails range from easy to rugged. The Visitor Center, renovated in 2008, includes interactive exhibits explaining

Alexandria Convention and Visitors Association

OLD TOWN ALEXANDRIA

the natural and cultural history of the area, and there are games, puzzles, and a please-touch table geared especially toward children. Entrance to the park, $3 per person, $5 per vehicle; $20 for annual pass.

♂ & **Lake Anna State Park** (540-854-5503; www.dcr.virginia.gov/state_parks /lak.shtml), off Hwy. 208 in Spotsylvania. Open daily. You can get out on the 13,000-acre lake in a pontoon boat or swim at a lifeguarded beach, go fishing, or pan for gold at the old Goodwin Gold Mine from the early 1800s. Thirteen miles of wooded trails and lakeshore picnicking are also popular. If the parking lot fills, officials close the park until it empties out enough to accommodate more visitors, so arrive early to ensure a spot. Interpretive programs available. Cabins and campgrounds for those who want to stay overnight. $2–3 on weekends. Additional fees for horse trailers or boat launching.

Meadowlark Botanical Gardens (703-255-3631; www.nvrpa.org/parks/meadow lark_botanical_gardens), 9750 Meadowlark Gardens Court, Vienna. Open 10 AM, closes between 5 and 8, depending on the month (see Web site for details). A 95-acre display garden of ornamentals and native plant collections with walking trails, lakes, gazebos, and myriad birds and butterflies. You'll see more than 20 varieties of cherry trees, and blossoming flowers such as irises and peonies. Gardening and horticultural workshops are popular. $5 adults, $2.50 ages 7–17 and 55 and over, free for under age 7.

Mount Vernon Estate Gardens (see "Mount Vernon Estate" under "Historic Sites").

Mount Vernon Trail, a wide, paved path that runs for 18 miles along the Potomac River, offers spacious views of Washington, D.C., and green parks along the water, quiet passages through marshland, and wooded and windy pathways all the way to Mount Vernon. It's used by bicyclists, runners, in-line skaters, and strollers. The passage through Alexandria shows off its waterfront parks and views, and Old Town restaurants and shops are right off the trail if you want to stop for refreshment or a bit of touring. We like Gravelly Point, where families picnic on the grass under the path of airplanes taking off and landing at National Airport.

Prince William Forest Park (703-221-7181; www.nps.gov/prwi), Rte. 619 near I-95, see directions on Web site. Open daily. This 15,000-acre wooded park is crisscrossed with 37 miles of hiking trails and 21 miles of bike-accessible roads and trails. Deer, wild turkeys, and beavers are best seen at dusk; migratory birds flock here in spring and fall. Fishing for bass, bluegill, perch, pickerel, crappie, and catfish in the park's streams and lakes requires a Virginia fishing license; regulations are available at the Visitor Center.

The park's history spans early English colonists cultivating tobacco in the 1600s, the Revolutionary and Civil Wars, the rise of a pyrite mine, and the New Deal project to create a recreation area. Later, the Civilian Conservation Corps built five rustic cabins for inner-city kids. The cabins still stand (and can be rented by groups for overnight camping). During World War II, the area was used as a top secret military installation, and recruits practiced spying in nearby communities. $5 per vehicle for seven days, walk-in $3 per person age 16 or older; $20 annual pass.

✐ ☃ **Theodore Roosevelt Island** (703-289-2500; www.nps.gov/this), off George Washington Memorial Parkway heading north, just north of Arlington National Cemetery. Open daily 6 AM–10 PM. This island oasis of green is just off the parkway, with trails through the woods and views of the Potomac River, plus a 47-foot monument to Teddy, a nature lover famous for preserving much of our national parkland. Ranger-led tours shed light on the wildlife found here, including beavers, box turtles, and opossums. The airplanes taking off and landing at nearby National Airport make for a noisy nature retreat, but the views are soothing. Free.

✳ Lodging

HOTELS, RESORTS, AND LODGES

Alexandria

🔗 ♿ (ᵞ) **Embassy Suites—Old Town** (703-684-5900; 1-800-EMBASSY; www.embassysuites1.hilton.com), 1900 Diagonal Road, is located directly across the street from the King Street Metro and a short walk away from the heart of Old Town Alexandria. The heated indoor pool and fitness room are a nice plus, as is the complimentary cooked-to-order breakfast and nightly manager's reception (think free drinks and snacks) and a free shuttle to destinations within a 2-mile radius. The 268 two-room suites include living room and bedroom (or in some cases, two bedrooms), two televisions, fridge, and microwave plus the usual coffeemaker.

♿ (ᵞ) **Hampton Inn—King Street Metro** (703-299-9900; http://hamptoninn.hilton.com), 1616 King Street. The Old Town Trolley stops right outside the door, and the King Street Metro is a block away from this 80-room hotel in Old Town Alexandria. Suites are available; each room comes with free Internet access. A fitness center and outdoor pool plus complimentary breakfast (they'll give it to you "to go" if you're in a hurry) are nice additions. $115–205.

🐾 ♿ (ᵞ) **Hawthorn Suites by Wyndham** (703-370-1000; 1-800-368-3339; www.hawthornsuitesalexandria.com), 420 North Van Dorn Street, is a mile and a half from the Van Dorn Metro stop, and the 184-suite hotel provides free shuttle service there. The one- and two-bedroom suites were recently redecorated and feature fully equipped kitchens, free wireless Internet access, plasma TVs, and DVD players. The full breakfast is complimentary, and the "manager's reception," a light dinner with free beer and wine, is served Mon.–Thu. evenings. $110–210.

🔗 ♿ (ᵞ) **Lorien Hotel and Spa** (703-894-3434; 1-877-956-7436; www.lorienhotelandspa.com), 1600 King Street. Both luxury boutique hotel and full-service spa, this Kimpton property is nestled amongst the historic brick façades of Old Town. The 107 rooms follow an elegant Vicente Wolf design, and service includes such extras as a free morning newspaper, French press coffee (by request), designer linens, iHome docking station, and Aveda bath products to go with the "bath butler"—someone who actually draws the bath for you. Which makes sense, as this hotel is also a spa: You can get massage, facial, manicures and pedicures, waxing, and body scrubs. Lorien also touts itself as a green advocate and uses eco-certified cleaning supplies, offers organic snacks and organic and fair-trade coffee, tea, and other beverages; and has installed low-flow toilets, showers, and faucets, as well as efficient lighting fixtures. The hotel restaurant, Brabo, and its sister, Brabo Tasting Room, is headed by Robert Wiedmaier, known locally for his upscale Marcel's and Brasserie Beck in Washington, D.C. The hotel accepts dogs without fees and without any restriction on size or weight. From $169.

🔗 🐾 (ᵞ) **Morrison House Hotel** (703-838-8000; 1-866-834-6628; www.morrisonhouse.com), 116 South Alfred Street, is a stately Federal-style brick, four-star hotel with just 45 rooms and suites. In the luxurious accommodations more like those you'd find in a bed-and-breakfast than in a hotel, designers have combined Federal-style reproduction furniture such as four-poster beds and mahogany armoires with such modern conveniences as Wi-Fi and the requisite terry cloth bathrobes that mark high-end establishments. Some rooms have fireplaces. Run by Kimpton Hotels, Morrison House has been on *Condé Nast Traveler's* Gold List since 2005 and has been featured in *Travel and Leisure's* 500 best hotels. It is pet-friendly and family-friendly, with cribs and playpens, highchairs, and safety kits with electrical outlet covers, toilet latches, and nightlights, plus recommended children's activities and a gift for the kids on arrival. From $159.

&. (ᵠ) **Residence Inn by Marriott** (703-548-5474; 1-800-331-3131; www.marriott.com), 1456 Duke Street, in Old Town. This 240-room hotel is designed for extended stays, with suites featuring separate living, sleeping, and eating areas and full kitchens, as well as complimentary breakfast and light supper and drinks Mon.–Thu. Indoor pool and fitness center, wired and wireless Internet connection, free newspapers, and coffee in the lobby. From $129.

Arlington
&. (ᵠ) **Embassy Suites Crystal City** (703-979-9799; 1-800-EMBASSY; www.embassysuites1.hilton.com), 1300 Jefferson Davis Highway, use 1402 South Eads Street for GPS. 267 spacious suites with separate bedroom and living areas allow travelers to spread out and find a bit more privacy than the average hotel room might otherwise provide. The full American buffet breakfast and complimentary

"manager's reception"—a two-hour happy hour—present added value. Free shuttle to National Airport, the Pentagon City Mall, and the Metro station. $129–329.

&. (ᵠ) **Hilton Garden Inn Arlington, Shirlington** (703-820-0880; 877-782-9444; http://hiltongardeninn .hilton.com), 4271 Campell Avenue. Right in Shirlington, a neighborhood anchored by the award-winning Signature Theatre and vibrant with shops and restaurants, this 142-room hotel is also close to Arlington and Washington, D.C., attractions. It includes all the standard amenities: free Internet access, microwave, frig, an indoor pool and whirlpool, and a fitness center. There is an on-site restaurant, but we love **Busboys and Poets** food (703-379-9757; www.busboysand poets.com), 4251 South Campbell Avenue, for artsy, politically progressive, local flavor and great, or **Capitol City Brewing Company** (703-578-3888; capcitybrew.com), 4001 Campbell Avenue, a brewpub/restaurant, for beer brewed on site and reliable American fare. Free parking is a nice perk. Rates as low as $109 increase dramatically depending on the season—the highest rate, on the Fourth of July, is $302.

&. **Hyatt Arlington at Washington's Key Bridge** (703-525-1234; http: //Arlington.hyatt.com), 1325 Wilson Boulevard, in the Rosslyn section of Arlington, has some rooms with beautiful views of Washington, D.C., just across the Potomac River. Its 317 rooms (including five suites) are convenient to Arlington's memorials and a short walk from the scenic Key Bridge that leads into D.C.'s Georgetown neighborhood, a hub of shopping and nightlife. Rosslyn itself is a busy commercial center with a Metro stop that puts visitors a short ride from area attractions. Rooms were recently redesigned in a crisp, contemporary style and include the usual amenities—Internet access, coffeemaker, flat-screen television—but no refrigerator or microwave. $259–369, weekend rates are generally lowest.

&. (ᵩ) **Key Bridge Marriott** (703-524-6400; 1-800-228-9290; www.marriott.com), 1401 Lee Highway. On the banks of the Potomac River, with views of Washington, D.C., from many rooms and from the rooftop restaurant, this 585-room hotel is centrally located for visitors touring Washington, D.C., and northern Virginia. The nearby Key Bridge makes it a short walk to D.C.'s Georgetown neighborhood, and a free shuttle takes you to the Rosslyn Metro station. $270–325.

☃ (ᵩ) **Residence Inn by Marriott—Arlington Courthouse** (703-312-2100; 1-800-331-3131; www.marriott.com), 1401 North Adams Street. New in 2009, this 176-room Marriott is in Courthouse Village, surrounded by restaurants, shopping, and recreational facilities, and a short walk from the Courthouse Metro stop. Each suite has a fully equipped kitchen with microwave, fridge, dishwasher, and coffeemaker, and wired and wireless Internet access. Studios and one- and two-bedroom suites are also available. A pool, whirlpool, and on-site gym are available to guests. The bargain comes with the full buffet breakfast, and a "manager's reception" that is actually dinner (think spaghetti and meatballs, burgers, or hot dogs) on Mon.–Wed. nights. $119–329.

Fredericksburg

There are dozens of big chain hotels in and around Fredericksburg, and many small bed-and-breakfasts beyond those listed here. Go to www.visitfred.com for more choices or to request a visitors guide with an updated, multipage section on lodging.

☃ &. (ᵩ) **Comfort Inn Southpoint** (540-898-5550; www.comfortinn.com/hotel-fredericksburg-virginia-VA105), 5422 Jefferson Davis Highway. This is a standard hotel located near Mary Washington University, with 125 rooms, indoor swimming pool, sauna, and fitness room. Complimentary deluxe continental breakfast at the on-site restaurant. From $90.

☃ &. (ᵩ) **Dunning Mills Inn All-Suite** (540-373-1256; www.dunningmills.com), 2305 Jefferson Davis Highway. This all-suite hotel is designed for extended stays. Each suite includes a fully equipped kitchen with a full-size refrigerator, four-burner range with oven, microwave, pots and pans, dishes, and cutlery. There is an outdoor pool, and pets are accepted. From $69.

&. (ᵩ) **Hampton Inn and Suites Fredericksburg South** (540-898-5000; www.fredericksburghampton.com), 4800 Market Street. The Hampton Inn offers a combination of hotel rooms and suites, with 121 rooms in all. An indoor pool and fitness facilities are available on-site, and a complimentary hot breakfast is included. Suites include under-the-counter refrigerators, microwave, and a more spacious living area. From $94.

(ᵩ) **Inn at the Old Silke Mill** (540-371-5666; http://innattheoldesilkmill.com), 1707 Princess Anne Street. Not quite as historic as some of its colonial neighbors, this inn was built around 1930 but maintains a flair for the distant past, with antique furnishings and a "parlor" with a working fireplace and a piano guests can play. The 30 rooms (with televisions and refrigerators) make this feel more like a hotel than a bed-and-breakfast, but continental fare is provided for breakfast each morning. $89–159.

☀ ⚹ (ᵚᵖ) **Residence Inn by Marriott** (540-786-9292; www.marriott.com), 60 Towne Centre Boulevard, is a 124-suite hotel designed for extended stays. Outdoor patio with fire pit plus library, fitness room, and indoor pool. Each suite features a fully equipped kitchen (including dishwasher) and HDTV flat-screen television. Complimentary breakfast buffet and evening receptions Mon.–Thu. From $140.

Other areas of northern Virginia
⚹ (ᵚᵖ) **Country Inn and Suites by Carlson Manassas** (703-393-9797; 1-800-596-2375; www.countryinns.com /manassasva), 10810 Battleview Parkway, Manassas, right off I-66 and near Old Town and Civil War battlefields, has 75 hotel rooms with standard microwave, refrigerator, and cable TV. Indoor pool and fitness center, plus complimentary breakfast. $90–145.

♂ **Oakland Green Farm** (540-338-7628; www.oaklandgreen.com), Lincoln (near Leesburg). You can either rent a suite, or a suite plus bedroom at the log house portion of this historic farmhouse, built of logs, stone, and brick in the 1730s. Ten generations of the Brown family have lived here and continue to run the property as a working cattle farm, with 50 head of Black Angus, two horses, and several cats, set on 200 acres. Guests can use picnic tables set out around the property, swim in the pool, explore woodland trails, or fish in the stocked

pond. Historic buildings such as the pre–Civil War barn are also of interest. $130–235.

⤴ ☀ (ᵚᵖ) **Ritz-Carlton, Tysons Corner** (703-506-4300; www.ritzcarlton .com), 1700 Tysons Boulevard, McLean. This luxury hotel, attached to the popular Tysons Galleria shopping mall, includes a day spa and 398 recently improved rooms, including 50 suites and 34 "club level" rooms (for members who enjoy such amenities as a separate lounge, food and beverages, and dedicated concierge staff) with views of Washington, D.C., or the Blue Ridge mountains. Features include a fitness center, indoor pool, sauna, and steam bath; oversize marble bathrooms and the fluffy terry cotton bathrobes the Ritz loves to flaunt—plus featherbeds and down comforter. The in-house restaurant, Entyse, features an organic approach to comfort foods. Named one of the top 50 hotels in the United States by *Condé Nast Traveler* Reader's Choice; Virginia Green Lodging Certified. Dogs 30 pounds or less are allowed for an extra $250 fee per stay. $175–355.

BED & BREAKFAST INNS

Alexandria and Arlington
Alexandria and Arlington Bed and Breakfast Network (703-549-3415; 1-888-549-3415; www.aabbn.com) lists 13 bed-and-breakfasts in Alexandria and six in Arlington, plus one each in Falls Church, McLean, and Tysons Corner. Most are one- to three-room homes; many are in Old Town. Prices, locations, and descriptions are available on the Web site.

(ᵚᵖ) **The Kenmore Inn** (540-371-7622; 1-800-437-7622; www.kenmore inn.com), 1200 Princess Anne Street.

In keeping with historic Fredericksburg, the Kenmore Inn dates back to 1793 and has been closely linked to George Washington family properties; it survived Civil War shelling (evidence can still be seen in the roof supports) and housed Union horses on its lower level during the Battle of Fredericksburg. Today, it is furnished with four-poster beds and other antiques, and four of its nine guest rooms feature working fireplaces. Other rooms, in the 1933 addition, do not, but every room comes with complimentary sherry, flat-screen cable TV, and wireless Internet service. Besides guest rooms, the inn has a dinner restaurant with a garden room, pub, and sunken patio. $130–175.

Fredericksburg

❀ ♂ **The Richard Johnston Inn** (540-899-7606; 1-800-557-0770; www.therichardjohnstoninn.com), 711 Caroline Street. Nine rooms. One of the original signers of the Declaration of Independence, architect John Taylow, built this home in 1770. By the 1800s, it was home to the mayor of Fredericksburg, Richard Johnston, for whom it is named. Just across the street from the Visitor Center, the inn, now run as a bed-and-breakfast, is within walking distance of many of the historic sites in Old Town. Guest rooms are furnished with period antiques; two suites are also available. $110–275.

Other areas of northern Virginia

♪ ❀ ♂ **Briar Patch Bed and Breakfast** (1-866-327-5911; www.briarpatchbanb.com), 23130 Briar Patch Lane, Middleburg, is a historic 1805 farm on 47 acres with views of the Blue Ridge Mountains. This eight-room bed-and-breakfast has the not-uncommon antique furnishings but also a swimming pool and hot tub, and offers a separate cottage for rent. Pets and children are welcome. Four miles east of Middleburg, the property is near wineries, Civil War battlefields, and small towns with antique shops and restaurants. The property is frequently used for events such as weddings and cooking class weekends, so call ahead to be sure of a spot. Some rooms have shared baths. $95–165, cottage $210–265.

♂ **Poplar Springs Inn** (540-788-4600; 1-800-490-7747; www.poplarspringsinn.com), 9245 Rogues Road, Casanova. 21 rooms. Along with the Manor House Restaurant, the on-site dining room, this country inn, just an hour from Washington, D.C., feels a world away. The large stone manor house is situated on 200 wooded acres. Walk the gardens and paths, play tennis, swim in the outdoor pool, or pull up a chair and read on the shaded patio. For an extra treat, enjoy a massage at the inn's own spa. Several packages bundle lodging with meals and spa services. With the Saturday Night All-Inclusive, for example—a room, dinner, and breakfast—is $262 per person, double occupancy, or $385 for one person. Girlfriends Getaway Package for two nights, double occupancy, includes lodging, daily afternoon tea, light lunch, one dinner, and one massage, facial and manicure, $724 per person plus tax and service charge. Check with the inn for other packages. Three-course dinner Thu.–Sat. $74; rooms $209–279.

♈ **The Red Fox Inn** (540-687-6301; 1-800-223-1728; http://redfox.com), 2 East Washington Street, Middleburg, built as a tavern in 1728, is listed on the National Register of Historic Places. Made of local fieldstone, it was originally called Mr. Chinn's Ordinary (after owner Joseph Chinn) and was a popular spot among early colonists, including George Washington. It became part of Middleburg in 1787, a town so named because it was the midway point for travelers by coach or horseback, between Alexandria and Winchester—and thus, a popular resting stop. Its rich history includes use by the Confederates during the Civil War (the pine service bar in the Tap Room was once a field operating table); and in more recent history, it hosted President Kennedy, Elizabeth Taylor, and Pamela Harriman. It is still popular among celebrities visiting for hunt country events and regional tourism. Fourteen rooms are spread out among three historic buildings; an on-site restaurant with original stone fireplaces and hand-hewn ceiling beams features local food and wine from nearby farms and vineyards. $170–245.

✳ Where to Eat

Alexandria
♈ **Bilbo Baggins** (703-683-0300; http://bilbobaggins.net), 208 Queen Street, is a cozy bar and comfy restaurant frequented by locals who favor the warm ambience created not only by the 10 beers on tap (or choose from 80 bottles) and 32 wines at its Green Dragon Pub, but also by the upbeat music, stained-glass art, and warm wood tones of the interior. The extensive menu offers popular tapas (firecracker shrimp on Asian slaw; spinach and artichoke dip; spicy cilantro fries, and more), "gourmet" pizza, salad plates (the Thai shredded beef salad and smoked duck salad look especially interesting), and such

main courses as grilled lamb chops with butternut squash, cinnamon pork loin, and grilled portobello chicken on wild mushroom polenta. The Sunday brunch menu has standard pancakes, French toast, and various Benedicts plus quesadillas and chicken hash. Main courses $17–24.

Cheesetique (703-706-5300; www
.cheesetique.com), 2411 Mount Vernon Avenue. A specialty shop with a case full of gorgeous cheeses, from the familiar Camembert to Robioloa Bosina, and including local products like Monacacy Ash goat cheese, this spot doubles as a wine-and-cheese bar. You can buy cheese to take home, or nosh on samples, from cheese boards augmented by fresh bread, crackers, quince paste, cornichons, and grapes. Or you can order sweet or savory nibbles such as glazed Greek figs, black olive tapenade, and red pepper spread to accompany the *fromage*. A full menu of cheese-influenced soups, salads, and main courses lets you try Parrano cheese on a portobello melt, quiche, or a grilled cheese jacked up with three-year Cheddar, Dragon's Breath, Dubliner, and pimiento peppers melted on grilled sourdough. To go with it, you can order many wines by the glass (helpful descriptions assist in pairing different cheeses with different wines), plus unusual beers. $5–25.

♈ **Columbia Firehouse Restaurant and Barroom** (703-683-1776; www
.columbiafirehouse.com), 109 South St. Asaph Street, Old Town. Set in an old firehouse (ca. 1883), this rustic restaurant still shows off the exposed brick walls of its 19th-century history. It has a barroom feel, with lots of polished wood and soft lighting, and there's plenty of pub food, such as

ribs and barbeque, sliders, fries, and chili. But the menu also ventures into more refined selections, such as grilled branzino with shaved fennel salad and house-made egg noodles to go with bison Stroganoff. You can get mussels three different ways, and oysters come on the half shell or deviled with Parmesan, mushrooms, and bacon. Families and foodies mix easily here, and tourists are as likely to be patrons as are locals. $16–24.

♈ **Evening Star Café** (703-549-5051; http://eveningstarcafe.net), 2000 Mount Vernon Avenue, is a lively, unpretentious spot with a neighborhood feel and locally sourced, elegant food. The menu includes interesting combinations of high-quality ingredients, such as rare seared tuna with green peppercorn lentils and carrot caramel sauce; or stuffed chicken breast with bacon-braised greens with blue cheese and jalapeño mac and cheese. The wine list is influenced by sister establishment Planet Wine, with more than 1,000 selections; you can choose your wine from there and have it served to you at Evening Star for an extra fee. Two separate bars give you the choice of a down-to-earth bar (downstairs) or comfy couch–style bar (upstairs) with craft beers and live music. $18–27.

FireFlies Delray (703-548-7200; www.firefliesdelray.com), 1501 Mount Vernon Avenue. You'll get live tunes with your meal four nights a week at this venue for local musicians, plus your choice of seven draft microbrews, 70 bottles, and 15 wine selections. The menu runs from salads, burgers, and sandwiches to typical bar munchies such as hummus, wings, and tater skins—though there are a few curveballs in there, such as fried

olives and Scotch eggs. There's also pasta and pizza, plus main courses such as brisket and pecan-crusted tilapia, and a couple of good vegetarian options. $7–15.

Fish Market Restaurant and Anchor Bar (703-836-5676; www.fishmarketva.com), 105 King Street. Open daily 11:30–11. It seems appropriate to buy fish in a historic seaport, and the Fish Market, just steps from the waterfront, makes it easy. If you're seated near the restaurant's Anchor Bar, you'll get a serving of boisterous activity too: the Fish Market hosts theme nights, ladies nights, and DJs and on big game nights the eight HD TVs and drink specials attract plenty of sports fans. The restaurant menu seems typical of seafood restaurants in many coastal towns: all sorts of shellfish (oysters, shrimp, clams, mussels) and a few fin fish (tuna, tilapia, mahi-mahi) in various combinations like the Captain's Platter, Skipper's Platter, etc. plus some specialties like Crab Norfolk and Seafood Jambalaya. $10–27.

Gadsby's Tavern (703-548-1288; www.gadsbystavernrestaurant.com), 138 North Royal Street. Open Mon.–Sat. 11:30–3, 5:30–10, Sun. 11–3, 5:30–10. Gadsby's is situated in a tavern that was once frequented by George Washington and other founding fathers. Next door is a museum exhibiting the colonial lifestyle, and while the restaurant holds to the theme, its food is the focus, rather than a gimmick. Costumed wait staff, a cozy fireplace, and tables set with tin plates and hurricane lamps establish the time period, and the kitchen turns out period dishes, but with modern attention to detail. "George Washington's favorite" is grilled breast of duck with scalloped potatoes, corn pudding, *rhotekraut* (a red cabbage dish), and port wine orange glace. The Gentleman's Pye is a lamb, beef, and red wine stew with a whipped potato and pastry topping; there are also crab cakes, shellfish Newburg, and crispy fried oysters. Main courses $22–30.

Ÿ **Hank's Oyster Bar** (703-739-HANK; www.hanksdc.com), 1026 King Street, is the second location for a casual restaurant that nevertheless has chef-driven, mindful preparations of all things oyster. If you want something beyond seafood, this isn't such a great choice—most selections revolve around the bivalve: There are oyster shooters, broiled oysters, fried oyster poboys, and, of course, several types of oysters on the half shell plus Hog Island–style BBQ oysters (an Eastern Shore specialty). You'll also find shrimp (peel-and-eat or popcorn), clams (fried), lobster (as in lobster roll—we're going for casual here), and crab cakes. As a nod to landlubbers, daily specials, called "meat and two [sides]" offer ribs, chicken schnitzel, steaks, and pork loin with interesting sides such as sesame snow peas, Old Bay French fries, and marinated beets. Main courses $18–23.

Hard Times Café (703-837-0050; www.hardtimes.com), 1404 King Street (also in Clarendon, Fairfax, Fredericksburg, Manassas, Springfield, and Woodbridge). The original location of this local chain, Hard Times is an icon among chili lovers. The menu always offers four kinds of chili: Texas, Cincinnati, Terlingua Red, and Vegetarian—served up in combinations with macaroni ("chili mac"), cheese, onions, and beans or in dishes such as chili taters (Tater Tots smothered in chili) or Frito Chili Pie (a bowl of Fritos topped with chili, cheese, tomatoes, and sour cream). There are also sliders and hot dogs, salads, chicken sandwiches, ribs, grilled salmon, and fish-and-chips. $9–17.

King Street Blues (703-836-8800; www.kingstreetblues.com), one block off King Street on St. Asaph Street South, Old Town (also in Crystal City, Arlington Court House, Kingstowne, and Stafford). This is the original site of a locally owned mini-chain of Southern-flavored restaurants-cum-roundhouses. Decorated with enormous papier-mâché characters and nostalgic murals in bright colors, King Street Blues is an upbeat spot to enjoy a menu of comfort food such as ribs and barbecue, New Orleans–style poboy sandwiches with shrimp instead of oysters, and bowls of chili, gumbo, or red beans and rice. There are salads topped with pork or chicken barbecued or blackened chicken, fried catfish, and plenty of hush puppies and corn bread. $13–21; a Southern supper of meat plus three sides $15.

♪ **Lavender Moon Cupcakery** (703-683-0588) 116 South Royal Street. A tiny bakery with big flavor, Lavender Moon focuses solely on cupcakes—and it shows. The cakes are moist and flavorful, and the selections are mouthwateringly tempting. They change daily, but a sampling from a recent summer afternoon included flourless chocolate with sea salt and almonds, triple Belgian chocolate, blood orange Dreamsicle, carrot, cashew and cardamom, and Jersey peach and blueberry. $3–4 per cupcake.

Restaurant Eve (703-706-0450; www.restauranteve.com), 110 South

Pitt Street, is one of the most coveted reservations in the D.C. area, consistently rated by food critics as among the finest high-end restaurants. If you're ready to splurge, come here for Chef Cathal (don't pronounce the *h*) Armstrong's tasting room menu, which was relying on locally sourced ingredients—as local as the chef's own vegetable garden and home-cured pork belly—long before the practice became trendy. The adjoining **Bistro**, with its separate menu, also relies on local, seasonal foods. Think heirloom tomato tart with (organic) garden basil, and butter-poached Maine lobster with Eastern Shore corn, or (local) Polyface Farm pasture-fed beef rib eye; Maryland crab cakes with baby greens and rémoulade, and pan-roasted veal sweetbreads with fried oysters and country ham. As fine an experience as this is, the restaurant avoids pretention with a scaled-down décor and the still upscale but more casual (and less expensive) bistro and bar. Bistro main courses, $34–40; Tasting room five-, seven- and nine-course menus, $110–150.

Taqueria Poblano (703-548-8226; www.taqueriapoblano.com), 2400B Mount Vernon Avenue (also at 2503A North Harrison Street, Arlington) is consistently reviewed as one of the best spots around for friendly service and great Mexican food that's not too heavy, just tasty. Plus, their margaritas are made with all-fresh ingredients—no mixes here. Taquitos, rolled tortillas filled with pork or chicken and fried to a crisp, are a great choice from among the appetizers; tacos come with fun choices for fillings, such as cumin-poached chicken, adobo-seasoned pork, lime-marinated

duck, grilled shrimp, or beer-battered and fried mahi-mahi. Outside seating allows locals bring their dogs, who are ubiquitous in this Del Ray neighborhood. $5–14.

Vermilion (703-684-9669; www.vermilionrestaurant.com), 1120 King Street, was voted best upscale casual restaurant by the Restaurant Association of Metropolitan Washington, and has been a consistent listing in the best restaurant guides for the area. Its locally sourced, seasonal menu relies on purveyors so integral to the restaurant's success that they are listed by name on the Web site. You can expect creative, chef-driven touches here, such as walnut froth with a beet and goat cheese salad, spearmint in the arugula salad and, rather than an entire softshell crab, a softshell "bit" served with fried green tomato, curly endive, bacon tuiles, and whipped avocado. The atmosphere is cozy, with exposed brick and warm lighting. Main courses $14–33.

The Warehouse Bar and Grill (703-683-6868; www.warehousebarandgrill.com), 214 King Street, is as amusing for its caricatures of local political and social figures as it is for its food; the walls are lined with drawings and paintings, some with sculptured features giving them a three-dimensional element. Menu specialties are prime aged steaks and seafood with a bit of New Orleans flavor: There's steak Pontchartrain, a filet mignon topped with jumbo lump crab and sauce béarnaise; pecan-crusted chicken with a spicy Creole mustard cream sauce; and a pasta jambalaya with shrimp, andouille sausage, pork, and chicken. Atmosphere is casually elegant. $10–33.

Arlington

Ⓨ **Busboys and Poets** (703-379-9757; www.busboysandpoets.com), 4251 South Campbell Avenue, is the hip place to be for food, poetry, music, and conversation. Just look at its lineup of events, such as an organic beer happy hour, a Habitat for Humanity fundraiser, a band called Funky Folk, and an open mic poetry reading. An adjacent bookstore gives you something to do while you wait for a table, and food for conversation over dinner. You might think with all this attention to social justice, the food might suffer, but you'd be wrong: The extensive menu here is great, with everything from vegan coconut-tofu bites to a corned beef Reuben, from gourmet shrimp and grits or scallop risotto to sandwiches, pizza and burgers, a generous list of desserts, and even breakfast. A full bar with craft beers and organic wines plus plenty of coffee drinks completes the picture. $9–17.

Ⓨ **Capital City Brewing Company** (703-578-3888; www.capcitybrew .com), 4001 Campbell Avenue. The first brewery to open in the District after Prohibition was over, Capital City now has three locations in the area. Arlington's offers a view of the pedestrian promenade in Shirlington, where cafés, shops, and theatergoers make for great people watching. The beer here is brewed on site, and the taps run with seven or eight different choices every night, including the house brews Capital Kolsch, Pale Rider Ale, Amber Waves Ale, and Prohibition Porter. The menu trends toward hearty fare, with lots of burgers, sandwiches, nachos, and chili as well as full-on main courses of seafood, beef, chicken, and a home-made meat loaf with caramelized onions. $9–20.

Cassatt's (703-527-3330; www .cassattscafe.com), 4536 Lee Highway near North Glebe Road, in the Lee Heights Center. It's not often you find a New Zealand–themed restaurant, so this spot is especially fun. Inspired by an eight-month stay in New Zealand, the proprietor has tried to recreate the café atmosphere there with a cozy, art-filled space and a menu that includes such kiwi specialties as the dessert, pavlova; "flat white," a sort of cappuccino drink; meat and vegetable pies; green-lipped mussels; and lamb, along with more standard items. The place is named for Mary Cassatt, the American impressionist, and exhibits local artists who tend toward impressionism. $10–19.

Earl's (703-248-0150; http://earlsin arlington.com), 2605 Wilson Boulevard, is a local mainstay for its extensive menu of generous hot and cold sandwiches. Earl's roasts its own turkey, beef, and pork, hand cuts its French fries (served with or without gravy, cheese sauce, or chili), roasts its own red peppers, and makes soups, such as New Orleans–style gumbo, from scratch. Signature sandwich sauces are especially enticing: tangy barbecue, chipotle mayonnaise, pesto, or homemade garlic mayo. Roasted turkey variations include some with cranberry and gravy, just like for Thanksgiving; a pork sandwich topped with French fries is another favorite. Veggie combinations include the Mona Lisa, with roasted eggplant, red pepper, garlic, mushrooms, and provolone on ciabatta. $8–12.

Jaleo (703-413-8181; www.jaleo .com), 2250A Crystal Drive, Crystal City. Celebrity chef José Andrés has a miniature empire of Spanish restaurants, including three Jaleo locations in the D.C. area—but the quality at each is uncompromised. Jaleo is a tapas restaurant, focusing on small plates of many different types of food. Diners can sample numerous authentic Spanish dishes between sips of sangria (or anything else from the full bar). You can nibble on creamy chicken croquettes or bacon-wrapped dates, marinated mussels, or garlicky sautéed shrimp, potato-laden tortillas, or Moorish chickpeas and spinach. There are hot and cold items, vegetables, and meats and seafood, and the small dishes are made for sharing. Small dishes $7–32.

Liberty Tavern (703-465-9360; www .thelibertytavern.com), 3195 Wilson Boulevard, near the Clarendon Metro stop. Chef Liam LaCivita focuses on modern American cuisine, using seasonal, regional ingredients. Two wood-burning ovens influence the menu with selections such as Neapolitan pizzas, fresh whole and filleted fish, and thick-cut steaks. Unexpected twists include the orange and lavender on the roasted branzino, and an anise-garlic sauce with spinach/baby snail raviolini. Breads, pastas, sausages, ice creams, and other desserts are made in-house; a menu of artisan cheeses offers almost a dozen selections from area dairies. Much of the meat is locally sourced. Main courses $10–25.

Minh's (703-525-2828), 2500 Wilson Boulevard, between the Clarendon and Courthouse Metro stops, turns up as a favorite among Vietnamese food fans, and is a years-long member of the "very best restaurants" list at the well-respected *Washingtonian* magazine. Best bets are green papaya

salad, spring rolls, caramel pork, and lemongrass chicken. If you can't decide on an appetizer, you can opt for the sampler: shrimp cake, spring roll, and rice roll. Service is family style, so this is an especially good place to come with a crowd—and prices make it affordable, with nothing over $15 and most main courses between $9 and $12.

Pupatella (571-312-7230; pupatella.com), 5104 Wilson Boulevard. Once a little red food cart parked outside the Ballston Metro stop, Pupatella opened a storefront in 2010 and now has a brick pizza oven turning out Neapolitan-style pies. The baker, Enzo Algarme, was raised in Naples, so you know these are authentic. The oven, built in Naples using volcanic ash from Mount Vesuvius, reaches 800 to 1,000 degrees Fahrenheit, baking the pies in just one minute. Pizza aficionados will recognize San Marzano tomatoes for the sauce, which is simple—just crushed tomatoes and salt. Besides pizza, there are Neapolitan specialties such as fried calzone and arancini (fried risotto balls), plus gelato, beer, and espresso.

Ray's Hell-Burger (703-841-0001), 1725 Wilson Boulevard, was made famous when President Obama came here to stand in line for one of the best burgers in the area—and many say the best, bar none. Perfectly cooked to order and adorned by various accoutrements such as cognac- and sherry-sautéed mushrooms, charred jalapeños, and even foie gras, plus several different sorts of cheeses, these generously portioned burgers make foodies rave and tourists flock. Be ready for a crowd, and a wait. Also, don't expect much in the way of ambience: The place is small and *unpretentious* is an understatement. A plain burger is around $12, so even with sides such as sweet potato fries and root beer, you can leave without having spent more than $20. The nearby Ray's Hell-Burger II (no phone; 1713 Wilson Boulevard) also offers game meats, such as wild boar and venison, plus a vegetarian portobello mushroom "burger" option.

Ray's the Steaks (703-841-7297), 2300 Wilson Boulevard, near the Courthouse and Rosslyn Metro stops. Open Mon.–Thu. 5–10, Fri. and Sat. 5–11. This place became famous for flouting the usual über-expensive steakhouses and offering up similarly high-end cuts for far more affordable prices and in a more casual, neighborhood atmosphere. The cowboy and hanger steaks are especially good deals, but you won't regret going to the surf side of the menu, either: crab bisque is chock-full of chunky crabmeat and seared scallops are divine. All the meat is butchered by proprietor Michael Landrum, who runs four other Ray's enterprises, in Silver Spring, Maryland, and Washington, D.C. $20–37.

Ravi Kabob (703-522-6666; http://ravikabobusa.com), 305 North Glebe Road. You will not find an enchanting atmosphere at Ravi Kabob, but the food you eat off your plastic fork is some of the best Pakistani fare in the area. Beef, lamb, and chicken kabobs and stews are juicy and flavorful, having been slow-cooked or charcoal-grilled. The spice-laden *seekh kabob* of minced beef, and a similar treatment of lamb, *the seekh-kabob karahi*, are good choices if you want to explore this cuisine beyond the hunks of succulent meat. Much of this meat

fest is accompanied by fluffy white rice or naan, a soft flatbread great for sopping up sauces. Prices are low: appetizers $1.25–2.50, main courses $9–17.

Tallula (703-778-5051; http://tallula restaurant.com), 2761 Washington Boulevard, in the Clarendon neighborhood, is an upscale eatery known for its deep wine list and creative cuisine from chef Barry Koslow. As for the wine, more than 70 varieties are available by the glass and selections include many smaller producers difficult to find elsewhere. Food emphasizes locally grown, seasonal fare with a few twists: such as gnocchi with braised wild boar. One summer, appetizers ranged from chilled tomato and cantaloupe soup with blue crab, to fava bean bruschetta; three housemade pastas included sweet corn and smoked potato agnolotti with rapini and garden basil, and saffron fettuccine with rock shrimp, calamari, and chorizo; and main courses went from Southern-influenced Pennsylvania pork loin and bacon with black-eyed peas, collards, and okra and tomato stew; to Peking duck with roasted peaches, turnips, watercress, and vincotto. Main courses $20–30. Tallula's sister restaurant at the same location, *⊘ EatBar Gastro Pub*, is more casual: It hosts Saturday morning cartoons at brunch, Sunday evening movies, and offers more casual fare, including baby burgers and corn dog bites. $10–12.

Fredericksburg

Ψ **Bistro Bethem** (540-371-9999; www.bistrobethem.com), 309 William Street. With a vaulted ceiling, local art, and a 300-year-old pine bar, Bistro Bethem pays close attention to décor, but the menu is where owner-chef Blake Bethem's training comes through. He stays true to his local roots—he grew up in Dale City—but uses his culinary training on a menu that includes fresh fish, wild game, and house-made charcuterie, breads, and desserts. The menu changes daily, to incorporate the freshest, locally sourced seasonal ingredients, and includes pork and grass-fed beef from nearby farms (e.g., pork belly confit, grass-fed burgers). $16–25.

Y **Capital Ale House** (540-371-2337 www.capitalalehouse.com), 917 Caroline Street, has no fewer than 60 beers on tap, 250 in bottles, and two cask-conditioned ales for beer aficionados. There's also a (less extensive) wine list and full menu with hearty fare: three kinds of mussels; bar-type appetizers including frites, fried pierogi, Bavarian pretzels, and cheese-and-sausage plates; and main courses that mix brats and other sausages with ribs, jerk chicken, chile-lime crab cakes, salads, sandwiches, and desserts. Menu notes help you pair the right beer with your food selection. $9–13.

✆ **Carl's Ice Cream**, 2200 Princess Anne Street. Open mid-Feb.–mid-Nov. Sun.–Thu. 11–11, Fri. and Sat. 11–11:30. An iconic ice-cream stand that first opened in 1947, Carl's is marked by a brilliant, retro neon sign and draws crowds who stand in long (but fast-moving) lines for their frozen custard–like ice cream. It comes in just three flavors, the basic chocolate, vanilla, and strawberry, and it's made in 1940-era Electro Freeze ice-cream machines, visible from the counter. Folks rave about the flavor. And you can get cones, cups, sundaes, shakes, or malts. $4–14.

Hyperion Espresso (540-373-4882; http://hyperionespresso.com), 301

William Street. Open Mon.–Sat. 7–10 and Sun. 8–8. A community hangout as much as a place to get espresso, cappuccino, and other elaborate coffee drinks, Hyperion has an artsy feel, with mismatched furniture and local artists' work on the walls. A light menu includes sweets as well as savories such as croissant sandwiches. $3–10.

La Petite Auberge (540-371-2727; http://lapetiteaubergefredericksburg .com), 311 William Street. In 1981 when Nice-born chef Christian Renault left his restaurants in Washington, D.C.—La Niçoise, Le Canard and Le Pescadou—he moved his family to Fredericksburg and continued to cook in his new place, La Petite Auberge. Still drawing on his first lessons from his French mother and grandmother, as well as his culinary school training, he and his family present traditional French cuisine and regional dishes, fueled by locally farmed produce and fresh seafood. The menu ranges from sauced veal scaloppine or calf's liver to crabmeat Norfolk or grilled mahi-mahi. A prix fixe early menu is offered from Mon.–Thu. 5:30–7 for $23. Otherwise, entrees $19–31.

Poppy Hill Tuscan Kitchen (540-373-2035; www.ciaopoppyhill.com), 1000 Charles Street. Named among the top farm-to-table restaurants by Epicurious.com, Poppy Hill emphasizes locally sourced ingredients for its chef-driven menu of "seasonally charged" food. Chef Scott Mahar, who worked in big-name Washington, D.C., restaurants before moving to Fredericksburg, combines his Cordon Bleu, New England training with a love of Tuscan food to present house-made pastas, creative salads (try a

Cobb salad with roast organic chicken, avocado, tomato, Gorgonzola, bacon, and organic romaine), and main courses infused with flavor (e.g., blackberry balsamic pork tenderloin or prosciutto-wrapped tilapia with shrimp risotto) in a cozy basement eatery. $13–24.

Sammy T's (540-371-2008; http ://sammyts.com), 801 Caroline Street, has a long history: Built in 1804, it was an auction house and store, then the Fredericksburg Post Office, an auto supply store, and, from 1930 to '80, a restaurant called Dugan's. Since then, it's been Sammy T's, a casual restaurant with indoor and outdoor dining and a full menu of soups, salads, and sandwiches. It has a kids' menu, a beer and wine list, and homemade desserts, plus lots of vegetarian options, such falafel, tempeh burgers, and bean burritos. $7–23.

Other areas of northern Virginia
2941 (703-270-1500; www.2941.com), 2941 Fairview Park Drive, Falls Church. Named for its address, 2941 offers a high-end fine dining experience from Chef Bertrand Chemel, who worked at New York's highly regarded Boulud before coming here. The influence tends toward French, with some Asian elements, and the result is an experience that consistently lands on the best-restaurants list of food critics. You'll find such delicacies as foie gras with roasted peach, praline brioche, and lemon verbena; sturgeon with smoked potato, cauliflower, summer truffle, and beet sauce; and corn ravioli with shrimp, Maitake mushroom, and curry (though of course the menu varies from season to season and day to day). Views of the landscaped woods, waterfalls, and

koi ponds are an elegant touch. Four- or six-course tasting menu, $58–110; standard menu main courses, $32–46. A weekday lunch of three courses goes for $23.95.

Mount Vernon Inn (703-780-0011; www.mountvernon.org), at Mount Vernon Estate, Mount Vernon. You might expect a restaurant at a tourist attraction to be less than savory, but at Mount Vernon Inn, you'd be wrong. The ambience, with cozy (working!) fireplaces and wall murals of estate scenes, is cheery; the service is attentive; the décor is colonial but not overbearingly so; and the food is delicious as well as interesting. The restaurant is famous for its peanut soup, a thick, rich concoction that tastes like liquid peanut butter, but better—it was apparently a colonial staple. Other stabs at colonial fare include a turkey "pye," a potpie with pastry crust; hoecakes that are certainly better than what they were cooking over field fires back in the day; roast duck with George Washington's "favorite" apricot sauce, and a venison mixed grill. Drinks feel authentic, too, with hot buttered rum, Dominion Oak Barrel stout, Mount Vernon Harvest Ale, and hot mulled cider. Save room for dessert or hot chocolate. Dinner main courses, $19–22.

Ⴘ **Tuscarora Mill** (703-771-9300; www.tuskies.com), 203 Harrison Street, Leesburg. A café, bar, and bakery in the middle of historic Leesburg, Tuskie's, as it is known locally, is in a historic 19th-century mill, where mill equipment still hangs over the bar and exposed brick reminds visitors of its provenance. Long a proponent of the "eat local" movement, the

FEASTING IN LITTLE VIETNAM

Northern Virginia has one of the largest populations of Vietnamese immigrants in the United States—and that means it has some of the best Vietnamese restaurants, as well. Many of them are located at the Eden Center, northern Virginia's "Little Vietnam," a shopping complex that feels like a foreign country has plopped right down in the middle of Wilson Boulevard in Falls Church, Virginia. Some say it is a center for Vietnamese Americans all up and down the East Coast.

This sprawling set of shops and restaurants—some facing the winding corridors of small indoor shopping malls, others facing the parking lot, strip-mall style—buzzes with people of all ages, chatting away in Vietnamese as they linger over bowls of *pho* (noodle soup) or sip bubble tea through oversized straws. There are plenty of shopping opportunities, which makes this place a vibrant spot even when it's not mealtime: There are hairdressers; music shops and jewelry stores; gift shops with Buddha statues of all sizes; places where you can buy electronics, get a pedicure or manicure, or buy a plane ticket and a trip to . . . Vietnam. There is karaoke. There are bars. And cafés. And a Chinese herb shop. And delis, where you can buy exotic produce such as sapodilla, pomelo, guava, and papaya, or premade treats such as shredded spicy dry squid or packets of sticky sweet rice wrapped neatly in banana leaves.

Presiding over all of it is the Eden Center Clock Tower, a replica of the clock tower in Saigon, and an intricately carved lion arch at the Wilson Boulevard Entrance.

What we like best here is the food. There are so many quick carry-outs and leisurely sit-down restaurants, it's hard to decide where to go; but whatever spot you choose, be prepared for a mixture of familiar dishes and some more unusual ones. You'll probably recognize spring rolls; noodle soups with beef, chicken, or seafood; stir-fried vegetables with or without meat; and egg

chef here relies heavily on locally available produce, cheese, wine, and livestock, so you'll see such things as local goat cheese mousse with figs, rack of lamb made with local meat, and a vegetarian tikka masala crafted with local produce. A nice wine list includes a number of local bottles as well.

✳ **Entertainment**

Arlington Cinema & Drafthouse (703-486-2345; www.arlingtondrafthouse.com), 2903 Columbia Pike, Arlington. A fun place to combine food and film, or, on Thursday nights, stand-up comedy. Situated in a 1950s-era movie house, the Cinema & Drafthouse offers a full menu of piz-

noodles with various combinations of meats, tofu, and vegetables. There's also caramelized seafood and meat, lemongrass-flavored dishes, and "hot pot" soups in various combinations. We enjoy the ground beef–stuffed grape leaves and summer rolls wrapped in thin rice paper and stuffed with carrots, cilantro, and shrimp. Some of the more unusual selections include jellyfish, salty fried squid, and pork blood in stir-fries and soups.

If you're on the go, pop into a deli and get a bubble tea. Usually fruit-based, these sweet drinks come with tapioca pearls, or "bubbles," that give them an unexpected texture. Another favorite: Vietnamese iced coffee, its intensity cut with creamy, sweetened condensed milk.

For those unfamiliar with Vietnamese food, here are a few pointers:

- Sauces are key. You'll find them already on your table, or delivered with your meal. Ask which go with which dishes, or experiment: You'll have many from which to choose, including hot chili sauce, fish sauce (which tends to be salty), bean sauce, soy sauce, and vinegar-based sauces. Some will be quite spicy, so proceed with caution.
- Fresh herbs are delivered in piles of fragrant leaves, still on their stems— typically basil, mint, and cilantro. Use them liberally. They're especially delicious with noodle soups (*pho*) and eggy, savory crepes called *bánh xèo*, as they help cut the richness of both dishes.
- Be prepared for raw meat if you order pho. This clear-brothed dish, usually beef-based, comes as a bowl of noodles and piping-hot broth, which cooks the raw beef as you stir. Piles of bean sprouts and herbs plus liberal use of sauces will make this dish especially flavorful.
- Vietnamese desserts are unlike those to which most Americans are accustomed. Many are based on sweet sticky rice; others involve red beans, coconut, and gelatin.

zas, sandwiches, a few main courses, and munchies with tableside service, a mix of comfy theater seats and tables, and a range of current and vintage films. There are microbrews and wine as well. Movies are $5.50.

The Birchmere Music Hall (703-549-7500; www.birchmere.com), 3701 Mount Vernon Avenue, Alexandria. This legendary music hall has helped launched the careers of such luminaries as Mary Chapin Carpenter, Lyle Lovett, Shawn Colvin, Jerry Jeff Walker, Dave Matthews, Vince Gill, John Prine, Emmylou Harris, Linda Ronstadt, and k.d. lang. The intimate atmosphere lends itself to down-to-earth singer-songwriters and rockin' bands. There are tables and chairs— and a full menu—in the Music Hall;

the Bandstand is meant for dance-oriented bands, and some shows there are standing only. The kitchen opens at 6 PM, most shows begin around 8, but many people arrive early to get a seat. The food is surprisingly good, given that the focus here really is the music: bar food plus generous salads, some sandwiches, pizza, grilled salmon, and ribs. Music reigns supreme. $14–18.

Fairfax Symphony Orchestra (703-827-0600; http://fairfaxsymphony.org), performances at George Mason University's Center for the Arts in Fairfax, and the Hylton Performing Arts Center on the GMU campus in Manassas. This nationally respected orchestra, which is more than 50 years old, presents more than 100 events each year, with prestigious guest musicians and classical favorites like Tchaikovsky, Mozart, and Beethoven. Free summer concerts in Fairfax County parks; regular tickets $25–55.

Signature Theatre (703-527-1833; www.signature-theatre.org), 4200 Campbell Avenue, Arlington. One of the go-to theaters for the entire Washington region, Signature has grown from its roots in an Arlington garage to a glistening modern building in Shirlington Village; along the way, it's built a fine reputation for itself as a premier spot for contemporary musicals and plays, winning a Tony Award for Regional Theater in 2009. Its spacious lobby is great for hanging out over drinks and snacks before or after the shows, which consistently get favorable reviews from national theater critics. Signature is best known for its musicals and has become a definitive Sondheim showcase; it promotes itself as taking on challenging work, both new and reworked. Among recent shows:

Dirty Blonde, Show Boat, I Am My Own Wife, and *Sweeney Todd.* $70–100.

Synetic Theater (1-800-494-8497; www.synetictheater.org), 4041 South 28th Street, Crystal City neighborhood of Arlington. A unique theater company that emphasizes movement over sound, Synetic performs such classics as *Hamlet*, and *Romeo and Juliet*—with no words. Calling itself "simultaneously avant-garde and accessible," the award-winning theater performs a mix of dance, mime, drama, and movement at big D.C. venues such as the Kennedy Center for the Performing Arts and the Shakespeare Theatre Company's Lansburgh Theatre as well as its home theater in Crystal City. Tickets generally $30–50.

Wolf Trap National Park for the Performing Arts (703-225-1900; 703-255-1860; www.wolftrap.org), 1624 Trap Road, Vienna. This regional venue for performing arts draws national audiences for a broad range of entertainment, mostly music and dance, to its 6,800-seat outdoor amphitheater or the 382-seat indoor "Barns." From May through September, visitors typically buy stadium seats under a shelter and close to the stage, or lawn tickets, joining hundreds of people who spread picnic blankets on the grass and pop bottles of wine while they listen to favorite bands. Genres are all over the map, from country western, Cajun, and rock and roll to opera, blues, pop, orchestra, and theater. The Barns is open year-round. Concessions are available; there's a restaurant, Ovations, on-site; and you can order a picnic basket if you don't have time to pack one yourself. Typically, tickets are $20–85.

NIGHTLIFE: BARS, CLUBS, EATERIES

Alexandria

Ⓨ **Grille Piano Bar**, Morrison House (703-838-8000; www.morrisonhouse.com), 116 South Alfred Street. Open Thu.–Sun. 8 PM–10 PM. Serving bistro fare, the piano bar in the Morrison House sets a refined tone with paneled walls, fireplace, and leather club chairs. The place tends to attract a "seasoned" crowd. $17–29.

Ⓨ **Murphy's Irish Pub** (703-548-1717; www.murphyspub.com), 713 King Street. Open Tue.–Sat. 4–late, Sun. 11–2. Wash down your Irish meat and potato pie with a pint of Guinness at this traditional Irish pub. Then, toe-tap along to the live Irish music performed nightly. $7–15.

Ⓨ **PX** (703-299-8384; www.eamonns dublinchipper.com), 728 King Street. Open Wed.–Sat. 6 PM–late. Inspired by speakeasies, PX doesn't have a sign. Instead look for the blue light. Like the members of 1920s clubs, patrons dress for drinks. *GQ* magazine included PX in a list of the 25 best cocktail bars in America. $6–9.

Arlington

Ⓨ ⒴ **CarPool** (703-532-7665; www.gocarpool.com), 4000 Fairfax Drive. Open Mon.–Fri. 11:30 AM–2 AM, Sat. noon–2 AM, Sun. noon–1 AM. There's lots of game playing here on the 10 pool tables, four shuffleboard courts, and seven dartboards. Sports enthusiasts like the 30-plus televisions. $8–13.

Ⓨ **Clarendon Ballroom** (703-469-2244; www.clarendonballroom.com), 3185 Wilson Boulevard. Rooftop only open Wed. 5 PM–midnight in warm weather. rooftop and ballroom Thu.–Fri. 5 PM–2 AM. Meet, mingle and dance with the young professionals who frequent this popular place known for its rooftop. Typically, no cover.

WOLF TRAP NATIONAL PARK FOR THE PERFORMING ARTS

Visit Fairfax

♉ **Galaxy Hut** (703-525-8646; www .galaxyhut.com), 2711 Wilson Boulevard, Clarendon neighborhood of Arlington. A hip but tiny music venue, bar, and restaurant, Galaxy Hut is especially popular among artsy 20- and 30-somethings who gather around for craft and imported beer (20 taps and 30 bottles), pinball, tabletop video games, and a jukebox (except on Sundays and Mondays, when there is live music). While some see much of Clarendon as a collection of upscale chain stores, Galaxy Hut is a hangout for those who'd rather fight convention. Cover $5.

♉ **Guarapo** (703-528-6500; www .latinconcepts.com/guarapo.php), 2039 Wilson Boulevard. Open Mon.– Thu. 5–10:30, Fri. and Sat. 5–11:30; lounge Thu.–Sat. 9 PM–1 AM. The Latin flair extends to the South American tapas and much of the music. Live bands and DJs in the lounge. $8–17.

♉ **Iota Club and Café** (703-522-8340; www.iotaclubandcafe.com), 2832 Wilson Boulevard, Clarendon neighborhood of Arlington. Open Mon.–Fri. 6:30 AM–late, Sat. and Sun. 8 AM–late. This combination café and no-frills club is a popular venue for local and up-and-coming musicians. The café has a full and thoughtful menu and an intimate, cozy ambience; the club is small and crowded (on a good night), but everyone makes room to dance. You can get bar food (burgers, nachos, fries) in the club. Bands are generally singer-songwriters with roots rock, bluegrass/rock, folk, and quirky (ukulele, anyone?) fare. Performance tickets are inexpensive, around $12.

♉ **Velocity Five** (703-243-4900; www .velocityfiverestaurant.com/arlington),

2300 Clarendon Boulevard. Open daily 11 AM–2 AM. Music, dancing, and entertainment after 10 PM. Part of a chain of sports bars, this one has 5,200 square feet indoors plus 30 large-screen televisions. The place is known for its chicken wings. $10–19.

Manassas
City Tavern (703-330-0076; www .citytaverngrille.com), Open Mon.– Sat. 11 AM–2 AM, Sun. 10 AM–2 AM. In between munching on traditional American fare of burgers or chicken seafood, dance nightly to music by DJs or watch sports on the several televisions. $10–17.

✽ **Selective Shopping**

Alexandria
Arts Afire (703-838-9785; www.arts afire.com), 1117 King Street. Contemporary American crafts heavy on glass art, such as beads, jewelry, and kaleidoscopes (they even offer a kaleidoscope-making workshop) plus pottery, fiber art, turned wood, and functional objects that double as art. More than 400 local and international artists are featured here.

Artcraft (703-299-6616; www.artcraft online.com), 132 King Street. A fun collection representing some 500 artists and their eclectic crafts, many of them functional: hand-painted furniture, candles, handbags, turned wooden bowls, pottery, and more in all sorts of styles, from art deco to American craft. Expect some quirky items in the mix, such as bracelets made of recycled aluminum cans and pewter measuring cups adorned with birds.

The Fibre Space (703-664-0344; www.fibrespace.com), 102 North Fayette Street. A knitting and crochet store packed full of brightly colored yarns and knitting knickknacks, this is also home to a community of knitters, with comfortable places to take out your needles and knit a few rows yourself, plus classes for all skill levels.

Gossypia (703-836-6969; www .gossypia.com), 325 Cameron Street. An eclectic boutique on two floors of a historic townhome, Gossypia features a trove of Latin American folk art (including nativity sets and Day of the Dead items), fun and funky jewelry, wearable art, and more practical women's clothing, from Flax and Eileen Fisher to one-of-a-kind informal wedding and special-occasion dresses.

The King's Own Gift Shoppe (703-836-6686), 213 King Street, Alexandria. You'll be greeted by a Renaissance-costumed clerk when you walk into this quirky shop and browse through an eclectic stock of hand-carved chess sets, suits of armor, handmade furniture, and a collection of fairy figurines. The shop is associated with Medieval Madness at Renaissance Hall, 1121 King Street, a weekends-only medieval-themed dinner theater.

La Cuisine: The Cook's Resource (703-836-4435; http://lacuisineus .com), 323 Cameron Street. With a staff and owners who call themselves the Cuisinettes, you know you'll get service with a sense of humor at this kitchen store. Designed for serious and playful cooks, the shop carries high-end pots and pans, canning supplies, grills and grill tools, and all sorts of other useful tools and fun kitchen accoutrements, from chocolate chippers to chile pepper lights to children's cookbooks. They do not carry

what their literature describes as "trendy gadgets with dubious uses which take up too much drawer space and spawn innumerable yard sales," and they claim they test all goods before they select them for their shelves.

Scottish Merchant (703-739-2302; www.scottishmerchant.com), 215 King Street This shop celebrates the fact that Alexandria was founded by Scottish people, and offers wares from the homeland: tartan scarves and ties, kilts and skirts, clan crest plaques, and the opportunity to order your own clan's tartan and have it tailored to fit. There are also Scottish music, books, Celtic jewelry, and, yes, bagpipes. The shop is combined with **John Crouch Tobacconist**, with imported cigars, pipes, cigarettes, snuff, and smokers' paraphernalia.

Arlington
The Fashion Centre at Pentagon City (703-415-2401; www.simon.com /mall/?id=157), 1100 South Hayes Street, Arlington. One of the closest megamalls to Washington, D.C., Pentagon City has three floors with more than 170 stores and restaurants. Anchors include Macy's, Nordstrom, the Ritz-Carlton, Ann Taylor, and Apple. There's also a Banana Republic, bebe, Coach, Cole Haan, J.Crew, J.Jill, Kenneth Cole, and Guess.

Le Village Marché (703-379-4444; www.levillagemarche.com), 4150 Campbell Avenue, Suite 101, in Shirlington Village. Voted best place to find an unusual gift, Le Village Marché has a distinctive French flair, flea market style, with stacks of French linens and tea towels, fragrant soaps and bath products, vintage porcelain, and antique armoires. Inspired by turn-of-the-century Paris

DEL RAY

If you've had enough of Old Town Alexandria's cobblestones and colonial history, head up King Street and out to Del Ray, a neighborhood known more for its artists and quirky cafés than for 18th-century tradition.

Not that there's no history here—it's just more recent. A designated historic district, Del Ray was one of the first commuter suburbs, connected to Washington, D.C., by electric rail. Its buildings date to the early 20th century but also span the 1940s and '50s. Victorian gingerbread mixes with bungalows and ramblers, with a few colonials and row houses thrown in for good measure.

The neighborhood is more affordable than Old Town (but not so affordable—homes still go for $400,000-plus), so residents tend to be younger. Many are professionals who work in the city and commute by the nearby Metro, but there are also many artists and musicians, and it seems, a healthy share of alternative health practitioners—think acupuncture, body work, and New Age spa. There is a real sense of community here. The area motto is, "Del Ray, Where Main Street Still Exists," and it's not unusual to see clusters of neighbors hanging out, usually with dogs on leashes, catching up on the local news.

For visitors, Del Ray is a charmingly funky collection of restaurants and gift shops and the friendly folks running them. Like old-time communities, there is a butcher, a baker—and instead of a candlestick maker, a cheese shop and a place called **Planet Wine**, with artisan wines and craft beers—the butcher, **Let's Meat on the Ave** (703-836-6328), 2403 Mount Vernon Avenue; the baker, **Caboose Bakery** (703-566-1283; www.caboose-cafe.com), 2419 Mount Vernon Avenue; the cheese shop **Cheesetique** (703-706-3800; cheesetique.com), 2411 Mount Vernon Avenue. One of our favorite spots is the **Dairy Godmother** (703-683-7767; www.thedairygodmother.com), 2310 Mount Vernon Avenue, a popular ice-cream parlor where locals follow the "forecast" of flavors and plan visits accordingly. The shop serves vanilla and chocolate frozen custard plus one flavor that changes daily, such as banana pudding, caramel Heath bar, or lemon meringue pie. There are also

and the lost generation, the shop allows rustic and refined to bump elbows in a mix of merchandise that recalls the City of Light.

Random Harvest (703-527-9690; www.randomharvesthome.com), 4522

Lee Highway. Originally from the Upper West Side of New York City, Random Harvest now has locations in Old Town Alexandria, Georgetown, and Bethesda, MD, as well as this Arlington spot. Its eclectic collection

innovative sorbets such as lemon lavender and mango lassi, plus ice pops in lemon basil, apricot, and saffron, and ice pops for dogs.

For coffee, **St. Elmo's Coffee Pub** (703-739-9268; www.stelmoscoffeepub .com), 2300 Mount Vernon Avenue, is the gathering place, with muraled walls and local art exhibited, mismatched comfy couches and chairs, coffee drinks, smoothies, sandwiches, and salads and the ubiquitous community bulletin board that shows up in many businesses along "the Avenue"—Mount Vernon Avenue, the neighborhood's Main Street. **Artfully Chocolate/Kingsbury Confections** (703-635-7917; www.thecocoagallery.com), 2003A Mount Vernon Avenue, specializes in hot chocolate combinations named for divas, such as Bette, Marilyn, and Eartha—no last names required.

For noncomestibles, you'll find fun shops. **A Show of Hands** (703-683-2905; www.ashowofhands.biz), 2301 Mount Vernon Avenue, is an artists' collective of eclectic crafts and paintings, photography and jewelry, complete with vintage lawn chairs set around the outdoor patio for visiting. **Clay Queen Pottery** (703-549-7775; http://theclayqueen.com), 2303 Mount Vernon Avenue, has a small gallery of high-fired, functional stoneware and porcelain as well as a schedule of classes for potters and wannabes. Visit **Kiskadee** (703-549-0813; http://kiskadee shop.com), 2205 Mount Vernon Avenue, for resort-style women's and men's clothing, jewelry, and gifts.

On Saturdays from 8 in the morning until noon, a farmers' market draws neighbors together to buy locally grown produce. Every first Thursday of the month is Thursday on the Avenue, with shops open late, live music, food specials, and different themes such as "dog days of summer" and "taste of Del Ray." There's also an art market with local artisans every first Saturday from June through September and November, at the **Del Ray Artisans Gallery** (703-838-4827), 2704 Mount Vernon Avenue. In October, **Art on the Avenue** attracts more than 40,000 visitors and locals to browse arts and crafts from hundreds of vendors, from painters and potters to photographers and fabric artists.

For more on the Del Ray neighborhood, and to get a street map and list of shops, services, and restaurants, go to www.visitdelray.com.

includes a mixture of antique, vintage, and new furniture, as well as decorative objects such as mirrors, lamps, pillows, and prints. Expect a mix of genuine antiques and well-wrought reproductions set up in a spacious shop that, despite the many items displayed, manages not to feel cluttered.

Woodmont Weavers/Ellipse Fine Crafts (703-469-1892; www.stcoletta .org), Ballston Common Mall. When you buy the handcrafted place mats, pillows, totes, scarves, and hats at this gallery/studio, you are supporting the artisan group of adults with cognitive disabilities that makes them. In addition to producing lovely wearable and workable art (jewelry, pottery, glass sculptures, and more) the work helps teach independence and social skills.

Fredericksburg

Art First Gallery (540-371-7107; www.artfirstgallery.com), 824 Caroline Street. Open Mon.–Thu. 11–7, Fri. and Sat. 11–9, Sun. noon–7. Founded in 1992, this is Fredericksburg's first artists cooperative. More than 30 local artists here cover a wide range of creative territory, with acrylics, oils, watercolors, pastels, prints, photography, jewelry, and fiber arts. Member exhibits change monthly.

The Griffin Bookshop and Coffee Bar (540-899-8041; http://thegriffin bookshopcoffeebar.com), 723 Caroline Street. This cozy shop, with comfy chairs, a fireplace, and shelves of new and used books, is also a neighborhood meeting place where friends can share a coffee drink (made with free-trade, organic coffee) and a sweet, or listen to live music (on Friday and Saturday nights). Along with the books, the Griffin sells tea sets, tea pots, mugs, and other unusual gifts. An outdoor patio is open in warm weather.

Liberty Town Arts Workshop (540-371-7255; www.libertytownarts.com), 916 Liberty Street. Open Mon.–Thu. 10–6, Fri. and Sat. 10–5, and Sun. noon to 4. You can get a big dose of local artists here, as Liberty Town hosts 25 artists' studios and more than 50 artists and craftspeople. Paintings, fiber art, decorative ceramics, pottery, handcrafted jewelry, and more are for

sale, but that's not all: Artists also teach classes at the pottery school and exhibit in the art and craft gallery.

The Wounded Bookshop (540-373-1311), 109 Amelia Street. Operated by the nonprofit Fredericksburg Athenaeum and dedicated to supporting the arts and letters, this eclectic space is part art gallery, part used bookstore, and part venue for poetry readings, book signings, music, and other cultural events.

Other locations in northern Virginia

Potomac Mills (703-496-9301; www .simon.com/mall/default.aspx?id=1260), 2700 Potomac Mills Circle, Woodbridge. This megamall just of I-95 has more than 200 retail stores (including a number of discount outlets), plus restaurants and a movie theater. Anchors include Neiman Marcus Last Call, Saks Fifth Avenue Outlet OFF 5TH, Nordstrom Rack, Costco, Off Broadway Shoe Warehouse, and Modell's Sporting Goods. There are also factory outlets for Coach, J.Crew, Polo Ralph Lauren, Brooks Brothers, and Banana Republic.

Tysons Galleria (703-827-7730; www.tysonsgalleria.com), 2001 International Drive, McLean. The upscale megamall caters to high-end-brand shoppers, hosting more than 120 retailers and six restaurants. Among the most popular are Burberry, Cartier, Chanel, and Versace; there's also Lacoste, Thomas Pink, Eileen Fisher, and Stuart Weitzman, plus Ann Taylor, Coach, J.Crew, and Anthropologie. Restaurants include Maggiano's Little Italy, Legal Sea Foods of Boston, and P. F. Chang's China Bistro.

FREDERICKSBURG ANTIQUES

Surrounded by all that colonial history, you'll want to wander Old Town Fredericksburg and poke in and out of small antique shops, which is a lovely way to spend an afternoon—or you could hit multiple antique dealers at once by visiting one of the following collectives:

Fredericksburg Antique Gallery (540-373-2961), 1023 Caroline Street, Mon.–Sat. 10–5 and Sun. noon–5. A wide variety of 18th- and 19th-century furniture, Civil War items, antique jewelry, paintings, glassware, quilts, porcelain, silver, china, rungs, lamps, Majolica, and more from 35 dealers.

Fredericksburg Antiques Mall (540-372-6894), 211 William Street, Mon.–Sat. 10–5 and Sun. noon–5, features 35 dealers offering furniture, fine art, jewelry, prints, linens, pewter, toys, antique clocks, primitives, books, china, quilts, pottery, and other collectibles.

R&R Antiques Shop (540-371-0685), 1001 Caroline Street, Mon.–Sat. 10–5, Sun. noon–5. This is the biggest antique mall in Old Town Fredericksburg, where you'll find mahogany, cherry, oak, country, and wicker furniture, toys, linens, stained glass, flo blue glass, depression glass, jewelry, dolls, books, comics, mirrors, Fiestaware, and collectibles.

River Run Antique Mall (540-371-4588), 925 Caroline Street, Mon.–Sat. 10–6, Sun. noon–6, more merchants with country and primitive items, coins, clocks, and sports memorabilia.

Upstairs, Downstairs Antiques (540-373-0370), 922 Caroline Street, Mon., Tue., Thu., and Fri. 10–4, Sat. 10–5, Sun. noon–5, has 30 dealers with furniture, glassware, collectibles, jewelry, toys, Wedgewood, sterling flatware, and Boy Scout and fishing items.

✳ Special Events

February: **George Washington's Birthday Celebration** at Mount Vernon, President's Day Weekend (703-780-2000; www.mountvernon.org), 3200 Mount Vernon Memorial Highway, at the south end of George Washington Memorial Parkway. You can join "George Washington" at his favorite breakfast (hoecakes drenched in butter and honey, cooked over an open fire), watch a parade with fife and drum corps, see a Revolutionary War battle demonstration, and visit with costumed characters all day in celebration of the birthday boy.

September: **Alexandria Festival of the Arts**, early September (954-472-3755; http://artfestival.com). From Washington Street to the Potomac

River, King Street fills with paintings, life-size sculptures, photography, glass, wood, jewelry, collage, and ceramics from more than 200 artists and crafts people. The juried exhibit is designed to be diverse, and includes both international and local artists. Artwork is both on exhibit and for sale, with prices ranging from $25 for hand-designed earrings to $20,000 for metal sculptures.

Rosslyn Jazz Festival, early September (http://rosslynnva.org), Gateway Park, 1300 Lee Highway, at the base of the Key Bridge, Rosslyn neighborhood of Arlington. A mix of national and local acts, this festival is held on the banks of the Potomac and has featured such musicians as Joe Henderson, Dave Valentine, Nnenna Freelon, and Ahmad Jamal. A street festival also includes food and artisans.

October: **Art on the Avenue**, early October (www.artontheavenue.org), Mount Vernon Avenue. Some 350 artisans and thousands of area residents turn up for this art festival in the creative, funky Del Ray neighborhood of Alexandria. In addition to exhibits and the art works and crafts for sale, there are hands-on art activities, live music, and kids' activities, plus food, dance, and yoga demonstrations, and a pie-baking contest.

Hot Air Balloon, Wine & Music Festival, mid-October, Long Branch Historic House and Farm (540-837-1856; 1-877-868-1811; www.historic longbranch.com).

December: **Scottish Christmas Walk Weekend and Parade**, early December (703-548-0111; www .scottishchristmaswalk.com), Alexandria. Bagpipes herald this annual event, which involves more than 100 clans and pipe and drum bands—with their Scottish terriers and hounds—marching the historic streets of Alexandria (with its rich Scottish heritage). Nearly 30,000 people come out to see the spectacle and participate in activities scheduled throughout the weekend, including a Christmas Marketplace, a heather and greens sale, a tour of decorated homes, a children's tea party, and a Taste of Scotland food event.

Central Virginia 4

CENTRAL VIRGINIA

Steeped in history, central Virginia is also thoroughly modern. Richmond, the state's capital, lures visitors with its sophisticated dining, the excellent Virginia Museum of Fine Arts, and trendy shopping. Charlottesville is home to the gem of the state's higher education system, the University of Virginia. Lynchburg, 60 miles south of Charlottesville and 95 miles from Richmond, swells during the academic year with students at Liberty University, founded by the Reverend Jerry Falwell, who also established the city's Thomas Road Baptist Church, 25,000 members strong.

The Richmond, Lynchburg, and Charlottesville regions draw history buffs as well. Significant Civil War battles bloodied the lands surrounding Richmond and Lynchburg. In Richmond, the Confederate capital, tour the Museum and White House of the Confederacy. The American Civil War Center at Historic Tredegar interprets the Civil War from three perspectives: Union, Confederate, and African American. Just south of Richmond is Petersburg, site of a 292-day Union siege that helped define the last days of the war. In Bedford, near Lynchburg, at what is now Appomattox Court House National Historical Park, General Robert E. Lee surrendered to General Ulysses S. Grant. Charlottesville has one of America's great, historic homes: Thomas Jefferson's Monticello. Nearby are the homes of two other presidents, James Monroe's Ash Lawn–Highland and James Madison's Montpelier.

But central Virginia is not all bustling cities and "big" history. Canoe and kayak on the James River, play on the region's many golf courses; bike along back country roads; and ski, hike, and simply hang out at the Blue Ridge Mountains' Wintergreen Resort.

TOWNS AND COUNTIES Bedford County. With a population of about 67,000, Bedford County is one of Virginia's fastest-growing counties. Consisting of 764 square miles in the western central portion of Virginia, the rich Piedmont land nurtures five wineries, with more expected. The town of Bedford, about 28 miles southwest of Lynchburg, is the site of the National D-Day Memorial.

Charlottesville and Albemarle County. Charlottesville, long associated with Thomas Jefferson, who lived at Monticello and designed the original buildings of

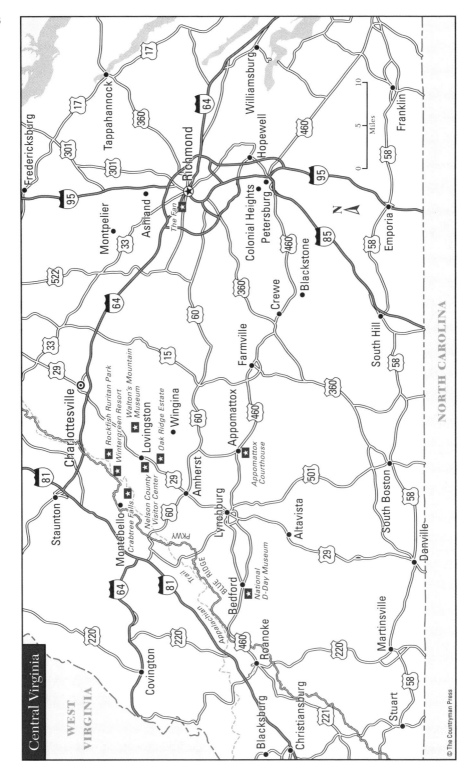

Central Virginia

WEST VIRGINIA

NORTH CAROLINA

© The Countryman Press

Miles
10
5
0

N

Fredericksburg
Tappahannock
17
17
301
301
360
64
Williamsburg
Hopewell
460
95
Franklin
58
58
Emporia
85
58
Richmond
The Fan
Montpelier
33
Ashland
522
95
81
Staunton
Charlottesville
29
33
64
Rockfish Ruritan Park
Wintergreen Resort
Walton's Mountain Museum
Lovingston
Oak Ridge Estate
Wingina
Nelson County Visitor Center
Montebello
Crabtree Falls
60
29
Amherst
15
60
Farmville
360
60
Crewe
Blackstone
South Hill
360
58
Appomattox
460
Appomattox Courthouse
501
Lynchburg
BLUE RIDGE PKWY
Appalachian Trail
Bedford
National D-Day Museum
81
64
220
Covington
220
460
Roanoke
Blacksburg
221
Christiansburg
Stuart
58
Martinsville
220
Altavista
29
South Boston
58
Danville
Colonial Heights
Petersburg
460

the University of Virginia's campus, is a Southern charmer of a city, steeped in tradition and set in the scenic Blue Ridge Mountain foothills. Although Jefferson never realized his dream of quality vineyards, others have. The Monticello Wine Trail leads to the region's many wineries. Charlottesville's county, Albemarle, has nurtured many future presidents whose homes may be toured.

Lynchburg. Nestled at the foothills of the Blue Ridge Mountains, Lynchburg, also known as the "City of Seven Hills," has a population of 68,000, and is about 60 miles south of Charlottesville and 95 miles from Richmond. Lynchburg is also often called the "City of Churches" because of its 281 such facilities. Jerry Falwell founded the Thomas Road Baptist Church, now a major Lynchburg institution with 25,000 members and a 1-million-square-foot facility. Civil War buffs head to the city for its significant sites.

Nelson County. Adjacent to Albemarle County, more rural Nelson County is midway between metropolitan Charlottesville and Lynchburg. If you've ever watched the television series *The Waltons,* then you have something of a sense of Nelson County, at least as it was during the Depression. The series took its inspiration from author Earl Hamner Jr.'s writings about his childhood there during the 1930s. The James River borders the county's east and the Blue Ridge Mountains form the western border, which has 30 miles of the scenic Blue Ridge Parkway. Farmland and orchards dot the valley's rolling hills, and hikers and skiers

VIRGINIA MUSEUM OF FINE ARTS

Bilyana Dimitrova

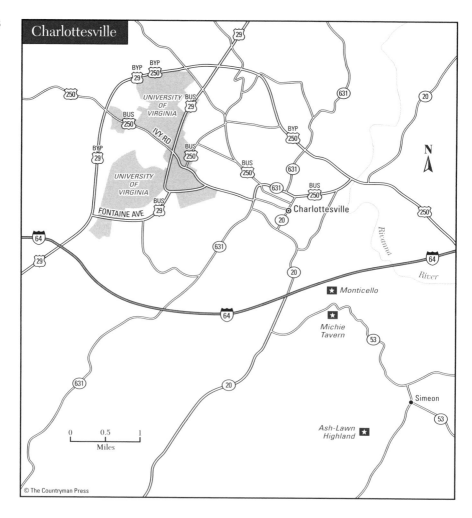

Charlottesville

take to the mountains and the Appalachian Trail in season. Nelson County has long served as a recreational getaway for work-weary urbanites in Virginia and neighboring states.

Petersburg. After the Union forces failed to vanquish Richmond, Union general Ulysses Grant stated, "The key to taking Richmond is Petersburg." Situated on the Appomattox River 23 miles south of Richmond, Petersburg also had five railroad lines. Grant knew that if he cut off supplies from Petersburg to Richmond, then he could win the capital of the Confederacy. It was at Petersburg that the last decisive engagement of the Civil War was fought.

Richmond. Virginia's capital since 1780, Richmond is a cosmopolitan city with deep Southern roots. As the capital of the Confederacy from 1861 to 1865, Richmond is rich in Civil War sites. In addition to history, Richmond offers beautiful gardens and intriguing museums, including the expanded Virginia Museum of Fine Arts, and vibrant neighborhoods. The Fan District blooms with restored homes, Monument Avenue has elegant mansions and Shockoe Slip and Carytown offer restaurants, shopping and nightlife.

GUIDANCE **Albemarle Visitor Information County Office Building** (434-293-6789; 1-877-386-1103; www.visitcharlottesville.org), 401 McIntire Road. Open Mon.–Fri. 9–5. **Albemarle County Virginia** (www.albemarle.org).

Bedford Welcome Center (540-587-5681; 1-877-447-3257; www.visitbedford .com), 816 Burks Hill Road, intersection of Rtes. 460 and 122.

Charlottesville Albemarle County Downtown Visitor Center (434-293-6789; 1-877-386-1103; www.visitcharlottesville.org), 610 East Main Street, Charlottesville. Open daily 9–5. Closed Thanksgiving, Dec. 25, and Jan. 1.

Lynchburg Regional Convention and Visitors Bureau (434-847-1811; 1-800-732-5821; www.discoverlynchburg.com), 216 12th Street.

Nelson County Tourist Information (434-263-7015; 1-800-282-8223; www.nelsoncounty.com; www.virginia.org), 8519 Thomas Nelson Highway, Lovingston.

Petersburg Visitor Center (804-733-2400; www.petersburg-va.org), 19 Bolling-brook Street.

Petersburg Area Regional Tourism (1-877-730-7278; www.petersburgarea .org), P.O. Box 1776.

Richmond Metropolitan Convention & Visitors Bureau (804-783-7450; 1-800-370-9004; www.visitrichmondva.com), 405 North Third Street, Richmond.

GETTING THERE *By air:* The nearest commercial airport to Charlottesville is the **Charlottesville-Albemarle Airport** (434-973-8341; www.gocho.com), 201 Bowen Loop, about 8 miles from downtown Charlottesville and 40 miles from Wintergreen Resort. **Lynchburg Regional Airport** (434-582-1150; www.lynch burgva.gov/airport), 4308 Wards Road, no. 100, is about 6 miles from Lynch-burg.

Richmond International Airport (804-226-1227; www.flyrichmond.com), 1 Richard E. Byrd Terminal Drive. Richmond is about 13 miles from Richmond, and is one of two airports convenient to Petersburg. The other is the **Newport News/Williamsburg International Airport** (757-877-0221; www.nnwairport .com), 900 Bland Boulevard, Newport News.

By bus: **Charlottesville**, the nearest major city to Wintergreen Resort, is serv-iced by **Greyhound Bus Line** (434-295-5131; 1-800-231-2222; www.greyhound .com), 310 West Main Street. **Lynchburg** is also serviced by **Greyhound**, 1301 Kemper Street. **Greyhound** travels to Richmond, 2910 North Street, Rich-mond, and to **Petersburg**, 108 East Washington Street.

By car: **Charlottesville and Albemarle County:** Charlottesville is about 120 miles (2½ hours) southwest of Washington, D.C. From D.C., take I-66 to Rte. 29 south. Charlottesville is about 65 miles from Richmond and about 58 miles from

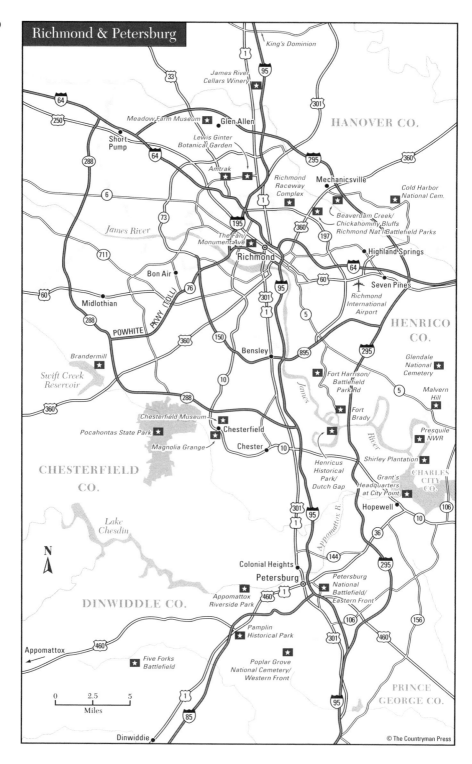

Richmond & Petersburg

King's Dominion

James River
Cellars Winery

Meadow Farm Museum   Glen Allen

Short
Pump

Lewis Ginter
Botanical Garden

HANOVER CO.

Cold Harbor
National Cem.

Amtrak

Richmond
Raceway
Complex

Mechanicsville

Beaverdam Creek/
Chickahominy Bluffs
Richmond Nat'l Battlefield Parks

James River

The Fan
Monument Ave.

Richmond

Highland Springs

Bon Air

Seven Pines

Richmond
International
Airport

Midlothian

HENRICO
CO.

POWHITE PKWY (TOLL)

Bensley

Brandermill

Glendale
National
Cemetery

Swift Creek
Reservoir

Malvern
Hill

James River

Fort Harrison/
Battlefield
Park Rd

Fort
Brady

Presquile
NWR

Chesterfield Museum

Pocahontas State Park

Chesterfield

Chester

Shirley Plantation

Magnolia Grange

Henricus
Historical
Park/
Dutch Gap

Grant's
Headquarters
at City Point

CHARLES
CITY
CO.

CHESTERFIELD
CO.

Hopewell

Lake
Chesdin

Appomattox R.

N

Colonial Heights

Petersburg

Petersburg
National
Battlefield/
Eastern Front

DINWIDDLE CO.

Appomattox
Riverside Park

Appomattox

Pamplin
Historical Park

Five Forks
Battlefield

Poplar Grove
National Cemetery/
Western Front

PRINCE
GEORGE CO.

0   2.5   5
Miles

Dinwiddie

© The Countryman Press

Lynchburg. From Richmond, take I-64 West to Charlottesville. From Lynchburg, take 29 North to Charlottesville.

Lynchburg is about 180 miles (nearly 4 hours) from Washington, D.C. From Washington and Baltimore, take US 50 west and continue I-66 West. Take I-81 south and I-64 east and continue to US 250 east toward US 29 South. Take VA 130 west to State Rte. 669. Lynchburg is about 115 miles (2½ hours) from Richmond. From Richmond, take VA 195 east toward I-64 and continue onto US 29 South to VA 130 west and take route 669.

Petersburg is about 131 miles from Washington, D.C., 25 miles from Richmond and 76 miles from Norfolk. From D.C. and Baltimore, take I-395 south and continue on I-95 south. From Richmond, take VA 195 east onto I-95 south. From Norfolk, take I-264 east to I-64 west and continue on I-295 toward US 60. Continue onto I-295 south and take VA 36 west.

Richmond is about 107 miles (2 hours) from Washington, D.C. From D.C. and Baltimore, take I-395 south to I-95 south and continue onto I-195 south toward VA 195 east and then take US 301. From Norfolk/Hampton Roads, take I-264 east to I-64 west.

Wintergreen Resort and Nelson County: Since much of **Nelson County** is rural, **Wintergreen Resort** (www.wintergreenresort.com) serves as a landmark from which to measure distance. The resort is about 150 miles (3½ hours) from Washington, D.C. From Washington, D.C., take I-66 to Rte. 29 south to I-64 to Rte. 250 to Rte. 151 South to Rte. 664. Wintergreen Resort is also about 100 miles (2½ hours) from Richmond via I-64 west to near Charlottesville to Rte. 29 south, to Rte. 6 to Rte. 151 south to Rte. 664. Wintergreen Resort is 45 miles southwest of Charlottesville.

By train: **Amtrak** (1-800-872-7245; www.amtrak.com), 810 West Main Street, services **Charlottesville** and is the nearest major train station to Nelson County and Wintergreen Resort. Amtrak services **Lynchburg**, 825 Kemper Street; **Richmond**, 1500 East Main Street; and **Petersburg**, 3516 South Street.

GETTING AROUND *By bus and trolley:* Charlottesville Area Transit (CAT) (434-970-3649; www.catchthecat.org), Downtown Transit Station, 615 East Water Street, operates buses in the greater Charlottesville area. CAT also has a convenient and free trolley service that runs along Main Street, making stops every 15 minutes Mon.–Sat. 6:40 AM–11:45 PM, Sun. 8–5:45. The Greater Lynchburg Transit Company (GLTC) (434-455-5090; www.gltconline.com) provides bus service. In Richmond, the GRTC Transit System (804-358-4782; www.ride grtc.com) provides transportation. In Petersburg, the Petersburg Area Transit (PAT) (804-733-2413) offers bus service Mon.–Sat.

By car: A car is convenient and also necessary in **Charlottesville** if you want to tour the surrounding region, visiting the wineries, Monticello, and other sites. In **Nelson County**, a car is necessary; and in **Lynchburg, Richmond**, and **Petersburg** a cars is advisable.

WHEN TO COME In **Charlottesville**, **Lynchburg**, and **Richmond**, spring and summer are high seasons and fall can be busy, too, with homecoming and football games at their respective universities. Spring and summer are high seasons for Petersburg as well. Winter is low season for Charlottesville, Lynchburg, Richmond, and Petersburg.

For **Wintergreen Resort**, ski season rates are the highest. Ski season typically starts in early December and runs through mid-March, depending on the snow and the weather. From mid-March–mid-April (unofficially known as "mud season") and most of November, except for Thanksgiving, until the beginning of ski season, rates are low. Spring, summer, and fall are "shoulder seasons," although these months are gaining in popularity.

MUSEUMS AND HISTORIC LANDMARKS, PLACES, AND SITES

Charlottesville

& **Ash Lawn–Highland** (434-293-8000; www.ashlawnhighland.org), 1000 James Monroe Parkway, 4½ miles southeast of Charlottesville on County Road 795 and 3 miles southwest of Monticello. Open Apr.–Oct. daily 9–6, Nov.–Mar. daily 11–5. Closed Thanksgiving, Dec. 25, and Jan. 1. Unlike nearby Monticello, Ash Lawn–Highland, the estate of James Monroe, fifth president of the United States, isn't a grand manor. In fact, what you see is actually larger than the home Monroe occupied on this site (selected for him by Jefferson, a close friend.) Most people during this era lived in even smaller places than what was built here initially; Monroe's farmhouse originally had five rooms, and later two more were added. Although modest in scale, the home has some distinctive furniture, including the Monroe's carved, four-poster bed, a French mantel clock, and a drop-leaf table constructed from Honduras mahogany sent to Monroe by the people of Santo Domingo (now the Dominican Republic) in gratitude for his policy discouraging intervention by Europe into Western Hemisphere affairs, later known as the "Monroe Doctrine." The property has great views of the Blue Ridge Mountains. On selected summer weekends, the plantation offers hands-on crafts and colonial games. $10 adults, $5 ages 6–11.

& **Kluge-Ruhe Aboriginal Art Collection** (434-244-0234; www.virginia.edu /kluge-ruhe), 400 Worrell Drive, Peter Jefferson Place. Open Tue.–Sat. 10–4, Sun. 1–5. Part of the University of Virginia, the facility features aboriginal paintings from the collections of businessman John Kluge and Edward Ruhe. This off-the-beaten path museum is a great place for art lovers. Free admission.

& **Michie Tavern** (434-977-1234; www.michietavern.com), Hwy. 53, 683 Jefferson Davis Parkway. Open daily 9–5 for tours, restaurant 11:15–3; Living History tours Apr.–Oct. Opened in 1784 as an "ordinary," a place to dine, rest, and socialize along the stagecoach route, Michie (pronounced "mik-ee") Tavern is more than a restaurant, although most of the people on the tour buses have come for its platefuls of fried chicken, pork barbecue, and fixings, and for the souvenirs in the shops. The food is okay (see *Where to Eat*) and the tours of the tavern, one of the oldest homesteads still standing in Virginia, are fun. On the regular tour, learn such colonial tidbits as how commoners slept—head-to-toe on shared rope beds—and how payment for rented candles was determined—by the amount of melted wax. "Mind your beeswax" comes from the colonial admonishment to pay attention to burning too much of your expensive candle wax. On the Living History tour, learn to dance a colonial reel and write with a quill pen, and also taste a tavern punch. Tour only $9 adults, $4.50 ages 6–11. Reduced tour rates with a lunch purchase.

& **Monticello** (434-984-9822; www.monticello.org), 931 Thomas Jefferson Parkway, Rte. 53. The house and visitor center are open year-round, Mar.–Oct. daily 8–5 and Nov.–Feb. 10–4; garden and plantation tours Apr.–Oct. In 1768, Thomas Jefferson had the mountaintop cleared. In 1769, construction began, and in 1770, he moved to Monticello (pronounced "Mont-i-chello"), although he continued building and changing the home's design for more than 40 years, until 1809. The 100-foot-long, mountaintop plantation house is an architectural gem, with 21 rooms, 13 skylights, and eight fireplaces. Touring the manor house affords one a glimpse of the public Jefferson—a politician whose office displays busts of John Adams and George Washington—as well as Jefferson the innovator and Jefferson the plantation owner and family man.

MONTICELLO, HOME OF THOMAS JEFFERSON

Virginia Tourism Corporation

Tours start at the **Thomas Jefferson Visitor Center.** The 15-minute introductory film, *Thomas Jefferson's World*, shown three times each hour, provides background information. Galleries present various aspects of Jefferson's views on architecture, liberty, and other matters. In the **Stacy Smith Liss Gallery**, step on a word such as "Monticello," "Slavery," or "Government," and key phrases with those words taken from Jefferson's writings appear. In the **Griffin Discovery Room**, kids can construct their own plantation, play draughts (checkers), and figure out secret codes with a cipher wheel. After all, Jefferson had to send coded messages sometimes.

The house tour takes 35 minutes and most of the furnishings are original. The hallway features the seven-day calendar clock, designed by Jefferson, which still works. An avid reader, Jefferson said, "I am afflicted with bibliomania." In his private rooms, floor-to-ceiling bookshelves line the walls (the books displayed are replicas, however). As an inventor and innovator, Jefferson improved upon a number of items to make life easier, including the "duplicator" or "polygraph," a two-pen device that enabled him to make a copy of whatever he was writing. He also designed the dining room with dumbwaiters to make it easy to bring wine up from the cellar. As an architect, he did not like to waste space. His bed is set in an alcove between his office and his sleeping chamber. Because staircases took up floor space, Jefferson made Monticello's narrow or hidden. He brought additional light into the house with skylights and windows that function as doors.

PLANTATION TOUR: SLAVES AT MONTICELLO

Only the footprint of some slave dwellings remain, but as you walk with the guide on the Plantation Tour, Apr.–Oct., you learn about Jefferson's complicated relationship with slavery. Jefferson fought for liberty of the individual and he believed slavery was wrong, yet during his lifetime 600 slaves passed through Monticello. Some died, some he gave to relatives, and he sold more than 100, even though he didn't like that practice. The details presented about a few of them make vivid the harsh reality of slavery, even at Monticello. For example, Jefferson gave Robert Hemings permission to hire himself out when his owner was away. Joseph Fossett, a member of the Hemings family, loved Edith Hern, whom Jefferson took with him to the White House as a cook. Joe ran away to see Edith, but was arrested and taken back to Monticello. Joe waited eight years for Jefferson to return to Monticello with Edith so the couple could marry; they would have 10 children together. In Jefferson's will, Joe was one of five men to be freed 12 months after Jefferson's death. Joe worked 11 years to free Edith and several of their children, but he could not obtain freedom for all of them. In around 1840, the family moved to Ohio, a free state.

After the house tour, on your own you may view the kitchen, gardens, and cellar. Allow time to walk down the hill to see Jefferson's grave. House and garden $17–22 adults, $8 ages 6–11.

&. **The Rotunda and the Academical Village, University of Virginia** (434-924-7969; www.virginia.edu/academicalvillage), Rotunda, University Avenue and Rugby Road. Open daily 9–4:45. Thomas Jefferson, founder of the University of Virginia, designed its first buildings, the Rotunda and the "Academical Village" that lines the green lawn on either side of the Rotunda. Then as now the village houses faculty and students. Edgar Allan Poe was a student here, and his living quarters (Room 13, West Range) are open for public viewing. The Rotunda, modeled after Rome's Pantheon, was designed by Jefferson to be the university's library; it is still used for lectures and academic events, much as he intended. Free admission.

&. **Virginia Discovery Museum** (434-977-1025; www.vadm.org), 524 East Main Street, east end of the Downtown Mall. Open Tue.–Sat. 10–5, Sun. 1–5. This is a good place to take young children for a couple of hours. Despite the fact that the museum states its objective as targeting tots through 10-year-olds, most children older than around age seven would be bored by the exhibits. But for little ones, the place is a find. For parents, the museum is conveniently located on the Downtown Mall. Along with exhibits that change every four months, the permanent galleries allow kids to read a book in the hollow of the Treehouse, create art projects at Open Studio, walk into a kaleidoscope, and dress up for performances in the Barnyard Theater. $6, free for under age 1.

Orange County
Montpelier (540-672-2728; www.montpelier.org), 11395 Constitution Highway, 28 miles northeast of Charlottesville on Hwy. 20, 4 miles southwest of the town of Orange. Open Apr.–Oct. daily 9–5, Nov.–Mar. daily 9–4. Closed Thanksgiving and Dec. 25. Situated on 2,650 acres, Montpelier is the home of James Madison, fourth president of the United States. Madison grew up on the estate and brought Dolley here after their marriage. The property has been restored, returning the manor house to its original 22 rooms from the 55-room behemoth that William duPont Sr. created out of the original structure. Tours of the house are available, but the building is still in the process of being decorated and furnished. Along with the manor home, the site has several other attractions, including a freedman's farm, a slave cemetery, active archaeological digs, an archaeological lab, and the Madison family cemetery, as well as the two-acre Annie duPont formal garden and James Madison's Landmark Forest (see *Green Spaces*). $16 adults, $8 ages 6–14.

MONTPELIER, HOME OF PRESIDENT JAMES MADISON

Virginia Department of Transportation

Lynchburg area

♿ **National D-Day Memorial** (540-586-3329; 1-800-351-DDAY; www.dday.org), 3 Overlook Circle, Bedford. Open Tue.–Sun. 10–5. This memorial commemorates the Normandy invasion of June 6, 1944 (also called D-Day), an epic air, land, and sea invasion involving a dozen nations. The Allied Forces launched 5,333 ships, 11,000 airplanes, 50,000 military vehicles, and more than 154,000 soldiers. More than 4,500 Allied personnel died in Normandy. Bedford, with a population of 3,200 in 1944, lost 19 men—the highest per capita loss of any single community in the United States, which is why Bedford was chosen as the site of this memorial. Among the elements of the 88-acre outdoor site are a 44-foot-high granite arch that opens onto the Victory Plaza and a 16-foot story wall with a series of reflecting pools. Guided walking tours are 45 minutes long and cost additional $3 adults, $2 students; admission $7 adults, $5 ages 6–18.

Petersburg

Battersea (804-732-9882; www.batterseafound.org), 1289 Upper Appomattox Street. Open for tours by appointment. Built in 1768, Battersea, on the banks of the Appomattox River, was the home of Petersburg's first mayor, Colonel John

THOMAS JEFFERSON'S POPLAR FOREST

Although Monticello, a stunning mountaintop plantation, is the house most associated with Thomas Jefferson, a visit to Jefferson's other home—Poplar Forest, Lynchburg—reveals much about the famed statesman and president in later life. For Jefferson, Poplar Forest, 60 miles from his beloved Monticello, took shape as a personal retreat, a place for solitude and renewal far from the frequent visitors who descended upon his home, sometimes staying for months.

While completing his second presidential term in 1806, he began construction on the unique house he designed for Poplar Forest, a 4,000-acre plantation he inherited in 1773. Even though a suburban enclave now surrounds Poplar Forest, the property still conveys a sense of what Jefferson wanted for his retirement. Like many prospective retirees, he delighted in planning his dream house.

Instead of constructing a classic, Federal-style home, one with a central hall flanked by two rooms on either side, Jefferson craved increased light and better ventilation. That's why he fashioned an octagonal building and placed a 16-foot skylight above the dining room, located in the heart of the structure. The design, with its emphasis on sun and a central gathering place, feels much more 20th than early 19th century. Poplar Forest also illustrates Jefferson's admiration for European elements, still the time-honored model for a new nation. Instead of the typical pine floors used in most Vir-

Tony Hall, Virginia Tourism Corporation

NATIONAL D-DAY MEMORIAL

ginia homes of that era, he installed white oak floors, popular in Europe, and created a sunken lawn, then all the rage in France.

Jefferson visited Poplar Forest many times between 1809 and 1823. The
sunny south parlor features floor-to-ceiling windows, two fireplaces, and what
Jefferson called his "siesta chair," a semireclining lounger that he favored after
1819 when his arthritis made it painful for him to lie down or sit straight for long
periods. In 1821, when he was 78, he wrote the following to William Short: "I
have an excellent house there [Poplar Forest] . . . am comfortably fixed and
attended, have a few good neighbors, and pass my time there in tranquility and
retirement much adapted to my age and indolence."

Five tulip poplars dating from Jefferson's era still grace the lawn. Gazing at
them from the front portico, it's easy to envision the elder statesman handing off
his stallion to a groomsman after the two-day horseback ride from Monticello,
then climbing the stairs to kick off his boots by the fire in the sunlit south parlor.

Monument Terrace, Ninth and Church streets. This monument, set atop 139
steps, honors the Lynchburg-area soldiers who fought in wars from the Civil War
to Vietnam.

Thomas Jefferson's Poplar Forest (434-525-1806; www.poplarforest.org), 1542
Bateman Bridge Road, Rte. 661, Forest. Open Mar. 15–Dec. 15 daily 10–4. $14
adults, $7 college students, $6 ages 12–18.

THE LYNCHBURG AREA'S CIVIL WAR HERITAGE

Lynchburg served as a supply and communications base for the Confederate Army during the Civil War. Recognizing the city's importance, General Ulysses Grant ordered General David Hunter to invade in 1864. That encounter, the Battle of Lynchburg, mostly took place on the city's outskirts. The Confederates won. Not far from Lynchburg, at what is now Appomattox Court House National Historical Park, General Robert E. Lee surrendered to General Ulysses S. Grant.

Appomattox Court House National Historical Park (434-352-8987; www.nps.gov/apco), main visitor parking, Rte. 24, about 2 miles northeast of Appomattox Court House. Open daily 8:30–5. Closed federal holidays. Twenty miles east of Lynchburg. General Lee surrendered to General Grant at the McLean House on April 9, 1865. You can visualize the epic yet simple surrender in the plain parlor with its two tables, one for Lee and one for Grant.

APPOMATTOX COURT HOUSE NATIONAL HISTORIC PARK

Will Simmons, Virginia Tourism Corporation

Banister. Banister fought in the Revolutionary War and helped craft the Articles of Confederation. A noted feature of the home is its Chinese Chippendale staircase. Each year on the third weekend in April, a reenactment of the Battle of Petersburg, fought April 25, 1781, takes place. Donation suggested.

Richmond area

Agecroft Hall (804-353-4241; www.agecrofthall.com), 4305 Sulgrave Road. Open Tue.–Sat. 10–4, Sun. 12:30–5. Agecroft Hall is an oddity, but a beautiful

Grant gave Lee generous terms, saying, "Hand over all your military gear and go home." Three days later, the soldiers of Lee's Army of Northern Virginia marched before the Union Army, stacked their weapons, laid down their flags, and went home. The village, closed to vehicles, has been restored to the way it looked on that fateful day. Videos at the reconstructed courthouse, which serves as the Visitor Center, provide background.

Most of the 27 structures on the site can be entered by the public. The Living History interpreters, on site at selected times, Memorial Day–Labor Day, bring the era's events to life. A favorite of ours is Ernie Price, a Northern journalist sent down to report on the Southern recovery. "It's easier to talk about emancipation than to do it," he stated as he chronicled some of the choices made by former slaves and townspeople he'd met.

Battle of Lynchburg Driving Tour (www.discoverlynchburg.com). This CD driving tour takes you to eight sites that proved crucial to the Battle of Lynchburg, June 17–18, 1864.

Fort Early (434-847-1811; www.discoverlynchburg.com), Memorial and Fort streets. This Civil War earthen redoubt helped provide the outer defense during the Battle of Lynchburg.

National Civil War Chaplains Museum (434-582-2087; www.chaplains museum.org), Mountain View Boulevard. Open Tue.–Fri. and Sun. 1–5, Sat. 10–4. People say there are no atheists in a foxhole. This museum, the only such U.S. facility, focuses on the priests, chaplains, and rabbis who served the troops in the Civil War.

Old City Cemetery and Pest House (434-847-1465; www.gravegarden.org), 401 Taylor Street. Open daily dawn to dusk. The Confederate section contains more than 2,000 graves of soldiers from 14 states. Although you cannot enter the facility, an audiotape provides history of the Pest House Medical Museum, which served as the quarantine hospital for Confederate soldiers during the war. A registered historic landmark, this cemetery also has a rose garden and a medicinal herb garden. Its oldest gravestone dates back to 1807. Free admission.

one. The 15th-century manor house stood in Lancashire, England, for hundreds of years until wealthy Richmonder Thomas Williams Jr., had it dismantled, brought to Richmond in 1925, and reassembled. The home features period antiques, huge fireplaces, beautiful oak paneling, and impressive leaded glass windows. Its period gardens include an Elizabethan knot garden, featuring ornamental shrubs intertwined in patterns with one another, plus an herb garden. Richmond Shakespeare stages plays on the grounds in summer (see *Special Events*). $8 adults, $5 students.

PETERSBURG'S CIVIL WAR HERITAGE

The last decisive battle of the Civil War took place in Petersburg, 23 miles south of Richmond. After unsuccessful attempts to take Richmond, Union general Ulysses S. Grant realized that the way to make Richmond fall was to capture Petersburg, thus cutting off supplies via rail to Richmond. On June 15, 1864, Grant aimed his forces at Petersburg. The siege lasted 292 days, nearly 10 months. Grant headquartered at City Point (now Hopewell), a town at the confluence of the James and Appomattox rivers, 8 miles northeast of Petersburg. By mid-March 1865, the Union troops controlled all the rail lines except for the South Side Railroad, which General Phillip Sheridan captured on April 2, causing General Robert E. Lee's forces to retreat. Approximately 28,000 Confederate and 42,000 Union soldiers were killed, wounded, or captured during the Petersburg campaign. Lee surrendered to Grant at one week later. Major Civil War sites in Petersburg include the following:

Petersburg National Battlefield (804-732-3531; www.nps.gov/pete), Eastern Front Visitor Center, 5001 Siege Road. Open daily 9–5. Closed Thanksgiving, Dec. 25, and Jan. 1. A 13-stop, 33-mile-long self-guided driving tour winds through the 2,500-acre battlefield, explaining the 10-month siege of the city. The Visitor Center provides background presentations and maps. Park rangers offer guided walks and tours at selected times with more programs during June through August; check the schedule. Probably the park's most fascinating—and sobering—site is the Crater, a deep depression caused by the explosion that occurred after Union volunteers dug a 500-foot-long mine shaft that ended under a Confederate fort, then replaced the soil with black powder that they ignited, killing 278 Confederate soldiers. Grant's Headquarters at City Point is furnished with period pieces and comes with an introductory video. More than 6,000 soldiers are buried at Poplar Grove National Cemetery. Weeklong pass $5 car, $3 individual.

Old Blandford Church (804-733-2396; www.petersburg-va.org), 319 South Crater Road. Open Mon.–Sat. 10–4, Sun. noon–4. Old Blandford Church possesses one of the largest collections of Tiffany windows in the world. Built in 1735, the church was abandoned in 1806 in favor of a new one in town. The grounds contain the graves of 30,000 Confederate soldiers. In 1901, the Ladies' Memorial Association of Petersburg began a restoration project, turning the church into a memorial to the Confederate soldiers. The association chose Louis Comfort Tiffany to design the church's 15 memorial windows, 14 of which were sponsored by the former Confederate states and the local association; Tiffany donated his stunning *Cross of the Jewels* window. The reception center has exhibits that include Civil War artifacts. $5 adults, $4 children.

&. **Pamplin Historical Park and the National Museum of the Civil War Soldier** (804-861-2408; 1-877-PAMPLIN; www.pamplinpark.org), 6125 Boydton Plank Road. Open Tue.–Sun. 9–5. Closed Thanksgiving, Dec. 25, and Jan. 1. The 422-acre, privately owned park consists of several museums and antebellum homes, plus a military encampment, as well as the Breakthrough Battlefield of April 2, 1865, the place where Union troops commanded by General Grant finally, after a nearly 10-month siege of Petersburg, broke through the defenses of General Lee. Begin your visit at the **National Museum of the Civil War Soldier**, designed to immerse you in the life of an everyday soldier fighting in the Civil War. Before you enter, choose one of 13 "soldier comrades," real people who fought in the Civil War: you will be given an MP3 player through which you hear your comrade describe his experiences. At the end, you learn your comrade's fate.

Tudor Hall, small by manor house standards, has been restored to its mid-19th-century use as a home and military headquarters for South Carolina general Samuel McGowan. The Field Quarter, a depiction of 19th-century slave life, includes two cabins and a chicken coop, corn crib, and well house, plus plots where cotton, tobacco, corn, and wheat grow. One cabin contains a frank video, featuring six characters from the late 1850s who share their opinions on slavery. At the Military Encampment, kids can step inside the tents and try on Civil War uniforms. The Battlefield Center museum focuses on the April 2 Union attack that caused the Confederates to retreat. From there, you enter the Breakthrough Trail, several paths that take you through the battlefield. The trail's exhibits provide information, as does your borrowed MP3 player. Check the schedule for guided tours. $12 adults, $7 ages 6–12.

Siege Museum (804-733-2404; www.petersburg-va.org), 15 West Bank Street. Mon.–Sat. 10–4 Sun. noon–4. An 18-minute film plus exhibits explore how the citizens of Petersburg lived before and during the roughly 10 months they were under siege (the longest any city was under attack during the entire Civil War). Learn how women hid food, ammunition, and supplies in their hoop skirts. You can also see one of only two revolving cannons ever built. $5 adults, $4 children.

RICHMOND AREA'S CIVIL WAR HERITAGE

Richmond, as the capital of the Confederacy from 1861 to 1865, is rich in historic sites related to the Civil War. The city's position as a political and manufacturing hub added to its importance. Union troops attacked Richmond seven times. As Virginia commemorates the Civil War's 150th anniversary from 2011 to 2015, check with the following special events.

Start your Richmond Civil War history tour at the **American Civil War Center at Historic Tredegar**] (804-780-1865; www.tredegar.org), 500 Tredegar Street. Open daily 9–5. The center, located on factory land along the James River, interprets the Civil War from three perspectives: Union, Confederate, and African American. During the Civil War, Tredegar, an ironworks factory, manufactured cannons and armored plates for the CSS *Virginia*, the former USS *Merrimack*. In the Cause of Liberty, the center's signature exhibit, explores the causes of the conflict and presents rotating war artifacts. Downloadable podcasts offer additional commentary and background. At the Center's Richmond National Battlefield Park Visitor Center, obtain a map of the Richmond Battlefield. $8 adults, $2 ages 6–12.

Hollywood Cemetery (804-648-8501; www.hollywoodcemetery.org), 412 South Cherry Street. Open daily 8–5. Along with 25 generals and 18,000 Confederate soldiers, Jefferson Davis, president of the Confederacy, and his family are

STATUE OF LINCOLN AND SON, TREDEGAR IRONWORKS

Richmond Metropolitan Convention & Visitors Bureau, Virginia Tourism Corporation

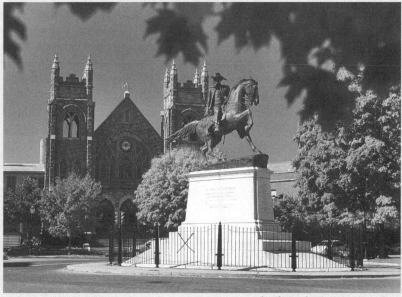

Richmond Metropolitan Convention & Visitors Bureau

MONUMENT AVENUE

buried in this cemetery named for its holly trees. Also interred on the grounds are U.S. presidents James Monroe and John Tyler. Free admission. Reserve ahead for walking tours offered Apr.–Oct. Sat. 10 AM, $7.

Monument Avenue (www.visitrichmondva.com). Impressive houses and imposing monuments line this iconic Richmond street. Statues do honor to such Confederate Civil War leaders as Robert E. Lee, Stonewall Jackson, and Jefferson Davis, but the avenue came into the 20th century by dedicating a statue to Richmond native and African American Arthur Ashe, the noted tennis star, on July 10, 1996. Monument Avenue is one of the only U.S. streets on the National Register of Historic Places. Free admission.

The Museum and White House of the Confederacy (804-649-1861; www .moc.org), 1201 East Clay Street. The museum is wheelchair accessible but the White House of the Confederacy is not. The museum doesn't glorify the Confederates or the Confederacy; instead, it presents artifacts and a historical interpretation. The War Comes Home, which debuted February 2011, explores how Southerners, particularly those living in Richmond, coped during the war years. Next door, the **White House of the Confederacy** was home to President Jefferson Davis and his family during that period. Many of furnishings are original, making the mansion a wonderful example of mid-Victorian style. Note just how close Davis's formal office was to the family's living quarters and how intertwined were the family's political and personal lives. $9 adults, $5 ages 7–18.

Slavery Reconciliation Statue (www.visitrichmondva.com), 15th and East Market Street, Shockoe Bottom. Located on Richmond's Slave Trail in the Shockoe Bottom neighborhood near the former slave market, the *Slavery Reconciliation Statue* depicts two people melded together. Sculpted by Stephen Broadbent, the statue, identical to ones in Liverpool, England, and the Republic of Benin, two points of the bustling slave trade, is part of the city's acknowledgment of its part in the odious practice. In the pre–Civil War era, more than 300,000 people were sold as slaves in Richmond alone.

&. **Richmond National Battlefield Park** (804-226-1981; www.nps.gov/rich), 3215 East Broad Street. Open year-round daily dawn–dusk, closed Thanksgiving, Dec. 25, and Jan. 1. This park commemorates the four sieges for control of Richmond. A complete battlefield tour requires an 80-mile drive of 13 sites. For Civil War buffs who want to see it all, obtain a CD of the battlefield from the Visitor Center. The park has podcasts for certain stops. Check out the small visitor centers at Cold Harbor, where 7,000 of Grant's men were killed or wounded in just thirty minutes, and the Glendale Cemetery Lodge (seasonally). Chickahominy Bluff, Malvern Hill, Fort Harrison, and Drewry's Bluff have interpretive signs and audio stations. At Chimborazo Medical Museum, see how the wounded and sick were cared for on and off the battlefield. Free admission.

Black History Museum and Cultural Center of Virginia (804-780-9093; www.blackhistorymuseum.org), 00 Clay Street. Open Tue.–Sat. 10–5 Located in Jackson Ward, once known as the "Harlem of the South," the museum, while not large, presents interesting changing exhibits showcasing the work of African American artists as well as presenting African art. $5 adults, $3 age 12 and younger.

Edgar Allan Poe Museum (804-648-5523; 1-888-21E-APOE; www.poemuseum .org), 1914–16 East Main Street. Open Tue.–Sat. 10–5, Sun. 11–5. Four buildings display some of Richmond native Poe's manuscripts and memorabilia, one of the largest collections in the world of the writer's original materials. The Raven Room features a video of the poem and illustrations by James Carling that were inspired by this chilling tale. The museum is in the Old Stone House, built in 1737, which is Richmond's oldest building. $6 adults, $5 ages 7–12.

✍ **Henricus Historical Park** (804-748-1613; www. henricus.org), 251 Henricus Park Road, Chester. Open Tue.–Sun. 10–5. Established by 300 settlers who left Jamestown in 1611, traveling 80 miles up the James River, Henricus

& **Virginia State Capitol** (804-698-1788; www.virginiacapitol.gov), 1000 Bank Street. Open Mon.–Sat. 8–5, Sun. 1–5. The Virginia State Capitol, designed by Thomas Jefferson in 1785, features a central dome and other classic Jeffersonian architectural touches. When Jefferson designed the capitol, he was minister to France, and he modeled the building after an ancient Roman temple in Nîmes. The Confederate Congress met here from 1861 to 1865. The one-hour guided tours are informative. Free admission.

SLAVERY RECONCILIATION STATUE

Richmond Metropolitan Convention & Visitors Bureau

(named for Henry, Prince of Wales, James I of England's eldest son) was the second successful English settlement in the New World. Henricus Historical Park, an outdoor living history museum, re-creates the early years of the settlement. At the Indian Village, observe "natives" (costumed interpreters) craft a canoe or cultivate tobacco. See musket demonstrations at the Soldier's House, blacksmith's crafting farm tools at the Forge, and cooking over an open hearth at the Planter's House, and learn about the medicinal herb garden at Mount Malady, called the first "guest-house," or hospital, in the New World. Henricus is important for another reason as well: Pocahontas, after being captured in 1613, was brought to Henricus, where she converted to Christianity. $8 adults, $6 ages 3–12.

& **St. John's Church** (804-648-5015; www.historicstjohnschurch.org), 2401 East Broad Street. Tours Mon.–Sat. 10–4, Sun. 1–4. Patrick Henry issued his famous "Give me liberty or give me death" speech here in 1775. In the summer on Saturdays at 2 PM, you can watch a free reenactment of the famous 1775 debate among the founding fathers. The 1741 church is itself noteworthy as the oldest

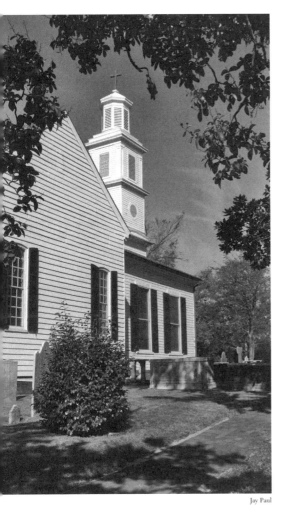
ST. JOHN'S CHURCH

Jay Paul

wooden church building in Virginia. It still has an active Episcopal congregation. $6 adults, $4 ages 7–18.

☼ ♿ **Science Museum of Virginia** (804-864-1400; 1-800-659-1727; www.smv.org), 2500 West Broad Street. Open Tue.–Sat. 9:30–5, Sun. 11:30–5. Closed Thanksgiving and Dec. 24 and 25.

Hundreds of exhibits enable kids to bounce as though they are on the moon, test air-pressured hovercraft chairs, or explore life science with a five-story DNA strand. Science Saturdays offers special hands-on activities. The facility has an IMAX theater and planetarium. $10 ages 13–59, $9 ages 4–12 and 60-plus.

The Valentine Richmond History Center (804-649-0711; www.rich mondhistorycenter.com), 1015 East Clay Street. Open Tue.–Sat. 10–5, Sun. noon–5. Although relatively small, the Valentine Richmond History Center has some interesting exhibits, both permanent and changing, but for some visitors the highlights are the museum's historic tours of neighborhoods by foot and by Segway. With guides, explore Church Hill, home to the largest number of antebellum structures in the city, as well as Carytown, a former buffalo trail. Reserve these tours in advance. The History Center was established by Mann Valentine Jr., a Richmond businessman and his brother Edward, a sculptor. The museum primarily focuses on Richmond's development from the 19th century to the present. The site includes Edward Valentine's sculpture studio and the Wickham House, built in 1812. Settlement to Streetcars, a permanent exhibit, explores how this mode of transportation boosted development of the outer city. Driving and walking tours are available. $8 adults, $7 ages 7–18.

♿ **Virginia Museum of Fine Arts** (804-340-1400; www.vmfa.state.va.us), 200 North Boulevard. Open Sat.–Wed. 10–5, Thu. and Fri. 10–9. Closed Thanksgiving, Dec. 25, Jan. 1, and July 4. The new, three-story atrium, part of a $120 million expansion and renovation completed May 2010, creates a bright space for this important Richmond facility. Outside, a parking lot has morphed into a 3.5-

Richmond Metropolitan Convention & Visitors Bureau

VIRGINIA MUSEUM OF FINE ARTS

acre sculpture garden with paths and greenery. The museum houses an exceptional collection of jewel-encrusted Fabergé eggs and other items created at the beginning of the 20 century for the Russian tsars, as well as paintings by Degas, Van Gogh, Picasso, and other masters plus impressive galleries of works from South Asia, the Himalayas, and Africa. Free.

COCHRANE ATRIUM, VIRGINIA MUSEUM OF FINE ARTS

Bilyana Dimitrova

✳ To Do

AMUSEMENT PARKS 🖉 ⅃ **Kings Dominion** (804-876-5000; www.kingsdominion.com), 1600 Theme Park Way, Doswell. Open late May–Sept. daily 10:30–10, Apr.–May and Labor Day–Oct. Sat. and Sun. 10:30–8 At Kings Dominion, 20 miles north of Richmond, get your thrills on the 15 "scream machines." Intimidator 305, the park's newest roller coaster, zips you down 300 feet at an 85-degree incline, careening at speeds nearing 90 mph. Planet Snoopy and KidZville engage young kids with pint-size rides and youngsters meet the Peanuts Gang at live shows. At Water

KINGS DOMINION

Works, 20 acres of wet fun, splash down slides, float on a Lazy River, and buck the surf at Big Wave Bay, a 650,000-gallon wave pool. Ask for the park's guide for guests with disabilities. $43 for guests 48 inches and taller, $35 children age 3 (under 48 inches), free for age 2 and younger.

APPLE PICKING AND FARMS

Charlottesville

Carter Mountain Orchard (434-977-1833; www.cartermountainorchard .com), 1435 Carters Mountain Trail, Charlottesville. Open mid-Apr.–Nov. daily and Dec. weekends; hours vary. Especially pretty in spring when the orchard blooms with acres of pink blossoms, Carter Mountain Orchard is the place to pick your own peaches in summer; bushels of apples starting in mid-August; and later in fall, pumpkins. In spring and fall, the orchard hosts crafts festivals. The on-site country store sells apple butter, jams, preserves, and local crafts. Aunt Sarah's bakery is famous for its apple cider doughnuts.

KINGS DOMINION

Nelson County

Nelson County grows acres upon acres of apples. In fall, you can buy apples, and in summer, other fresh produce. **Dickie Brothers Orchard**

(434-277-5516; www.dickiebros.com), 2552 Dickie Road, Roseland, is one place to stop. Open July–Aug. Mon.–Fri. 8–5; Sept.–Oct. Mon.–Sat. 8–5, Sun. 10–5; Nov. Mon.–Fri. 8–5, Sat. 10–4. Always closed noon–1 PM for lunch.

✐ **Drumheller's Orchard** (434-263-5036; www.drumhellersorchard.com), 1130 Drumheller Orchard Lane, off Hwy. 29, Lovingston. Open fall Mon.–Sat. 9–5, Sun. noon–5. At the apple festivals, held the last weekend in September and the third weekend in October, enjoy hayrides, a corn maze, and lots of food.

Heaven and Earth Acres (434-361-1824; www.heaven-earth.biz), 450 Phillips Lane, Nellysford. This apple orchard sells 21 varieties of heritage apples, most of which were developed between 1535 and 1887, as well as herbs. The orchard sells the apples at the **Nelson Farmers' Market** (434-244-2399; www.nelson county.com), 3079 Rockfish Valley Highway, Nellysford. Open May–Oct. Sat. 8–noon.

BICYCLING

Nelson County

Pedal along gentle hills in the valley or opt for more challenging routes. For additional routes, contact the **Nelson County Department of Parks and Recreation** (434-263-7130).

The Blue Ridge Parkway, a 22-mile ride, begins at milepost 16 in Love and continues south to the Tye River Gap and back again. The **Walton's Mountain Museum** 31-mile loop crosses rivers and picnicking spots and returns to the museum. Those wanting a challenge can head out on the winding, 5½-mile **Delfosse Trail at Deer Creek**, open mid-Nov.–Jan. 1. Sun. 9–dusk Access is through the winery. The trail, used by hikers and ATV riders, leads up a mountain and through a forest, affording scenic views.

Lynchburg

Blackwater Creek Bikeway, Blackwater Creek Natural Area and Trail (434-847-1640; 1-800-732-5821; www.discoverlynchburg.org), 1700 Old Langhorne Road. The 3-mile-long paved bikeway is part of the city's Blackwater Creek Natural Area and Trail.

Lynchburg University trails offer 60 miles of biking and hiking trails. (See "Hiking.")

BREWPUBS AND HARD CIDERIES

Nelson County

BrewRidgeTrail.com (www.brewridgetrail.com) shows off the region's brew pubs and hard cideries.

Albemarle CiderWorks (434-297-2326; www.vintagevirginiaapples.com), 2545 Rural Ridge Lane, North Garden. Open Wed.–Sun. 11–5. Thomas Jefferson grew the dozen heirloom varieties of apples that this family-run cidery mixes with other types to produce their hard ciders. At tastings, you can try the company's four varieties.

Ψ **Blue Mountain Brewery** (540-456-8020; www.bluemountainbrewery.com), 9519 Critzers Shop Road, Rte. 151, Afton. Open Mon.–Sat. 11:30–10, Sun. 11:30–9. This farm brewery grows its own hops as well as crafts its own beer. At the 2010 Great American Beer Festival, the brewery's Sandy Bottom won a gold medal and its Kolsch 151 earned a bronze. The casual restaurant also serves pizza and sandwiches. $9-21.

Ψ **Devil's Backbone Brewing Company** (434-361-1001; www.dbbrewing company.com), 200 Mosbys Run, crossroads of Rtes. 151 and 664, Roseland, not far from Wintergreen Resort. Open daily 11:30 AM–late. The casual eatery serves burgers, pasta, wraps and seafood, but draws locals for its four to six microbrews on tap. The Vienna Lager won a silver medal at the 2009 Great American Beer Festival, and the Golf Leaf Lager won gold medals at the 2009 and 2010 festival. $8-22.

Wild Wolf Brewing Company (434-361-0088; www.wildwolfbeer.com), 2773A Rockfish Valley Highway, Nellysford, also near Wintergreen Resort. Depending on the season, you might find some of the following on tap: pumpkin beer, American lager, Weiz Wolf, Alpha Ale, Smoked Scottish Ale, and American Stout. Bring or buy a growler (a glass half-gallon jug) for a fill-up.

CANOEING AND KAYAKING From the Charlottesville area it's easy to paddle along the James River.

James River Reeling and Rafting (434-286-4386; www.reelingandrafting .com), 265 Ferry Street, Scottsville. Open Apr.–Oct. 8–6. This is the outfitter closest to Charlottesville. Choose from day or overnight guided canoe and kayak trips that paddle through Class 1, 2, or 3 rapids. Tubing is offered as well. Guided canoe or rafting trips $25–40, tubing $22.

James River Runners (434-286-2338; www.jamesriver.com), 10092 Hatton Ferry Road, 5 miles beyond Scottsville. Open Apr.-Oct. 8–6. This outfitter offers day and overnight guided river trips, as well as rentals of canoes, kayaks, rafts, inner tubes, and fishing gear. Day trips $25–62, overnight trips $56–68.

CRUISES

Richmond
River District Canal Cruises (804-649-2800; www.venturerichmond.com), Dock and 14th Street, Canal Turning Basin. Cruises operate Apr. and Oct.–mid-Nov. Fri. and Sat. noon–7, Sun. noon–5; May and Sept. Thu.–Sat. noon–7, Sun. noon–5; June–Aug. Wed.–Sat. noon–7, Sun. noon–5. A guide relates historic information on this 40-minute canal cruise. $5 adults, $4 ages 5–12.

FARMERS' MARKETS

Charlottesville
City Market (434-970-3371; www.charlottesville.org), Water and First streets Apr.–Oct., Sat. 7–noon. Thanksgiving–Christmas, the market relocates to the Downtown Mall, Sat. and Sun. 10–5. Vendors sell ceramics, local wine, artisanal cheeses, handcrafted jewelry, and other handmade or home-grown items.

Richmond Metropolitan Convention & Visitors Bureau

KAYAKER

Nelson County
Nelson Farmers' Market (434-244-2399; www.nelsoncounty.com), 3079 Rock-fish Valley Highway, Nellysford. Open May–Oct. Sat. 8–noon. The market sells a variety of seasonal fruits and vegetables. Look for peaches in summer and apples in fall.

Richmond
17th Street Farmers' Market (804-646-0477; www.richmondgov.com), 100 North 17th Street. Open Sat. 8:30–4, Sun. 9–4. On Saturdays, check out the fresh produce and the home-baked goodies; on Sun, browse for crafts and collectibles.

FISHING (See "Lakes.")

GARDENS

Richmond
🐾 & **Lewis Ginter Botanical Garden** (804-262-9887; www.lewisginter.org), 1800 Lakeside Avenue. Open June–Aug. daily 9–5, Tue. 5 PM–8:30 PM. Closed Thanksgiving, Dec. 24 and 25, and Jan. 1. The garden has 40 acres of plants and pathways. Highlights include the Rose Garden, blooming with 1,800 roses; the Perennial Garden, adorned with 770 species of bulbs, trees, and shrubs; the Lucy Payne Minor Garden, bright with daylilies and daffodils; the Children's Garden, with a water play area and farm plants; and the Conservatory, an 11,000-square-foot space housing palms, orchids, and other exotic plants. $10 adults, $6 ages 3–12.

✔ ♿ **Maymont House and Park** (804-358-7166; www.maymont.org), 2201 Shields Lake Drive, Byrd Park. Open grounds daily 10–5, mansion Tue.–Sun. noon–5. Tram, carriage, and hayrides June–Aug. The Victorian house with its stained-glass windows, grand staircase, and opulent furnishings is interesting for lovers of antiques, but we think the 100 acres of grounds and gardens, studded with gazebos, are the most fun for children and adults alike. At the Children's Farm, kids can see (and sometimes feed) piglets, chickens, sheep, donkeys, goats, and cows. Maymont's 40-acre wild park functions a preserve for bison, deer, bobcats, foxes, black bears, and other species that once were or are native to Virginia. A 20-foot waterfall cascades near the Nature Center that showcases river otters, fish, and other species. Fountains, geometric planting beds, and a pergola grace the Italian Garden; water features, stones, raked sand, and pruned shrubs create the soothing Japanese Garden and plants that attract butterflies grow in the Butterfly Garden. In summer, explore the property by tram or hay wagon. At selected times, Maymont offers horse-drawn carriage rides. Free admission, but $5 donation suggested. Children's Farm, $2 per person.

GOLF Listed here are a sampling of public courses as well as those resort or private courses that accept nonmembers.

Albemarle County
Keswick Club, **Keswick Hall at Monticello** (434-929-3440; 1-800-274-5391; www.keswick.com), 701 Country Club Drive, Keswick. Located on the grounds of Keswick Inn, a country hotel (see *Lodging*). $115–130.

Richmond area
Belmont Golf Course (804-501-5995; www.henrico.va.us), 1600 Hilliard Road, Henrico County. Open 7 AM–7:30 PM, weather permitting. The 18-hole golf course is open to the public. Greens fees $25–28.

HIKING AND WALKING Wintergreen Resort Nature Foundation (434-325-8169; www.twnf.org), maintains 30 miles of nature trails and offers guided group hikes with a naturalist on Wednesdays and Saturdays, spring through fall. Maps are also available at the main check-in desk at the Mountain Inn, Wintergreen's main lodge, as well as at Trillium House, the headquarters for the Nature Foundation. Because there can be bears in the woods at Wintergreen, it is recommended that you never hike alone and always talk or make noise so that you don't surprise a bear.

Lynchburg
Liberty University trails (1-800-543-5317; www.libertyu.com), 1971 University Boulevard. Founded by Jerry Falwell, the university offers 60 miles of hiking and biking. These facilities are open to the public. Free admission.

Nelson County
Appalachian Trail (304-535-6331; 1-800-282-8223; www.nelsoncounty.com; www.appalachiantrail.org) winds through the county, creating 25 miles of moderately challenging to difficult hiking paths.

MONTICELLO GOLF TRAIL

Monticello Golf Trail (434-774-8350; www.monticellogolftrail.com), 304 Hickman Road, Suite B, Charlottesville, consists of five courses in the Charlottesville, Albemarle County, Nelson County, and surrounding regions. Check the site for special discounts to golfers signed up for a Monticello Golf Trail card. Its courses:

Birdwood Golf Course (434-293-GOLF; www.boarsheadinn.com), 200 Ednam Drive, west of Charlottesville off Rte. 250, Albemarle County. Open year-round, weather permitting. Tee times daily from 8 AM. The 500-acre course, formerly owned by the AAA Four Diamond Boar's Head Inn, is now managed by the University of Virginia. The 18-hole course, home to the school's golf teams, is open to the public. Greens fees from $21.

Poplar Grove Golf Club (434-946-9933; www.poplargrovegolf.com), 129 Tavern Lane, Amherst. Sam Snead and Ed Carton designed Poplar Grove, located 45 miles from Charlottesville. The 18-hole course opened in 2005 was ranked by *Golf Digest* as the Eighth Best New Upscale Public Facility in 2005.

Rivanna Golf Course (434-589-3730; www.rivannaresort.com), 45 Friendship Drive, Palmyra, Fluvanna County. At press time, the 18-hole course was being redesigned.

Wintergreen Resort (1-800-266-2444; www.wintergreenresort.com; see "Snow Sports" as well as *Lodging*) has two golf courses. The 18 holes of the **Devil's Knob Golf Course** (434-325-8250; www.wintergreenresort.com), the highest golf course in Virginia, stretch along a mountain ridge at an elevation of 3,850 feet. The thin air adds extra carry to the balls, but the relatively narrow fairways demand accuracy. Greens fees $50–80. The 27-hole **Stoney Creek Golf Course** in the valley offers views of Lake Monocan and the Blue Ridge Mountains. Open year-round, weather permitting. Greens fees $40–75.

✄ **Crabtree Falls** (1-800-282-8223; www.nelsoncounty.com), 11581 Crabtree Falls Highway, Montebello. The highest cascading waterfall east of the Mississippi River, Crabtree Falls descends 1,200 feet in a series of five cascades visible from several overlooks. With young kids, it's easy to walk the few hundred feet from the parking lot to the first falls' overlook. In summer, the woods along the 2½-mile one-way trail are shady, and in spring and winter when the water is high, the billowing falls are most dramatic.

Richmond

Richmond Riverfront Canal Walk (www.venturerichmond.com), River District. Access points on almost all blocks between Fifth and 17th streets. To improve trade with the west, George Washington proposed linking Richmond's James River with the Kanawha River in West Virginia that flowed into Ohio. Richmond has restored 1¼ miles of its canal between Tobacco Row and Tredegar Iron Works (See "Richmond Area's Civil War Heritage" sidebar).

Rockfish Valley

Blue Ridge Rail Trail (1-800-282-8223; www.nelsoncounty.com), 3124 Patrick Henry Highway, Piney River. Open sunrise–sunset. The multiuse trail—hiking, biking, and horseback riding—runs along the Piney River; it begins at Rte. 151 and ends in Roses Mill on Rte. 674.

Fortune's Cove Nature Preserve, from Rte. 29, Rte. 718 to Rte. 651, contains a 5.3-mile hiking trail within the mountainous property. Other features are seven viewpoints and a stream. A parking area and informational kiosk at the base of the cove will help orient visitors.

Rockfish River and Reid's Creek (434-263-7015; 1-800-282-8223; www.nelson county.com), park your car at Spruce Creek Park, old Wintergreen, southwest side of the Rte. 151 bridge over the Rockfish River. Open sunrise–sunset. Part of the Virginia Birding and Wildlife Trail, the 4-mile dirt path is relatively flat and provides mountain views.

HORSEBACK RIDING

Nelson County

Appalachian Horse Adventures at Montebello Camping and Fishing (540-377-2650; www.montebellova.com), 15072 Crabtree Falls Highway, Montebello. Open for rides Mar.–Oct. Choose from one-, two-, or four-hour trail tides. The facility also offers 30-minute riding lessons. $30–95.

LAKES

Bedford County

Smith Mountain Lake, Smith Mountain Lake Regional Chamber of Commerce (540-721-1203; 1-800-676-8203; www.visitsmithmountainlake.com), 16430 Booker T. Washington Highway, Moneta. Equidistant from Roanoke and Lynchburg (40 miles from each city) and nestled in the Blue Ridge Mountains, scenic Smith Mountain Lake features 500 miles of shoreline, making the lake Virginia's second largest. You can boat, fish, canoe, Jet Ski, swim, and cruise the lake aboard the replica 19th-century paddlewheeler the **Virginia Dare** (540-297-7100; www.vadarecruises.com), 3619 State Rte. 853, Moneta. Cruises Apr.–Oct.

Smith Mountain Lake State Park (540-297-6066; 1-800-933-PARK; www.dcr .virginia.gov), 1235 State Park Road, off Rte. 626, Smith Mountain Lake Parkway, Huddleston. Occupying 1,056 acres on the northern side of the lake, the park has 16 miles of lakefront, including a 500-foot-long beach great for swimming. At select times, rangers offer guided canoe trips and night hikes. The park's 13 trails wind through forests and along the shore's coves. Swimming fees $3–4.

John H. Kerr Reservoir, also known as **Buggs Island Lake**, is located within **Occoneechee State Park** (434-374-2210; 1-800-933-PARK; www.dcr.virginia .gov), 1192 Occoneechee Park Road, Rte. 58, 1 mile east of Clarksville. Located near the North Carolina border, Buggs Island Lake rates as the state's largest lake, constituting a whopping 48,000 acres. Swimming is forbidden because of the heavy boat traffic and the deep drop-offs near the shore. However, the lake lures anglers for its plentiful bass, bluegill, crappie, and perch. Pontoon and fishing boats are available for rental from **Clarksville Water Sports & Clarksville Marine Rental** (434-374-2755; www.clarksvilleboats.com), Occoneechee State Park. Open summer Mon.–Sat. 8–5, Sun. 8–noon; winter Mon.–Fri. 8–5, Sat. 8–noon. Pontoon boats $20–25 per hour, daily $175–230, weekly $875–1150.

SCENIC DRIVES **The Blue Ridge Parkway** (828-298-0398; www.blueridge parkway.org), Blue Ridge Parkway Association, P.O. Box 2136, Asheville, NC, stretches for 469 miles, cutting through sections of Virginia, North Carolina, and Tennessee. Milepost zero, the northernmost part of the parkway, as well as 30 miles of scenic roads, are in Nelson County. (See also "Southern Shenandoah Region and the Blue Ridge Parkway" in chapter 5.)

Journey Through Hallowed Ground (540-882-4929; www.hallowedground .org; www.byways.org). Established as a scenic byway in 2010, Journey Through Hallowed Ground stretches for 180 miles from Gettysburg, PA, to Charlottesville, VA. Much of the route is along U.S. Hwy. 15. The trail served as a transportation path in the Revolutionary War, a way to freedom on the Underground Railroad, and a place where Confederates and Union forces fought during the Civil War. In central Virginia, the suggested 52.6-mile drive begins at **Montpelier**, continues to the **Barboursville Ruins** located on the winery, then leads to **Ash Lawn–Highland**, James Monroe's home, and on to **Monticello**, Thomas Jefferson's estate, before ending in downtown **Charlottesville**. (See these individual attractions in this chapter.)

SNOW SPORTS

Lynchburg

✤ **Liberty Mountain Snowflex Centre**, Liberty University (434-582-3539; 1-866-504-7541; www.liberty.edu), 4000 Candlers Mountain Road. Open Mon.–Thu. noon–midnight, Fri. noon–1 AM, Sat. 10 AM–1 AM, Sun. 1 PM–midnight. The facility offers year-round skiing, snowboarding, and tubing on slopes made of Snowflex, an artificial material that is supposed to emulate the feel and grip of snow. $5–7 per hour, not including rentals.

Nelson County

✤ **Wintergreen Resort** (1-800-266-2444; www.wintergreenresort.com), Rte. 664, Wintergreen. The property, 43 miles southwest of Charlottesville, has comprehensive ski programs and classes for kids and adults as well as other year-round activities and a variety of lodgings. This family-friendly resort sprawled on 10,800 acres in the valley and in the Blue Ridge Mountains offers some of the mid-Atlantic's best skiing and snowboarding from December through mid-March.

Wintergreen's powerful snowmaking system can cover all 24 slopes and trails. Snowboarders and skiers can practice tricks at two terrain parks. Never-evers, whether kids (minimum age 3) or adults, can learn to ski and snowboard. For children, the resort offers the half-day or full-day Mountain Explorers and Mogul Monkeys programs as well as child-care programs for nonskiing tots. Off the slopes, enjoy ice skating and sliding down 900-foot tubing. The slopes are open to non–resort guests. Lift tickets $34–57. (See *Lodging.*)

SPAS

Nelson County
Wintergreen Resort (1-800-266-2444; www.wintergreenresort.com), Rte. 664, Wintergreen. The Wintergarden Spa offers thirteen rooms for massages and wraps. The facility has saunas, steam rooms, hot tubs, and a Jacuzzi. Fees vary. (See *Lodging.*)

Ben Blankenburg. Virginia Tourism Corporation
SNOWBOARDING, WINTERGREEN RESORT

WINERIES

Albemarle, Nelson, and nearby counties
The **Bedford Wine Trail** (540-587-5681; 1-877-447-3257; www.bedford winetrail.com), in Bedford County, leads to four wineries. Grapes and other fruit grow well in the soil of the Piedmont plateau, an area of mild winters and warm summers.

Hickory Hill Vineyards & Winery (540-296-1393; www.hickoryhillvine yards.com), 1722 Hickory Cove Lane, Moneta. Apr.–Nov. Thu.–Mon. 11–5, Mar. and Dec. Sat. noon–5. At the complimentary wine tastings and tours, try Hickory Hill's Chardonnay and Cabernet Sauvignon as well as their Lake Series, lighter wines named for the wineries location near Smith Mountain Lake. Free tours.

SKIING, WINTERGREEN RESORT
Ben Blankenburg, Virginia Tourism Corporation

THE MONTICELLO AND THE BEDFORD WINE TRAILS

The Monticello area as well as Albemarle, Orange, and other nearby counties lay claim to being the "birthplace of American wine" because of Thomas Jefferson's early, but unsuccessful, attempts to grow European wine-producing grapes. "We could, in the United States," noted Jefferson, "make as

OCTAGON

great a variety of wines as are made in Europe, not exactly of the same kinds, but doubtless as good." Plant diseases and the region's humid summers and cold winter defeated his attempts, but 19th-century growers reaped success by planting American and European hybrids. However, the Civil War, the growth of California vineyards, then Prohibition, the Great Depression, and two World Wars vanquished Virginia's wine industry. In the 1970s, six Virginia wineries took root. Now, more than 140 wineries lace Virginia's countryside.

"It's all about learning the climate and the soil," says Luca Paschina, the winemaker at noteworthy Barboursville Vineyards. "You cannot control the weather, but you have to learn how to adapt to it." Barboursville, set on a 900-acre historic estate, keeps about 150 acres planted in vines.

"We produced about 380,000 bottles in 2009; that makes us the fourth or fifth in volume, but the second largest in acres planted," says Paschina. The winery started when the Zonin family, owner of one of Italy's largest wine companies, purchased the Barboursville estate in 1976. Now Barboursville, winners of many medals, ranks as one of Virginia's top wineries.

Signature wines include a Cabernet Franc and Pinot Grigio as well as the estate's Octagon, whose 2006 vintage won Virginia's Monticello Cup in 2009. Octagon, as the winery notes, "proves the vitality of the Bordeaux style in the New World. " Jefferson would certainly approve.

Barboursville is one of the 23 vineyards on the **Monticello Wine Trail**; www.monticellowinetrail.com. **Kluge Estate Winery and Vineyard**, which underwent foreclosure in December 2010, is now Grand Cru Properties. However, currently little is known about whether the estate will remain as a winery.

Our favorite wineries to visit include:

Barboursville Vineyards (540-832-3824; www.barboursvillewine.net), 17655 Winery Road, Barboursville. Tastings Mon.–Sat. 10–5, Sun. 11–5. Winery tours Sat. and Sun. noon–4. Allow time to see the ruins of Governor Barbour's mansion, an impressive brick structure designed by Thomas Jefferson, which burned during Christmas 1884. You can still see the outlines of the octagonal parlor, a signature design element of Jefferson's. You can dine at the vineyard's restaurant, **Palladio** (see *Where to Eat*) and stay at the on-site **1804 Inn** (see *Lodging*). At the tastings, sample 16–20 wines, $5.

Jefferson Vineyards (434-977-3042; 1-800-272-3042; www.jeffersonvine yards.com), 1353 Thomas Jefferson Parkway, Charlottesville. Open daily 10–6 for tours. The winery takes its name from the fact that its vines grow on the site of Thomas Jefferson's original plants. The vineyard produces 4,000 to 8,000 cases each year. Tastings, $5.

King Family Vineyards (434-823-7800; www.kingfamilyvineyards.com), 6550 Roseland Farm, Crozet. Open Mon.–Fri. 9–5, Sat. and Sun. 11–5. Tours Sat. and Sun. noon and 3. This boutique winery, founded in 1998, went from producing 500 cases per year to 5,000 cases annually. Tastings $5.

New Kent Winery (804-932-8240: www.newkentwinery.com), 8400 Old Church Road, New Kent. Open Tue.–Sun. 10–6. Although listed on the Chesapeake Bay Wine Trail, the New Kent Winery is located between Richmond and Williamsburg.

LeoGrande Vineyards and Winery (540-586-4066; www.leograndewinery .com), 1343 Wingfield Drive, Goode. Open Mar.–Dec. for tastings (no tours) Wed.–Sun. 11—6. Black Angus cattle, horses, and goats roam the 400-acre farm that has scenic views of the Blue Ridge Mountains. The winery produces Sauvignon Blanc and Chardonnay. Visitors enjoy tastings and can use the picnic tables. Tastings $5.

Peaks of Otter Winery (540-586-3707; www.bedfordwinetrail.com), 2122 Sheep Creek Road, Bedford. Open Jan.–Mar. Sat. and Sun. noon–5, Apr.–Dec. daily noon–5. This winery specializes in fruit wines created from the apples, berries, and plums grown on its 200-plus acres of farmland. The wines include Blueberry Muffin, a mix of apple and blueberry; Cinfulicious, apple-cinnamon; Pumpkin Pie, from pumpkins; and Kiss the Devil Chili Pepper made from 30 varieties of peppers and geared more for "basting than tasting." Free tours.

Virginia Wine Country by Limousine (434-990-9070; www.camryn-limo .com), offers five different tours, each to four or five area wineries. Rates vary.

Prince Michel Vineyards & Winery (1-800-800-WINE; www.princemichel.com), 154 Winery Lane, Leon. Jan. 2–Mar. 31 Mon.–Thu. 10–5, Sun. 10–6; Apr.–Dec. daily 10–6. Located 35 miles north of Charlottesville, Prince Michel is home to both its namesake winery and Rapidan River Wines. Self-guided tours of the winery are free. Tastings $5.

GRAPE HARVESTING

Virginia Tourism Corporation

✳ Green Spaces
(See also "Hiking.")

Charlottesville
Rivanna Trail (434-970-3589; http://rivanna.avenue.org), Riverside Avenue, Riverview Park. Open 6 AM–9 PM. Part of the Virginia Birding and Wildlife Trail, the 2.3-mile Rivanna Trail starts at Riverview Park and winds along the Rivanna River.

Riverview Park (434-970-3021; www.charlottesville.org), Chesapeake Street and Riverview Avenue. Open 6 AM–9 PM. Picnic, jog, and people watch in this 26.6-acre park that borders the Rivanna River.

Lynchburg
Blackwater Creek Natural Area and Trail (434-847-1640; 1-800-732-5821; www.discoverlynchburg.org), 1700 Old Langhorne Road. The 8-mile trail follows the creek and tributaries of the James River as they cut through Lynchburg. (See also "Biking.")

James River Heritage Trail (www.lynchburgva.gov), Jefferson Street, consists of the Blackwater Creek Bikeway (see "Biking") and **RiverWalk**, a 3½-mile paved trail that begins downtown at Jefferson Street and continues into Amherst County.

Orange County

James Madison's Landmark Forest at Montpelier (540-672-2728; www .montpelier.org), 11395 Constitution Highway, 28 miles northeast of Charlottesville on Hwy. 20, 4 miles southwest of the town of Orange. Open Apr.–Oct. daily 9–5, Nov.–Mar. daily 9–4. Closed Thanksgiving and Dec. 25. A variety of easy walking trails wind through the 200-acre, old-growth forest, one that consists of native species grown without human intervention.

Richmond

Lewis Ginter Botanical Garden (804-262-9887; www.lewisginter.com), 1800 Lakeside Avenue. (See "Gardens.")

Maymont House and Park (804-358-7166; www.maymont.org), 2201 Shields Lake Drive, Byrd Park. (See "Gardens.")

✳ Lodging

HOTELS AND RESORTS

Bedford area

((ᵞ)) **Bernard's Landing Resort & Conference Center** (540-721-8870; 1-800-572-2048; www.bernardsland ing.com), 775 Ashmeade Road, Moneta. Rent a one- to three-bedroom condominium, townhouse, or home, each with a kitchen. The resort has two outdoor pools and fronts Smith Mountain Lake. Five- to seven-night rates available. One-bedroom condo $195–245 per night.

Charlottesville and surrounding area

& **Boar's Head Inn** (434-296-2181; 1-800-476-1988; www.boarsheadinn .com), Hwy. 250. The inn was built in 1965 but has history surrounding it. The Boar's Head, which grew from a smaller inn, is now a 170-room property offering accommodations in the main building, Ednam Hall, the Hunt Club, and Lakeside. The property has a golf course, spa, and tennis. $160–575.

Keswick Hall at Monticello (434-929-3440; 1-800-274-5391; www .keswick.com), 701 Country Club Drive, Keswick. 48 rooms. Keswick Hall, an Orient-Express property, is a grand country hotel on 600 acres in the rolling hills outside of Charlottesville. Rooms combine antiques and period pieces with comfortable settees and wing chairs. The smallest rooms, the Hall rooms, are a manageable 350 square feet. The Balcony Signature rooms feature countryside or golf views. Keswick Hall has an 18-hole golf course, an outdoor pool, tennis courts, a spa, casual meals at the **Palmer Room Restaurant**, and great food at **Fossett's** (see *Where to Eat*). $295–600.

🐾 & **Omni Charlottesville Hotel** (434-971-5500; www.omnihotels .com), 235 West Main Street. 208 rooms. Conveniently located at the west end of the Downtown Mall. There are indoor and outdoor pools. $115–190.

Lynchburg

& **Craddock Terry Hotel** (434-455-1500; www.craddockterryhotel.com), 1312 Commerce Street. 44 rooms. Located in historic Lynchburg in the reinvigorated Bluffwalk neighborhood, the hotel occupies two historic landmarks: a former 1906 shoe factory and a former 1896 tobacco warehouse. Buster Brown, the hotel's pet wire-haired terrier, may greet you. The rooms are a nice mix of period and contemporary pieces. $139–299.

Nelson County

💧 **Wintergreen Resort** (1-800-266-2444; www.wintergreenresort.com), Rte. 664, Wintergreen. Wintergreen, best known as a ski resort (see "Snow Sports"), also offers plenty of activities in spring through fall. The property extends to nearly 11,000 acres in the Blue Ridge Mountains and in the valley. The Mountain Inn offers hotel rooms and the resort also rents some 300 condominiums or homes. In the valley, there's a 20-acre lake for boating as well as a golf course. Another golf course is situated on the mountaintop, as are tennis courts, an adventure center (Ridgely's Fun Park) that has rock climbing, Wii, and other activities, plus the property has indoor and outdoor pools and a spa. Naturalists also lead guided hikes. In summer, on holidays, and on selected weekends, the resort offers a Kids in Action program for ages 2½ to 12. With Kids Night Out (Friday and Saturday evenings, July through Labor Day), ages 6 to 12 enjoy swimming and movies in the evening. In fall, Wintergreen is glorious, as the mountainsides are covered with brilliant red, orange, and yellow foliage. The chairlifts provide easy and spectacular mountain views. The resort also offers nature hikes and craft workshops. $139–855.

Petersburg

& 🛜 **Country Inn & Suites by Carlson** (804-861-4355; www.countryinns.com), 130 Wagner Road. 52 hotel rooms and 18 one-bedroom suites. Rates include continental breakfast. Rooms $90–100.

Hampton Inn Petersburg-Fort Lee (804-732-1400; hamptoninn.hilton.com/Petersburg), 11909 South Carter Road. 77 standard hotel rooms. Rates include hot breakfast. $110–120.

Richmond

♂ 🛜 **Berkeley Hotel** (804-780-1300, 888-780-4422; www.berkeleyhotel.com), 1200 East Carey Street. 55 rooms. An AAA Four Diamond property, the boutique hotel is located on the edge of the Shockhoe Slip dining and shopping district. $230–280.

🛜 **Hilton Garden Inn Hotel Downtown Richmond** (804-344-4300, hiltongardeninn.hilton.com), 501 East Broad Street. 250 rooms. Located in the former Miller & Rhoads department store, the hotel offers comfortable, standard rooms at moderate prices. $110–225.

🐾 🛜 **Jefferson Hotel** (1-800-424-8014; www.jeffersonhotel.com), 101 West Franklin Street. 262 rooms. First opened in 1895, the Jefferson Hotel, renovated several times, is Richmond's grande dame property, winning AAA Five Diamond rating for 18 consecutive years. Rooms $310–395.

🐾 & 🛜 **Westin Richmond** (804-282-8444; www. westin.com), 6631 West Broad Street. 250 rooms. This AAA Four Diamond property has a welcoming contemporary décor and some pet-friendly rooms. $135–335.

BED & BREAKFAST INNS

Albemarle County
Guesthouses Bed and Breakfast Reservation Service (434-979-7264; www.va-guesthouses.com), P.O. Box 5737, Charlottesville. Office hours Mon.–Fri. 9–5. This service books stays in private houses, guest cottages, and traditional bed-and-breakfast accommodations in Charlottesville and the surrounding area. Rates vary.

🐾 ♂ **Clifton Inn** (434-971-1800; www.cliftoninn.net)1296 Clifton Inn Drive. 17 rooms. A Relais & Châteaux property, the Clifton Inn sits on 100 acres. Rooms are in the main house as well as in the stables or former carriage house on the grounds. The inn is known for the good food at its restaurant (see *Where to Eat*). $195–375.

High Meadows Vineyard Inn (434-286-2218; www.highmeadowsinn.com), 55 High Meadows Lane, Scottsville. Seven rooms. A combination of two homes, one dating to 1832, High Meadows offers a country retreat on 13 acres that include vineyards. Antiques and comfortable furnishings create a pleasing décor. $150–350.

Charlottesville area (Orange County)
The 1804 Inn and the **Vineyard Cottage** (540-832-5384; www.the1804inn.com), Barboursville Vineyards, 17655 Winery Road, Barboursville. The gracious 1804 house where the Barbours once lived now offers three suites furnished with antiques owned by the Zonin family. $350–550. The 18th-century Vineyard Cottage includes a sitting room and a small kitchen. $240–260.

♿ **Inn at Willow Grove** (540-672-7001; www.theinnatwillowgrove.com), 14079 Plantation Way, Orange. 14 rooms. This stately manor house in Virginia's horse country comes with porches, rockers, fireplaces, and good food at **Vintage**, the on-site restaurant (see *Where to Eat*). And did we mention the butler service? $250–695.

Nelson County
Acorn Inn (434-361-9357; www.acorninn.com), 2256 Adial Road (Rte. 634), 2 miles from Nellysford. Kathy and Martin Versluys have been welcoming guests to their European-style bed-and-breakfast inn for more than 20 years. The inn's style is a mixture of Dutch practicality, tasty health food, and low-cost touring. The 10 rooms, brightened with quilts, are in a renovated stable, and each is as big as—you guessed it—a horse stall. Shower rooms, one for men and one for women, are down the hall. The former barn area has a common room for gatherings. $55–85.

🐾 **Mark Addy Inn** (434-361-1101; www.mark-addy.com), 56 Rodes Farm Drive, intersection of Hwy. 151 and Rte. 613. 10 rooms with private baths. The inn sits on land that once belonged to Charles Everett, a friend of and physician to Thomas Jefferson. The inn offers a welcome stay, furnished with a mix of antiques, comfortable pieces, and eclectic items. The Tiger Lily room houses the owner's collection of Indian elephants. A former smokehouse has a pool table and an HDTV for guests. The inn also serves dinner (reservations required). Some rooms are pet-friendly, but call ahead. Rates include breakfast. $140–230.

Orchard House Bed and Breakfast (434-262-7747; 1-877-603-7477; www.orchardhousebb.com), 9749 Thomas Nelson Highway, Rte. 29, Lovingston. Five rooms. Enjoy the mountain views from a rocking chair on the porch of this 1874 farmhouse. $105–135.

Richmond

Grace Manor Inn (804-353-4334; www.thegracemanorinn.com), 1853 West Grace Street. Four rooms. Nicely located in Richmond's Fan District, the impressive home with high ceilings and period pieces is a welcoming bed-and-breakfast inn. $165–205.

✳ Where to Eat

Bedford

Artisan Café (540-587-8878; www.artisancafe4u.com), 207 East Depot Street. Open Tue.–Sat. 10–2. The café is situated in Bedford's Electric Company, an arts complex located in (what else?) the town's former electric company building. The café uses organic lettuce and vegetables plus homemade bread for its sandwiches and salads named after artists. $6–8.

Bedford Social Club (540-586-9454; www.bedfordsocialclub.com), 124 South Bridge Street. Tue.–Fri. lunch 11:30–2, Wed.–Sat. dinner 5 PM–closing. The owners refer to this restaurant as offering "fine dining in a casual atmosphere." The entrées show a wide range of influences. Among them are Maryland crab cakes, Montego Bay chicken, beef Wellington, and salmon Maui. $14–28.

Charlottesville and surrounding area

Clifton Inn (434-971-1800; www.cliftoninn.net), 1296 Clifton Inn Drive. Open daily 6 PM–9 PM. This noted restaurant divides its menu into "delicate," "light," "full-bodied," and "robust." "Delicate" includes seared tuna; "light," a mushroom flan with tofu; "full-bodied," a roasted striped bass; and "robust," grilled rib eye. Four courses $58, five courses $74, six courses $89.

Fossett's, Keswick Hall at Monticello (434-929-3440; 1-800-274-5391; www.keswick.com), 701 Country Club Drive, Keswick. Breakfast Mon.–Fri. 7 AM–10 AM, Sat. and Sun. 7 AM–11 AM; brunch Sun. 11 AM–1:30; dinner daily 6 PM–9:30 PM. The setting lovely at Fossett's and so is the food. From the dining room or outdoor patio enjoy views of the grounds with the peaks of the Blue Ridge Mountains in the distance. For dinner, the award-winning restaurant serves American cuisine with other influences. $19–26.

Ivy Inn (434-977-1222; www.ivyinnrestaurant.com), 2244 Old Ivy Road. Open for dinner Mon.–Sat.5–9:30. The family-owned restaurant, a Charlottesville area favorite since

1995, serves locally inspired American cuisine. The restaurant is located in an 1816 home that was formerly an inn. $20–35.

Palladio (540-832-7848; www.bar boursville.net), Barboursville Vineyards, 17655 Winery Road, Barboursville, serves lunch Wed.–Sun. 12–2:30 and dinner Fri. and Sat. 6:30–9; reservations required. Closed January. The fare is inspired by northern Italian cuisine. Four courses $75, with wine $100.

Michie Tavern (434-977-1234; www .michietavern.com), Hwy. 53, 683 Jefferson Davis Parkway. Open daily 9–5 for tours. Lunch daily 11:15 AM–3 PM. The restaurant's costumed hostesses welcome you as "stranger," the 18th-century term for "traveler." The "ordinary" log cabin serves tasty fried chicken, pork barbecue, and other lunch fare at a bountiful buffet. $17 adults, $11 ages 12–15. $7 ages 6–11. Discounted tour rates are available with lunch.

Vintage (540-317-1206; www.theinn atwillowgrove.com), Inn at Willow Grove, 14079 Plantation Way, Orange. This restaurant serves modern American cuisine in the impressive setting of the Inn at Willow Grove (see *Lodging*). $24–39.

Lynchburg

Hot & Cold Café (434-846-4976; www.hotcoldcafe.com), 205 Ninth Street. Open Mon.–Fri. 10–7, Sat. 11–6. The Indian-Mediterranean fare at this casual eatery includes sandwiches, tabbouleh, wraps, and curries. $7–15.

Shoemaker's American Grill, Craddock Terry Hotel (434-455-1500; www.shoemakersdining.com), 1312 Commerce Street. Open Mon.–Fri.

lunch 11–2:30, dinner 4:30–10; Sat. dinner 4:30–10. With its exposed brick walls and leather banquettes, Shoemaker's is trendy but comfortable and the steaks are good. Also available are seafood and chicken entrées. $15–25.

Nelson County

Basic Necessities (434-361-1766; 2226 Rockfish Valley Highway (State Hwy. 151), Nellysford. Open Tue.–Thu. 10–6, Fri. and Sat. 10–10, Sun. 10–3. The shop sells cheese, wine, bread, and some other "basic necessities" and the café offers salads and sandwiches. For dinner, the restaurant serves pasta, vegetarian, seafood, meat, or poultry entrées. $8–25.

Blue Mountain Brewery (540-456-8020; www.bluemountainbrewery .com), 9519 Critzers Shop Road, Rte. 151, Afton. Open Mon.–Sat. 11:30–10, Sun. 11:30–9. Along with serving its own beers, the casual restaurant offers pizza and sandwiches (see "Brew Pubs"). $9–21.

Ⴠ **Devil's Backbone Brewing Company** (434-361-1001; www.dbbrew ingcompany.com), 200 Mosbys Run, crossroads of Rtes. 151 and 664. Open daily 11:30 AM. This is a popular spot for its microbrews and its pizza. The casual eatery also serves burgers, pasta, wraps, and seafood. The restaurant is located at the turnoff to the road that leads to Wintergreen Resort. If you're headed to the resort, consider calling ahead to Devil's Backbone for a pizza to go (see "Brew Pubs"). $8–22.

Fountain Room at the Mark Addy Inn (434-361-2324; www.mark-addy .com), 56 Rodes Farm Drive, intersection of Hwy. 151 and Rte. 613, serves dinner to nonlodgers by reservation. $18–28.

Petersburg

Eley's Barbecue (804-732-5861; www.eleysbarbecue.com), 3221 West Washington Street. Open daily 11–8:30, Sat. and Sun. breakfast 7 AM–10:30 AM. Along with tasty barbecue, Eley's also offers burgers, sandwiches, fish, chicken wings, and steak. $8–19.

King's Famous Barbecue (804-732-0975; www.kingsfamousbarbecue .com), 2910 South Crater Road. Open Wed.–Sun. 11–8:30. Since 1946, King's has been serving slow-cooked, pit-smoked barbecued pork, beef, and chicken. The menu also includes fried chicken. $8–20.

Richmond

Arianna's Grill (804-353-6002; www .ariannasgrill.com), 700 North Sheppard Street. Open Mon.–Thu. 11–10, Fri. and Sat. 11–11, Sun. noon–10. Come here for pizza, pasta, and Italian subs. $7–16.

Ƴ ♂ **Bank** (804-648-3070; bankand-vault.com), 1005 East Main Street. Open Mon.–Thu. 11–11, Fri. 11 AM–2 AM, Sat. 6 PM–2 AM. Enjoy New American cuisine in a renovated, turn-of-the century bank that has refashioned the original marble counters into a bar and turned the bank president's office into a martini lounge. The menu includes burgers, shrimp and grits, fish, and pork chops. Downstairs is the Vault nightclub (see *Nightlife*). $10–30.

Caliente (804-340-2920; www.cal ienterichmond.com), 2922 Park Avenue. Mon.–Fri. Lunch 11:30–2, Mon.–Sat. dinner 5–closing. The casual eatery serves Cajun, Caribbean, Thai, and South Carolina low-country fare. In addition to sandwiches, entrées include coconut shrimp, jerk chicken, and tequila flank steak. $9–18.

Ƴ **Havana 59** (804-780-CUBA; www.havana59.net), 16 North 17th Street. Tue.–Sat. bar opens 4:30, dinner service 5–10. Evoking Cuba in the 1950s in décor and cuisine, the restaurant serves such entrées as salmon over red beans and rice, rib eye with Cuban steak fries, and paella. $16–25.

Strawberry Street Café (804-353-6860 421; www.strawberrystreet cafe.com), 421 North Strawberry Street. Open Mon.–Thu. 11–10:30, Fri. 11–11, Sat. 10 AM–11 PM, Sun. 10 AM–10:30 PM. At this local favorite in the Fan District, a Victorian bathtub contains part of the salad bar. Popular items include pasta, burgers, crab cakes, and quiche. $7–16.

✴ Entertainment

Charlottesville

Ash Lawn Opera Festival (434-979-1333; www.ashlawnopera.org), Paramount Theater, 215 East Main Street. Opera, concerts, and lectures, July–Aug.

Charlottesville Pavilion (434-245-4910; 1-877-CPAV-TIX; www.char lottesvillepavilion.com), east end Downtown Mall, 700 East Main Street, hosts outdoor concerts.

Paramount Theater (434-979-1333; www.theparamount.net), 215 East Main Street, Downtown Mall, hosts headliners at live concerts.

Lynchburg

Academy of Fine Arts (434-528-3526; www.academyfinearts.com), 600 Main Street, is a combination performance and gallery space.

Dance Theatre of Lynchburg (434-846-6272; www.dancelynchburg.org), 722 Commerce Street, offers dance performances.

Richmond

Richmond CenterStage (804-327-5755; www.richmondcenterstage .com), 600 East Grace Street. The multiuse complex houses an art gallery and three stages. Along with presenting local talent and Broadway shows, the facility showcases perform-ances by the Richmond Philharmonic, the Richmond Symphony and the Richmond Ballet.

Richmond International Raceway (1-866-455-RACE; www.rir.com), 600 East Laburnum Avenue. For those like gunning engines and burning rubber battles for track position, this raceway hosts NASCAR competitions. Prices vary.

NIGHTLIFE: BARS, CLUBS, EATERIES

Charlottesville

♉ **Blue Light Grill and Raw Bar** (434-295-1223; www.bluelight grill.com), 120 East Main Street. Open daily for dinner 4:30–10, late-night menu Thu.–Sat. 11 PM–1 AM. The raw bar features clams and oys-ters, seafood dominates the entrées, and professionals in their 20s to 40s populate the bar. $17–23.

♉ **Miller's Restaurant** (434-971-8511; www.millersdowntown.com), 109 West Main Street. Open Mon.–Sat. 11:30 AM–2 AM, Sun. 12:30 PM–2 AM. Before being discovered, Dave Matthews waited tables and played music at this popular restau-rant and bar. That's fueled the feeling that late-night performers are, as

Miller's states, "soon-to-be-famous musicians." $9–11.

♉ **South Street Brewery** (434-293-6550; www.southstreetbrewery.com), 106 South Street. Open Mon.–Thu. 5–10, Sat. and Sun. 5–10:30; late-night menu Fri. and Sat. 10:30–midnight. The converted, 1800s grain warehouse still has its old brick walls and thick timbers. The place serves handcrafted ales and lagers, including the award-winning J. P. Ale and the popular Satan's Pony Amber Ale Kebabs, nachos, sandwiches burgers, BBQ chicken, stuffed trout, and salads are some of the items served. $9–17.

♉ **The Virginian** (434-984-4667; www.virginianrestaurant.com/the virginian), 1521 University Avenue. Open Mon.–Sat. 11 AM–2 AM, Sun. 10 AM–2 AM. Wooden booths, pressed-tin ceilings and decades of photographs of the city's beloved University of Vir-ginia decorate this restaurant and bar handily located opposite the universi-ty on "the Corner," University Avenue near the Chapel. After 10 PM, dinners give way to bar food. The place fills with UVA students. $9–17.

♉ **X Lounge** (434-244-8439; www .the-x-lounge.com), 313 Second Street SE. Open Tue.–Sat. 5:30 PM–2 AM. Along with serving small plates and entrées, the place has two lounges with DJ music. The crowd is often dominated by young profession-als in their 20s and 30s. Entrées include spaghetti and meatballs, beer-battered fish and chips, maple -glazed duck, and New York strip loin. $12–20.

Lynchburg

♉ **Jimmy's on the James** (434-845-1116; www.jimmysonthejames.com), 610 Commerce Street. Open Tue.–

Thu. 5–11, Fri. and Sat. 5–midnight. Jimmy's calls itself a "Southern American bistro and speakeasy." In addition to burgers, the menu features Lynchburg City Tavern Pie, pasta jambalaya, and a jerked Creole chicken sandwich, plus for dessert, deep-fried Oreos. The owner, Jim Dudley, might sing a few tunes, and others may perform as well. $10–25.

Ⓨ **Phase 2** (434-846-3206; www.Phase2Club.com), 4009 Murray Place. Open daily dinner 5–10, bar 4–late. Part sports lounge, part dance club, and part restaurant, Phase 2 hosts DJs along with live performances of Top 40 rock and country music.

Ⓨ **White Hart Café** (434-455-1659; www.inklingswhitehart.com), 1208 Main Street. Open Mon.–Sat. 7:30 AM–10 PM. An addition to Inklings Bookshop, the White Hart Café creates an English pub ambience in the adjoining space and hosts live music on Friday and Saturday evenings.

Richmond
Ⓨ **The Camel** (804-353-4901; www.thecamel.org), 1621 West Broad Street. Open daily 5 PM–late. The Camel serves typical pub grub of salads, sandwiches, pizza, and pasta, attracting 20- and 30-somethings for their live music and occasional poetry readings. $7–12.

Ⓨ **Capital Ale House** (804-780-ALES; www.capitalalehouse.com), 623 East Main Street. Open daily 11 AM–1 AM. Richmond's downtown beer oasis, the Capital Ale House has 53 beers on tap and 100-plus in bottles, as well as a menu of burgers, soups, salads, and some entrées. The Music Hall hosts live bands on weekends as well as at other times. $7–28.

Ⓨ **The Tobacco Company** (804-782-

9555; www.thetobaccocompany.com), 1201 East Carey Street. Open for lunch Mon.–Thu. 11:30–2:30, Fri. and Sat. 11:30–2:30, Sun. 11:30–2; dinner Mon.–Thu. 5:30–10. Fri. and Sat. 5:30–10:30, Sun. 5:30–9:30;. bar and lounge daily 3:30 PM–2 AM. The restaurant offers American cuisine—pasta, meat loaf, crab cakes, chicken, and steak. Live music takes place in the atrium bar and lounge Wednesday through Saturday night from 9:30 PM. $20–35.

Ⓨ **Vault Night Club** (804-648-3070; www.bankandvault.com), 1005 East Main Street. Open Thu. 9 PM–1 AM, Fri. and Sat. 10 PM–2 AM. At the same location as the Bank restaurant, Vault was voted the best nightclub in Richmond by *Richmond Magazine*. Thursday nights, the place hosts Pump, a lesbian, gay, bisexual, and transgendered DJ dance party, but the rest of the time the place appeals to everyone.

✳ Selective Shopping
Bedford
The Electric Company (540-586-1990; www.artisancafe4u.com), 207 East Depot Street. Open Tue.–Sat. 10–4. The former 1890 electric company building houses an arts center offering galleries, workshops, classes, shops, and a café. **Art on Depo** showcases ceramics, glassworks, and paintings of more than 30 artisans and artists, and **Book Nooky** sells new and used books.

Charlottesville
Downtown Mall (434-295-9073; www.downtowncharlottesville.net) along East Main Street. More than 30 restaurants and 120 shops line the 7-block-long pedestrian mall. A free

trolley connects the Downtown Mall to the University of Virginia.

Gearharts Fine Chocolates (434-972-9100; www.gearhartschocolates .com), 416 West Main Street, no. C. Open Mon.–Sat. 10–6. Chocolatier Tim Gearhart uses fine Venezuelan chocolate to handcraft these tasty treats. The mint julep is a favorite. This site is the flagship shop and production kitchen; Richmond has another shop. $1.75 per piece.

Richmond

Carytown (804-422-2279; www.cary town.org) This nine-block area along West Cary Street from Thompson Street to the Boulevard has nearly 200 restaurants, clothing boutiques, bakeries, antiques dealers, bookstores, and gift shops.

Gearharts Fine Chocolates (804-282-1822; www.gearhartschocolates .com), 306 B, Libbie Avenue. Open Mon.–Fri. 11–6, Sat. 10–6. This shop sells chocolatier Tim Gearhart's hand-crafted chocolates. The mint julep is a favorite. $1.75 per piece.

Shockoe Bottom (www.shockoe slip.org) East Cary Street from 12th to 14th Streets. The former ware-houses in this neighborhood, Rich-mond's oldest, now house restaurants, boutiques, and clubs. At the **Sunday Vintage Market** (804-646-0477), 17th Street Farmers' Market, 100 North 17th Street, Apr.–Dec. Sun. 9–3, poke around the stalls and you just might find that Hopalong Cassidy lunchbox, turquoise Formica kitchen table, or other throwback from your or your parents' childhood.

Warm Springs Gallery at Char-lottesville (434-245-0800; www.warm springsgallery.com), 105 Third Street NE. Open Wed.–Sat. 11–5, Sun. 1–3.

This gallery presents a nice selection of glass, paintings, ceramics, and pho-tography. Warm Springs has a sister gallery.

✴ Special Events

February: **Virginia Indie Film Festival** (1-800-854-6233; www.film virginia.org), Richmond. View films and shorts by Virginia filmmakers.

March: **Kite Festival & Taste and Sounds of Henrico County** (804-501-1611), Dory Park, Richmond area. Enjoy hot-air balloon rides, kite-flying, music, and food.

March–early April: **A Million Blooms** (804-262-9887), Lewis Ginter Botani-cal Garden, Richmond. The orchids, cherry blossoms, daffodils, tulips, and irises are spectacular.

April: A **Battle of Petersburg** reen-actment takes place every third week-end at Battersea, a historic home in Petersburg.

June: **River of Time (Batteau) Fes-tival** (434-528-3950), Lynchburg. Replicas of the flat-bottomed mer-chant boats parade on the river. Fes-tivities include music, entertainment, and storytelling.

June–September: **Richmond Shake-speare** (804-232-4000), Richmond, puts on outdoor productions of the Bard's plays at Agecroft Hall.

July: **African-American Cultural Festival** (434-979-0582; www.cville african-amfest.com), Charlottesville. Music, dance, storytelling, crafts, and food are part of the celebration of the African American heritage.

July–August: **Ash Lawn Opera Fes-tival** (434-979-1333; www.ashlawn opera.org), Paramount Theater, 215 East Main Street, Charlottesville.

Opera, concerts, and lectures, July–Aug.

August: **Albemarle County Fair** (434-293-6789; www.albemarle countyfair.com), Charlottesville, features livestock and tractor pulls as well as crafts, music, and typically a Civil War reenactment.

October: **Fall Fiber Festival & Montpelier Sheep Dog Trials, Montpelier Estate** (434-296-85333; www.fallfiberfestival.org), Charlottesville. Sheep-shearing demonstrations, sheep dog competitions, fleece sales, and craft demonstrations held on the grounds of James Madison's Montpelier estate.

Western Virginia: Shenandoah Region

NORTHERN SHENANDOAH REGION
AND SHENANDOAH NATIONAL PARK

SOUTHERN SHENANDOAH REGION
AND THE BLUE RIDGE PARKWAY

Virginia Tourism Corporation

INTRODUCTION

S tretching for 200 miles between the Blue Ridge and Allegheny mountain chains, the Shenandoah Valley is one of Virginia's most beautiful regions. The rolling hills support farms, apple orchards, and vineyards and hide underground caverns that reveal fantastical formations thousands of years-old. The area's gem, Shenandoah National Park, covers more than 197,000 acres, with hiking trails, waterfalls and scenic overlooks.

Two of America's great drives are here. Skyline Drive winds through Shenandoah National Park and the Blue Ridge Parkway stretches for 469 miles, linking Virginia's Shenandoah National Park with North Carolina's Great Smoky Mountains National Park. Much of the 1.9 million-acre George Washington Jefferson National Forest also lies in the Shenandoah region. Hikers, nature lovers, and work-weary urbanites find trails, wildlife, and solace in the hills. Skiers can take to the slopes at Bryce, Massanutten, and the Homestead resorts, all of which offer golf and hiking in summer. The grande dame Homestead Resort adds fine dining as well as soaks in the same mineral springs that soothed Thomas Jefferson and Alexander Hamilton. Romantic country inns bloom along the back roads and in the region's small towns.

The Shenandoah region is also rich in Civil War history and sites. Known as the "breadbasket of the Confederacy," the area saw fierce fighting. Control of Winchester, for example, changed more than 70 times during the Civil War years. Among the major confrontations was the Battle of Cedar Creek.

Because the Shenandoah is a big area, we have divided it, for convenience, into two sections: Northern Shenandoah Region and Shenandoah National Park, and Southern Shenandoah Region and the Blue Ridge Parkway

NORTHERN SHENANDOAH REGION AND SHENANDOAH NATIONAL PARK

TOWNS Front Royal. One of the gateway towns for Shenandoah National Park and the town nearest the start of Skyline Drive, Front Royal is worth a pre- or post-park visit for several reasons. The town is a good place to eat or to stay while visiting the park, exploring Skyline Caverns, or the George Washington National Forest. Also, at Front Royal, the north and south forks of the Shenandoah River join, making the area a popular place for canoeing.

Luray. Luray, about 9 miles west of Skyline Drive on US 211, is famous for its caverns, Virginia's largest and the most popular caverns on the East Coast.

Middletown, **New Market**, and **Strasburg.** In these towns find Civil War battlefields and other historic sites.

Winchester. George Washington used his surveying and building talents to supervise the construction of Fort Loudon, built to protect Virginia's border in the French and Indian Wars. Washington required each of the tenants on his lands to plant 4 acres of apples, one of the reasons apple orchards surround Winchester. During the Civil War, Winchester changed hands more than 70 times, including 13 times in one day.

GUIDANCE Front Royal-Warren County Visitor's Center/Chamber of Commerce (1-800-338-2576; http://discoverfrontroyal.com), 414 East Main Street, Main Street, Front Royal.

Luray-Page County Chamber of Commerce (540-743-3915; 888-743-3915; www.luraypage.com), 46 East Main Street.

Shenandoah County Tourism (540-459-6227; 888-367-3965; http://shenandoah travel.org), 600 North Main Street, Woodstock, for information about Strasburg.

Shenandoah National Park (540-999-3500; 1-800-999-4714; www.nps.gov /shen; www.visitshenandoah.com), 3655 U.S. Hwy. 211 East, Luray. The Dickey Ridge Visitor Center, mile 4.6 near the Front Royal Entrance Station. This visitor center has maps of the park as well as the *Shenandoah Overlook*, a

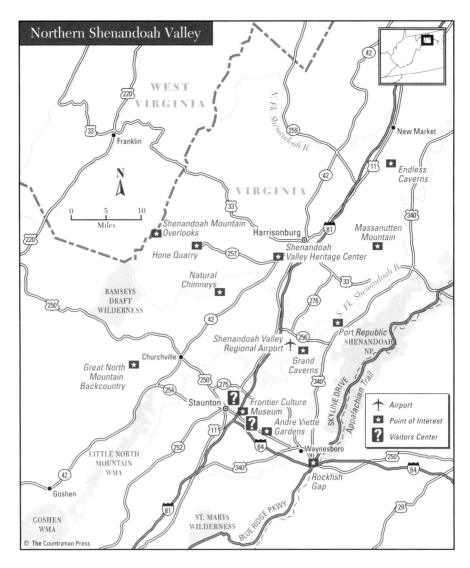

Northern Shenandoah Valley

publication that will tell you about the park. Open daily but closed from the end of November through the end of March. The Byrd Visitor Center (mile 51), is open daily from April through the end of November. Loft Mountain Information Center (mile 79.5) is open intermittently; call ahead.

Shenandoah Valley Visitor Center and Travel Association (540-740-3132; 1-877-VISIT-SVA; www.visitshenandoah.org), 277 West Old Cross Road, New Market.

Winchester-Frederick County Convention and Visitors Bureau (540-542-1326; 1-877-871-1326; www.visitwinchesterva.com), 1360 South Pleasant Valley Road, Winchester, also provides information on Middletown.

3570), 229 Stokes Airport Road, Front Royal, is about 10 miles from Strasburg and about 30 miles from the Shenandoah National Park. **Luray Caverns Airport** (540-743-6070), 1504 Airport Rd., Luray, is about 2 miles from Luray. **Winchester Regional Airport** (540-662-5786) is located at 491 Airport Rd.

For **Shenandoah National Park, Washington Dulles International Airport** (703-572-2700; www.metwashairports.com), 1 Saarinen Circle, Dulles, is 65 miles from the **Thornton Gap Entrance**. **Shenandoah Valley Regional Airport** is 27 miles from Swift Run Gap and the **Charlottesville-Albemarle Airport** is 31 miles from Swift Run Gap.

By bus: There is no public bus service to Front Royal, Luray, Middletown, Strasburg, or Winchester.

By car: **Front Royal:** From Washington and Baltimore, take I-66 west to VA 79. From Richmond, take VA 195 east to I-95 north onto I-64. Continue to US 17 north to I-66 west, and then take VA 79 to Front Royal. From Norfolk/Hampton Roads, take I-264 east onto I-64 west to I-295 north and take I-95 north to US 17 north and then take I-66 west to VA 79/Front Royal.

Luray: From Washington and Baltimore, take I-66 west to VA 79 toward VA 55 west. Continue to US 340 south. From Richmond, take I-95 north toward I-64 west and then take US 15 north to US 340 north. From Norfolk/Hampton Roads, **New Market** is about 13 miles west of Luray on Rte. 211.

Shenandoah National Park: From Washington and Baltimore, take I-66 west to VA 79. Continue onto John Marshall Highway/VA 55 to VA 55 west and follow US 340 south. From Richmond, take VA 195 east to I-95 north onto I-64. Continue to US 15 north to US 33/Bus west to US 340 north. From Norfolk/Hampton Roads, take I-264 east onto I-64 west to US 15 north to US 33 west. The park stretches for 105 miles from its northern entrance at **Front Royal** (park milepost 1 is nearby) Rte. 340 near I-66, to its southern entrance at **Rockfish Gap** (park milepost 105), Rte. 250 and I-64, near Waynesboro. The middle two park entrances are at **Thornton Gap** (mile 31.5) via Rte. 211, and **Swift Run Gap** (mile 65.5) via Rte. 33.

Strasburg: From Washington and Baltimore, take US 50 west onto I-66 west and then take 1-81 south toward US 11. From Richmond, take VA 195 east onto I-95 north toward I-64. Take US 17 north onto I-66 west and continue on I-81 south to US 11 to Strasburg. From Norfolk/Hampton Roads, take I-264 east to I-64 west onto I-295 north and take that to onto I-95 north. Take US 17 north to I-81 south and then take US 11 toward Strasburg. **Middletown** is about 5 miles north of Strasburg on Rte. 11.

Winchester: From Washington and Baltimore, take US 50 west to I-66 west toward I-81 north and continue on US 17. From Richmond, take VA 195 east to I-95 north and continue on I-64 toward US 17 north to I-81 north and then take US 17 north. From Norfolk/Hampton Roads, take I-64 west for I-295 north. Take US 17 north to I-81 north and go US 17 north.

By train: **Amtrak** (1-800-872-7245; www.amtrak.com). Culpeper is that closest Amtrak station to **Front Royal**, 32 miles from Culpeper; **Luray**, 28 miles from

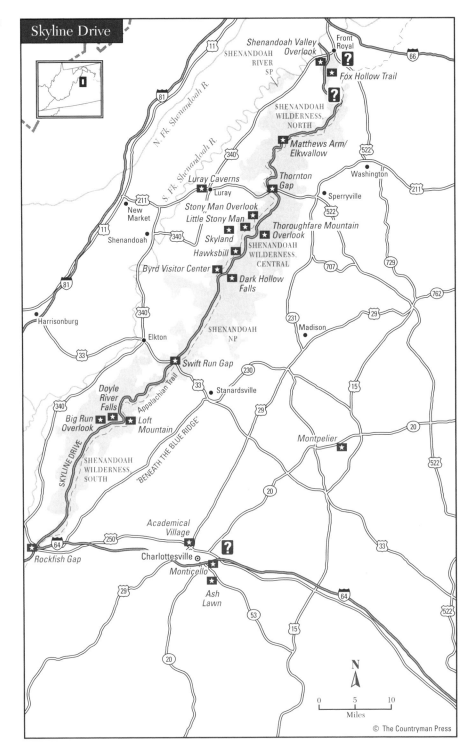

Skyline Drive

Shenandoah Valley Overlook
Front Royal
SHENANDOAH RIVER SP
Fox Hollow Trail
SHENANDOAH WILDERNESS, NORTH
Matthews Arm/ Elkwallow
Luray Caverns
Luray
Thornton Gap
Washington
Stony Man Overlook
Little Stony Man
Sperryville
New Market
Thoroughfare Mountain Overlook
Shenandoah
Skyland
SHENANDOAH WILDERNESS, CENTRAL
Hawksbill
Byrd Visitor Center
Dark Hollow Falls
Harrisonburg
Elkton
SHENANDOAH NP
Madison
Swift Run Gap
Doyle River Falls
Stanardsville
Big Run Overlook
Loft Mountain
Montpelier
SHENANDOAH WILDERNESS SOUTH
"BENEATH THE BLUE RIDGE"
SKYLINE DRIVE
Appalachian Trail
Academical Village
Rockfish Gap
Charlottesville
Monticello
Ash Lawn

N. Fk. Shenandoah R.
S. Fk. Shenandoah R.

WESTERN VIRGINIA: SHENANDOAH REGION

N

0   5   10
Miles

© The Countryman Press

Culpeper; and **New Market**, 28 miles from Culpeper. Martinsburg, WV, is the closest Amtrak station for **Strasburg**, 39 miles away, and **Winchester**, 22 miles from Martinsburg.

GETTING AROUND In Front Royal, **Front Royal Area Transit** (www.front royalva.com) provides bus service; and in Winchester, **Winchester Transit** (http://winchesterva.gov/transit) operates public buses. However, a car is advisable to explore the region.

WHEN TO COME Summer is high season; spring and fall bring nice walking weather and fewer crowds. Skiers, of course, like winter at the region's mountain resorts.

MUSEUMS, HISTORIC LANDMARKS, AND SITES

Clarke County
Long Branch Historic House and Farm (540-837-1856; 1-877-868-1811; www.historiclongbranch.com), 830 Long Branch Lane, Millwood. Open 9–5. Guided tours Wed.–Sun. noon–4. Construction on the historic mansion began in 1805. Baltimore businessman Harry Isaacs purchased the home in 1986, restoring it to its former glory and furnishing the manor house with period antiques. The 400-acre farm features English-style gardens and serves as a horse-boarding and therapeutic riding facility. The property hosts an annual Hot-Air Balloon, Wine & Music Festival, typically in late September or mid-October. $8 admission. Private tours $10.

Winchester
George Washington's Office Museum (540-662-4412; www.winchesterhistory .org), 32 West Cork Street. Open Apr.–Oct. Mon.–Sat. 10–4, Sun. noon–4. From September 1755 to December 1756, when Washington was supervising the construction of Fort Loudon in the north end of Winchester, he used the middle room of this log building as an office. The fort, which no longer exists, was built to defend the 300-mile frontier of Virginia during the French and Indian War. $5 adults, $2.50 ages 7–18.

& **Museum of the Shenandoah Valley** (540-662-1473, 888-556-5799; www .shenandoahmuseum.org), 801 Amherst Street. Open Tue.–Sun. museum 10–4, gardens and mansion Mar.–Nov. 10–4. The complex consists of the 50,000-square-foot museum, the 18th-century Glen Burnie Historic House, and 6 acres of gardens. The museum provides interesting background for any visit to the Shenandoah Valley, detailing the region's geographical features, history, and crafts. Quilts, paintings, and furniture are displayed in the Shenandoah Valley Gallery, and the R. Lee Taylor Miniatures Gallery showcases five miniature houses whose tiny furnishings were crafted by 75 regional artists. The house, filled with period furnishings, is open by guided tour. The gardens feature boxwood, roses, a water garden, and other soothing elements. Combination ticket house/gardens/museum $12 adults, $10 ages 7–18.

CIVIL WAR HERITAGE NORTHERN SHENANDOAH VALLEY

The Shenandoah Valley saw fierce fighting during the Civil War. The northern valley has some 10 battle sites. During the Civil War, Winchester, the northernmost city under Confederate control, changed hands more than 70 times. Middletown saw the Battle of Cedar Creek, also known as the Battle of Belle Grove, the last significant encounter in the Shenandoah Valley. For more information, contact the **Shenandoah Valley Battlefields Foundation** (540-740-4545; www.shenandoahatwar.org), 298 West Cross Road, New Market. Among the sites are:

Middletown

Belle Grove Plantation (540-869-2028; www.bellegrove.org), 336 Belle Grove Road. Open for guided tours Apr.–Oct. Mon.–Sat. 10:15–3:15, Sun. 1:15–4:15, and selected Nov. weekends. Free self-guided tours late Mar.–Dec. Mon.–Fri. 10–4, Sun. 1–5. At one time, this 1797 limestone manor house served as the centerpiece of a 7,500-acre plantation with 103 slaves. Belle Grove is a National Historic Landmark. Guided tours $8 adults, $4 ages 6–12.

Cedar Creek and Belle Grove National Historical Park (540-869-3051; www.nps.gov/cebe), intersection of I-81 and I-66. The park consists of the Cedar Creek Battlefield and Belle Grove Plantation. At selected times, park rangers offer interpretive programs, including a two-hour guided driving tour (you follow the ranger in your car).

Cedar Creek Battlefield (540-869-2064; www.cedarcreekbattlefield.org), 8437 Valley Pike. The last major Shenandoah Valley confrontation took place on October 19, 1864, between Union general Philip Sheridan and Confederate general Jubal Early. In the morning, Early took the Union forces by surprise. Initially, Federal forces retreated north across Belle Grove Plantation. Sheridan heard the cannon fire in Winchester, where he had gone for a meeting. He mounted his horse, Rienzi, and rode hard for 23 miles to the battlefield, where he rallied his troops. Later in the day, the Confederate soldiers tired and the Union Army regrouped, Sheridan pushed the Confederates back toward Middletown. By night, he had broken Confederate resistance. Historians credit this Union victory with helping President Abraham Lincoln win a second term in office. Every October, thousands of reenactors gather to recreate the battle, including artillery and cannon demonstrations.

New Market

♿ **New Market Battlefield State Historical Park and Hall of Valor Civil War Museum** (540-740-3101; 1-866-515-1864; www2.vmi.edu/museum) Rte. 305

(George Collins Parkway). Open daily 9–5. Closed Thanksgiving, Dec. 24–25, and Jan. 1. The 300-acre battlefield and the museum commemorate the 257 Virginia Military Institute students whose fighting on May 15, 1864, contributed much to the Union retreat. The cadets, some as young as 15 (although the average age was 18), were supposed to be kept in reserve. If called, they were to be placed far back. Instead these schoolboys ended up on the front lines, facing the Union troops. The cadets held the line for 30 minutes, forcing the Union troops to withdraw. Ten VMI students were killed and 47 were wounded. Much of the fighting took place around the Bushong farm, now among the buildings that interpret farm life in the mid-19th century. At the time of the encounter, the farm's spring wheat was growing north of the house in a field notorious for some of the bloodiest fighting. After five days of rain, the ground turned to mud, sucking the shoes from the soldiers; an award-winning film shown at the museum, interpreting the battle, is called *Field of Lost Shoes*. Another film screened at the museum discusses Confederate general Stonewall Jackson's Shenandoah campaign. In summer, VMI cadets lead one-hour guided tours. You can also walk the 1-mile trail by yourself. A battle re-enactment takes place in mid-May. $10 adults, $6 ages 6–12.

NEW MARKET BATTLEFIELD CIVIL WAR REENACTMENT

Virginia Tourism Corporation

Winchester

Fort Collier Civil War Center (540-662-2281; www.fortcollier.com), 922 Martinsburg Pike.

What remains on this 10-acre site are the earthworks constructed by the Confederate infantry. These were no match for Union general George Custer's cavalry charge—one of the largest in U.S. history—on September 18, 1864. Union forces prevailed. Free.

Old Court House Civil War Museum (540-542-1145; www.civilwarmuseum .org), 20 North Loudon Street. Open Wed.–Sat. 10–5, Sun. 1–5. This museum, located in the Frederick County Court House, housed both Confederate and Union prisoners during the Civil War, depending on which side had control of the city. As a result, the 1840 building still bears graffiti from both sides, including, on the south wall, a strongly worded curse regarding Jefferson Davis, president of the Confederacy. $5 age 6 and older, free for under age 6.

Stonewall Jackson's Headquarters Museum (540-667-3242; www.win chesterhistory.org), 415 Braddock Street. Open Apr.–Oct. Mon.–Sat. 10–4, Sun. noon–4. From November 1861 to March 1862 General Thomas J. "Stonewall" Jackson coordinated his Shenandoah Valley campaign from this house. On the guided tour, you see the table he used as a desk, maps, and artifacts of Jackson and other Civil War soldiers. The building was originally owned by Colonel Lewis T. Moore, great-grandfather of actress Mary Tyler Moore; the colonel invited Jackson to use the house while headquartered in Winchester. $5 adults, $2.50 ages 7–18.

Third Winchester Battlefield (1-800-298-7878; www.shenandoahatwar.org), Redbud Road, east of Rte. 11 north. The 5-mile walking trail has interpretive signs. Free.

✳ To Do

Winchester

APPLE PICKING Winchester and the surrounding Frederick County are known for their apple orchards. The Visitor Center offers a Follow the Apple Trail audio driving tour for purchase. (see "Scenic Drives"). Orchards along the way include:

Follow the Apple Trail (540-542-1326; www.visitwinchestervirginia.com), 1360 South Pleasant Valley Road. The 45-minute audio driving tour, available on CD, winds you through Frederick County's scenic apple country.

Marker-Miller Orchards (540-662-1391; www.markermillerorchards.com),

3035 Cedar Creek Grade. Open Mon.–Sat. 9–5, summer also Sun. 9–5. Locals love the orchards' apple cider doughnuts.

Pumpkin Patch at Hill High Farm (540-667-7377; www.thepumpkin-patch .com), 933 Barley Lane. Open mid-Sept.–Oct. 10–5. The farm celebrates the harvest with apples, apple dumplings, bluegrass music, and farm animals to pet.

CANOEING, KAYAKING, AND RAFTING

Front Royal

Front Royal Canoe Company (540-635-5440; 1-800-270-8808; www.front royalcanoe.com), 8567 Stonewall Jackson Highway. Open Apr.–Oct. Mon.–Fri. 9–6, Sat. and Sun. 7–7. Explore the Shenandoah River on a guided canoe, kayak, or raft trip. Day trips range from 3-mile jaunts that are a relaxing one to two hours, to 19-mile journeys that take six to seven hours. Many excursions wind through the Shenandoah River State Park. For more time on the river in a place that gets you farther from the day trippers, consider a two-to-four-day trip. The Full Moon Floats are nice as well. Rates vary. Day trips for a two-person canoe $45–70.

Luray

Shenandoah River Outfitters (540-743-4159; 1-800-6-CANOE2; www.shen andoahriver.com), 6502 South Page Valley Road. Open Apr.–Nov. 9-5 daily. Paddle at your own pace after renting a canoe, kayak, raft or even a tube for floating with the current. The company also rents campsites and cabins.

CAVERNS The underground wonders of limestone pillars, "secret tunnels," flowing streams, and "rooms" as big as cathedrals delight children (and adults). No matter how hot it may be above ground, especially on a humid Virginia summer afternoon when the mercury hits 92 degrees F, Virginia's caverns remain cool, about 55 to 56 degrees F. Remember to bring a sweater or a sweatshirt and to wear close-toed shoes, preferable ones with rubber soles, as walkways may be slippery in places.

Front Royal

✔ **Skyline Caverns** (540-635-4545; 1-800-296-4545; www.skylinecaverns.com. 10344 Stonewall Jackson Highway, 1 mile south of Front Royal on U.S. Hwy. 340. Open Mar. 15–June 14 and Labor Day–Nov. 14 Mon.–Fri. 9–5, Sat. and Sun. 9–6; June 15–Labor Day Mon.–Fri. 9–6, Sat. and Sun. 9–6; Nov. 15–Mar. 14, Mon.–Fri. 9–4, Sat. and Sun. 9–4. Skyline Caverns gains fame for its clusters of shimmering white calcium carbonate crystals called anthodites. These rare, slow-growing formations gain only 1 inch every 7,000 years, compared to the 120 to 125 years required for similar growth in stalagmites and stalactites. On the guided tour, kids like the various formations as well as Rainbow Falls, an underground waterfall that plunges more than 37 feet, and, above-ground, a miniature-train ride around the grounds, and making their way through the Enchanted Dragon Mirror Maze. A snack bar and gift shop are on site. Remember, the temperature in the caverns is a cool 54 degrees F. $16 adults, $8 ages 7–13.

❧ **Luray Caverns** (540-743-6551; www.luraycaverns.com), 970 Highway 211 West. Open Apr.–June 14 and Labor Day–Oct. daily 9–6; June 15–Labor Day daily 9–7; Nov.–Mar. Mon.–Fri. 9–4, Sat. and Sun. 9–5. The largest cavern in Virginia and the most popular on the East Coast, Luray amazes with its cathedral-like chambers, some as high as 140 feet, its massive formations, and its Great Stalacpipe Organ, billed as the world's largest natural musical instrument. When plungers tap the stalactites, "music" comes forth. The tunes resonate throughout the chamber when plungers tap the stalactites. If you only have time or patience for one cavern tour, consider Luray, a U.S. National Natural Landmark. Admission includes a one-hour cavern tour plus access to the Luray Valley Museum and the Car and Carriage Caravan of Luray Caverns, a collection of 100-plus vehicles that includes a 1892 Mercedes-Benz, an 1840 Conestoga wagon, and a 1913 Stanley Steamer. Make your way through a garden maze made more mysterious with mist (extra fee). Shops sell child-pleasing souvenirs and the property has a café. Underground, the temperature is a constant 55 degrees F. $23 adults, $11 ages 6–12.; maze $7 adults, $6 ages 6–12.

New Market and surrounding area

❧ **Endless Caverns and RV Resort** (540-896-2283; 1-800-544-2283; www.endlesscaverns.com), 1800 Endless Caverns Road. Open daily 9-5. Closed Christmas. Named "endless" for its complex web of passageways that seem never to end, the cavern offers more than 5 miles of trails. Guided tours take approximately 75 minutes and the temperature is about 56 degrees F. $16 adults, $8 ages 4–12.

❧ **Shenandoah Caverns** (1-888-4CAVERN; www.shenandoahcaverns.com), I-81 exit 269, Quicksburg. The property features an eclectic group of attractions. Cavern highlights include Beyond the Veil, a row of stalactites illuminated with colored lights, a huge snowmanlike mound dubbed the "Capitol Dome" and striated formations called "Breakfast Bacon." At the Yellow Barn, see restored 19th-century farm wagons, a Model T and other vehicles, plus, sometimes, live entertainment. Kids like the 35-foot-tall tree house inhabited by five-foot-tall squirrels, the live farm animals, and American Celebration's collection of more than 30 floats from Rose Bowl and other parades. Of course there's a gift shop. $23 adults, $10 ages 6–10.

FARMERS' MARKETS (See also "Apple Picking.")

Winchester

Virginia Farm Market (540-665-8000; www.visitwinchesterva.com), 1 mile north of Winchester, 1881 North Frederick Pike. Open Apr.–Dec. 8–1. Shop for farm-fresh food. Summer brings cantaloupes and other fruit as well as vegetables, and in fall, buy apples and fresh apple cider and choose from among 15,000 pumpkins.

GOLF

Luray

Caverns Country Club Resort (540-743-7111; 888-443-6551; www.luray caverns.com), 910 T. C. North Boulevard. The 18-hole golf course plays out on gently rolling terrain overlooking the Shenandoah River. $30–40.

Shenvalee Golf Resort (540-740-9930; 888-339-3181; www.shenvalee.com), 9660 Fairway Drive. Swing through 27 holes of golf on three different courses. The property also has an outdoor swimming pool as well as motel-like accommodations.

HISTORY WALKING TOURS
New Market
New Market Walking Tours (540-740-3747; www.new-market-virginia-walking -tours.com), 9317 North Congress Street. Open May–Oct. Mon.–Sat. 10:30am. Evening tours by appointment. Choose from two 90-minute tours combining local history and lore that are led by a storyteller/historian in 19th-century attire. In Boys, Bugles and Skirts, find out about what happened to locals who sympathized with the Union, who helped nurse the Confederate wounded, and how one wife and mother outwitted the invading Union forces. New Market: An All-American Town details the town's colonial and revolutionary history. $10 adults, $5 age 12 and younger.

HORSEBACK RIDING A great way to savor the Shenandoah region's spectacular beauty is from atop a horse. Guided trail rides lead you through shady woods, across meadows to spectacular overlooks.

Luray area
Fort Valley Stable (540-933-6633, 888-754-5771; www.fortvalleystable.com), 299 South Fort Valley Road, Fort Valley. Open year-round, Nov.–Mar. weather permitting; call ahead. The rides lead you through the scenic Massanutten Mountains of the George Washington National Forest or along miles of the ranch's trails. All-day rides go to high peaks for panoramic views. Sixty- to 90-minute rides $28–38. Full-day ride to park or forest ridges comes with lunch, $165.

Jordan Hollow Stables (540-778-2623; 1-800-419-0599; www.jordanhollow stables.com), Judy Lane, Stanley, about 7 miles south of Luray. Open Memorial Day–Labor Day and Oct. Guided trail rides at 10, 1, and 3:30; reserve ahead. Rides leave from the facility's Bar M Boarding Stable and go through the property's 140 acres. Ninety- to 120-minute rides $38–58. All-day rides in either Shenandoah National Park or George Washington National Forest, $175.

Winchester
Rocking S. Ranch (540-678-8501; www.therockingsranch.com), 564 Glazie Orchard Road, offers trail rides.

SCENIC DRIVES (Also see "Shenandoah National Park" sidebar.)

Winchester area
Follow the Apple Trail (540-542-1326), 1360 South Pleasant Valley Road. This 45-minute audio driving tour, available on CD, winds you through Frederick County's scenic apple country, especially beautiful in spring when whitish-pink apple blossoms lace the hillsides. (See "Apple Picking.")

SHENANDOAH VALLEY WINERIES

The rich soil of the Shenandoah Valley nurtures several vineyards. The following are some of the region's wineries open for tours.

Linden Vineyards (540-364-1997; www.lindenvineyards.com), 3708 Harrels
Corner Road, Linden. Open Apr.–Nov. Wed.–Sun. 11–5; Dec.–Mar. weekends
11–5. Free tours Sat. and Sun. 11:30. Jim Law, vintner and co-owner, purchased the farm in 1983 and opened the winery in 1988. Linden now produces 5,000 cases annually. The *Oxford Companion to the Wines of North
America* calls Linden "a small but prestigious winery . . . offered stylish, elegant, polished wines." It's a peaceful place; you won't find bus tours here,
as groups may not be larger than six people. Regular tasting $5, cellar
reserve tasting $15.

Shenandoah Vineyards (540-984-8699; www.shentel.net/shenvine), 3659
South Ox Road, Edinburg. Open daily 10-5 daily. Located between Strasburg
and New Market, Shenandoah Vineyards, founded in 1976, is the oldest winery in the Shenandoah Valley. Tours and tastings available. $3.

Vino Curioso (703-447-0648; www.virginiawine.org), 1334 Perry Road, Winchester. Open Sat. and Sun. 11–5, but call ahead for a reservation as space
is limited. The boutique winery produces fewer than 1,000 cases a year.
Tours are free. Tastings $3.

✳ Green Spaces

Elizabeth Furnace Recreational Area, within the **Lee Ranger District**
(540-984-4101; www.fs.usda.gov), 109 Molineau Road, Edinburg, is about 9
miles from Front Royal. Elizabeth Furnace, named for the pig iron produced in
the area during the 19th century, has a campground as well as several trails. Both
the.3-mile **Pig Iron Trail loop** and the **Charcoal Trail loop**, 0.6 miles, are
easy walks. For more difficult hiking, try the **Bear Wallow Trail**, a 4½-mile
loop, or the **Signal Knob Trail**, a 10.2-mile loop.

George Washington and Jefferson National Forest (540-265-5100; www
.fs.usda.gov), Supervisor's Office, 5162 Valleypointe Parkway, Roanoke. Open
Mon.–Fri. 8–4:30. A good portion of this 1.9-million-acre recreational area lies in
the Shenandoah region. In Virginia, the forest runs from near Winchester in the
north to Abingdon in the south. What was formerly called the George Washington National Forest occupies the northern region, including the Allegheny, Massanutten, and Blue Ridge mountain ranges and what was formerly called the
Jefferson National Forest occupies the southern end. Administered by the U.S.
Forest Service, the entire area is now considered one national forest and divided
into three regions; the **northern region** lies north of Rte. 250 and I-64. A forest
this big offers many recreational opportunities. Popular places in the northern
section include:

SHENANDOAH NATIONAL PARK

Shenandoah National Park (540-999-3500; 1-800-828-1140; 1-877-444-6777 for emergencies; www.nps.gov/shen; www.visitshenandoah.com), 3655 U.S. Hwy. 211 East, Luray. Most areas open mid-May–late Oct.; other months, call ahead to see what sections remain open. One- to seven-day pass Mar.–Nov. individual $8, vehicle $15; Dec.–Feb. individual $5, vehicle $10.

Shenandoah National Park, the Shenandoah Valley region's gem, celebrated its 75th anniversary in 2011. The park's 197,438 acres of forests, mountains, and streams preserves the region's legendary beauty. The park

Shenandoah National Park

HAWKSBILL SUMMIT, SHENANDOAH NATIONAL PARK

serves as a refuge, a "green getaway" for work-weary urbanites throughout Virginia and nearby states, but especially for those in Washington, D.C., a mere 75 miles from the park's northern entrance at Front Royal. No one is certain of the derivation of the word "Shenandoah," which is reputed to mean "daughter of the stars" or "river of high mountains" in a Native American language. Either name fits. We have spent many soothing walks within the sound of the park's streams and waterfalls, and many evenings admiring the stars as they pop and glow in the purple sky.

HIKING With more than 100 hiking trails covering 500 miles, the park has paths to suit every ability. Along the way, you might see deer, hawks, falcons and other birds, and maybe even black bears. Popular hikes include the following (distances are one-way unless otherwise noted):

Easy hikes: **Little Stony Man Cliffs** (mile 39.1) is a relatively easy hike of 0.9 miles with a 270-foot elevation gain and mountain views. **Limberlost Trail** (milepost 43), meets former (not current) ADA requirements. The 1.3-mile loop has benches and passes through forest and mountain laurel grove, especially beautiful when blooming in June.

Moderately difficult hikes: **Dark Hollow Falls** (mile 50.7) near the Byrd Visitor Center, is a moderate hike of 1.4 miles to a view of the cascading waters, one the closet waterfalls to Skyline Drive. Save your energy because it's a 440-foot climb back to the trailhead. For those searching for a more challenging hike, try **Doyles River Falls** (mile 81.1). This hike starts near Loft Mountain Information Center, a 2.7-mile round-trip with an 850-foot change in elevation. Allow at least three hours. The trail leads to a waterfall surrounded by trees. Some places are steep. For the waterfall lovers, **Overall Run** (mile 22.2) is a great hike, moderately steep, and also leads to the park's highest waterfall. Allow at least five and a half hours.

Difficult hikes: The **White Oak Canyon** trail (mile 42.6) rewards you with views of six waterfalls as you hike the 7.3-mile trail through a gorge. Count on all day, as it's a 2,160-foot climb back to the start.

EarthCache Adventures adds both challenges and learning components to your hikes. Think of these outings as educational scavenger hunts using 21st-century technology. All you need is a GPS device (think of your smartphone). To play, sign on to www.geocahing.com/membership and sign up (basic membership is free). Then select a region of the park and an Earth-Cache link or trail. (You can download and print these out ahead of your visit.) At each of several places along the route, you are given some information and asked to observe something and write down what you see or think. For example, one part of a trek in the North District leads you to Compton Peak. Once there, your assignment includes taking a digital photo and writing down what you find most remarkable about the view. Unlike some other EarthCache quests, ones in Shenandoah (and other national parks) do not involve leaving or taking anything from the park or going off-trail.

HORSEBACK RIDING

Skyland Stables (540-999-2210), near Skyland Lodge (mile 41.7) Open Apr. 2–Nov. The stable offers one-hour guided trail rides for adults. Reserve ahead as horseback riding is popular. $35–55.

RANGER PROGRAMS

Although park rangers offer lectures and activities year-round, spring through fall brings an

TRAIL RIDE

Shenandoah National Park

abundance of these free programs. Go on guided, often easy hikes (as well as a few difficult ones); listen to talks about birds, bears, and other critters; and participate in evening campfire talks and walks. These programs take place at or depart from the park's two lodges, Skyland and Big Meadows.

SCENIC DRIVES AND OVERLOOKS **Skyline Drive** cuts through the park, stretching 105 miles across the crest of the Blue Ridge Mountains from Front Royal to Rockfish Gap. The scenic road can be accessed from all four park entrances. The mile markers start after the Front Royal Entrance Station in the north, at milepost 1, and end at the Rockfish Gap Entrance Station in the south just after milepost 105. (Whole numbers are "mileposts"; markers that indicate any fractional distance are designated "mile"). The maximum speed limit on this curving, scenic road is 35 mph. According to park rangers, on a clear day with no traffic (not in the heart of leaf-peeping season), three hours would get you from beginning to end. But that would be without stopping. Take time to pause and admire the vistas of mountains and sky at some of the 76 scenic overlooks. Also remember that for some people—especially children—a little bit of a twisting road goes a long way—you don't have to do it all. Among the popular overlooks offering valley and mountain views are **Shenandoah Valley Overlook** (mile 2.8); **Stony Man Overlook** (mile 38.6); **Franklin Cliffs Overlook** (milepost 49); and **Big Run Overlook** (mile 81.2), one of the park's most beautiful.

During autumn, prime foliage season, when the mountains area ribbon of yellow and gold leaves, the Skyline Drive can come to a near crawl. Typically, the colors are at their peak in mid-October. If you visit during leaf-peeping season, be ready for crowds: Prepare to go slow and have patience. For the latest foliage updates, contact Skyline Drive/Shenandoah National Park (540-999-3500; 1-800-828-1140; www.nps.gov/shen; www.visitshenandoah.com).

HOTELS AND LODGES IN THE PARK Within the park are two hotels and two groups of self-serve cabins that may be rented. The hotels basic but clean and serviceable accommodations, the majority of which do not have air-conditioning. Some do not have televisions and many do not have in-room phones. Remember why you came here—to be outside, in nature. Reserve up to a year in advance for popular fall and summer getaways.

Skyland Resort (540-483-2100; 1-800-999-4714; www.visitshenandoah.com), mile 41.7, P.O. Box 727, Luray. Open late Mar.–late Nov. Situated at 3,680 feet, this historic lodge, opened in the late 1800s, is situated at the highest point of Skyline Drive, making for spectacular valley views. None of the accommodations offer in-room phones or Wi-Fi. On 36 acres, Skyland Resort has 179 guest units, including some more modern rooms, plus three family cabins that sleep six to eight people. Facilities include a restaurant and evening entertainment in season. $109–267.

Big Meadows Lodge (540-483-2100; 1-800-999-4714; www.visitshenandoah .com), mile 51.2, P.O. Box 727, Luray. Open mid-May–early Nov. On the National Register of Historic Place, Big Meadows offers views of the Shenandoah Valley. The property has 97 rooms, 25 of which are in the main lodge built in 1939 as a Civilian Conservation Corps project. In addition, there are 72 other units in other buildings. Televisions and air-conditioning are available in some, but not all, guest rooms. The lodge has an on-site restaurant and often presents nightly entertainment in summer and fall. $109–187.

Lewis Mountain Cabins (mile 57.5). Apr.–8-Nov.6. Choose from semirustic studio cabins and two-bedroom cabins, each with private baths and heat; linens are provided. Cooking facilities include a fireplace, grills, and picnic tables in the connecting outdoor area. $109.

WHERE TO EAT IN THE PARK We always like packing a picnic and pausing at a scenic spot to eat lunch. The park has six designated picnic areas: **Dickey Ridge**, mile 4.6; **Elkwallow**, mile 24.1; **Pinnacles**, mile 36.7; **Big Meadows**, mile 51.2; **Lewis Mountain**, mile 57.6; and **South River**, mile 62.9.

The two lodges in the park have restaurants. **Skyland Resort Pollock Dining Room** (540-483-2100; 1-800-999-4714; www.visitshenandoah.com), mile 41.7. Open late Mar.–late Nov. breakfast 7:30–10, lunch noon–2, dinner 5:30–9. The American fare includes fried chicken, mountain trout, turkey platter, pasta, and beef tenderloin. $13–22.

Big Meadows Lodge Spottswood Dining Room (540-483-2100; 1-800-999-4714; www.visitshenandoah.com), mile 51.2. Open mid-May–early Nov. breakfast 7:30–10, lunch noon–2, dinner 5:30–9. The American fare for dinner includes fried chicken, meat loaf, grilled salmon, trout, steak, and pasta. $13–25.

The State Arboretum of Virginia (540-837-1758; www.virginia.edu/~blandy), 400 Blandy Farm Lane, Boyce, 10 miles east of Winchester. Open daily dawn–dusk. The arboretum's 170 acres of trees and meadows, part of the 700-acre Blandy Experimental Farm, a University of Virginia research facility, offers walking and bridle trails (bring your own horse). In summer concerts are held at the Margaret Byrd Stimpson Amphitheater.

Wayside Food stores sell breakfast items, sandwiches, burgers, snacks, and groceries to go. **Big Meadows Wayside** (mile 51.2). late March–late Nov. $7–9. **Elkwallow Wayside** (mile 24.1). Open mid-Apr.–early Nov. $7–9. **Loft Mountain Wayside** (mile 79.5). Open early Apr.–early Nov. $7–9.

VISITOR CENTERS Dickey Ridge Visitor Center (540-999-3500), mile 4.7 near the Front Royal Entrance Station. Open late Mar.–late Nov. daily 8:30–5. An exhibit and a film introduce visitors to the park. Maps, books, and other items for sale.

The Byrd Visitor Center (540-999-3500), mile 51. Open late Mar.–late Nov. daily 8:30–5. This center has interpretive exhibits, plus a good selection of books, maps, trail guides, and park-related items.

Loft Mountain Information Center, mile 79.5, will be closed in 2011.

BIG MEADOWS LODGE

Shenandoah National Park

Todd Lake Recreational Area, within the **North River Ranger District** (540-828-0187; www.fs.usda.gov), 401 Oakwood Drive, Harrisonburg, is about 15 miles from Bridgewater or 25 miles from Staunton. Swim and fish in the lake, as well as take the easy 1-mile loop trail around the water. (See also *Green Spaces* in "Southwestern Shenandoah Region.")

✳ Lodging

HOTELS, RESORTS, AND LODGES

Front Royal

Hampton Inn (540-635-18812; 1-800-HAMPTON; www.hamptoninn .hilton.com), 9800 Winchester Road. Located 5 miles from Skyline Drive, the moderately priced property has 75 rooms. $90–120.

🐾 ♿ (ᵖ) **Quality Inn Skyline Drive** (540-635-3161; 1-800-228-5151; www .qualityinn.com), 10 Commerce Avenue. Rates at this moderately priced hotel include a continental breakfast. $70–100.

Shenandoah River Cabins (540-743-4159; 1-800-622-6632; www .shenandoahrivercabins.com) 6502 South Page Valley Road. A branch of the Shenandoah River Outfitters, this company offers six log cabins for rent, some with hot tubs. Rates vary with the season and rentals are available year-round. Mar.–Nov. $140–180.

Luray

🐾 ♿ **Best Western Intown of Luray** (540-743-6511; 1-800-528-1234; www.bestwestern.com), 410 West Main Street. 40 rooms, and an outdoor pool. $80–120.

🐾 (ᵖ) **Days Inn Luray** (540-743-4521; www.daysinn-luray.com), 138 Whispering Hill Road. 108 rooms, plus an outdoor pool. $70–160.

♿ (ᵖ) **Mimslyn Inn** (540-743-5105; 1-800-296-5105; www.mimslynninn .com), 401 West Main. 45 rooms. The hotel, dating to 1931, has been renovated and a spa added, turning it into one of Luray's nicest inns. $115–325.

New Market

(ᵖ) **Quality Inn-Shenandoah Valley** (540-740-3141; 1-800-228-1AAA; www.qualityinn.com), 162 West Old Cross Road. 100 rooms. The property has an outdoor pool and free Internet. $65–120.

Winchester

♿ (ᵖ) **George Washington Hotel, Wyndham** (540-678-4700; 1-800-WYNDHAM; www.wyndham.com), 103 Piccadilly Street. This 1924 hotel was once the jewel of Winchester. After a $30-million restoration, the property shines again. Amenities include an indoor pool and a jazz lounge. $120–290.

Hampton Inn (540-667-8011; 1-800-HAMPTON; www.hampton-inn.com), 1655 Apple Blossom Drive. The hotel is close to restaurants and historic sites. Continental breakfast is in-cluded in room rates. $80–115.

Holiday Inn Express & Suites (540-542-1326; 1-877-871-1326; www .visitwinchesterva.com), 1360 South Pleasant Valley Road, Winchester. Free breakfast, an indoor pool, and high-speed Internet access are included in the rates of rooms. $90–125.

BED & BREAKFAST INNS

Front Royal area

Inn at Narrow Passage (540-459-8900; 1-800-459-8002; innatnarrow passage.com), Rte. 11 at Chapman Landing Road, Woodstock. 12 rooms. This was once an overnight stop for travelers along the Great Wagon Road. Parts of this historic inn date to 1740, and during the Civil War, Stonewall Jackson stayed here for part of his Shenandoah campaign. The inn is furnished with a mix of antiques,

SHENANDOAH REGION MOUNTAIN RESORTS

At the region's mountain resorts, enjoy panoramic views, swimming, golf, and hiking.

Bryce Resort (540-856-2121; 1-800-821-1444), 1982 Fairway Drive, Basye. Located on 400 acres in the Allegheny Mountains, in winter Bryce offers skiing and snowboarding on eight slopes, as well as snow tubing. Spring through fall, enjoy golf, fishing, and boating on Lake Laura, hiking, and a zip line. Many property owners put their condominiums or homes in the rental pool for select times. Bryce does not offer a hotel. Rates vary.

Massanutten Resort (540-289-9441; www.massresort.com), 1822 Resort Drive, McGaheysville. In winter, ski and snowboard on 14 trails; in summer, play 27 holes of golf, hike the trails, and relax at the spa. The resort has both an outdoor and a year-round indoor water park. The property has about 140 hotel rooms and 800 condominiums that are timeshare properties. Some may be available for rental. Prices vary. Hotel rooms $150.

period reproductions, and comfortable modern pieces. $135–175.

New Market

Apple Blossom Inn Bed & Breakfast (540-740-3747), 9317 North Congress Street. Open year-round. Instead of renting just a room, you rent the entire house, which has two bedrooms and 1½ baths plus a parlor, music room, and screened garden gazebo. The New Market Walking Tours begin from this B&B. $125–135.

Cross Roads Inn Bed and Breakfast (540-740-4157; www.crossroads innva.com), 9222 John Sevier Road. 6 rooms. A wrap-around porch with rocking chairs, bedrooms with canopy or four-poster beds and down comforters ad to the welcoming nature of this home. $75-135.

(ᵃ) **Jacob Swartz House** (540-740-9208; jacobswartz.com), 574 Jiggady Road. Open February through New Year's Day. The guest cottage, a converted cobbler's shop has two bedrooms, but is rented to just one couple or group at a time. Relax in the living area with its wood-burning stove or sit on the screened-in porch. A full breakfast is served. $150.

New Market area

Strathmore House (540-477-4141, 888-921-6139; wwww.strathmore house.com), P.O. Box 499, Mount Jackson. Four guest rooms. A Queen Anne–style country home 5 miles from New Market and near the Meem's Bottom covered bridge, this inn is comfortably furnished with antiques and caters to romantic getaways. $140–180.

Strasburg

🐾 **Hotel Strasburg** (540-465-9191; 1-800-348-8327; www.hotelstrasburg.com), 213 South Holliday Street. 29 rooms. Built as a hospital in 1902, this inn has a restaurant and its rooms are decorated with Victorian antiques. $100–190.

The Wayside Inn (540-869-1797; 1-877-869-1797; www.alongthewayside.com), 7783 Main Street, Strasburg. Dating to 1797, the Wayside, at the foot of the Massanutten Mountains, offers 22 rooms with canopied beds, French Provincial and Victorian period pieces and collectibles, plus modern conveniences such as televisions. There is an on-site restaurant. $100–170.

White Post

L'Auberge Provençale (540-837-1375; 1-800-638-1702; www.laubergeprovencale.com), P.O. Box 190. Eleven rooms. Open to the public for dinner Mon.–Sat. 6–10, Sun. 5–10. We have been coming to this inn for weekend getaways for years. The décor and the atmosphere re-create a bit of southern France in Virginia hunt country. Lodging is either in the main house or in adjacent cottages (we like the cottage rooms best). With their bright colors, floral prints, wine racks, and country antiques, the rooms conjure up Provence. $235–325.

Winchester Area

The Inn at Vaucluse Spring (540-869-0200; 1-800-869-0525; www.vauclusespring.com), 231 Vaucluse Spring Lane, Stephens City. 15 rooms. Set on 100 acres of rolling hills near Winchester's orchards and Front Royal's entrance to Shenandoah National Park, the inn offers guest rooms in six buildings, including the Manor House, an 1850s log house, and the Gallery, a two-story cottage with a pool. Rates include afternoon tea and a full breakfast. $160–320. Dinners are available by reservation Fri. $40, and Sat. $63. Wines additional.

✷ Where to Eat

Front Royal

Royal Dairy Ice Cream Bar & Restaurant (540-635-5202), 241 Chester Street. Open Sun.–Thu. 5:30 AM–9 PM, Fri. and Sat. 5:30 AM–9:30 PM. Ice cream is still a highlight of this local eatery, opened in 1947, but now the place also serves burgers and sandwiches. $4–10.

Soul Mountain Café (540-636-0070; www.restaurant.com), 300 East Main Street. Tue.–Sat. lunch noon–3:30 PM, dinner 5:30–9; Sun. lunch noon-4. The small yet pleasant restaurant offers an interesting blend of Caribbean, Cajun, and American cuisine. $14–22.

South Street Grill (540-636-6654), 424 South Street, no. A. The local eatery with a retro 1950s feel serves old favorites such as milkshakes, peanut butter and jelly sandwiches, and burgers, as well as soups, salads, and chicken. $7–15.

Luray

🍸 **Speakeasy Bar & Restaurant**, Mimslyn Inn (540-743-5105; 1-800-296-5105; www.mimslynninn.com), 401 West Main. Open Mon.–Thu. 5–9, Fri. and Sat. 4–10, Sun. 5–8. Locals like this casual restaurant and bar whose specialties include chicken potpie, meat loaf, pork sandwiches, soups, and other comfort foods. Live music is offered Thursday and Friday nights. $9–25.

Middletown

Y **Irish Isle Restaurant & Pub** (540-868-9877; www.theirishisle.com), 7843 Main Street. Open Tue.–Fri. 4 PM–closing, Sun. noon–closing. The owner, Brian Coughlan, is from Limerick. He mixes traditional Irish fare—sausages in pastry, corned beef and cabbage—with salads, chicken, burgers, and other pub foods. Several nights every week, he and others perform Irish, Scottish, and English folk tunes. The pub, notes Brian, even has a resident ghost—benign—whom Brian has named George. $8–25.

New Market

Johnny Appleseed Restaurant (540-740-3141), Quality Inn Shenandoah Valley, I-81, exit 264, 162 West Cross Road. Open daily 6:30 AM–9 PM. The restaurant offers fried chicken, country-fried steak, crab cakes, and other regional fare. $10–19.

Strasburg

Hotel Strasburg (540-465-9191; www.hotelstrasburg.com), 213 South Holliday Street. Open Mon.–Sat. lunch 11:30–2:30; Mon.–Thu. dinner 5–8; Fri. and Sat. dinner 5–9; Sun. breakfast 8–10:30, lunch 11:30–2, and dinner 4-8. Converted from a hospital to an Edwardian hotel in 1915, the hotel's restaurant serves international cuisine plus regional specialties in a dining room accented with antiques and collectibles. $12–18.

White Post

L'Auberge Provençale (540-837-1375; 1-800-638-1702; www.lauberge provencale.com), P.O. Box 190. 11 rooms. Open to the public for dinner Mon.–Sat. 6–10, Sun. 5–10. We have been enjoying Chef Alain Borel's modern Provençale cuisine for years. The Zagat survey has rated the inn's restaurant as number 57 on a list of the top 100 hotel restaurants in the United States. Three-course prix fixe menu $58, Five-course $88.

Winchester

One Block West (540-662-1455; www.oneblockwest.com), 25 South Indian Alley. Tue.–Sat. lunch 11-2, dinner 5–closing. Named for its location one block west of Winchester's downtown pedestrian mall, this is one of Winchester's best restaurants. Chef and owner Ed Matthews serves seasonal American cuisine. $22-33.

Snow White Grill (540-662-5955; www.snowwhitegrill.net) 159 North Loudon Street. Open Mon.–Fri. 10–6, Sat. 10–4, plus Fri. and Sat. 11 PM–2:30 AM. Opened in 1949 as part of a regional family chain, the grill, with its traditional diner feel, was taken over in 2008. The owners still keep the famous mini-hamburger on the menu and still serve ice cream and shakes. $1.50–6.

✴ Entertainment

Middletown

Wayside Theatre (540-869-1776; www.waysidetheatre.org), 7853 Main Street, Rte. 11. Box office open Mon.–Fri. 10–5. Virginia's second-oldest professional theater presents drama and musicals. Ticket prices vary.

Winchester

Shenandoah Summer Music Theatre (540-665-4569; 1-877-580-8025; shenandoahsummermusictheatre.com), Shenandoah University, 1460 University Drive. The company puts on four Broadway musicals in the summer season. $25–28.

✳ Selective Shopping

Strasburg

Strasburg Emporium Antiques
(540-465-3711; www.strasburgem
porium.com), 160 North Massanutten
Street. Sun.–Thu. 10–5, Fri. and Sat.
10–6. The emporium houses about
100 dealers under one roof, selling
antiques, collectibles, books, and
glassware.

✳ Special Events

May: **Shenandoah Apple Blossom
Festival**, Winchester, is carnival featuring fireworks and a firefighters'
parade that is reputed to be the
world's largest. Early May **Annual of
Ale & History Beer Festival at
Belle Grove Plantation** (540-869-
2028), Middletown. Enjoy food, beer
and rugby on the lawn.

Mid-May: **Battle of New Market
Reenactment** gathers 2,000 reenactors (540-740-3101; 1-866-515-
1864), in New Market. **Wildflower
Weekend in Shenandoah National
Park**, generally the second weekend
in May, offers special walks and
exhibits that highlight the park's
spring flowers.

August–September: **Shenandoah
County Fair**, held in Woodstock, has
midway rides, greased-pig contests,
prize livestock, country music concerts, harness races, and bubble
gum–blowing contests.

September: **Apple Harvest Arts &
Crafts Festival**, Winchester. One of
the area's largest annual events, with
music, apple-butter making, square
dancing, and lots more, takes place
the third week in September.

SHENANDOAH APPLE BLOSSOM FESTIVAL

Christopher Hunter Photography, Virginia Tourism Corporation

October: **Annual Hot Air Balloon, Wine & Music Festival**, Long Branch Historic House and Farm, Millwood, mid-October, has more than 30 hot-air balloon launches, powered parachutes, wine tastings, and events for kids.

Battle of Cedar Creek Reenactment, Long Branch Historic House and Farm, Millwood. The October 19, 1864, Civil War Battle of Cedar Creek is relived during the third week of October, while visitors can also browse Civil War merchants' stalls, listen to period music, and go on candlelit tours of the camps.

Heritage Days Fall Festival, in late October every year, presents food and games in New Market.

SOUTHERN SHENANDOAH REGION AND THE BLUE RIDGE PARKWAY

TOWNS AND COUNTIES Bath County. Bath County has no incorporated towns as well as no traffic lights. What the region offers is quintessential mountain scenery. Forested mountains account for 89 percent of the county's land. The George Washington Jefferson National Forest, for example, encompasses 170,000 acres of it. On a drive along the winding roads, you pass country towns and rolling meadows nestled among the Allegheny Mountain peaks. Settled by pioneers around 1745, the county is famous for its healing springs that gave rise to the Homestead Resort, an area fixture since 1766. Both Warn Springs and Hot Springs are located in this county.

MENNONITE BUGGY NEAR DAYTON

Virginia Department of Tourism

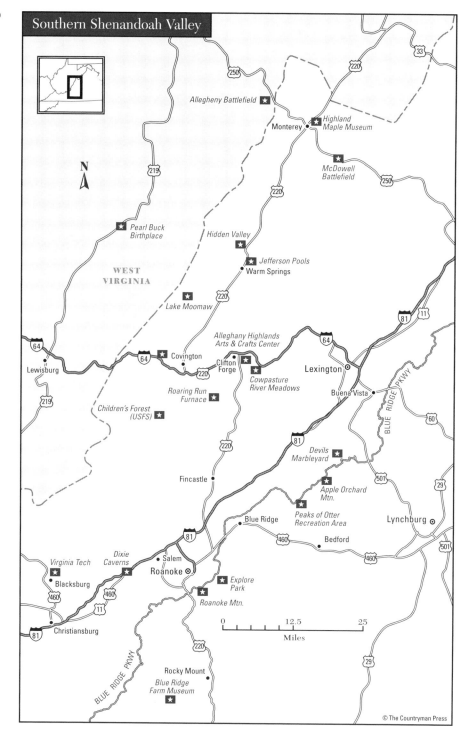

Southern Shenandoah Valley

Allegheny Battlefield

Monterey · ★ Highland
Maple Museum

★ McDowell
Battlefield

N

Pearl Buck
Birthplace

Hidden Valley

★ Jefferson Pools
Warm Springs

WEST
VIRGINIA

Lake Moomaw

Alleghany Highlands
Arts & Crafts Center

64

64

Covington

Lewisburg

Clifton
Forge

Lexington

Cowpasture
River Meadows

Roaring Run
Furnace

Buena Vista

Children's Forest
(USFS)

BLUE RIDGE PKWY

Devils
Marbleyard

Fincastle

Apple Orchard
Mtn.

Peaks of Otter
Recreation Area

Blue Ridge

Lynchburg

Bedford

Dixie
Caverns

Salem

Virginia Tech

Roanoke

Blacksburg

Explore
Park

Roanoke Mtn.

Christiansburg

0   12.5   25

Miles

BLUE RIDGE PKWY

Rocky Mount

Blue Ridge
Farm Museum

© The Countryman Press

Lexington and Natural Bridge. Steeped in traditions and lively with college students, Lexington, 35 miles south of Staunton, is home to the Virginia Military Institute (VMI) and to Washington and Lee University. **Natural Bridge** isn't a town as much as a group of attractions that grew up around the natural limestone bridge, a site admired and once owned by Thomas Jefferson.

Roanoke. About 54 miles south of Lexington, off milepost 120 on the Blue Ridge Parkway, Roanoke, population 260,000, is the parkway's largest city. Roanoke calls itself the "Star City of the South" for many reasons, including the massive, illuminated star that shines year-round from the top of Mill Mountain. The city has a strong railroad heritage and is home to the Norfolk Southern Railway.

Staunton. One of the oldest cities west of the Blue Ridge Mountains, Staunton (pronounced "Stan-ton"), 11 miles west of the southern end of Skyline Drive at Waynesboro, is the birthplace of Woodrow Wilson. His former home serves as a museum.

GUIDANCE Bath County Chamber of Commerce(540-839-5409; 1-800-628-8092; www.bathcountyva.org; www.discoverbath.com), US 220, P.O. Box 718, Hot Springs. Open June–Oct. 9–1.

Lexington and Rockbridge County (540-463-3777; www.lexingtonvirginia .com), 106 East Washington Street. **The Roanoke Valley Convention and Visitors Bureau Visitor Information** (540-342-6025; 1-800-635-5535; www .visitroanokeva.com), 101 Shenandoah Avenue.

Staunton-Augusta Travel Information Center (540-332-3972; 800-332-5219; www.staunton.va.us; www.visit staunton.com), 1290 Richmond Road. **Staunton Visitors Center** (540-332-3971; 1-800-342-7942), 35 South New Street.

GETTING THERE *By air:* **Shenandoah Valley Regional Airport** (540-234-8304), 77 Aviation Circle, Weyers Cave, off Interstate 81, is about 50 miles from **Lexington** and about 20 miles from **Staunton**. **Roanoke Regional Airport** (540-362-1999) is 6 miles from **Roanoke.**

By bus: There is no regularly scheduled bus service to Lexington and Staunton. The **Roanoke** Greyhound bus terminal (1-800-231-2222; www .greyhound.com) is at 26 Salem Avenue SW.

AERIAL VIEW OF ROANOKE
CameronDavidson, Virginia Tourism Corporation

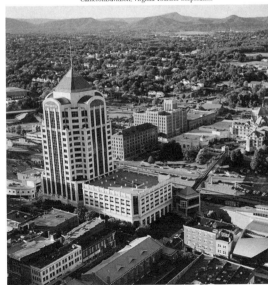

Kathy Frazier

BEVERLEY STREET, STAUNTON

By car: **Lexington:** From Washington and Baltimore, take 1-66 west to I-81 south toward US 60 west. From Richmond, take VA 195 east to I-95 north onto I-64. Continue on I-64 west to I-81 south to US 60 west. From Norfolk/Hampton Roads, take I-264 east onto I-64 west to I-81 south to US 60 west toward Lexington.

Roanoke: From Washington and Baltimore, take I-66 west onto I-81 south toward Roanoke. Take US 220 south and take I-581 south and continue on US 11 south. From Richmond, take VA 195 east to I-95 north to I-64 west and continue on I-81 south. Take US 220 south and continue on I-581 south to US 11 south. From Norfolk/Hampton Roads, take I-64 west toward Richmond. Continue on I-81 south to US 220 south toward I-581 south. Continue on US 11 south to Roanoke.

Staunton: From Washington and Baltimore, take I-66 west to I-81 south toward Roanoke and then take VA 262 south. From Richmond, take VA 195 east to I-95 north. Take I-64 onto I-81 north and then take US 250 west toward Staunton. From Norfolk/Hampton Roads, take I-264 east to I-81 north and then take US 250 west toward Staunton.

By train: **Amtrak** (1-800-872-7245; www.amtrak.com) has several stops in this area. From **Clifton Forge's** station, it is 22 miles to **Lexington;** 13 miles to **Hot Springs**; and 38 miles to **Roanoke. Staunton's** station is located at 1 Middlebrook Avenue.

GETTING AROUND A car is a must, especially for exploring the back roads, state parks and national forests. In **Roanoke**, **Valley Metro** (540-982-2222; www.valleymetro.com) provides public bus transportation and **Staunton, Staunton-Augusta Travel Information Center** (540-332-3972; 1-800-332-5219; www.staunton.va.us; www.visitstaunton.com), has free downtown trolley service.

MUSEUMS, HISTORIC LANDMARKS, AND SITES

Lexington

Downtown Lexington (540-463-5375; www.downtownlexington.com), downtown. Listed on the state and national registers of historic places, Lexington's downtown retains its 19th-century look while brimming with cafés, boutiques, shops, and art galleries. Pick up a walking tour brochure at the Visitor Center. The **Lexington Carriage Company** (540-463-5647) offers tours in season.

Lee Chapel and Museum (540-458-8768), 11 University Place, campus of Washington and Lee University. Open Apr.–Oct. Mon.–Sat. 9–5, Sun. 1–5 Nov.–Mar. Mon.–Sat. 9–4, Sun. 1–4. Closed Thanksgiving Thu. and Fri., Dec. 24 and 25, and Jan. 1. Constructed in 1867 under the supervision of General Robert E. Lee, the chapel is noted for Charles Willson Peale's portrait of George Washington and Edward Valentine's recumbent sculpture of Lee, who served as president of the college from the end of the Civil War until his death in 1870. Afterward, Lee's name was added to that of the university. Lee and his family are buried beneath the chapel and Traveller, Lee's beloved horse, is interred in a marked plot outside. $5 donation suggested.

STAUNTON'S TROLLEY

Jean Boyd

&. **George C. Marshall Museum** (540-463-2083; www.marshallfoundation .org), VMI Parade Grounds. Open Mar.–Dec. Tue.–Sat. 9–5, Sun. 1–5, Closed Thanksgiving, Dec. 24–25, and Jan. 1. The facility houses the Marshall Research Library as well as the museum. Marshall, a 1901 VMI graduate, served as a five-star general in World War II. Artifacts include his 1953 Nobel Peace Prize for his Marshall Plan, which was to stimulate the recovery of war-torn Europe. $5 adults, $2 students, free for under age 12.

&. **Virginia Military Institute Museum** (540-464-7334; www. vmi.edu /museum), 415 Fletcher Avenue, VMI Parade Grounds. Open daily 9–5. Closed Thanksgiving, Dec. 25, and Jan. 1. Presenting a history of the former VMI cadets who went on to military and other career, the museum houses 15,000 artifacts in its permanent collection. General Stonewall Jackson's mounted horse "Little Sorrel" is here, as well the coat Jackson wore when he was shot. The Henry Stewart 19th Century Antique Firearms Collection presents 50 weapons, including the air rifle carried by Lewis and Clark for hunting in their expeditions.

Roanoke

O. Winston Link Museum (540-982-5465; www.linkmuseum.org), 101 Shenandoah Avenue NE. Open Mar.–Dec. daily 10–5, Jan.–Feb. noon–5. Closed Easter, Thanksgiving, Dec. 25, and Jan. 1. A must-see for both lovers of photography and train buffs, the museum showcases hundreds of O. Winston Link's black-and-white photographs of trains, primarily 1950s Norfolk & Western Railway's steam locomotives, the last of their era. Soon afterward, diesel power took over.

VIRGINIA MILITARY INSTITUTE

Virginia Department of Tourism

Virginia Tourism Corporation

TAUBMAN MUSEUM OF ART

Link's engaging images capture not only the big, belching locomotives, but the era as well: Trains chug by drive-in movies, laundry hang on the line, and kids splash in a river. The museum also hosts temporary exhibits. $5 adults, $4 ages 3–11.

✈ ⟳ **Science Museum of Western Virginia** (540-342-5710; www.smwv.org), One Market Square. Open Wed.–Sat. noon–5. Closed Easter, Memorial Day, Labor Day, Thanksgiving, Dec. 24 and 25, and Jan. 1. At this museum's kid-friendly interactive exhibits, visitors learn hands-on about science and the ecology of western Virginia. At the Living River, see how mountain streams and rivers connect to the ocean and handle horseshoe crabs and sea stars in the touch tank. Admire sparkling mineral samples at Earth Treasures; broadcast rain or sun at the Weather Gallery; make your hair stand on end in the Light & Sound Gallery; and view pythons, box turtles, and snakes at the Live Animals exhibit. Watch the stars at the planetarium or be immersed in movies at the MegaDome, which has a 40-foot dome-shaped screen with surround sound. $8 adults, $6 ages 3–12; Planetarium and MegaDome cost extra.

⟳ **Taubman Museum of Art** (540-342-5760; www.taubmanmuseum.org), 110 Salem Avenue NE. Open Tue., Wed., Fr., and Sat. 10-5, Thu. 10–8 (5–8 free), Sun. noon–5. You can't miss this museum because of its striking glass façade. The 81,000-square-foot facility concentrates on American modern and contemporary art, but also has 19th-century and some earlier works; a Japanese print collection; and to the delight of fashionistas, a Mixed Bag Gallery with Judith Leiber purses. Check the museum' schedule for afternoon concerts and performances by the Roanoke Symphony Orchestra. $10.50 adults, $8.50 students, $5.50 ages 5–12.

NATURAL BRIDGE

❧ **The Natural Bridge** (540-291-2121; 1-800-533-1410; www.naturalbridgeva .com), 15 Appledore Lane, 12 miles south of Lexington. Bridge open daily 8 AM–dusk; Cedar Creek Trail open 9 AM–dusk; Drama of Creation Apr.–Oct. daily at dusk, winter on select weekends at dusk; Monacan Village Apr.–mid-Nov. daily 10–5; Wax Museum and Toy Museum daily 10–5. This limestone arch, 215 feet high and 90 feet wide, was formed by erosion. Carved eons ago by Cedar Creek, a tributary of the James River, Natural Bridge is an impressive geological feature, a Virginia and a National Histori- cal Landmark. A Monocan Indian legend states that the bridge magically appeared just as the tribe needed a way to escape from enemies. George Washington surveyed the bridge for Lord Fairfax (you can see where he was believed to have carved his initials), and Thomas Jefferson, so taken by the bridge's beauty, purchased the arch and the surrounding land. A number of attractions have developed around the bridge. Mile-long **Cedar Creek Trail** leads to Lace Falls. **The Drama of Creation** is a nightly sound-and-light show. At the **Monacan Indian Living History Village,** reached by a nature trail, watch interpreters in Native American clothing tan hides, weave mats, build shelters, and create bowls and baskets. The Monacans were one of the powerful tribes Captain John Smith encountered when he landed in what was to him and the Europeans, a "New World." Children may like the **Wax Museum**, although they may need help figuring out the identities of some of the 150 wax statues concerning Virginia history. No explanation needed for the **Toy Museum** that displays 45,000 items, some of which date back to 1740. Along with its colonial dolls, kids can see Star Trek toys, 1930s mechanical toys, GI Joe and other early action figures, and much more. $18

❧ & **Virginia Museum of Transportation** (540-342-5670; www.vmt.org), 303 Norfolk Avenue. Open Mon.–Sat. 10–5, Sun. 1–5. Train buffs love this place. The yard has more than 40 real pieces of equipment, including steam, diesel, and vintage electric locomotives; cabooses and a railway postal car; plus inside model trains move along on 600 feet of track. The museum focuses on other means of transportation, showcasing road and air travel. The car collection high- lights some greats, including a 1904 Curved Dash Olds, a1925 Ford Model T, a 1948 Packard Super Eight, an Oldsmobile Cutlass Supreme SX, and a 1983 Ford Mustang GLX convertible. The Wings Over Virginia Aviation Collection is tem- porarily closed because of storm damage. The museum store is a great source of transportation-related toys and gifts. $8 adults, $6 ages 3–11.

adults, $10 ages 5–12. Admission package to the bridge, Drama of Creation, Monacan Village, Wax Museum, and Toy Museum is $26 adults, $14 ages 5–12.

Natural Bridge Caverns, open Mar.–Nov. 10–5. Highlights include the stalagmites, stalactites, a large flowstone formation, and what's called the "Colossal Dome" room—a large, high-ceilinged natural formation. The caverns remain a constant 54 degrees F. $14 adults, $9 ages 5–12.

✧ **Virginia Safari Park** (540-291-3205; www.virginiasafaripark.com), 229 Safari Lane. Open mid-Mar.–May 29 daily 9–5, last car admitted 4 PM; May 30–Sept. 5 daily 9–6, last car admitted 5 PM; Sept. 6–Thanskgiving weekend, 9–5, last car admitted 4 PM (closed Thanksgiving Day); Memorial Day–Labor Day daily 9–6. Here, exotic animals live in expansive enclosures while the people stay caged in their cars and drive through. The 180-acre park gives kids (and adults) the chance to see zebras, antelope, ostriches, elk, bison, and other animals roaming "free" (sort of). The park provides specialty grains and other edibles, should you wish to feed the critters. When a big elk ambles over to munch from your kids' bucket is an experience your child will long remember. At the Giraffe Feeding Station, part of the walk-through section, climb the steps to get eyeball-to-eyeball with the long-necked wonders. As you feed them, watch how they reach for your treats with their big, purple tongues. Enjoy close encounters with beautiful birds at the free-flight aviary and admire rainbow-colored lorikeets as they sip nectar from a cup you hold at the Lorikeet Landing. The best way to tour is to hop aboard the safari wagon for a 60-minute guided run. Since the sides are more open than those of a car, you see more; and with someone else driving, everyone gets to have fun. $14 adults, $10 ages 3–12. Bucket of grain $3. Safari ride $4, includes one bucket of animal feed. You may want to purchase another bucket or two.

Roanoke area

✧ ♿ **Booker T. Washington National Monument** (540-721-2094; www.nps .gov/bowa/), 12130 Booker T. Washington Highway, Hardy. Open daily 9–5. On April 5, 1856, Booker T. Washington was born into slavery in the kitchen of this 19th-century tobacco plantation. His mother was the farm's cook. Washington lived here until the age of nine, when he was freed by the Emancipation Proclamation. Later, he became a respected educator and founder of the Tuskegee Institute in Alabama, as well as an adviser to presidents. For grade school–age children and teens, a visit here illuminates Washington's humble beginnings, the evils of slavery, and how determination plays an important part in one's life. The film at the Visitor Center provides background. A walk along the.25-mile-long

✐ MILL MOUNTAIN ATTRACTIONS

Roanoke Star/Overlook (540-342-6025; 1-800-635-5535; www.visitroanoke va.com), J. P. Fishburne Parkway and Prospect Road. Open 24/7. What's a city without a symbol? Roanoke's is a 100-foot-tall, concrete and steel star illuminated with 2,000 feet of neon tubing. Initially erected by business owners in 1949 as a Christmas decoration, the star proved so popular that it has been glowing above the city ever since from the top of **Mill Mountain**, Mill Mountain Park. Also atop the mountain is the **Mill Mountain Zoo** (540-343-3241; www.mmzoo.org), J. P. Fishburne Parkway and Prospect Road. Open spring–fall daily 10–4:30, winter 10–4:30; grounds close at 5. View red pandas, Siberian tigers, hawks, snow leopards, reptiles, and other critters at this zoo. Be aware that the animals are in cages, not moat-ringed habitats. $7.50 adults, $5 ages 3–11. While you're on the mountain, check in at the **Discovery Center** (540-853-2236; www.roanokeva.gov), 2000 J. P. Fishburne Parkway. Open Apr.–Oct. Mon.–Sat. 10–4, Nov.–Mar. Mon.–Sat. noon–4. Kids can learn about the mountain's geology, plants, and wildlife. Free admission.

Plantation Trail loops you to the restored buildings. Kids also like the farm animals. Free admission.

FRONTIER CULTURE MUSEUM
Staunton Convention & Visitors Bureau

Staunton

✐ ᕫ Frontier Culture Museum

(540-332-7850; www.frontiermuse-um.org), 1290 Richmond Road. Open Apr.–Nov. daily 9–5 30, Dec.–Mar. 31 daily 10–4, but guided tours only. Closed Thanksgiving, Dec. 25, and Jan. 1 No interpreters in winter. This living history museum pays tribute to the pioneers who came to this region, in re-created 17th- to 19th-century homesteads from West Africa, England, Ireland, Germany, as well as three American farms illustrating the 1740s, 1820s, and 1850s. Although guided tours are available in the winter, it's best to visit from April through fall, when interpreters in period attire illustrate the customs and the hope that the hardy immigrants brought with them and planted in the fertile

Virginia soil. A bonneted matron at the 18th-century German farmstead charmed my daughter when she was young by teaching her how to card wool, carefully picking the straw and hay from the fibers. At the Irish cottage, we pulled up "creepie stools" (because you crept closer to the fire for warmth as the night wore on) and learned how to cook Donegal pie in the open-hearth fireplace. At the American log house, we flailed wheat and imagined folks readying for a barn dance to celebrate the harvest. Check the calendar for special events geared to the seasons and holidays. Enjoy watching sheep shearing during May Wool Days, fly kites on July Fourth, dance at Oktoberfest, and listen to ghost tales during Halloween. $10 adults, $9 ages 13–college, $6 ages 6–12.

♿ **Trinity Church** (540-886-9132; www.trinitystaunton.org), 214 West Beverley Street. Open June–Aug. Mon.–Thu. 1–4, Sept.–May Mon.–Fri. 1–4. Founded as Augusta Parish in 1746, the existing church building dates to 1855. The church features 12 stained-glass windows by Tiffany Studios. Free admission.

♿ **The Woodrow Wilson Presidential Library & Museum** (540-885-0897; 1-888-496-6376; www.woodrowwilson.org), 18–24 North Coalter Street; Open Mar.–Oct. Mon.–Sat. 9–5, Sun. noon–5; Nov.–Feb. Mon.–Sat. 10–4, Sun. noon–4. Closed major holidays. Woodrow Wilson, the 28th president of the United States, was born in this house on December 28, 1856, and lived here with his family until he was two. The home has period furnishings, including Wilson's baby crib and other family memorabilia. The museum, housed next door, details Wilson's public life, concentrating on his presidency from 1913 to 1921. Scholars have access to the Wilson Library and Archives. Kids particularly enjoy a glimpse of the presidential limousine in the garage: a 1919 Pierce-Arrow. Take time to stroll the garden. $14 adults, $7 students age 13 and older, $5 ages 6–12. Free admission on December 28, Wilson's birthday.

✷ To Do

CANOEING, KAYAKING, TUBING

Lexington area
Twin River Outfitters (540-261-7334; www.canoevirginia.com), 917 Rockbridge Road, Glasgow. Go for an easy half-day float with a few light riffles on the James River.

April to June, add a few thrills on the Maury River. Cool off by floating down the James River in an inner tube. $25–25, tubing $15–20.

Wilderness Canoe Company (540-291-2295; www.wildernesscanoecampground.com), 631 James River Road, Natural Bridge Station, Glasgow. The company rents canoes, kayaks, and tubes, and transports you to the put-in location. You paddle back to the site on your own. Experts can try the 7-mile guided Balcony Falls kayak trip with Class III and IV rapids. Rentals $30–60, tubes $15, guided trips $50.

CAVERNS (See "Natural Bridge" sidebar.)

Virginia Department of Tourism

FAMILY FARM OUTSIDE LEXINGTON

FARMERS' MARKETS

Lexington

Lexington Farmers' Market (no phone; www.lexingtonvirginia.com), Southern Inn parking lot between Washington and Nelson streets. May–Oct. Wed. 8 AM– 1 PM. Peruse fresh vegetables, fruits, eggs, and meat as well as flowers and crafts.

Rockbridge Farmers Market (540-463-9451; www.lexingtonvirginia.com), front parking lot, Virginia Horse Center (540-464-2950; www.horsecenter.org), 487 Maury River Road. May–Oct. Sat. 8–noon. Vendors sell fresh fruits, vegetables, and other edibles.

Roanoke

Historic Roanoke City Market (540-342-2028; www.downtownroanoke.org), Campbell Avenue and Market Street. Open Mon.–Sat. 8–5, Sun. 10–4. Closed Dec. 25 and Jan. 1. Known also as the **Farmers' Market**, the market dates to 1882, making the place one of the oldest, continuously operated open-air markets in Virginia. For foodies, this is the place to find farm-fresh fare. You can also buy pastries and breads and browse craft items.

Staunton

Staunton/Augusta Farmers' Market (540-332-3802; www.safarmersmarket .com), Wharf parking lot, Johnson Street. Open April–Thanksgiving Sat. 7–noon. Vendors sell fresh flowers, eggs, fruits, and vegetables.

GALLERIES (See also Selective Shopping.)

Lexington

Nelson Gallery (540-463-9827; www.nelson-gallery.com), 27 West Washington Street. Open Mon., Tue., and Thu.–Sat. 11–5, Presents a variety of fine art shows of prints, drawings, paintings, and sculpture.

Staunton

Staunton Augusta Art Center, R. R. Smith Center for History and Art (540-885-2028; http://saartcenter.org). Open Mon.–Fri. 10–5, Sat. 10–2.

GOLF

Lexington

The Vista Links (540-261-4653; www.thevistalinks.com), 100 Vista Links Drive, Buena Vista. The Vista Links is a links-style, 18-hole par-72 championship golf course and the area's only public golf course. Located on 180 acres of rolling countryside, it offers many panoramic views of the mountains and Buena Vista. The course features bentgrass greens and fairways, bluegrass roughs, and native grasses throughout, while with five sets of tees for those golfing. $25–45.

Staunton

Gypsy Hill Golf Club (540-332-3949; www.staunton.va.us), Gypsy Hill Park, 600 Churchville Avenue. Open 7:30 AM–8 PM, weather permitting. Play 18 holes at this public golf course. $25.

HIKING (See also *Green Spaces and Lakes* for trails in the George Washington Jefferson National Forest.)

Lexington

Chessie Nature Trail. The former Chesapeake & Ohio railbed is now a 6-mile walking path along the Maury River.

SCENIC DRIVES

Lexington area

Avenue of Trees (www.lexingtonvirginia.com). Drive past farms and mountain scenery and along a road canopied by mature maple trees. From Lexington, follow Rte. 11 north to Rte. 606 west to Rte. 252 south to Rte. 39, which loops you back to Lexington.

Blue Ridge Parkway. Enjoy the overlooks on this scenic route. Local access is from Buena Vista, Rte. 60 east. (See "Blue Ridge Parkway" sidebar.)

Goshen Pass (www.lexingtonvirginia.com). From Lexington, follow Rte. 39 west past Rockbridge Baths. On a drive through this scenic mountain gorge, enjoy the rocky cliffs and rushing water of the Maury River.

SKIING

Bath County

Homestead Ski Area (540-839-1766; 1-800-838-1766; www.thehomestead .com), 7696 Sam Snead Highway, Hot Springs. The 45-acre ski area operated by

Virginia Department of Tourism

KAYAKERS ENJOY THE FALL COLORS ALONG THE SCENIC BYWAY, RTE. 39, NORTHWEST OF
LEXINGTON, WHERE THE MAURY RIVER CUTS THROUGH GOSHEN PASS.

the Homestead Resort is best for beginners and those looking for fun, not thrills.
The ski school gets kids and adults ready for Alpine runs and snowboarding. You
can also snow-tube and, at the resort, ice skate. Lift tickets $39–59.

SPA

Hot Springs and Warm Springs

Homestead Resort (540 839-1766; 1-800-838-1766; www.thehomestead.com),
7696 Sam Snead Highway. Open year-round. The historic property began in
1766 as a place to Experience the healing waters of Hot Springs. You can soak in
a tub filled with water from the same mineral springs at the spa. The full-service
spa offers a range of massages, wraps and treatments. Prices vary; for example,
30-minute tub soak $65, 50-minute Swedish massage $145. The Homestead also
operates the **Jefferson Pools** (540-839-7741), Rte. 220, 5 miles north of the
Homestead, Warm Springs. Open June–Oct. daily noon–5. The men's pool dates
to 1761 and is named for the third president, who stayed at the Homestead in
1818 in hopes the healing minerals would ease his arthritis. He found the soaks
beneficial. In 1836, a Ladies Pool House opened. History buffs and believers in
mineral waters should soak in these centuries-old pools. A nice touch: The resort
offers family soaking hours daily noon–2. $17.

Roanoke

Salem Red Sox Baseball (540 389-3333; www.minorleaguebaseball.com), P.O. Box 842, Salem Memorial Stadium, 1004 Texas Street, Salem. Open April-Labor Day. The Boston Red Sox's top Class A Minor League Baseball team plays ball at Salem Memorial Stadium.

WINERIES

Staunton area

Barren Ridge Vineyards (540-248-3300; barrenridgevineyards.com), 984 Barren Ridge Road, Fishersville. Open Mon.–Sat. 11–6, Sun. 1–6. One of the region's newer wineries, the first vineyards were planted in 2008. Free tours and tastings.

Rockbridge Vineyard (1-888-511-WINE; www.rockbridgevineyard.com), 35 Hill View Lane, Raphine. Open Tue.–Sat. 10–6, Sun.–Mon. noon–5. The winery has won medals for its Tuscarora red and white wines. Tasting $3.

✳ Green Spaces and Lakes

(See also "Blue Ridge Parkway" sidebar.)

Bath County

& **Douthat State Park** (540-862-8100; 1-800-933-PARK; www.dcr.virginia.gov), 14239 Douthat State Park Road, Rte. 629, Millboro. The park straddles Bath

HOMESTEAD RESORT ICE RINK

BLUE RIDGE PARKWAY

The 469-mile Blue Ridge Parkway, which climbs mountains and dips into valleys, is one of America's great drives. The road links Shenandoah National Park, VA, to the Great Smoky Mountains National Park, NC. A getaway following the parkway offers a combination of country and city sights. Although you may be tempted to drive the entire 469 miles, don't. The road curves and speed limits are low. Instead, alternate between motoring along the parkway's scenic roads and making up time on faster I-81, parallel to the parkway. The parkway starts in Virginia near Waynesboro and crosses the North Carolina border at milepost 218.

VISITOR CENTERS AND INFORMATION The parkway passes by farms, forests, and wooded areas, as well as near towns and cities. Even though, unlike Skyline Drive, it is not surrounded by national park or forests, the road leads to trailheads for hiking. Many of these paths begin near the visitor centers.

Blue Ridge Parkway (828-298-0398; www.blueridgeparkway.org), P.O. Box 2136 Asheville, NC.

Rockfish Gap Visitor Center (540-943-5187; www.waynesboro.va.us), mile 0, northern end of the parkway. Open daily 9–5.

INTERPRETER QUILTING AT HUMPBACK ROCKS VISITOR CENTER. BLUE RIDGE PARKWAY MILEPOST 5.

Jeffrey Greenberg, Virginia Tourism Corporation

Humpback Rocks Visitor Center, mile 5.8. Open late Apr.–Oct. 31 daily 9–5. Has picnic grounds and scenic trails, as well as a collection of 19th-century farm buildings.

James River Visitor Center, mile 63.6. Open late May–Oct. 31 daily 9–5.

Peaks of Otter Visitor Center, milepost 86. Open late Apr.–Oct. 31 daily 9–5. Set in a picturesque landscape with views of the valley ringed by mountains and a lake, this visitor center is worth a stop. Check the schedule for ranger talks and guided tours. With a Virginia or North Carolina fishing license, you can try your luck at Abbott Lake. The Peaks of Otter Lodge offers rooms and a restaurant.

Scott K. Brown, Virginia Tourism Corporation

RV ALONG BLUE RIDGE PARKWAY

Rocky Knob Visitor Center, milepost 169, near Floyd. Open first 3 Sat. and Sun. in May 9–5, late May–Oct. 31 daily 9–5. (See chapter 6, "Blue Ridge Highlands and Southwestern Virginia.")

HIKING

Lexington Area
✐ Among the parkway's easy hikes in the Lexington area are: **Indian Rocks**, mile 47.5, a .3-mile walk to rock formations; **White Oak Flats**, mile 55.2, a 0.1-mile leg-stretching walk; and **Otter Creek**, mile 63.1, an 0.8-mile loop overlooking Otter Lake.

Natural Bridge and Peaks of Otter areas
Fallingwater Cascades National Scenic Trail, mile 83.4. A great hike with grade schoolers and older kids, the 1.6-mile loop's highlight is the waterfall. The hike is rated "moderate."

Abbott Lake Trail, mile 85.7, is an easy, scenic 1-mile loop around the lake; the **Elk Run Trail**, mile 85.9, is an easy 0.8-mile loop. The moderate 2.1-mile **Johnson Farm Loop**, mile 85.9, leads to a restored mountain farm.

Jeffrey Greenberg, Virginia Tourism Corporation
HUMPBACK ROCKS VISITOR CENTER, MILEPOST 5

Roanoke area

The **Roanoke River Trail**, mile 114.9, is a 0.35-mile loop along the river. A bit more difficult, the **Roanoke Mountain Summit Trail**, mile 120.4 is an 11-mile path to an overlook.

HISTORIC ATTRACTIONS Humpback Rocks Mountain Farm Buildings, mile 5.8. Open late May–Labor Day. Walk the Mountain Farm Trail to the collection of 19th-century farm buildings. In summer, interpreters demonstrate quilting and other mountain crafts.

SCENIC DRIVES All of the parkway offers a scenic drive, but a favorite portion runs from **Otter Creek**, mile 60.8 to **Roanoke Mountain**, mile 120.4. If you've packed sandwiches, pause at the picnic tables along the James River, mile 63.7. The nearby James River Trail leads to the Kanawha Canal Lock. Guided tours are available at select times. **Roanoke Mountain Overlook**, mile 120.4, is a 4-mile, one-way loop that affords beautiful views of Roanoke Valley and Mill Mountain.

LODGING Peaks of Otter Lodge (540-586-1081; www.peaksofotter.com), milepost 86, 85554 Blue Ridge Parkway. Open year-round. 63 rooms. Come for the views at this lodge just off the parkway. Overlooking Abbott Lake, the lodge sits in the valley between the two Peaks of Otter. Rooms are comfortable but not fancy. A favorite activity is riding the Sharp Top Bus (except in winter) to the top of Sharp Mountain for a breathtaking view without becoming breathless. The property also has a restaurant. $90–140.

and Alleghany counties. One of the Virginia's first six state parks opened in 1936, Douthat's 4,493 acres include a 50-acre lake for fishing, swimming, and boating, as well as more than 40 miles of wooded hiking trails.

Roanoke and Bath County areas

George Washington and Jefferson National Forest (540-265-5100; www .fs.usda.gov), Supervisor's Office, 5162 Valleypointe Parkway, Roanoke. Open Mon.–Fri. 8–4:30. **Warm Springs Ranger District** (540-432-0187), 422 Forestry Road, Hot Springs. Open Mon.–Fri. 8–4:30. A huge recreation area, the forests offer 1.9 acres with more than 2,000 miles of trails. In Virginia, the forest stretches from near Winchester in the north to Abingdon in the south. What was formerly called the George Washington National Forest occupies the northern region, including the Allegheny, Massanutten, and Blue Ridge mountain ranges; and what was formerly called the Jefferson National Forest occupies the southern end. Administered by the U.S. Forest Service, the entire area is commonly referred to as one national forest that is divided into the **northern region**, north of Rte. 250 and I-64; the **central section**, south of Rte. 250 and I-64 to north of I-77, and the **southern part**, south of I-77 (See chapter 6, "Blue Ridge Highlands and Southwestern Virginia"). Popular places in the central section include:

Hidden Valley, **Warm Springs Ranger District** (540-432-0187), 422 Forestry Road, Hot Springs, about 6 miles from Warm Springs. The Jackson River, dubbed "one of the 100 best trout streams in the country," is adjacent to the Hidden Valley campground.

Lake Moomaw, **James River Ranger District** (540-962-2214; www.fs.usda .gov), 810-A Madison Avenue, Covington, 19 miles north of Covington. At the scenic 2,530-acre lake, swim, fish, bike, and hike. You can pedal along the 1.1-mile **Morris Hill Bike Trail** or walk the 3.2-mile **Fortney Loop Trail.**

Natural Bridge area

James River Face Wilderness Area (540-291-2121; 1-800-533-1410; www .naturalbridgeVA.com), Rte. 781. The six trails in this 9,000-acre wilderness area gain in elevation from 650 to 3,073 feet, making most of these hikes best for experienced hikers who seek a challenge.

Staunton

✎ **Gypsy Hill Park** (540-332-3945; www.staunton.va.us), 600 Churchville Avenue. Open daily 5 AM–11 PM; train operates May–Oct. noon–6 PM. Little kids love the duck pond, playgrounds, green lawns, and the Gypsy Express, a mini-train that chugs through the 214-acre park. The park also has a public golf course and, in season, an outdoor swimming pool and free evening concerts. Train rides $1.

CIVIL WAR HERITAGE SOUTHERN SHENANDOAH VALLEY

Lexington

Stonewall Jackson Memorial Cemetery (540-436-2931;www.lexington virginia.com), 314 South Main Street. Open daily dawn–dusk. General Stonewall Jackson is interred here, along with his two wives (the first died in childbirth) and other family members. A statue of the general by Edward Valentine adorns the grave. Also buried here are 144 Confederate soldiers and two Virginia governors. Free admission.

Stonewall Jackson House (540-463-2552; www.stonewalljackson.org), 8 East Washington Street. Open Mar.–Dec. Mon.–Sat. 9–5, Sun. 1–5. Closed Jan. and Feb. Thomas Jonathan Jackson lived in Lexington from 1851 to 1861. At the nearby Virginia Military Institute, Jackson was a professor of natural and experimental philosophy, and he also taught artillery tactics. He lives in this home with his second wife Mary Anna—his first wife died in childbirth—from 1858 until April 1861, when he joined the Confederate Army. After the first battle of Manassas, Jackson earned the nickname "Stone-wall." Instead of emphasizing the general's military career, the museum focuses on Jackson the man, as church leader, professor, and husband. $8 adults, $6 ages 6–17.

Virginia Military Institute Museum (540-464-7334; www. vmi.edu/museum), 415 Fletcher Avenue, VMI Parade Ground. Open daily 9–5. Closed Thanks-giving, Dec. 25, and Jan. 1. Although there's much more at the museum than Civil War artifacts, two items of that era get wide attention: the taxidermic incarnation of "Little Sorrel," General Stonewall Jackson's favorite horse, who died in 1886; and the coat Jackson wore when he was accidentally shot in the left arm by one of his own troops on May 2, 1863, at Chancel-lorsville. Doctors amputated Jackson's arm, but he died of complications on May 10. $5 donation suggested. (See "Museums.")

Staunton

Fort Edward Johnson, Confederate Breastworks (no phone; www.visit staunton.com), Rte. 250, 20 miles west of Staunton. Only the breastworks of this Confederate fort remain, but the location, at 2,875-plus feet, offers sce-nic views. A ½-mile interpretive trail winds through the fort.

Thornrose Cemetery (540-886-8241; www.thornrose.org), 1041 West Bever-ley Street. More than 1,700 Confederate soldiers are buried in this cemetery, established in 1849.

✳ Lodging

HOTELS, RESORTS, LODGES

Lexington

&. (ᵠ) **Country Inn and Suites** (540-464-9000; 1-800-456-4000; www.countryinns.com), 875 North Lee Highway. 66 rooms. The hotel offers complimentary continental breakfast and an indoor pool. $70–200.

(ᵠ) **Hampton Inn Lexington-Historic District** (540-463-2223; http://hamptoninn.hilton.com), 401 East Nelson Street. 86 rooms. Yes, this is a Hampton Inn and also an 1827 manor home. Opt for one of the rooms in the main house or in the addition. Either way, rooms are comfortable, rates include breakfast, and the property has an outdoor pool. $140–200.

Natural Bridge

Natural Bridge Hotel & Conference Center (1-800-533-1410; www.naturalbridgeva.com), 15 Appledore Lane. 150 rooms. If you want to stay in Natural Bridge, the hotel is convenient. The rooms are comfortable with an old-fashioned, country décor. $90–140.

Roanoke

🐾 &. (ᵠ) **Best Western Inn at Valley View**; (540-363-2400; 1-800-362-2410; www.bestwestern.com), 5050 Valley View Boulevard. 85 rooms. These standard hotel rooms come with complimentary Internet service and the property has an indoor pool. $75–130.

&. (ᵠ) **The Hotel Roanoke & Conference Center** (540-985-5900; www.HotelRoanoke.com), 110 Shenandoah Avenue NE. 331 rooms. Built by the Norfolk and Western Railroad in 1882, the Hotel Roanoke is the city's grande dame. Restored and reopened in 1995, this Doubletree property sets an elegant turn-of-the-century tone with its wood-paneled lobby decorated with antiques. An outdoor pool is on-site. $110–230.

Staunton

&. (ᵠ) **Best Western** (540-885-1112; 1-800-752-9471; www.bestwestern.com), 92 Rowe Road. The property has serviceable rooms at good prices. $85–120.

🐾 &. (ᵠ) **Stonewall Jackson Hotel and Conference Center** (540-885-4848; 1-866-880-0024), 24 South Market Street. Restored to its 1924 décor, the 120-room hotel is the "belle" of Staunton. There is also an indoor pool. $115–200.

BED & BREAKFAST INNS (See also "Bath County" sidebar.)

Shenandoah Valley

Bed and Breakfasts of the Historic Shenandoah Valley (www.bbhsv.org) offers accommodations in farms, city homes, and country properties throughout the Shenandoah Valley. Prices vary.

Lexington area

↬ 🐾 **Applewood Inn & Llama Trekking** (540-463-1962; 1-800-463-1902; www.applewoodbb.com), 242 Tarn Beck Lane, Glasgow. Three rooms. Applewood, situated on 37 acres between Lexington and Natural Bridge, has walls of windows, making it easy to enjoy the scenic Shenandoah countryside, especially when sitting poolside. Quilts, antiques, and reproductions decorate the home. A special bonus: the llamas. You can admire them as well as book a two-hour llama trek with the clever critters. One pet-friendly room. Treks are available Apr.–Nov. $145–165.

MOUNTAIN MAGIC: BATH COUNTY LODGINGS

With its rolling hills and undulating mountains, Bath County delivers some of Virginia's most beautiful scenery. In 1861, General Robert E. Lee praised the region, saying "The views are magnificent, the valley so beautiful, the scenery so peaceful." That's still true. You can hike the many trails of George Washington and Jefferson National Forest and boat, fish, and swim in its lakes (see *Green Spaces and Lakes*). The therapeutic springs that drew the socially prominent—George Washington, Thomas Jefferson, and Alexander Hamilton, among many others—still exist. In fact, you can soak in the historic spring house dating to the 1830s, as well as "take the waters" the modern way, as part of a spa treatment at the upscale Homestead Resort (see "Spa"). The county has lodging for those who want luxury, as well as for those who prefer country comfortable rooms and prices

🍴 🏨 ♿ ((ŋ)) **The Homestead Resort** (540 839-1766; 1-800-838-1766; www.the homestead.com), 7696 Sam Snead Highway, Hot Springs. 483 rooms. This hotel dates its founding as 1766, when the land's owner built the first wooden structure to accommodate those soaking in the healing springs. Grown in size over the years and rebuilt in 1901 after a fire, the Homestead, an AAA Four Diamond property, maintains a mid-19th-century décor of wing chairs and other period furnishings. Regulars like the formal and maybe even a bit fusty feel whereas others may, at first, be taken aback by the somewhat staid ambience. It's a big resort, sprawled on 3,000 acres in the Allegheny Mountains. You'll find your spot. We like to read in the wood-paneled Washington room or sit in one of the wooden rocking chairs on the long front porch and admire the view.

There's much to do—and most of it costs extra. Swing through three 18-hole golf courses, go horseback riding, shoot clays, play tennis, and go mountain biking and hiking. In winter, go downhill at the 45-acre ski area or ice skate at the outdoor rink on the hotel's back lawn. Afterward, indulge with a spa treatment. Be sure to include a soak in the mineral-rich waters, still used today, which drew the gentry centuries ago. The Homestead KidsClub, for ages 3 to 12, operates year-round, with half-day and full-day supervised play. Although men don't need tuxedos, once de rigueur the Main Dining Room, the place offers formal service and fine food accompanied by live music. The casual casino offers less-pricey and informal meals. $185–550.

BED & BREAKFAST INNS For those who don't want to dress up, the county blooms with a range of bed-and-breakfast inns. Favorites include:

Fort Lewis Lodge (540-925-2314; www.fortlewislodge.com), 603 Old Plantation Way, Millboro. 19 rooms. Situated on the other side of the mountain from the Homestead, the Fort Lewis Lodge, also on 3,000–plus spectacular acres, is the antithesis of the Homestead. This farm dotted with cattle and laced by the Cowpasture River, emphasizes the *country* in *country inn.* You can float on the river in inner tubes, fish for trout, and splash in a natural swimming hole. Along the miles of hiking trails, keep an eye out for deer, grouse, hawks, or ducks. The innkeepers call the décor "Shaker style." Simple, country pieces of pine and wicker are accented with quilts and throw pillows. You may opt to stay in the main lodge, a converted barn, a log cabin with a fireplace, or the nearby Riverside House. The property has a restaurant and rates include dinner and breakfast. $215–310.

Inn at Gristmill Square (540-839-2231; www.gristmillsquare.com), Rte. 645, Old Mill Road, P.O. Box 359, Warm Springs. 20 rooms. Rooms are clustered in several buildings, including a farmhouse and converted hardware store. More country comfortable than fancy, some rooms come with sitting areas or fireplaces. You can also rent a two-bedroom apartment with a living area, kitchen, and deck. For dinner, try the inn's Waterwheel restaurant (see *Where to Eat*). $110–175.

King's Victorian Inn (540-839-3134; www.kingsvictorianbandb.com), 8833 Sam Snead Highway, Hot Springs. Maple trees surround this 1899 home graced with bays and turrets. Choose from six rooms in the antique-filled main house, or opt for one of the more informal, one- to four-bedroom cottages, some with kitchens. Most of the cottages are a short drive away and rates do not include breakfast. $139–350.

♂ **Meadow Lane Lodge & Cottages** (540-839-5959; www.meadowlanecottages .com), 646 Meadow Lane Trail. Closed Jan. 2–mid-Mar. On this 1,400-acre property you can fly-fish for rainbow trout on the Jackson River, hike the trails, swim in the pool, play tennis or croquet, pet the horses in the barn, or simply savor the views. Choose one of the six rooms in the main lodge or from among six vacation rental cottages, great for families. All are furnished with country-style comfortable pieces. The historic 1860 house provides the setting for weddings and meetings. $115–140.

Frog Hollow Bed and Breakfast (540-463-5444; www.froghollowbnb.com), 492 Greenhouse Road. Four units. Choose from two rooms or a suite in the main house, or a cottage with kitchen and fireplaces. Enjoy the rocking chairs on the porch and the Jacuzzi tub on the lawn. $115–155.

Hummingbird Inn (540-997-9065; 1-800-397-3214; hummingbirdinn.com), 30 Wood Lane, Goshen. Five rooms. The Gothic-style Victorian home, originally built in 1780 and enlarged in 1853, has long porches and a welcoming feel. $145–175.

Natural Bridge
Herring Hall Bed & Breakfast (540-460-3365; www.herringhall.com), 154 Herring Hall Road. Three rooms. Originally the manor home for a 600-acre plantation, Herring Hall, built in 1812, is a large brick home. Restaurant is on-site. $150.

✳ **Where to Eat**

Bath County
Homestead Resort (540 839-1766; 1-800-838-1766; www.thehomestead.com), 7696 Sam Snead Highway, Hot Springs. The Homestead Resort has several restaurants. For an inexpensive meal, grab a sandwich or salad to go from the property's market or eat at the Casino. The casual restaurant serves flatbread pizza, pasta, burgers and a typically a fish or steak entrée. $12–26. The food at the formal Main Dining Room is good but pricey, and dressing up is expected. Interestingly, there are two dinner menus. The "classic" features Homestead signature entrées such as mountain trout (delicious). These are the meals that guests come back for year after year.

The "new classic" menu appeals to those accustomed to trendy cuisine. The seared black bass with littleneck clams in a lobster redux is also delicious. You can mix and match appetizers, entrées, and desserts from either menu. Entrées $29–35.

Lindsay's Roost Bar & Grill (540-839-2142), Rte. 220, "Main Street," Hot Springs. Open daily 8–2. With its red vinyl bar stools, plastic tablecloths decorated with roosters, back room adorned with Elvis memorabilia, and moderate prices, this eatery has a retro 1950s feel. Except for Sam Snead's (a steakhouse primarily open for dinner), Lindsay's Roost is the only other sit-down restaurant in town and the only one's that's inexpensive (we're not counting the sandwiches to go from the **Duck In**, a deli and mini-market across the street). If you're looking for an inexpensive lunch spot within walking distance of the Homestead, Lindsay's is it. Kids will do fine with the burgers and chicken fingers as well as the side orders of macaroni and cheese. Tuna and other sandwiches are available, too. $4–6.

Waterwheel Restaurant (540-839-2231; www.gristmillsquare.com), Inn at Gristmill Square, Old Mill Road, P.O. Box 359, Warm Springs. Open daily 6 PM–9 PM, Sun. 11–2. This place takes its name from the large waterwheel that operated the former gristmill on this site. The atmosphere's casual, but the entrées are tasty and tend to include mountain trout, grilled rib eye, and roasted duck with apricots. The restaurant, part of the Inn at Gristmill Square (See "Bath County" in *Lodging*) is open to nonguests of the inn. $24–31.

Lexington

Bistro on Main (540-464-4888; www.bistro-lexington.com), 8 North Main Street. Open Tue.–Sat. lunch 11:30–2:30, dinner 5–9; also Sun. 11–2. The restaurant labels its cuisine "casual contemporary." Along with burgers, lasagne, and almond-encrusted chicken, oddly listed on the "light menu," you can order entrées that showcase the Bistro's various influences, such as Creole catfish, jambalaya, and Maryland crab cakes. $9–24.

A Joyful Spirit Café (540-463-4191), 26 South Main Street. Open Sun.–Thu. 11–3, Fri. and Sat. 9:30–3, Thu.–Sat. 6 PM–10 PM. Breakfast, bagels, pastries, and coffee, as well as sandwiches and wraps, plus vegetarian items make this a good choice for a casual meal. $4–9.

Southern Inn II (540-463-3612; southerninn.com), 465 East Nelson Street. Open Mon.–Sat. 11:30–10, Sun. 10–9. As a result of a fire, the restaurant has temporarily relocated to Nelson Street from its home at 37 South Main Street. Dinner entrées, which include burgers and Reuben sandwiches, range from fried chicken and meat loaf to mahi-mahi and roasted duck. $11–30.

Natural Bridge

Pink Cadillac Diner (540-291-2378; www.pinkcadillaconline.com), 4347 South Lee Highway. You'll know you've arrived when you see the pink Cadillac outside. Open daily 7 AM–9 PM. The 1950s-inspired eatery, with a dose of Elvis décor, serves burgers, hot dogs, omelets, sandwiches, chicken, and pasta at moderate prices. $5–12.

Roanoke

Downtown's **City Market** region is Roanoke's restaurant row. (See also *Nightlife.*)

Alexander's (540-982-6983; www.alexandersva.com), 105 South Jefferson Street. Open Wed. 11–2, Tue.–Thu. 5–9, Fri. and Sat. 5–10; Tue.–Sat. small plates and drinks at 4. A frequent winner of Roanoke's Best Restaurant award, Alexander's features imaginative American fare with Southern and Asian influences. $22–40.

Roanoker Restaurant (540-344-7745; www.theroanokerrestaurant.com), 2522 Colonial Avenue SW. Open Tue.–Sat. 7 AM–9 PM, Sun. 8 AM–9 PM. A longtime local favorite, this casual eatery serves good, basic Southern fare at moderate prices. $7–14.

In Staunton

The Beverley Restaurant (540-886-4317; www.thebeverleyrestaurant.com), 12 East Beverley Street. Open Mon.–Fri. 7–7, Sat. 8–3. Located in the Staunton's downtown historic district, this restaurant has been serving Staunton for 35 years. $7–8.

The Depot Grille (540-885-7332) 42 Middlebrook Avenue. Open Sun.–Thu. 11–10, Fri. and Sat. 11–11. Located in the old freight depot of the Staunton Train Station, this restaurant serves seafood and steaks as well as sandwiches, burgers, and pasta. $8–24.

Ϋ **Zynodoa** (540-885-7775; www.zynodoa.com), 115 East Beverley Street. Serving seasonal American fare, entrées might include such Southern favorites as shrimp and grits, chicken and dumplings, and Virginia rockfish. $21–27.

✶ Entertainment

Bath County
Garth Newel Music Center (540-839-5018; www.garthnewel.com), Rte. 220, P.O. Box 240, Warm Springs. Open Feb.–Oct. For music lovers, this center is a wonderful bonus to a Bath County getaway. The facility celebrates chamber music by presenting concerts, education programs, and workshops against the spectacular Allegheny Mountains backdrop. Along with performances of classical pieces, Garth Newel hosts evenings of bluegrass, acoustic blues, and other genres. You can combine a performance with a meal at the on-site restaurant and. The property also provides a few bed-and-breakfast rooms, $110. Tickets vary and some performances are free or are on a pay-what-you-wish basis.

Lexington
Clark's Ole Time Music Center (540-377-2490; www.lexingtonvir ginia.com), 1288 Ridge Road. Open seasonally 7:30–10; call ahead. Enjoy the performances of old-time mountain music by regional musicians. $5.

✄ **Hull's Drive-In Movie Theater** (540-463-2621; www.hullsdrivein .com), 2367 North Lee Highway. Open Apr.–Oct. Fri.–Sun. 6:30 PM. Go retro: Pull into the field and enjoy a double-feature movie from your car. $6 age 12 and older.

& **Lenfest Center for the Arts** (540-458-8000; www.wlu.edu), Washington and Lee University, 100 Glasgow Street. Chorale concerts, plays, and chamber music are just some of the more than 200 performances a year. Ticket prices vary.

Virginia Horse Center (540-464-2950; www.horsecenter.org), 487 Maury River Road. Open year-round. Check the schedule for horse shows at this 4,000-seat indoor arena. The 600-acre facility also presents the American Kennel Club Agility shows, the Old-Time Music Jam (July), and other events. Prices vary.

Roanoke
& **Jefferson Center** (540-345-2550; www.jeffcenter.org), 541 Luck Avenue. Along with providing studio space for artists, the Jefferson Center hosts performances by Opera Roanoke and the Roanoke Symphony Orchestra. Tickets vary widely by event, $10–80.

Opera Roanoke (540-982-2742; www.operaroanoke.org), Shaftman Performance Hall at Jefferson Center, 541 Luck Avenue. Offices, 1 Market Square SE. Box office open Mon.–Fri. 9–5. The company performs at the Jefferson Center. $20–90.

Roanoke Symphony Orchestra (540-343-9127; 1-866-277-9127; www.rso.com), Jefferson Center, 541 Luck Avenue SW. Box office open Mon.–Fri. 9–5. The largest professional orchestra in western Virginia, the Roanoke Symphony Orchestra performs classical, pop, and another concerts at three major venues in the city: Roanoke Performing Arts Theatre, Salem Civic Center, and the Shaftman Performance Hall at Jefferson Center. Ticket prices vary.

Staunton
& **American Shakespeare Center's Blackfriars Playhouse** (540-851-1733; 1-877-MUCH-ADO; www

American Shakespeare Center, Virginia Tourism Corporation

AMERICAN SHAKESPEARE CENTER, STAUNTON

.americanshakespearecenter.com), 10 South Market Street. Blackfriars recreates an indoor, Elizabethan theater that would be familiar to Shakespeare and his fellow playwrights (minus the electricity, bathrooms, and other modern conveniences). The company performs Shakespearean and Renaissance drama year-round. $20–40.

Oak Grove Theater (540-248-5005; www.oakgrovetheater.org), 845 Quick's Mill Road, Verona. Season runs May–Aug. For 58 years, this community theater has performed under the oak trees. However, tickets for individual performances may only be purchased by season ticket holders. If interested, ask if your lodging can get you a ticket. $15.

🍴 ♿ **Stonewall Brigade Band Concerts, Gypsy Hill Park** (540-213-3880; www.stonewallbrigadeband .com), 600 Churchville Avenue.

June–Aug 8 PM. Join the locals who gather in the park on summer evenings for free concerts.

NIGHTLIFE: BARS, CLUBS, EATERIES

Lexington

🍷 (🛜) **Brix** (540-464-3287; www.brix -winebar.com), 4 East Washington Street. Open Wed.–Sat. 4–11, Sun. 11–3. This wine bar serves small plates of Mediterranean-style fare. $15–25.

Roanoke

🍷 **202 Market** (540-343-6644; http ://202market.net), 202 Market Street SE. Open Tue.–Sat. lunch 11–2, Mon.–Sat. 4:30–late. At this popular restaurant and club, opt to sit in the CityBar with its market view, outdoor seating, and music (DJs, karaoke, and sometimes live performers) or in the quieter Gallery. CityBar $6–11, Gallery $13–45.

Staunton

Y **Pompei Lounge** (540-885-5553; www.thepompeilounge.com), 23 East Beverley Street. Open Tue.–Thu. 5 PM–1 AM, Fri. and Sat. 5 PM–2 AM. Located above Emilio's Italian restaurant, the Pompei Lounge has a rooftop terrace as well as indoor rooms where light dinner and desserts are served. Enjoy live music on weekends. $14–28.

DOWNTOWN STAUNTON
Virginia Tourism Corporation

✳ Selective Shopping

(See also "Galleries.")

Bath County

The Gallery at Seven Oaks (540-839-3054; www.thegalleryatseven oaks.com), Rte. 220, P.O. Box 959, Hot Springs. Open Fri.–Sun. 11–5. This eclectic gallery in a two-story house is worth a browse. In addition to Gangchen Tibetan carpets, the gallery showcases artists who work in glass, wood, and clay, as well as painters and photographers.

Warm Springs Gallery (540-839-2985; www.warmspringsgallery.com), 12 Katydid Trail, Warm Springs. Open by chance or appointment. This gallery, in a red-painted wooden house, offers an upmarket selection of ceramics, paintings, and other hand-crafted items. This isn't a huge place, but the selection is nice. The owner has a sister gallery in Charlottesville.

Lexington

Artists in Cahoots (540-464-1147), 1 West Washington Street. Open Mon.–Sat. 10–5:30, Sun. 11–3. A cooperative, the gallery presents the work of its 13 or so diverse artists. Browse the ceramics, handcrafted jewelry, decoys and bird carvings, landscapes, forged iron candlesticks, and other items.

Staunton

Staunton Antique Market (540-886-7277), 19 West Beverly Street. Open daily, hours vary. Forty dealers display a variety of antiques and collectibles.

Sunspots Studios and Glassblowing (540-885-0678; 1-800-659-8650; www.sunspots.com), 202 South Lewis Street. Open Mon.–Sat. 10–7, Sun. 11:30–5. Watch glassblowing demonstrations and browse the shop for handmade vases, perfume bottles, and other glass items, as well as handbags and silver jewelry.

✷ Special Events

February: **Staunton Winter Wine Festival**. Music, food, and Virginia wines.

July: **Lexington Hot Air Balloon Rally and Fourth of July Celebration**, the VMI parade grounds. Enjoy hot-air balloon rides, food, entertainment, and fireworks.

July: **Commonwealth Games of Virginia**, Roanoke. An amateur sports festival for all ages. Recognized by the U.S. Olympic Committee and National Congress of State Games, these are Virginia's Olympics, held in mid-July.

August: **Virginia Mountain Peach Festival**, Roanoke, first Friday and Saturday of the month. Peach shakes, sundaes, cobbler, and shortcakes, accompanied by live entertainment.

September: **Appalachian Folk Festival**, Roanoke. Music, storytelling, quilts, and crafts.

STAUNTON MUSIC FESTIVAL

Blue Ridge Highlands and Southwestern Virginia

6

.

BLUE RIDGE HIGHLANDS AND SOUTHWESTERN VIRGINIA

I n the **Blue Ridge Highlands and southwestern Virginia**, spectacular scenery mixes with mountain traditions. Less visited than areas closer to Washington, D.C. and Richmond, this region deliver some of the state's most unspoiled territory. Explore the trails, rivers, and lakes in the many state parks and in the George Washington Jefferson National Forest. Drive the Blue Ridge Parkway, pausing at scenic valley overlooks and country towns. Opt to stay in rustic state park cabins, funky mountain hotels, or welcoming bed-and-breakfast inns, or at Primland, an upscale mountain getaway sprawled on 12,000 acres and complete with a golf course, spa, and observatory.

There's something else that makes the region special: Their mountain heritage is alive and well. In Galax and Floyd, listen to old-time and bluegrass music at jamborees, local cafés, and large festivals. Artists' studios and galleries dot the hillsides and valleys from Abingdon to Blacksburg. Drive the back roads and browse the country towns for handcrafted quilts, pottery, and jewelry as well as contemporary works in glass, fiber, metal, and wood. It's worth the extra drive time to explore this rewarding region.

TOWNS Abingdon. Located near Virginia's border with Tennessee, Abingdon, population around 8,000, is known for its heritage arts and annual Highlands Festival. Established in 1778, Abingdon gains fame as the oldest English-speaking settlement west of the Blue Ridge Mountains. Daniel Boone named the site Wolf Hills for the packs that roamed the hills. In 1774, the name changed to Black's Fort with the erection of the fort. In 1778, the town was incor-

BLUE RIDGE PARKWAY
Virginia Department of Transportation

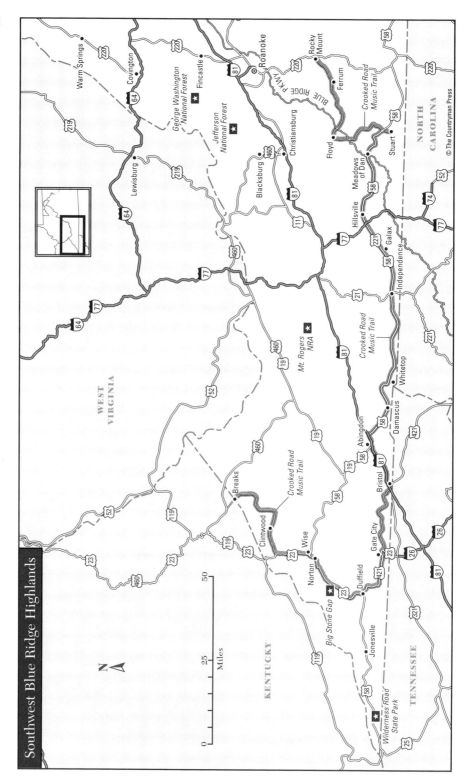

Southwest Blue Ridge Highlands

© The Countryman Press

Cameron Davidson

DOWNTOWN ABINGDON

porated as Abingdon, named after Martha Washington's English home, Abingdon Parish.

Blacksburg. A college town, Blacksburg is home to Virginia Tech (Virginia Polytechnic Institute and State University), one of the state's largest universities. With a population of 40,000, Blacksburg rates as one of region's largest cities.

Floyd. More than 30 miles of the Blue Ridge Parkway edge Floyd County, population 14,000. In 1768, the Cherokee Nation ceded land to the British. This became part of the land grant to "Light-Horse" Harry Lee, father of Robert E. Lee. The population of the town of Floyd, 40 miles southwest of Roanoke, hovers around 450. Part of the Crooked Trail, the region's music heritage drive, the town is popular with craftspeople and country musicians.

Galax. Since 1935, Galax has been hosting the Old Fiddler's Convention, the oldest and largest U.S. traditional mountain music festival. Pickin' and playin' are part of the town's heritage so much so that Galax, population 7,000, calls itself "the world capital of old-time mountain music."

Marion, population 6,500, is surrounded by the George Washington Jefferson National Forest and serves as a gateway to the Mount Rogers National Recreation Area as well as to the Grayson Highlands and Hungry Mother state parks.

Meadows of Dan, located at milepost 178 on the Blue Ridge Parkway, is part of the Crooked Road music heritage trail, the location of Fairy Stone State Park, and also home of Mabry's Mill, the much-photographed wood-sided grist mill.

Radford. Eighteen miles from Blacksburg, this Blue Ridge Mountain town has a population of 16,000 and hosts Radford University. Bordered on three sides by the New River, Radford serves as the gateway to Claytor Lake State Park.

GUIDANCE **Abingdon Convention and Visitors Bureau** (276-676-2282; www.abingdon.com, 335 Cummings Street.

Town of Blacksburg and Blacksburg Parks and Recreation (540-961-1135; www.blacksburg.va.us), 615 Patrick Henry Drive. Open Mon.–Fri. 9–5.

Floyd County Virginia (540-745-9300; 1-866-787-8806; www.floydcova.org), P.O. Box 218; also, **Floyd Chamber of Commerce** (540-745-4407; www.visit floyd.org), the Village Green, 201 East Main Street, open Mon.–Sat. 10–5; and **Floyd Virginia** (www.floydvirginia.com).

City of Galax Visitor's Center (276-238-8130; www.visitgalax.com), 106 East Grayson Street. **Chamber of Commerce of Smyth County** (276-783-3161; www.smythchamber.org), P.O. Box 92, Marion.

The Heart of Appalachia Tourism Authority (276-762-0011; www.heartof appalachia.com), 16625 Russell Street, Saint Paul.

Meadows of Dan: Blue Ridge Travel Association (1-800-446-9670; www .virginiablueridge.org), 468 East Main Street, Abingdon.

Montgomery County Chamber of Commerce (540-552-2636; www.mont gomerycc.org), 103 Professional Drive, Blacksburg. Mon.–Fri. Open 9–5.

Radford Visitors Center (540-276-3153; www.visitradford.com), 600 Unruh Drive.

MEADOWS OF DAN

GETTING THERE *By air:* **Abingdon: Tri-Cities Regional Airport** (423-325-6000), 2525 Hwy. 75, Blountville, TN, is about 30 miles from Abingdon.

Blacksburg: Raleigh-Durham International Airport (919-840-2123), Raleigh/Durham, North Carolina is the closest major airport (130 miles) to Blacksburg. **Virginia Tech Montgomery Executive Airport** (540-231-4444) is approximately 2 miles away. **New River Valley Airport** (540-674-4141), Dublin, is 16 miles away. **Roanoke Regional Airport** (540-362-1999), Roanoke, is 25 miles away. **Greenbrier Valley Airport** (304-645-3961), Lewisburg, WV, is 43 miles away. **Mercer County Airport** (609-882-1600), Princeton/Bluefield, WV, is 44 miles away.

Marion: Paducah Barkley Regional Airport (270-744-0521), 2901 Fisher Road, West Paducah, KY, is about 50 miles from Marion.

Meadows of Dan: Greensboro Piedmont Triad International Airport (336-665-5600), 6415 Bryan Boulevard, Greensboro, NC, is 50 miles from Meadows of Dan.

Radford: Roanoke Municipal Airport (540-362-1999) is 35 miles from Radford. **Bluefield Mercer County/Princeton Airport** (304-327-5308), Rte. 5, Box 202 Bluefield, WV, is about 60 miles away and the **Greenbrier Valley Airport** (304-645-3961), 219 North, Lewisburg, West Virginia, is also 60 miles away.

By bus: Marion has a **Greyhound** bus terminal (1-800-231-2222; www.greyhound.com), 141 Dabny Drive.

By car: **Abingdon:** From Washington and Baltimore, take I-81 to US 58/VA 75 toward Abingdon. From Richmond, take VA 195 east to I-95 north toward I-64 and continue on I-81 south to US 58/VA 75. From Norfolk/Hampton Roads, take I-64 west to I-81 south and then take US 58/VA 75 toward Abingdon.

Blacksburg: From Washington and Baltimore, take 1-66 west to I-81 south to Roanoke to US 460/US 11. From Richmond, take I-95 north to I-64 west/I-81 to US 460 west. From Norfolk/Hampton Roads, take I-64 west to I-95 north to Charlottesville to 1-81 south to Roanoke/Lexington to US 460/US 11.

Marion: From Washington and Baltimore, take I-81.

Meadows of Dan: From Washington and Baltimore, I-81 to Rte. 220 south to Rte. 419 to Floyd Highway north to Rte. 614. From Richmond, take 146, to Rte. 76 south, to I-95 to Danville Expressway, Rte. 29 south.

Radford: From Washington and Baltimore, take US 50 west to I-66 west to I-81 south to route 232 to Rte. 605. From Richmond, take VA 195 east toward I-64 west to I-81 south to Rte. 232 to Rte. 605.

GETTING AROUND To explore the region, a car is a necessity.

WHEN TO COME Spring brings wildflowers, summer is high season, and in fall the mountains billow with brilliant foliage. Check *Special Events* for the many regional mountain music and heritage festivals.

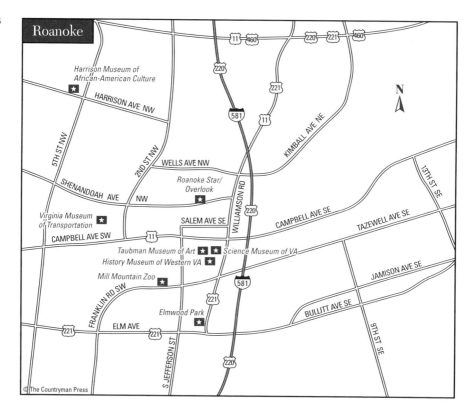

Roanoke

Harrison Museum of African-American Culture

HARRISON AVE NW

5TH ST NW

2ND ST NW

SHENANDOAH AVE NW

WELLS AVE NW

Roanoke Star/ Overlook

Virginia Museum of Transportation

CAMPBELL AVE SW

SALEM AVE SE

WILLIAMSON RD

CAMPBELL AVE SE

TAZEWELL AVE SE

13TH ST SE

KIMBALL AVE NE

Taubman Museum of Art   Science Museum of VA
History Museum of Western VA

Mill Mountain Zoo

FRANKLIN RD SW

ELM AVE

Elmwood Park

S. JEFFERSON ST

JAMISON AVE SE

BULLITT AVE SE

9TH ST SE

© The Countryman Press

✳ To See

MUSEUMS, HISTORIC LANDMARKS, AND SITES

Blacksburg

Historic Smithfield Plantation (540-231-3947; www.smithfieldplantation.org), 1000 Smithfield Plantation Road. Open Apr.–Dec. Mon.–Tue., Thu.–Fri. 7 10–5, Sat. and Sun. 1–5. When William Preston built Smithfield in 1775, the plantation edged the frontier. Costumed interpreters lead guided tours of the home, detailing what life was like at Smithfield in the 18th century. $7 adults, $4 age 12 through college, $3 ages 5–11.

Ferrum

♦ **Blue Ridge Institute and Farm Museum** (540-365-4416; www.blueridge institute.org), Rte. 40 west. Open mid-May–mid-Aug. Sat. 10–5, Sun. 1–5. Part of Ferrum College, the institute and museum showcase the traditions and crafts of Blue Ridge Mountains' residents. A series of log buildings, the Blue Ridge Farm re-creates life on a Virginia-German farm in 1800. Costumed interpreters drive oxen, cook over an open hearth, and perform other daily tasks. $8 adults, $5 ages 5–12.

♿ **Blue Ridge Institute & Museum galleries** present changing exhibits on various aspects of the region's history and crafts. Recent exhibits in the institute's

two galleries focused on Virginia's dulcimer, presenting 50 examples of the musical instrument from the 1700s to the present, and on Earl Palmer's photographs of women's crafts. Every October, on the fourth Saturday of the month, 10–5, the institute hosts the **Blue Ridge Folklife Festival.** Enjoy three musical stages of gospel, blues, bluegrass, and other types of mountain music. The festival also has a car show, a coon dog contest, and more than 50 artists who demonstrate traditional crafts such as tobacco twisting, basket making, and blacksmithing.

✳ To Do

BIKING

Blacksburg area
The Huckleberry Trail (540-231-5804; www.huckleberrytrail.org), 201 Clay Street SW. The former rail bed is a 5.8-mile paved bicycle and walking path connecting the Blacksburg library to the New River Mall.

Galax area
New River Trail State Park (276-699-6778; www.dcr.virginia.gov), 176 Orphanage Drive, Foster Falls. The scenic path follows the New River for 39 miles.

Radford
Radford Mountain Bike Park (540-267-3153; www.visitradford.com), The 100-acre park overlooks Claytor Lake Dam and offers 12 trails built according to International Mountain Biking standards. You must obtain a permit before biking in the park. Permits are available from the City Manager's Office, 619 Second Street, Mon.–Fri. 8:30–5.

CANOEING, KAYAKING

Galax and Radford areas
New River is popular for canoeing.

Blue Cat Outfitters (276-744-2027; www.bluecatonthenew.com), 5785 Fries Road, Galax; and (276-766-3729; www.bluecatonthenew.com), 2800 Wysor Highway, Draper. Blue Cat offers guided canoe trips as well as canoe, kayak, and inner tube rentals. Prices vary.

Tangent Outfitters (540-731-5202; www.newrivertrail.com), 1125 Norwood Street, Radford. The company offers guided canoeing and rafting trips on the New River as well as rents canoes, kayaks, and mountain bikes.

Canoeing is also available at **Claytor Lake State Park** and **Hungry Mother State Park** (see "State Parks" sidebar).

FARMERS' MARKETS

Abingdon
Abingdon Farmers' Market (276-698-1434; www.abingdonfarmersmarket .net), Cummings Street and Remsburg Drive. Open Tue. 3–6, Sat. 7–noon. The

MOUNTAIN MUSIC:
THE CROOKED ROAD

Toe-tapping fiddle and banjo tunes as well as blends of folk and popular music ring out against the mountains. The Blue Ridge Highlands and southwestern Virginia are home to a rich and lively tradition of mountain music. To let visitors discover what locals always knew and loved, the area created the Crooked Road, a music heritage trail. The path zigzags and meanders for 253 miles through 10 counties of the Appalachian Mountains. Joe Wilson, in his book *A Guide to the Crooked Road: Virginia's Heritage Music Trail,* details the venues—from local country stores to 40-year-old festivals—where you can admire, listen to, learn about, and dance to lively mountain tunes.

Scott Brown, Virginia Tourism
CROOKED ROAD, BLUEGRASS MUSIC TRAIL

Floyd

The Floyd Country Store (540-745-4563; www.floydcountrystore.com), 206 South Locust Street. Open Tue.–Thu. 10–5, Fri. 10 AM–11 PM, Sat. 10–5:30, Sun. noon–5:30. Yes, it's a country store, selling a little bit of a lot of items from hard-working jeans to bib overalls, crafts, and lotions, as well as hand-dipped ice cream. That serves the locals well, but it's the Friday night jamborees that draw visitors. Gospel music takes over the first hour, followed by two dance bands. Every Sunday afternoon, the store hosts a Mountain Music Jam Session, 2–5. Special events require tickets.

    ♿ **Hotel Floyd** (540-745-6080; www.hotelfloyd.com), 120 Wilson Street. Concerts May–Oct. Thu. 6 PM–9 PM. Floyd's downtown hotel hosts free concerts every Thursday evening in its outdoor amphitheater. Make an evening of it by purchasing food and drinks. (See *Lodging*.)

Galax

&. **Blue Ridge Music Center** (276-236-5309; www.blueridgemusiccenter.org), 700 Foothills Road, milepost 213 Blue Ridge Parkway, Galax. Open May–Oct. daily 9–5. The center, operated by the National Park Service and the National Council for the Traditional Arts, showcases mountain music. The center's museum, to open spring 2011, presents

BLUE RIDGE MUSIC CENTER
Cameron Davidson, Virginia Tourism Corporation

the Roots of American Music, an exhibit detailing how the African banjo and the European fiddle met and merged to create the lively rhythms of the mountain regions of Virginia and North Carolina. Enjoy live performances at the 3,000-seat outdoor amphitheater.

Old Fiddler's Convention (276-236-8541; www.oldfiddlersconvention.com), Felts Park, Main Street. Second weekend in Aug. Hear bluegrass and old-time rhythms played on mandolins, banjos, dulcimers, autoharps, and of course, fiddles at what's billed as the oldest traditional music event in the United States. The convention has been held every year since 1935. Watch flat-foot dancers (a mountain specialty) stomp in time to the ditties. Half the fun comes from watching the audience. They are down-home and dancing. Fans clog as performers play, and impromptu jam sessions break out in the parking lot and continue until the rooster crows. Musicians and bands from all over the world compete for prize money. Because motels book up fast, many of the spectators simply camp in town. If you plan on camping, arrive a week ahead of time.

&. **Rex Theater** (276-238-8130; www.rextheatergalax.com), 113 East Grayson Street. Live shows Fri. 8PM–10PM. Enjoy *Blue Ridge Back Roads,* live performances of old-time and bluegrass music, on Friday nights at the 475-seat theater owned by the city of Galax. Virginia station WBRF-98.1 broadcasts the performances live over the radio and the Web.

Hiltons, Clinch Mountain region

Carter Family Fold, Carter Family Memorial Music Center (276-386-9480; www.carterfamilyfold.org), A. P. Carter Highway. Since 1974, the music center has hosted old-time and bluegrass music every weekend in the Clinch area style—no electric instruments allowed. Established by Janette Carter to honor her parents, Sara and A. P. Carter as well as her aunt Maybelle, the performance hall is a regional icon. On the first weekend in August, the center hosts a festival with music, crafts, and food.

MOUNTAIN CRAFTS

Mountain crafts are alive and well in the Blue Ridge Highlands and south-western Virginia. Long known for its quilts, baskets, wood carvings, and pottery, the region blooms with craft galleries, artists' studios, and craft shops. Along with the traditional handmade items, the region also has artists and craftspeople creating contemporary interpretations of these mountain classics.

'Round the Mountain: Southwest Virginia's Artisan Network (276-492-2080; www.roundthemountain.org), 851 French Moore Jr. Boulevard, Suite 145, Abingdon. To promote and market the work of the region's artisans, the network has created an interactive online trip planner. You check off the type of work that interests you—fiber, glass, metal, wood—as well as the county, and the type of business—craft studio, store, gallery—and the planner generates an appropriate list. Check the site's calendar of events for shows. The trip planner makes it possible to find an artist even if he or she isn't having a current show.

Abingdon

The Arts Depot (276-628-9091; www.abingdonartsdepot.org), P.O. Box 2513. Open Thu.–Sat. 11–3. Along with workshops and classes, the facility show-cases area artists in its gallery.

Holston Mountain Artisans (276-628-7721; www.holstonmtnarts.com), 214 Park Street. Open Jan.–Feb. Thu.–Sat. 10–5:30, Mar.–Dec. Mon.–Sat. 10–5:30. The 40-year-old artists' cooperative showcases mountain artists in southwestern Virginia, northwestern North Carolina, and northeastern Tennessee. On display are quilts, wood carvings, baskets, pottery, stained glass, and jewelry.

Floyd

16 Hands (no phone; www.16hands.com), 1643 Starbuck Road SE. Open fourth weekend in November and first weekend in May. Eight Floyd area artisans open their studios twice yearly, creating a crafts tour. Among the artists are potters and furniture makers.

Jacksonville Center for the Arts (540-745-2784; http://jacksonvillecenter.org), 220 Parkway Lane South. Open Mon.–Fri. 10–3, Sun. 11–4. Browse works in two galleries, talk with resident artists, and sign up for arts classes.

Natural Woodworking Company (540-745-2665; www.naturalwoodworking co.com), 1527 Franklin Pike SE. Open workshop Mon.–Thu. 7–6. Producers of handcrafted solid wood furniture from sustainable woods.

Northwind Woodworks (540-745-3595; www.16hands.com), 297 Sumner Lane NE. Open by appointment. Creates contemporary furniture.

Tom Phelps Studio (no phone; www.potterystuff.com), 636 Stagecoach Run SE. Open by appointment. Among what Phelps calls his "functional and fanciful stoneware" are porcelain orbs, Christmas decorations, mugs with big noses, and totem pole sculptures.

Galax

Chestnut Creek School of the Arts (236-233-8340; www.chestnutcreekarts.org) 100 North Main Street. Take classes in jewelry making, woodworking, photography, and fiber arts, as well as in old-time banjo and fiddle playing. Admire local wares in the gallery.

Richlands

Appalachian Arts Center (276-596-9188; http://apparts.sw.edu), Southwestern Virginia Community College, Rte. 19, about 2½ miles south of the intersection with Rte. 460. Along with offering workshops and craft classes, the center showcases the work of regional artisans in seven galleries.

WOODCARVER, BRISTOL

Virginia Tourism Corporation

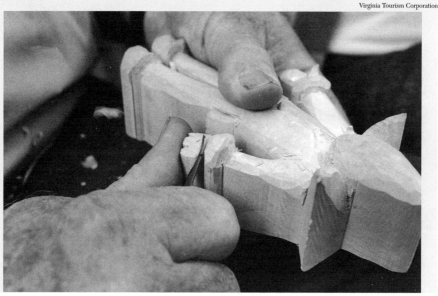

market offers homegrown and certified organic produce, homemade baked goods, honey, jam, jellies, and canned goods. Locally made wine, artwork, pottery, and other crafts are also available. Vendors sell plants and flowers, as well.

Blacksburg

Blacksburg Farmers' Market (540-239-8290; www.bbfarmersmarket.org), on the corner of Roanoke Street and Draper Avenue. Open Apr.–Oct. Sat. 8–2, Wed. 2–7 Nov.–Dec. Sat. 10–2, Wed. 2–6, Jan.–Mar. Sat. 10–2. Shop for fresh eggs, vegetables, meats, and flowers.

GALLERIES (See also "Mountain Crafts" sidebar and Selective Shopping.)

Blacksburg

Armory Gallery, Virginia Tech University, School of Visual Arts (540-231-5547; www.gallery.vt.edu), 203 Armory. The gallery showcases student work.

GOLF Highland Course at Primland Resort (276-222-3800; 1-866-960-7746; www.primland.com). 2000 Busted Rock Road, Meadows of Dan. European golf course architect Donald Steel designed the 18-hole course that offers expansive mountain scenery.

HIKING

Abingdon area

Virginia Creeper Trail (no phone; www.vacreepertrail.com), Daniel Boone walked this trail, a 34-mile path that leads from Abingdon through Damascus to the North Carolina state line near Whitetop, VA. In the 19th-century trains struggled up the railroad's steep grades, giving the line—and eventually the trail—the name Virginia Creeper. Walkers and bicyclists use this popular path.

(See also "Blue Ridge Parkway" sidebar and *Green Spaces*.)

GOLF AT PRIMLAND RESORT
Scott K. Brown. Courtesy Virginia Tourism Corporation

LAKES Claytor Lake State Park and Hungry Mother State Park have large lakes (see "State Parks" sidebar).

WINERIES AND CIDERIES

Abingdon

Abingdon Vineyard & Winery (276-623-1255; www.abingdon winery.com), 20530 Alvarado Road. Open mid-Mar.–mid-Dec. Tue.–Sat. 10–6, Sun. noon–6. Located on 53 acres along the South Holston River, the winery offers tasting room and picnic tables on its deck overlooking the river.

&. **Château Morrisette** (540-593-2865; www.chateaumorrisette.com), Blue Ridge Parkway, mile 171.5, 287 Winery Road SW. Open Mon.–Thu. 10–5, Fri. 10–6, Sun. 11–5. Château Morrisette, which released its first vintage in 1980, offers nearly 30 different wines. A black Labrador dog appears on its distinctive labels. The on-site restaurant serves lunch and dinner throughout the year. Tours are complimentary, but tastings cost $5.

Foggy Ridge Cider (276-398-2337; www.foggyridgecider.com), 1328 Pineview Road, Dugspur. Open May–early Dec. Sat. 11–5, Sun. noon–5. Foggy Ridge makes artisan hard cider from apples grown on its own orchards.

Villa Appalaccia Winery (540-3580357; www.villaappalaccia.com), 752 Rock Castle Gorge. Wine tastings Fri. 11–5, Sat. 11–6, Sun. noon–4, holiday Mon. 10–2. Located 5 miles from Primland Resort and 1 mile from the Château Morrisette Winery, Villa Appalaccia grows predominantly Italian grape varieties. Wine tastings $5.

✴ Lodging

HOTELS, RESORTS, CABINS, AND LODGES

Abingdon
((ᵧ)) **Martha Washington Hotel and Spa** (276-628-3161; 888-999-8078 www.marthawashingtoninn.com), 150 West Main Street. 51 rooms plus 11 suites. Built in 1832 as a private residence, the hotel served as a finishing school for young ladies, a hospital during the Civil War, and a women's college. The hotel offers a winning combination of 19th-century décor enlivened with modern amenities. Rooms augment antiques with comfortable wing chairs, flat-screen televisions, and modern bathrooms. The property has an indoor pool with a retractable roof, a spa, and restaurants. Rooms $250–275.

↬ ✵ &. ((ᵧ)) **Hotel Floyd** (540-745-6080; www.hotelfloyd.com), 120 Wilson Street. 14 rooms. By using bamboo flooring, sustainable fabrics. and a geothermal (heat from the earth) exchange system for heating and cooling, the builders created an eco-friendly hotel. The rooms feature art and furnishings made by local artisans, along with flat-screen televisions and coffeemakers. $80–180.

Marion
&. ((ᵧ)) **General Francis Marion Hotel** (276-783-4800; www.gfmhotel .com), 107 East Main Street. 36 rooms. The boutique lodging reopened in 2006 after an extensive renovation that brought back a sense of the hotel's 1920s stature as *the* place to stay in town. Rooms have flat-screen televisions and Internet access. $90–320.

Meadows of Dan
Meadows of Dan River Walk Cabins (336-312-1421; www.meadowsof danriverwalkcabins.com). 4444 J. E. B. Stuart Highway, Meadows of Dan. Situated on a 70-acre Christmas tree farm, the 730-square-foot, modern cabins have two bedrooms, a full kitchen, and a deck. You can hike to waterfalls and fish on the property. $160.

Radford
✵ &. ((ᵧ)) **Best Western Radford Inn** (540-639-3000; 1-800-628-1955; www

BLUE RIDGE PARKWAY

This great American drive starts near Waynesboro and winds for 469 miles through the Shenandoah Valley, connecting Shenandoah National Park to the Great Smoky Mountains National Park, NC. The parkway crosses into North Carolina at milepost 218. In the Blue Ridge Highlands and southwestern Virginia, the road cuts through southern Appalachia. Around a bend, enjoy the splendid mountain and forest views, and just off the parkway, explore the towns that keep alive traditions of mountain music and crafts. (See also chapter 5, Western Virginia: Shenandoah Region.)

GUIDANCE **Rocky Knob Visitor Center**, milepost 169, near Floyd. Open first three weekends in May Sat.–Sun. 9–5, late May–Oct. 31 daily 9–5.

BLUE RIDGE PARKWAY OVERLOOK

Blue Ridge Parkway, Overlook

.bestwestern.com), 1501 Tyler Avenue. 104 rooms. Rates include complimentary Internet and a continental breakfast. The property has an indoor pool. $75–125.

&. (ᵞ) **Comfort Inn & Suites** (540-639-3333; www.comfortinn.com), 2331 Tyler Road. 72 rooms. The hotel has an indoor pool and guests receive complimentary Internet access. $70–150.

BED & BREAKFAST INNS

Abingdon

Shepherd's Joy Bed and Breakfast Inn (276-628-3373; www.shepherds joy.com), 254 White's Mill Road. Four rooms. Situated in the Historic District of Abingdon, Shepherd's Joy is an 1892 Victorian home, with high ceilings and decorated with antiques, which is also a sheep farm. $140–160.

ATTRACTIONS **Blue Ridge Music Center** (276-236-5309; www.blueridge musiccenter.org), 700 Foothills Road, milepost 213 Blue Ridge Parkway, Galax. Open May–Oct. daily 9–5. Tap along to the lively tunes performed by regional musicians. (See "Mountain Music: The Crooked Road" sidebar in *Entertainment*.)

Mabry Mill (276-952-2947; www.blueridgeparkway.org), 266 Mabry Mill Road SE, milepost 176. Open May–Oct. This much-photographed park attraction is a restored, water-powered gristmill and sawmill. Interpreters demonstrate such mountain arts as blacksmithing and tanning.

HIKING AND SCENIC OVERLOOKS More than 15 miles of hiking trails may be accessed from the **Rocky Knob Visitor Center**, milepost 169.

Pine Spur Parking Overlook, mile 144.8, altitude 2,703 feet, is named for the white pine tree depicted on the parkway's emblem.

Rock Castle Gorge National Recreational Trail, mile 167.1, a 10.8-mile moderately difficult path, has streams, thick forests, and the rewards of scenic ridge overlooks.

Black Ridge Trail, milepost 169, is a 3.1-mile moderate loop that begins at the Rocky Knob Visitor Center.

Groundhog Mountain Parking Overlook, mile 188.8, at an altitude of 3,030 feet affords a panoramic view of the region.

LODGING **Rocky Knob Cabins** (540-593-3503; http://foreverlodging.com), milepost 174, near Meadows of Dan, 2 miles north of Mabry Mill. Seven cabins. Open May–early Nov. Civilian Conservation Corps workers built these rustic cabins in the 1930s. The cabins have electricity and either a two-burner stove or a hot-plate, sinks, and cold water, and come equipped with dishes, linens, and blankets. The ADA (Americans with Disabilities Act) cabin has its own bathroom, but the other six cabins share a bathhouse. $65.

Summerfield Inn (1-800-668-5905; www.summerfieldinn.com), 101 Valley Street NW. Seven rooms. Located in Abingdon's historic district, the 1920s home has a wraparound porch with rockers and gardens. Four guest rooms are in that main house and three are in the guest cottage. $165–195.

Blacksburg area
(((•))) **Clay Corner Inn** (540-552-4030; www.claycorner.com), 401 Clay Street SW. Nine rooms. One block away from Virginia Tech in downtown Blacksburg. Each room has a private bath, Wi-Fi, and a table for working. Comfortably furnished, the rooms' décor reflects the fact that these guest units are in a home and not a more formal inn. $119–129.

GEORGE WASHINGTON JEFFERSON NATIONAL FOREST (GWJNF)
The **Mount Rogers National Recreation Area (MRNRA)**, USDA Forest Service (276-783-5196; 1-800-628-7202; www.fs.fed.us/r8/gwj/mr), 3714 Hwy. 16, Marion, is a 200,000-acre section of southwestern Virginia's 690,000-acre portion of the George Washington Jefferson National Forest. The recreation area features hundreds of miles of hiking trails, scenic drives, and two lakes plus Mount Rogers, whose peak at 5,729 feet makes it Virginia's highest point. The park divides into three sections: West End, East End, and High Country.

West End highlights include the Virginia Creeper Trail and Beartree Lake. **Virginia Creeper Trail** (no phone; www.vacreepertrail.com), a 34-mile long, former Native American footpath, leads from Abingdon through Damascus (see "Hiking"). At 14-acre **Beartree Lake**, swim and fish for rainbow trout. The less-utilized **East End** has Hussy Mountain and Collins Cove Horse Camp and an interesting scenic overlook, **Comers Rock**. The 25,000-acre **High Country** is the heart of the recreation area and is adjacent to **Grayson Highlands State Park.**

Appalachian Trail winds through the MRNRA for 64 miles. About 55 miles lead through the Iron Mountains, making for difficult yet rewarding hikes for experienced hikers who like traversing the "rooftop of Virginia," so named because the mountains are among Virginia's highest. The remainder of the trail is in lower elevations.

Contact **George Washington Jefferson National Forest Supervisor** (540-265-5100; 1-888-265-0019; www. fs.fed.us/gw), 5162 Valleypointe Parkway, Roanoke, for more information.

MOUNT ROGERS NATIONAL RECREATION AREA, FALLS OVERLOOK

Virginia Tourism Corporation

♂ **Maison Beliveau** (540-961-0505; www.maisonbeliveau.com), 5415 Gallion Ridge Road/3860 Rue Maison Beliveau, Blacksburg. Five rooms. One of the owners leads an 8 AM, pre-breakfast hike through part of the 165-acre farm. The other owner is the cook, creating elaborate breakfasts and tasty dinners. Meet other guests at the evening for complimentary wine and cheese, 5–6 PM. In both 2009 and 2010, the B&B won "Best in Blacksburg Bed and Breakfast and Event Center." The property also hosts weddings. Some rooms come with private decks, fireplaces, or jetted tubs. $225–299.

《۹》 **Oaks Victorian Inn** (540-381-1500; www.theoaksvictorianinn.com), 311 East Main Street, Christiansburg. Five rooms plus one cottage. The Oaks has received an AAA Four Diamond rating for 16 consecutive years. Built in 1889, the Victorian house, on the National Register of Historic Places, has a wraparound porch surrounded by 300-year-old oak trees. Rooms feature antiques and comfortable pieces and come with mini-refrigerators. The Garden Cottage has a loft sleeping area and a private, outdoor hot tub. $139–209.

RESORTS

Mountain Lake Conservancy and Hotel (1-800-346-3334; www.mountainlake hotel.com), 115 Hotel Circle, Pembroke. Open May–Oct. daily, Nov. weekends. Only cabins remain open Dec.–May weekends. You've likely seen this place before. The resort starred, okay, *costarred* in *Dirty Dancing*—it was filmed here. Located on 2,600 acres, the resort stays true to its old-fashioned lake vacation heritage. Only cabins come with televisions and all the accommodations have simple furnishings. Some have fireplaces and kitchens. Spend your time boating and swimming in the lake and hiking some of the 22 miles of trails. The resort offers hotel rooms and one- to four-bedroom cottages. $150–245.

⇨ **Primland Resort Lodge at Primland** (276-222-3800; 1-866-960-7746; www .primland.com). 2000 Busted Rock Road, Meadows of Dan. Primland, at the opposite end of the spectrum from Mountain Lake, is a luxury resort with 26 rooms plus several one-bedroom cottages and two- to seven-bedroom homes. The eco-friendly property sprawls on 12,000 acres and includes an 18-hole golf course, a spa, tennis courts, an indoor pool, horseback riding and stargazing at the property's own observatory equipped with a high-powered telescope. The modern décor is simple, soothing, and suave. The smallest room is a generous 518 square feet. For casual dining, Stables Saloon serves breakfast and dinner. Elements, the more formal restaurant, serves breakfast and dinner as well. $259–1,200.

STATE PARKS

Duffield

⚓ **Natural Tunnel State Park** (276-940-2674; www.dcr.virginia.gov/state), 1420 Natural Tunnel Parkway. Visitor Center Memorial Day–Labor Day weekdays 10–5, weekends 10–6. Apr.–May, Sept.–Oct. weekends 10–4. As the name suggests, the highlight of the 950-acre park is the natural tunnel created by erosion. The massive tunnel is 850 -feet long and 100 feet high. Williams Jennings Bryan called the structure "the eighth wonder of the world." While we wouldn't go that far, the tunnel impresses kids who also like the easy trails—the longest is 1.1 miles—the chair lift and the park's 5,400-square-foot swimming pool.

Galax area

⚓ **New River Trail State Park** (276-699-6778; www.dcr.virginia.gov), 176 Orphanage Drive, Foster Falls. The 765-acre park stretches for 57 miles through Grayson, Carroll, Wythe, and Pulaski counties. Walk as well as bike along the **New River Trail**, a scenic former rail bed that parallels the New River for 39 miles. The trail passes the 75-foot-tall Shot Tower used in the making of ammunition in the 19th century. Shot Tower: Open Apr; 1–Memorial Day, Labor Day–Oct. Sat. and Sun. 10–6, Memorial Day–Labor Day daily 10–6. In season, you can climb the tower.

Marion area

⚓ **Hungry Mother State Park** (276-781-7400; 1-800-933-PARK; www.dcr.state .va.us/parks), 2854 Park Boulevard, Marion. The 2,215-acre park is noted for its woodlands and for its 108-acre lake. Kids like the swimming and the sandy beach, as well as canoeing and kayaking. Locals claim that the lake is the best place in the state to fish for northern pike. In summer, rangers offer guided canoe tours. The 3-mile Lake Trail that runs along the shore is easy. For more of a challenge, try the 1.1-mile Middle Ridge Trail that leads to an overlook. The park hosts a popular three-day arts festival on the third weekend in July. The Restaurant, the park's eatery, is open in season 11–3 for lunch and 5–8 for dinner.

Meadows of Dan area

Fairy Stone State Park (276-930-2424; 1-800-933-PARK; www.dcr.state.va .us/parks), 967 Fairy Stone Lake Drive, Stuart, about 23 miles from Meadows of Dan. Open lake swimming Memorial Day–Labor Day. The park takes its

pcopros

OVERNIGHT AND OTHER ACCOMMODATIONS AT HUNGRY MOTHER STATE PARK

name from the crosslike staurolite stones that, according to legend, were teardrops of fairies. In the 5,537-acre park, bike and hike 9 miles of trails and swim in the 168-acre lake.

Radford area

 ♿ **Claytor Lake State Park** (540-643-2500; 1-800-933-PARK; www.dcr.state .va.us/parks), 4400 State Park Road, Dublin. Created when Appalachian Power built a dam on the New River, Claytor Lake, the gem of this 472-acre park, is big: 4,500 acres, 21 miles long with 101 miles of shoreline. Swim, boat, and fish in the park. The park has a paved, wheelchair-accessible trail to the beach. Rent boats and go on lake tours with Claytor Lake Water Sports (540-731-8683; www.claytorlakewater sports.com). Open Memorial Day–Labor Day daily 8:30–6, Apr.–May, Sept.–Oct. Sat. and Sun. 8:30–6.

BIRD'S-EYE VIEW OF THE BEACH AT FAIRY STONE STATE PARK

pcopros

BLUE RIDGE HIGHLANDS AND SOUTHWESTERN VIRGINIA

pcopros

CLAYTOR LAKE STATE PARK

Volney area
⚓ **Grayson Highlands State Park** (276-579-7092; 1-800-933-PARK; www
.dcr.state.va.us/parks), 829 Grayson Highland Lane, Mouth of Wilson, about
35 miles southeast of Abingdon or 31 miles south of Marion. Open Memorial
Day–Labor Day daily, post–Labor Day–mid-Oct. Sat. and Sun. only. This

Marion
Windswept Bed and Breakfast
(276-783-1853; www.windsweptbnb
.net), 316 John Street. Three rooms,
each with bathrobes. Guests can use
the hot tub on the deck. The Emory &
Henry room is decorated with a country quilt and checked wallpaper; the
General's Room has a carved Victorian
bed; and the Blue Ridge Room has a
king-size bed. Located five minutes
from downtown Marion. $90–105.

Radford
Nesselrod on the New (540-731-
4970; www.nesselrod.com), 7535 Lee

Highway. Five rooms. On 9 acres
overlooking the New River, the home
is 1 mile from Radford University.
The Oriental Lily room has a sunken
tub and a fireplace. $99–200.

✳ Where to Eat
Abingdon
Alison's (276-628-8002), 1220 West
Main Street. Open Mon.–Thu. 11–9,
Fri. and Sat. 11–9:30. Famous for its
baked potato soup and ribs.
**The Café at Barter Theater Stage
II** (276-619-5462; www.bartertheatre

4,935-acre park appeals to many, especially families with young children. Nine hiking trails are a doable 1-mile or so long, and on summer weekends the Visitor Center presents live mountain music or demonstrations of quilting, basketry, or other regional craft. Fish for trout in the 10 miles of streams or pick blueberries in the woods (bring your own containers).

THE SCENERY AT GRAYSON HIGHLANDS IS UNPARALLELED.

pcopros

.com/cafe), 110 West Main Street. This restaurant offers salads, desserts, coffees, lattes, and iced drinks. Everything is made from scratch, and big deli sandwiches, panini, and wraps are both lunchtime and evening specialties.

Martha's Market (276-628-3161; www.marthawashingtoninn.com), 150 West Main Street, Martha Washington Hotel and Spa. Mon.–Sat. 10–3. The casual café serves salads and sandwiches. $8–14.

The Tavern (276-628-1118; www.abingdontavern.com), 222 East Main Street. Open Mon.–Sat. 4:30–9.

Located in the town's oldest building, a brick structure dating to 1779 that served as a stagecoach stop, the Tavern serves American-German fare. $25–34.

Blacksburg
Boudreaux's Restaurant (540-961-2330; www.boudreauxs.com), 205 North Main Street. Open Mon.–Fri. 5–10, Sat. and Sun. 10–10. Boudreaux's restaurant serves Cajun fare such as jambalaya, chicken Baton Rouge, and beans and rice, as well as salads and soup. $16–25.

Galax

Galax Smokehouse (276-236-1000; www.thegalaxsmokehouse.com), 101 North Main Street. Open Mon.–Sat. 11–9, Sun. 11–3. Eat Memphis-style barbecue, smoked chicken, and burgers. $4–16.

Meadows of Dan

Becky's Fried Pies and Bakery (276-952-6224; www.blueridgemtns .net/friedpies) 2588 J. E. B. Stuart Highway, Meadows of Dan. Tue.– Sun. 7–5. Homemade fried apple pies, cakes, cookies, and muffins are specialties; breakfast and lunch are served as well.

Mabry Mill Restaurant (276-952-2947), 266 Mabry Mill Road SE, Blue Ridge Parkway 176. Open daily 7 AM–8 PM. Located at the historic Mabry Mill, the convenient restaurant serves buckwheat pancakes, Virginia barbecue, and other country fare. $4–15.

Radford

BT's (540-639-1282; www.btsradford .com), 218 Tyler Avenue. Open daily 11 AM–1 AM. Established in 1983, BT's is popular with families and students. The eatery serves sandwiches, burgers, seafood, and pasta. $7–13.

✳ Entertainment

Abingdon

Barter Theatre, State Theatre of Virginia (276-628-3991; www.barter theatre.com), 133 West Main Street. Open Feb.–Dec. Founded in 1933, Barter claims fame as one of the oldest professional resident theaters in the United States. Barter performs on three stages: Barter Theatre Main Stage, Barter Stage II, and the Player Company for young people.

Blacksburg

Lyric Theatre (540-951-4771; www .thelyric.com), 135 College Avenue. Along with presenting movies, the Lyric stages live musical and theatrical performances.

NIGHTLIFE: BARS, CLUBS, EATERIES

Blacksburg

♈ **Big Al's Sports Bar** (540-951-3300; www.bigalssportsbar.com), 201 North Main Street. Open daily 11 AM–2 AM. Munch nachos, burgers, and salads while watching the big game on TV. $8–13.

♈ **The Cellar Restaurant** (540-953-0651; www.the-cellar.com), 302 North Main Street. Open daily 11:30 AM–2 AM. The casual eatery serves soups, salads, sandwiches, pasta, and pizza. Listen to blues, jazz, and rock-a-billy live music Tuesday and Thursdays. $4–12.

♈ **Hokie House** (540-552-0280; www.hokiehouse.com), 322 North Main Street. Open daily 11:30 AM–2 AM. The burgers, beer, and billiard tables draw the Hokies, college students from Virginia Tech. $7–12.

Sharkey's Wing & Rib Joint (540-552-2030; www.sharkeyswingandrib joint.com), 220 North Main Street. Open daily 10 AM–2 AM. At this sports bar, graze from the wing and pizza bar and fill up on half-pound burgers and barbecued ribs. Wash it down with more than 10-plus draft beers. The restaurant hosts trivia and DJ music on certain nights. $9–16.

Floyd

(See "Mountain Music: The Crooked Road" sidebar.)

Radford

Sharkey's Wing & Rib Joint (540-267-3434; www.sharkeyswingandrib joint.com), 1202 East Main Street. Open daily 10 AM–2 AM. The Radford branch of Sharkey's, a sports bar, has similar menus and events, but more beers on tap. $9–16.

✳ Selective Shopping

(See "Mountain Crafts" sidebar.)

VIRGINIA HIGHLANDS FESTIVAL

C. Cox, Virginia Tourism Corporation

✳ Special Events

April: **The Highlands Jazz Festival**, held in Abingdon, features many jazz greats as well as student jazz ensembles.

May: **Plumb Alley Day**, the third week in May, features yard sales, food, bagpipe music, craft vendors, dance performance, and other activities along the alley between Main and Valley streets in Abingdon.

June: **Wayne C. Henderson Music Festival**, the third weekend in June at Grayson Highlands State Park, includes a guitar competition and bluegrass mountain music concert.

July: **Hungry Mother State Park** Mountain Arts and Crafts Festival takes place the third weekend in Marion. **Floyd Fest**, a four-day celebration of music and art with more than 80 performers on seven stages, is the weekend in July, in Floyd.

August: **Virginia Highlands Festival**, held in Abingdon the first two weeks of the month, focuses on the arts and culture of the region and also stages one of the largest antique markets in the southern United States.

Old Fiddler's Convention (www.oldfiddlersconvention.com), the oldest and largest traditional music festival in the United States, takes place the second weekend of the month in Galax.

October: Enjoy three stages of mountain music and traditional crafts demonstrations at **Blue Ridge Folklife Festival**, at the Blue Ridge Institute & Museum in Ferrum, the fourth Saturday of the month.

INDEX